ENCOUNTER:

Group Processes for Interpersonal Growth

ENCOUNTER:

Group Processes for Interpersonal Growth

Gerard Egan

Loyola University of Chicago

Brooks/Cole Publishing Company
Belmont, California
A Division of Wadsworth Publishing Company, Inc.

L. C. Cat. Card No.: 71–113403
Printed in the United States of America
9 10

Preface

This book is about a small-group experience that has many names—a basic encounter group, a laboratory in interpersonal relations, sensitivity training, a basic human-relations laboratory, or an interpersonal-growth-oriented T-group. Whatever the name, all such experiences, together with group psychotherapy and group counseling, have this in common: the participants come together, most often under the "direction" of some kind of leader or facilitator, in order to grow in interpersonal effectiveness through the group experience. This book describes the goals and the kinds of interaction that constitute the backbone of such experiences. The emphasis here is not on counseling and therapy groups, but most of what is said applies also to such groups.

Although it is generally admitted that a sensitivity-training experience is almost impossible to describe, there have been several attempts made to let the reader "inside" a T-group so that he might get a feeling for the experience. No such attempt is made here. Rather, my purpose is to get at the "why's" behind the interactions that constitute encounter-group experiences and to suggest the kinds of individual and group action that are most likely to make the group experience as interpersonally growthful as possible. In order to establish a conceptual foundation for the encounter-group experience, I have drawn heavily on the psychological literature. The areas of self-actualization theory, counseling and psychotherapy, and social psychology, with special emphasis on the sub-specialty of group dynamics, have been most useful. The synthesis made in these pages, however tentative, is meant to be quite pragmatic; it is meant to subserve, in an immediate way, the interaction of the group. This, then, is a book of action and not just of theory.

As you read the following chapters, I would suggest one caution. There is an entire chapter devoted to a "contract" or structured approach to encounter groups, and the term "contract group" comes up frequently in other chapters. The quasi-structure provided by a contract that, in greater or lesser detail, governs a group experience may appear quite useful to some and relatively useless to others. The point is that the book is *not* specifically a justification of a contractual or structured approach to groups. In *any* group in which interpersonal growth (which, obviously, must be given some operational definition) is a primary goal, there are certain core interactions that take place—self-disclosure, expression of feeling, support, confrontation, self-examination, and, inevitably, various tendencies to flee the work of the group. My purpose here is to delve into the anatomy of such interactions, inasmuch as they constitute the warp and woof of the encounter-group experience. Therefore, most of what follows applies to all growth-group experiences, whether contractual (structured) or not. If, however, the reader believes that structure can be facilitative in encounter groups, then what is said about a contract approach may prove meaningful.

While the spread of the encounter-group phenomenon in contemporary society is striking, no one has yet scientifically documented the reasons for it. Undoubtedly, the reasons are multiple. One disturbing reason is the general failure of education as we know it in the United States to be a vehicle of putting people in growthful contact with one another. Fuller interpersonal living is not ordinarily one of the fruits of eight, twelve, or sixteen years of formal education. Therefore, encounter groups as we know them are to this extent remedial, and they will remain remedial until education grows up emotionally.

Usually the excesses, rather than the successes, of sensitivity training have been documented in the daily press and popular magazines. Occasional instances of poorly qualified trainers, poorly designed laboratories, training for the sake of training, people persuaded to participate in laboratory experiences under some kind of duress, and overemphasis on hostile and punitive confrontation have been treated as though they were representative of sensitivity training as a whole. Still, the well-run laboratory is an exhilarating and growthful, if sometimes painful, experience. The encounter group is not life, nor is it a viable substitute for it, but it can be an aid to more effective living. When the present movement loses its novelty and sheds its excesses, when participants stop expecting to find salvation in sensitivity training, and when adversaries stop condemning laboratory experiences as brainwashing or psychological rape, then perhaps the encounter group will be seen for what it is—just one (though a powerful one) of the instruments in the armamentarium of human growth experiences.

The inevitable problem arises of adequately thanking those who were of great help in the execution of a book. I am extremely grateful for the help and cooperation I received from Drs. Ronald Walker, William Hunt, and Michael O'Brien of the psychology department of Loyola University, Chicago. I would also like to thank Dr. Barbara Powell of the Malcolm Bliss Mental Health Center in St. Louis. We struggled through group experiences, discussions of theory, and a good deal of abortive research when we were together at Galesburg State Research Hospital, Galesburg, Illinois —all of which made it possible for me to sit down and write a bit more sensibly about group experiences.

A major debt of gratitude is to the members of the many groups in which I have participated and which I have directed. Without them nothing would have been written.

Thanks also go to Dr. Robert L. Helmreich of the University of Texas and Mr. Erle R. Kirk, Counselor/School Psychologist at Foothill College, Los Altos, California, who reviewed the manuscript and made many helpful suggestions.

Finally, I would like to thank my friends who have listened to me, who have opened themselves to me with feeling, and who have both supported and confronted me. Because of them and because of my experience with groups, I believe that I have begun to grow. That much remains to be done is evident to both them and me, but living is becoming, and in that lies its excitement.

Gerard Egan

Contents

1 **Introduction: The Contract Group in the Context of Laboratory Learning and Sensitivity Training   1**

The Burgeoning Phenomenon of Small Group Work   1
Toward a Definition of Sensitivity Training   4
Psychotherapy for the Normal?   11
The Contract-Interpersonal-Growth Group   17
The Question of Training Trainers   22
The Audience to Which This Study Is Addressed   24

2 **The Contract   25**

Groups as Natural and Groups as Contractual   25
Operationalizing the Group   31
Psychological versus Mere Formal Membership
in the Group   34
Ambiguity versus Clarity in Growth Experiences   35
Minimizing Manipulation   41
Group Participants as "Therapists" to One Another   42
Some Objections to Growth by Contract   43

A Variety of Contracts   50

A Sample Contract for a Laboratory in
Interpersonal Relations   51

A Contract for a Laboratory in
Interpersonal Growth   51

The Focused Contract   61

The Imposed versus the Freely Chosen Contract   61

Cautions in Contractual Approaches   62

The Contract and Research Possibilities   64

Concluding Remarks   67

Group Goals   68

Introduction   68

Ambiguity versus Clarity of Goals in
Laboratory Training   71

Varieties of Goals in Group Process   75

Contract Goals   78

Interaction Goals   82

Process Goals   82

Content Goals   96

Need Goals   99

The Overriding Goal—Interpersonal Growth—
Revisited   99

The Laboratory Method   104

Introduction   104

The Assumptions of Training Technology   111

Experimental Controls   115

Suspension of Judgment   115

What a Laboratory in Interpersonal
Relations Is Not   116

Artificiality-Reality Dimensions of Laboratory Life   117

Conclusion   121

Leadership   123

Introduction   123

The Trainer as Leader-Member   125

The Functions of the Leader-Member   126

The Leader as Guardian of the Contract   133

The Leader as Model   134

The Diffusion of Leadership   135

Leaderless Groups   136

Conclusion   139

6

Total Human Expression: The Elements of Human Dialogue: Pathos, Logos, Poiesis   141

Introduction   141

Pathos: Man as the Subject of Feelings and Emotions   143

The Flight from Emotion   143

The Phases of Emotional Experiencing   148

The Sensitivity Laboratory as Stimulator of Feelings and Emotions   156

Logos: Man's Translation of Himself into Language   159

Introduction   159

The Problems and Potential of Language   160

Different Kinds of Language   163

Language: Content, Invitation, and Self-Expression   167

The Function of Language in Organizing Reality   169

Translating Messages into Logos   170

Language and Self-Identity   172

Logos in the Contract Group   173

The Extra-Linguistic Dimensions of Speech   175

Logos: Nonverbal Communication in the Laboratory   175

Poiesis: Words Made Flesh   182

The Expression of Emotion   185

The Prevalence of Hostility   186

The Problems and Potentialities of Poiesis   188

7

Self-Disclosure   190

Introduction   190

Interaction Goals   191

Self-Disclosure: A Basic Step toward Growth   192

Deception and Concealment as Pathogenic or Growth-Stifling   193

Self-Disclosure and Cultural Taboo   199

Society and Truth   204

Intra-Individual Sources of Resistance to Self-Disclosure   207

The Many Faces of Guilt   213

An Example Illustrating the Four Species of Guilt   222

A Summary Word on Guilt   223

Shame and Self-Disclosure   223

Other Approaches to Self-Disclosure in the Training Group   231

The Mode or Quality of Self-Disclosure:
"Story" versus "History"   234

Levels of Self-Disclosure   238

Self-Disclosure at the Service of Behavior
Control: "Labeling"   240

Possible Dangers Associated with Self-Disclosure   242

Epilog   243

8   Supportive Behavior   246

Listening: The Sine Qua Non of Supportive
Behavior   248

Total Listening   248

Obstacles to Effective Listening   252

The Impact of the Speaker on Listening   258

The "Compleat" Listener   259

Listening as Diagnostic   259

Support: Creating a Climate for Growth   260

Antecedent and Consequent Support   262

The Forms of Antecedent Support   263

Consequent Support in Terms of Reinforcement   276

Failures in Support   282

The Problems in Receiving Support   285

Conclusion   286

9   Confrontation in Laboratory Training   287

Introduction   287

The Anatomy of Confrontation   293

The Nature of the Stimulus Act: The Forms of
Confrontation   294

The Natural Bias of the Confronter   310

The Relationship between the Confronter and the
Confrontee   311

The Motivation of the Confronter   312

The Manner of Confrontation   315

The Effect Confrontation Has on the Confrontee   327

Growthful Response to Confrontation   327

Areas of Confrontation   332

Summary: Suggested Rules for Confrontation   334

10   A Stance against Flight   336

Introduction   336

The Individual in Flight   338

The Group in Flight   348

Concluding Remarks   357

11   **Epilog**   **359**

The Problem of Agency   359
Research: Issues and Applications   362
The Ending of the Group   371

References   373

Indexes   413

ENCOUNTER:

Group Processes for Interpersonal Growth

Chapter One:
Introduction:
The Contract Group
in the Context of
Laboratory Learning
and Sensitivity Training

The Burgeoning
Phenomenon of
Small Group Work

There is no denying the phenomenon of the growing use of small group methods as a vehicle of learning and growth experiences. Popular articles referring to "sensitivity training" and "encounter" groups have recently appeared in newspapers and national magazines (e.g., Anonymous, 1968; Williams, 1968), and for years, business leaders have been interested in small-group laboratories as means of improving managerial skills, human relations acuity, and productivity in their organizations (Benne, 1964; Blake & Mouton, 1964, 1965; Campbell & Dunnette, 1968; House, 1967). The small group approach to problems in education (Fox & Lippitt, 1964) and in the wider community (Klein, 1965) is also on the rise.

The overly enthusiastic are claiming that all things can be done through groups. Individuals flock to sensitivity-training laboratories or encounter groups looking for a variety of self-actualization experiences, from hard-core psychotherapy to fellowship. Morton

Lieberman is currently studying the phenomenon of small self-actualization groups on the West coast. In one comparatively small city (population 50,000) he has discovered over 200 self-actualization groups of various kinds (personal communication). This seems to be merely the beginning, for the idea of growth through groups has just begun to catch the public imagination. Organizations in the turmoil of change are looking eagerly (or beleagueredly) to sensitivity training for some sort of help, if not salvation. Practitioners arise all around, many of them with doubtful qualifications, and still the supply does not approach the demand. Indeed, the professional community stands aghast at the number of nonprofessionals who have styled themselves "trainers." House (1967) expresses his concern over what is taking place in business and industry:

> The issue is one of some concern at this moment, because there are training directors, personnel managers, business consultants, and members of business school faculties not trained in psychological practice, who nevertheless engage in T-Group training. Are they perhaps getting beyond the area in which they are trained, and might they not evoke anxieties or problems which they are not capable of recognizing or handling? [pp. 26–27].

The problem may be even more acute outside business settings, for in these cases group experiences have an even greater similarity to group psychotherapy. Yet, despite the lack of qualified trainers, few professionals are engaged in the work of training trainers.

A striking amount of informal experimentation with small groups is going on—experimentation that is outside the pale of the group-dynamics subdivision of social psychology and that includes both normal and psychiatric populations. It ranges from the sensory-awareness experiments at the Esalen Institute (Gunther, 1968) and the self-actualization explorations of Herbert Otto and associates (1966) to Mowrer's "integrity-training" groups (1964, 1966); from the molar experimentation of such psychotherapeutic communities as Daytop Village (Shelly & Bassin, 1965) and Synanon (Casriel, 1963; Maslow, 1967; Yablonsky, 1962, 1965) doing pioneer work with sociopathic personalities to the more molecular experimentation with groups in university laboratories; from the organization-oriented laboratory approach delineated in such works as *The Managerial Grid* (Blake & Mouton, 1964) to the human-relations, personal-growth, community-relations, higher-education, and conflict-management laboratories sponsored by the National Training

Laboratories (Bradford, Gibb, & Benne, 1964) and the self-actualization exploration of Rogers (Hall, 1967; Rogers, 1967), Bugental (1965), and Thomas (1964, 1967).

The Research and Publication Gap. There is a fairly extensive literature on small-group laboratory learning (e.g., Blake & Mouton, 1961, 1964; Bradford, Gibb, & Benne, 1964; Campbell and Dunnette, 1968; Craig & Bittel, 1967; House, 1967; Miles, 1959, 1964; Schein & Bennis, 1965b; Tannenbaum, Weschler, & Massarik, 1961, to mention but a few). At least one journal (*The Journal of Applied Behavioral Science*) covers the field more or less directly, and some articles are beginning to appear in other journals. But, with few exceptions, what has been published concerning laboratory learning in general and, especially, what has been written specifically about sensitivity training has not yet made its way into the mainstream of psychological thinking. The practice of sensitivity training has outrun both theoretical formulation and organized research, and the resulting turmoil has made many behavioral scientists look upon the whole field of laboratory learning with suspicion and upon the subspecialty of sensitivity training with outright hostility. (For example, a colleague of mine, in counseling an undergraduate psychology major as to the advisability of counting a laboratory course in sensitivity training as part of his program, remarked to the young man: "We don't give credit for love-ins.")

Despite the fact that Schein and Bennis (1965b) render "particular thanks to Leland Bradford and Kenneth Benne whose efforts over the years to nurse the delicate child of laboratory training have now produced a robust viable adult [p. viii]," it seems that, in many ways, we are still dealing with the problems of an infant offspring of an adolescent science. Indeed, one of the strongest motivations underlying the writing of this book is the desire to put some order into one particularly chaotic area of laboratory learning—the use of the small group as a vehicle of personal and interpersonal growth, or, if you wish, a kind of psychotherapy or self-actualization or growth experience for the relatively normal. This I call "sensitivity training."

I think that the term "sensitivity training" is not a particularly happy one. For some people it has too many negative connotations, while for others it has so many meanings that it means nothing. But since the term is with us for better or for worse, and since it will be used with some frequency in the pages that follow, it is essential to give it as exact a definition as possible.

The Distinction between Laboratory Learning and Sensitivity Training. It is not my purpose here to present an extended treatment of laboratory training, for Bradford, Gibb, and Benne (1964) and Schein and Bennis (1965b) have already provided us with excellent overviews of this field. However, since I define laboratory training or learning as a genus of which sensitivity training is a species, and since it is the purpose of this book to explore group approaches to interpersonal growth including sensitivity training, it is necessary, first, briefly to point out the essentials of laboratory training and, second, to situate sensitivity training in this context. Only against such a background is it possible to formulate a specific approach to sensitivity training.

The Genus: Laboratory Training. Someone once said that it is better to feel compunction than to know how to define it. This sentiment, paraphrased and applied to laboratory learning, might read: It is easier to experience laboratory training than to describe it. Buchanan (1965) provides a compact description of the nature of laboratory training:

Training approaches meriting the name of laboratory (or T-Group) utilize (1) a face-to-face, largely unstructured group as a primary vehicle for learning, (2) planned activities involving interaction between individuals and/or between groups, (3) systematic and frequent feedback and analysis of information regarding what happened in the here-and-now and what effect it had, (4) dilemmas or problems for which 'old ways' of behaving for most of the participants do not provide effective courses of action (and thus for which innovative or 'search' behavior is required), and (5) generalization, or reformulation of concepts and values based upon the analysis of direct experience.

Schein and Bennis (1965c) outline some of the difficulties encountered in any attempt to write about it:

Many attempts have been made to characterize the nature of laboratory training, but most of them have not been successful for several reasons: (1) laboratories *vary tremendously* in goals, training design, delegate population, length, setting, making it difficult to describe this experience in general; (2) laboratories attempt to provide a *total* and integrated learning experience for the participants, making it difficult to communicate in written words the interdependence of the many separate aspects of the laboratory training design; (3) laboratories intend to provide the opportunity for the participants to explore the interdependence of emotional and intellectual learning. It is difficult without observing the process first-hand to describe and understand the nature of this emotional learning and its meaning to the learner [p. 10].

With this caution, let's look at the elements common to most, if not all, laboratory experiences.

Learning through Actual Experience in the Small Group. In most laboratory experiences, the most important learning takes place through the interactions in the small face-to-face conversation group itself. Learning may also take place through independent reading, lectures, and exercises that focus on various aspects of the group experience, but such learning is adjunctive and is important only to the degree that it leads to and enhances the quality of interactions in the T-group itself ("T" for "training"). The most important input during group sessions is the behavior of the participants themselves. Therefore, all laboratory experiences have a strong "here-and-now" flavor, and experiences outside the laboratory are considered valuable only to the degree that they can make some more or less direct contribution to the interactions in the T-group. The participants are learning how to learn from the behavior that they themselves produce during group sessions.

A Climate of Experimentation. Theoretically, if the group experience is to have an impact on behavior outside the laboratory, if it is to make a difference in day-to-day living, then it must be *different* from day-to-day experience. Interactions must in some way dramatize the overlooked dimensions of the kinds of behavior that are the focus of the laboratory, such as managerial styles, group decision making, and interpersonal relations. Therefore, participants are encouraged to experiment with their behavior during the laboratory—that is, to attempt new forms of behavior, kinds of behavior that previously have not characterized their style. Thus, the laboratory possesses a degree of behavioral freedom not always found in real-life situations. It provides the participants a kind of "cultural permission" to engage in forms of behavior (hopefully responsible forms) that the constrictions of their "back-home" environment do not allow. In fact, some of the exercises introduced during the laboratory are designed to shake the participants out of routine ways of acting. Admittedly, all of this can arouse a certain degree of anxiety, but anxiety itself, if kept within limits, becomes a stimulus to new forms of behavior.

Group Size. The group size has to be small enough to allow each participant the opportunity to contribute to the interaction of the group, but it must be large enough to allow the participants to space their contributions, not just according to the demands of the group, but also according to individual needs and capabilities. If the group is too small, each member is constantly "on call"; if the group is too large, it is too easy for an individual to hide in the crowd. Also, the group must be of a size that makes such factors as heterogeneity of contribution, diversity of opinion, coalition formation and other variables optimally productive in terms of learning. Another way of viewing group size is to say that the group should be large enough so that the absence of one or two members does not debilitate the group and yet small enough so that such absences are felt. In practice, groups range in size from about eight to about twelve or fourteen members, but optimal size is determined to a large extent by the nature of the group and its goals.

Feedback. Group members, both individually and corporately, try to reflect on the behavior in which they are engaged. The behavior itself (e.g., problem-solving work sessions, group decision-making conferences, managerial-planning sessions, discussion of interpersonal problems) is part of the input of the laboratory experience. The laboratory provides opportunities for both giving and receiving feedback with respect to input behavior; that is, the group processes its own behavior as a group and the behavior of the individuals in the group. All behavior is subject to scrutiny in terms of the group culture and goals, but process variables are subjected to particular scrutiny. Process variables are such factors as who speaks to whom and in what manner, the frequency of a person's contributions, what coalitions take place and how, whether the group atmosphere is one of cooperation, neutrality, or competition, and who are the cooperators, the neutrals, and the competitors.

Leadership. In laboratory experiences the leader is usually called a "trainer" (though some prefer the term "facilitator") and acts as a resource person for the group rather than an authoritarian figure imposing preconceived goals and types of interaction on the group. Seashore (1968) puts it well when he says that the "staff person's role is to facilitate the examination and understanding of the experiences in the group. He helps participants to focus on the way the group is working, the style of the individual's participation, or the issues that are facing the group [p. 1]." As a participant-observer, the trainer attempts to reveal to the group its own dynamics as it moves through various stages of group life. There is a wide variety of leadership styles; each trainer differs markedly from others with respect to such variables as frequency of intervention, directive tendencies, degree of self-involvement and self-revelation, and depth of confrontation. One reason he is called a trainer is that he is training group members to identify with his role of participant-observer; the participants learn from him how to observe what is happening in the group.

Communication and Emotion. In almost every laboratory, one of the principal emphases is the network of problems centering around intragroup communication processes. It is learned, often painfully, that it is impossible to deal with issues on a purely intellectual level, even though the laboratory might concern itself with a highly intellectual area, such as problem-solving. As Collins and Guetzkow (1964) note, any attempt to ignore human relations issues is self-defeating:

Meeting interpersonal obstacles contributes as much toward group productivity as meeting problems posed by task-environmental obstacles; in fact, because group members have a tendency to ignore interpersonal issues, interpersonal obstacles may be the major barrier to task effectiveness in many groups [p. 88].

This does not mean that laboratory training is directly psychotherapeutic. Rather, personal and interpersonal problems are dealt with insofar as they inhibit free communication within the group and stand in the way of the group's achieving its goals. Therefore, while emotional issues are not ordinarily the primary concern of the participants, they are not ignored but are dealt with to the extent called for by the goals of the group. In the laboratory experience outlined in the following chapters, self-actualization and interpersonal growth *are* the principal goals, and emotional issues *are* one of the principal focuses of the group.

Support. A laboratory is an opportunity for the responsible lowering of defenses that tend to rigidify the personality and distort reality. But if the laboratory deals with emotional issues, it must also provide a climate of support conducive to dealing effectively with them. This is one area in which many laboratories fail: they demand anxiety-arousing behavior from the participants and yet do not provide adequate security measures. This problem will be dealt with in the chapter on supportive behavior.

Ambiguity. The average laboratory experience contains a good deal of built-in ambiguity. The articulated goals of the laboratory are usually so general that one of the major perceptions of the participants is what Benne (1964) calls a "perception of goallessness [p. 217]." Since the trainer, true to his non-directive approach, does little to clarify either goals or procedure, the participants, with mounting anxiety, thrash around looking for viable ways of interacting with one another. Schein and Bennis (1965c) picture the situation in these terms: "The goals are unclear, the training staff provides minimal cues.... The general absence of expectations creates an unstructured, i.e., ambiguous situation. This serves to upset old routines and behavioral grooves and to open up new possibilities for the delegates [p. 44]." In the opinion of Schein and Bennis, "the ambiguous and unstructured situation creates a need to define and organize the environment [p. 31]." Each laboratory will have either marked or minimal ambiguity, in keeping with the nature of the laboratory and its goals. There is a tendency in the literature to consider a high degree of ambiguity essential to laboratory learning. However, in my opinion, excessive ambiguity can sometimes work counter to the principal goals of a laboratory and should, therefore, be mitigated or eliminated. This question, too, will be dealt with separately.

The General Goals of Laboratory Training. Since there are many kinds of laboratories, the specific goals of laboratory training will differ. However, certain general goals applicable to most laboratory experiences may be outlined, although the literature is slow to speak extensively about even these (e.g., Bradford, Gibb, & Benne, 1964). Schein and Bennis (1965a), however, claim that there "seems to be general agreement about the goals of laboratory training," and suggest the following: "(1) self-insight, or some variation of learning related to increased self-knowledge, (2) understanding the conditions which inhibit or facilitate group functioning, (3) understanding interpersonal operations in groups, and (4) developing skills for diagnosing individual, group, and organizational behavior [p. 35]." Most professionals engaged in laboratory training would probably maintain that all goals, both general and specific, must remain flexible and that it is essential to allow the group to create its own goals and to move in fruitful, though perhaps unexpected, directions.

Exercises. Exercises are used in most laboratories to stimulate participation, to introduce missing elements into the group experience, and to highlight various aspects of participant behavior. For instance, individual members might be given a problem to solve. Once they have reached an answer and have indicated their degree of certainty about it, they are placed in small groups in which members have different answers. They then discuss the problem and must eventually reach a single answer. Finally, after the answer has been presented, members discuss how they worked toward achieving consensus in the group and what emotional problems arose. Exercises may be verbal or nonverbal. Groups that focus on self-actualization processes and emotional issues tend to rely more heavily on nonverbal exercises. These will be discussed in greater detail in chapter 7.

Laboratory Populations. For the most part, participants are drawn from normal rather than psychiatric populations. However, special laboratory techniques have been used in psychiatric populations (Morton, 1965) and with a good deal of success (Johnson, Hanson, Rothaus, Morton, Lyle, and Moyer, 1965). Mowrer's (1967, 1968) and Mainord's (1968) approaches to group psychotherapy have laboratory features and, undoubtedly, further explorations in the use of laboratory methods with psychiatric populations will take place.

Differences in Laboratory Experiences. A group of executives may participate in a laboratory dealing with the relationship of managerial styles to human relations and productivity. A university laboratory course in group dynamics may learn about the nature and dynamics of small groups by actually becoming a group. It is obvious that the focus of learning of these two groups will differ.

What is not quite so obvious is that strikingly different kinds of growth and learning can take place even in similar groups participating in similar laboratories in the same residential center. Exactly what is learned or what kind of growth takes place depends on the style of leadership, the peculiar nature of each group, and the goals that it creates for itself as it moves through the laboratory experience. Investigations of molar activity have always been difficult for the behavioral sciences, but research in the area of laboratory training is even more difficult because of the diversities outlined here.

Sensitivity Training: A Species of Laboratory Learning. The distinction about to be made is not currently emphasized in the literature, but it governs the use of the terms "laboratory learning" and "sensitivity training" throughout this book. I am aware that some will find the definition of "sensitivity training" used here too restrictive, but I believe that the term must be defined and restricted if it is to be used with any kind of even quasi-technical clarity. Sensitivity training, as understood here, is a particular kind of laboratory learning *in which personal and interpersonal issues are the direct focus of the group.* Other goals, such as learning about group processes and developing skills for diagnosing group and organizational behavior, are not eliminated, but they are incidental and therefore subordinated to the goal of dealing with personal and interpersonal deficiencies and potentialities. Frankly, I prefer other terms to describe this kind of laboratory experience—for example, a self-actualization and interpersonal-growth experience, a laboratory in basic human relations, or a laboratory in interpersonal relations. Since these terms are less "loaded," I will frequently use them instead of "sensitivity training."

A sensitivity laboratory provides its members a unique opportunity for responsible learning about themselves on intrapsychic and interpersonal levels. Most laboratory experiences, whatever their specific goals, have sensitivity dimensions. The principal focus may be the dynamics of an organization, managerial styles, or group processes; however, the climate is such as to sustain and even demand examination of personal and interpersonal issues, especially insofar as such issues are interrelated with other aspects of the laboratory. House (1967) points to this interrelationship as one of the reasons trainers should be competent in clinical psychology:

Many of the T-Group properties deal with complex psychological and sociological variables. The T-Group is designed to induce anxieties and to stimulate interpersonal feedback, introspection, and self-evaluation. Although some may claim that the T-Group is not therapeutic, within the latitude of T-Group emphasis are methods which closely approximate methods utilized in overtly therapeutic processes. This being the case, I believe it is imperative that T-Group leaders have psychological training equivalent to that required for professional clinical psychology [p. 26].

Schein and Bennis (1965a) describe certain goals as "meta-goals" of laboratory training "rarely articulated by the trainer"—such as a spirit of inquiry (especially into oneself and one's interpersonal living), expanded consciousness and choice, authenticity in interpersonal relations, collaboration with other group members, and conflict resolution through rational means. These I see as direct goals of sensitivity training and see no reason why they should not be suggested or in some way articulated by the trainer. One purpose of this study is to show how the elements of laboratory learning outlined here apply to sensitivity training in general and, particularly, to the contract approach to interpersonal growth formulated here.

Psychotherapy for the Normal?

If sensitivity training as defined here deals directly with personal and interpersonal issues and only indirectly with group process and organization variables, then how does it differ from group psychotherapy? This is a valid but complex question. There is a growing demand among normal people for sensitivity experiences. In order to understand this phenomenon (if it is not just a fad), it is necessary to investigate the whole question of unused human potential.

The "Psychopathology of the Average." Early in the history of modern psychology, William James remarked that few men bring to bear more than about ten percent of their human potential on the problems and challenges of human living. Others since James have said substantially the same thing and few have challenged these statements. "Unused human potential" has even become the war cry of humanistic psychologists and humanistically oriented behavioral scientists and philosophers (e.g., Allport, 1955; Buber, 1937; Jourard, 1963, 1964, 1968; Laing, 1960; Maslow, 1968; May, 1958, 1961; Moustakas, 1956; Mowrer, 1964; Murphy, 1958; Otto, 1966; Rogers, 1961; Van Kaam, 1960; Wheelis, 1958, 1960, to mention but a few).

It is contended here that the problem of unused human potential outweighs the problem of emotional disorder, although it has been rightly claimed that, in terms of social welfare and national economy, mental illness is our most serious public health problem (Schofield, 1964). The problem of unused human resources is not as dramatic or visible as that of emotional disorder and it is not a public health problem, but it is a major problem of public welfare. Moreover, it is much more pervasive than mental illness; the problem of unused human potential affects every man.

Maslow (1968) remarks that "what we call 'normal' in psychology is really a psychopathology of the average, so undramatic and so widely spread that we don't even notice it ordinarily [p. 16]." Perhaps too much energy has been poured into the task of moving men from a state of mental illness to a state of mental health, while not nearly enough energy has been expended on the task of moving the mentally healthy in the direction of self-actualization. Mental health is like air-conditioning. Air-conditioning does not cause pleasure (except by initial contrast or as a status symbol). It gives relief. It renders a person's environment neutral and thus allows him the opportunity to make better use of his human potentiality, if he so desires.

Traditionally, the task of devising ways of developing a normal man's potentialities is the province of education in the broadest sense. Despite the importance of education, however, there is evidence to suggest that *formal* education has failed to serve the function of unfettering human potentiality (Jacob, 1957; Miles, 1964; Rogers, 1961, Chapter 13). For example, creativity among students, far from being encouraged, is often discouraged or repressed (Guilford, 1962; Holland, 1961). Some say that education, at least on primary and secondary levels in this country, is primarily an instrument of conformity rather than liberation (Friedenburg, 1963).

Thus, the problem of the "psychopathology of the average" must be attacked at its roots if there is to be any widespread success in dealing with it. Limbacher (1967a, 1967b) has suggested a training program in mental health for grammar school students. His program has a preventive-mental-health orientation rather than one of self-actualization. As it stands now, it seems to me too didactic and overly insight-oriented. Laboratory-learning approaches and sensitivity-like experiences would seem more suited to children of that age. However, he at least realizes that emotional education must accompany intellectual education in the school system itself.

Steinzor (1968) looks forward to the day when "the curriculum of our public and private institutions, from the earliest grades on, will have made the language of honest, warm dialogue a required part of general education [p. 9]." Full interpersonal living depends upon a person's ability to involve himself effectively, even creatively, with others, but this does not just happen, nor is it the result of a "gift" of creativity in human relationships. People have to *learn* how to interact with others. But until recently, children (and adults) have not been taught how to involve themselves with others. Children spend an enormous amount of their school time doing things next to, instead of with, others. Our society teems with this kind of "parallel" learning just as it does with "parallel" living. Therefore, it is essential, from the earliest years of education, to find ways of putting people into more effective human contact with one another. Interpersonal growth experiences, such as sensitivity-training laboratories, are showing us that people can learn how to live with themselves and with others more effectively. Human-relations learning is perhaps the most important kind of learning, but it is the most neglected. Perhaps it is presumed that such learning occurs naturally outside the classroom situation. Most often it does not; therefore, the majority of persons reach adulthood without being self-actualized on an interpersonal level.

D-needs, B-needs, and M-needs. Maslow (1968) sees the origin of neurosis in a person's "being deprived of certain satisfactions which I called needs in the same sense that water and amino acids and calcium are needs, namely that their absence produces illness [p. 21]." Some of these basic needs are for "safety, for belongingness and identification, for close love relationships and for respect and prestige [p. 21]." These are D-needs (for "deficiency"). Such needs, if unfulfilled, stand in the way of further human growth. Counter to D-needs are the B-needs (for "being") of the person whose D-needs have been adequately satisfied but who still feels a drive toward further self-actualization. For instance, a person may need B-love rather than D-love. D-love is "deficiency-love, love need, selfish love [p. 42]"; it is possessive and always characterized by a rather marked degree of anxiety and hostility. B-love, on the other hand, is "love for the Being of another person, unneeding love, unselfish love [p. 42]"; it is non-possessive, can never be sated, and possesses a minimum (almost non-existent) degree of anxiety and hostility. "B-lovers are more independent of each other, more autonomous, less jealous and threatened, less needful, more individual, more disinterested, but also simultaneously more eager to help the other toward self-actualization, more proud of his triumphs, more altruistic, generous and fostering [p. 43]."

I believe, however, that another category, M-needs (for "maintenance"), might be added to Maslow's scheme. While many men might not be grappling with marked D-problems, they still have not moved on to any significant pursuit of B-values, at least in key areas of life such as interpersonal relating. Rather, most of their energies are poured into maintenance functions. Such men work adequately, but often at uninteresting jobs; their home lives are rather neutral, neither hotbeds of neurotic interaction nor centers of interpersonal stimulation; they profess certain religious values, but these values are ritualistic and restraining, holding them back from doing wrong rather than impelling them to involve themselves more creatively in their communities. Such men exhaust their energy in M-functions, and there is relatively little left over for B-functions. Perhaps Phillips (1956) would include those who spend a disproportionate amount of time carrying out M-functions in his term "normally unadjusted adults." In such people, he notes, the approach gradient (the inertia that keeps them from the work of self-actualization) is the primary concern rather than the avoidance gradient (preoccupation with defense mechanisms).

Sensitivity-Training Populations versus Psychiatric Populations. It would be simple to state that sensitivity training is not group psychotherapy since the laboratory population is a normal rather than a diseased one (although, as noted above, laboratory methods are beginning to be applied to group psychotherapy). However, in making such a statement, one would overlook important issues. First of all, it is becoming more and more difficult to distinguish accurately between normal and psychiatric populations. Burton (1965) points out that studies of the non-diseased offer

the possibly novel thesis . . . that the psychically diseased and the non-diseased are not such polar opposites as we had formerly believed—that the existence of the diseased and non-diseased is fundamentally the same and differs only in the mode of being-in-the-world, i.e., in the expression of their humanness. Both have similar problems of being man, feel despair the same way. . . . Possibly only the crucial intensity of existence in each differs from time to time, and the historical and contemporaneous way in which the human condition is met [pp. 384–385].

Schofield (1964) would certainly sympathize with such a thesis, for he believes that the "psychiatrist has frequently expanded the domain of mental illness to include all degrees and kinds of psychological distress, failing to appreciate that the human suffers some pains not because he is sick but because he is human [p. 146]."

Hendin, Gaylin, and Carr (1965), in a study of the non-patient, also have difficulty with traditional ways of categorizing the mentally ill and the mentally well:

It is apparent that the distinction between patient and non-patient is not the same as between sick and well. The discrepancy between these individuals [the subjects of the study] and any textbook description of "healthy" or "ideal" adjustment is striking. The interesting question then arises as to what integrative forces permit individuals to function, often with purpose and adaptation, constructively and productively, in spite of underlying difficulties. ... It is somewhat disconcerting that in the present study the nurse whom the interviewer described as one of the most disturbed girls was also described as "dramatic and engaging," while the "colorlessness" of one of the most normal of the group led the interviewer to speculate on how depressing it would be if this is what constitutes "normality" [pp. 105–106].

Maslow (1968) and Rogers (1961, 1963) have also been studying normal groups in an effort to establish a baseline for psychotherapeutic treatment.

A total re-evaluation of the fruitfulness of the medical model in dealing with problems of living is taking place (Ellis, 1967; Kanfer and Saslow, 1965; Sarbin, 1967; Scheff, 1966; Szasz, 1960, 1961; Werry, 1968). As Schofield (1964) notes, "the total case load of those who are mentally and emotionally diseased is composed primarily of persons who are neither in need of, nor responsive to, specific medication, surgery, hospitalization, or other physical regimens [p. 1]." Given such turmoil even within the "healing guild," it would seem unwise to characterize any kind of sensitivity training as a psychotherapy for the normal, even though there are definite similarities between the two experiences. Though many people stand in awe of the term "psychotherapy," there is nothing mystic about it. Psychotherapy is a human growth experience that usually takes place in a relational context (as is a laboratory in interpersonal relations). The therapist variables (e.g., non-possessive warmth, genuineness, accurate empathy, responsible confrontation, concreteness) and patient variables (e.g., openness, a willingness to experiment with self-exploration, and other forms of growthful behavior) that characterize good psychotherapy do not differ significantly from the trainer and participant variables that characterize a good laboratory in interpersonal relations. However, the purpose of sensitivity training may be explained in terms of the D-, M-, and B-needs of relatively normal populations.

Sensitivity Training in Terms of D-, M-, and B-needs. Some experimenters feel, unrealistically, that participation in sensitivity-training experiences should be restricted to those in whom D-needs are no longer active factors and whose energies are not tied up in M-functions, so that the laboratory might center around B-needs, B-values, and B-functions exclusively. Bugental (1965) attempted to set up such a laboratory, terming it "Advanced Sensitivity Training." Members were chosen because of "functional excellence" in vocation, marriage, and friendship relations, because they manifested an observing and curious ego, and because they were highly motivated for group interaction. Also, they gave evidence of possessing adequate tolerance for psychic stress arising from ambiguity, intrapsychic conflict, interpersonal conflict, uncertainty, and risk. But, while everything looked fine on paper, things did not work out as well in practice:

Our hope to select a group freer than usual of the deterrents of psychic disturbance was in vain. The group was a fairly typical selection of twelve functional, reasonably socially effective people who nevertheless were beset by a clear range of emotional interferences with their functioning.

We, as trainers, were severely handicapped in attempting to give primary emphasis to positive forces in the participants' personalities by our own unresolved neurotic components and by our years of training and experience which have been largely in the frame of reference of psychopathology and dealing with deficiency motivations. Time and again we found ourselves most active in the familiar ways of pointing to interferences and distortions and least effective in facilitating growth, venturing, and creativity.

The participants, as faithful products of their culture and personal histories, seemed to be more ready to recognize and deal with that which was negative and pathologic within themselves and unsure and self-conscious about the positive and creative [p. 112].

Sensitivity training purports to deal with the whole man, and every man, even those most engaged in B-functions, must grapple to some extent with D-needs and M-functions all of his life.

If a sensitivity laboratory were composed principally of participants with unresolved D-needs, it would be much more similar to a traditional outpatient psychotherapy group than to the groups envisioned in this book. Slater (1966) even claims that "members of groups with which I am familiar benefit in inverse proportion to their therapeutic need [p. 253]"; it would be difficult, however, to validate such a statement, given the difficulty of measuring "benefit" and "therapeutic need." Sensitivity groups, as dealt with in the literature and here, are usually made up of participants with a mixture of D-problems, various degrees of M-function overinvolvement, and B-aspirations and skills. For most of the participants, D-needs are not the overriding interactional concern during group sessions; but nearly all of the participants express some D-concerns. Therefore, in almost all sensitivity groups, some time is spent in hunting down the sources of personal and interpersonal "noise-in-the-system." Or, as Bugental (1965) puts it, "much of the typical sensitivity-training program and most of psychotherapy have been concerned with exposing and (hopefully) overcoming those forces within individuals which limit their abilities to fully realize their potentialities [p. 107]."

A more important focus in sensitivity groups is M-involvement, or rather M-overinvolvement. In fact, it is the person who is overcommitted to M-operations in his personal and interpersonal living who is the principal victim of the "psychopathology of the average." In a laboratory in interpersonal relations, the participants can expect to be challenged to move beyond mere M-concerns in their interpersonal living.

Thus, the sensitivity-training laboratory deals with the D-, M-, and B-concerns of its participants, but the proportion of time and energy spent on each set of concerns, either in the case of an individual or of the group as a whole, depends on the composition of the group and the directions in which the group moves. It must be recognized that D-, M-, and B-concerns are interactive. For instance, overinvolvement in M-activity might lead to frustration and D-reactions. Or a participant might discover that experimentation with some kind of B-activity, such as practicing new ways of being responsibly present to the other members of the group, might eliminate some D-symptom, such as psychosomatic distress.

The Contract-Interpersonal-Growth Group

It is against the somewhat confused and ill-defined background of laboratory learning and sensitivity training that this study is written, a study that purports, first of all, to outline the major variables operative in any kind of group the purpose of which is interpersonal growth and, secondly, to establish a methodology for a particular kind of sensitivity-training group called, somewhat ungracefully, a "contract-interpersonal-growth group."

Ways in Which the Contract Group Differs from Traditional Sensitivity Training. The contract group has a much higher degree of structure and of "visibility" (the opposite of ambiguity) than do traditional sensitivity-training groups.

First of all, prospective participants realize what kind of experience they are about to undergo, for the major features of the contract experience are outlined for them, either by lecture or in writing, before or at the time they enter the group. Once they understand the principal features of the proposed laboratory, they are free to enter the experience or not. In other words, entry into the group takes place "by contract," the description of the sensitivity experience being the "contract" to which participants subscribe. In practice, I have found that if they freely choose to participate in a sensitivity-training experience, the contract need not be explicitly chosen but rather may be "imposed" as the defining structure of the experience. For good or ill, this eliminates a good deal of the ambiguity usually associated with the initial stages of the laboratory and also eliminates much of the anxiety resulting from this ambiguity. Anxiety, however, is by no means entirely eliminated; rather, its source and focus change. Once the participants realize, even in a general way, what is expected of them, their anxiety centers around their willingness and ability to fulfill the contract.

Secondly, the contract (chapter 2) provides a certain degree of structure for the laboratory; it establishes definite goals (chapter 3) and definite interactional means to achieve these goals (chapters 6–9); it defines the kind of leadership that is to characterize the group experience (chapter 5) and the general laboratory orientation of the group (chapter 4); finally, it points out the principal ways in which participants flee from sensitivity experiences and suggests ways in which members might take a stance against such flight (chapter 10).

The kinds of interaction seen as facilitating growth are self-disclosure (chapter 6), total human expression, including honest expression of emotion and the use of non-cliché language to translate oneself to the other members of the group (chapter 7), support (chapter 8), and responsible confrontation (chapter 9). At first glance, it might appear that the contract provides too much structure, but in practice, the structure is seen as facilitating rather than regulating and provides ample opportunity for both individual and group initiative. Therefore, chapter 2 explains in detail the reasons for sensitivity training by contract and subsequent chapters both explain the provisions of the contract and provide the rationale for each provision.

It is not suggested that the sensitivity-training contract described here is the only viable one. Many different kinds of contract could be set up for laboratories in general and sensitivity training experience in particular. The discussion here, therefore, is both a detailed account of a contract approach to one kind of laboratory experience and, perhaps more importantly, a paradigm for a wider variety of group experiences.

High visibility and the introduction of a good deal of structure (even to the definition of the modes of interaction demanded in the group) are actually rather radical departures from sensitivity-training theory and practice. Their potential value will be one of the principal emphases in this study.

The Parentage of the Contract Group: Therapy and Group Dynamics. The sources of the kind of group process suggested here are many. Of the three models of man described by Allport (1962)— man-as-reactive, man-as-reactive-in-depth, and man-as-a-being-in-the-process-of-becoming—the last has been the most influential, though the others have not been excluded. The immediate stimulus to formulate a methodology for sensitivity training came from my attempts to puzzle out for myself the difference between good and bad group process during t-group meetings of staff members and in group psychotherapy sessions with patients at Galesburg State Research Hospital, Illinois.

I have drawn on the theoretical formulations and the research findings of a number of fields: individual and group psychotherapy, laboratory training, social psychology in general, and group dynamics in particular. Theory and research in psychotherapy are very helpful in formulating programs for laboratories in interpersonal relations because the activities that take place in the context of psychotherapy are intense, growthful forms of relating. For instance, the patient begins to trust the therapist's genuineness, warmth, and acceptance and, therefore, is willing to disclose himself to the therapist, perhaps at some of the deepest levels of his being. The therapist responds with understanding and support and perhaps even self-disclosure. This kind of relationship is therapeutic because it is fully human, but because it is fully human, it belongs first of all in ordinary human life and only secondarily in the context of therapy. Many of us are afraid of intimacy, of deep human relations, and we would gladly relegate them to the therapeutic encounter. Laboratories in interpersonal relations have come into being in order to reintroduce men to deeper relationships, to challenge the assumption that the deepest human relationships may exist only between a client and his therapist. Much of the research, then, being done in the area of psychotherapy tells us a great deal about how to form closer, more growthful relationships with others.

Social psychology, because it deals with all forms of human relating, has much to tell the clinical psychologist. Unfortunately, too few clinicians read the social psychology literature. Those who reject a constricted medical model in dealing with problems and anxieties in human living desperately need to know how man relates to man in all areas of living. Clinicians frequently tend to see pathology everywhere because they do not have a sufficient feel for the wide range of human response found in the normal man, or at least in the man afflicted only with the "psychopathology of the average." Reading in the literature of social psychology can help counteract this tendency. This literature is referred to from time to time in the following pages, but it is just a beginning.

Since this study deals with groups, it seems only natural to refer to the group dynamics literature of social psychology. Although Lott and Lott (1965) claim that "since applications of so-called group-behavior principles are *often* urged in such fields as *group psychotherapy,* education, and community relations, it is vital to distinguish between validated and unvalidated hypotheses ... [p. 299, emphasis added]," it strikes me that the failure to make adequate use of group-behavior principles in the practice of group psychotherapy is one of the foremost problems in this field. Many group psychotherapists do little more than conduct individual therapy in front of an audience, completely failing to apply the laws of group interaction to the therapeutic process. Some psychotherapists, principally psychoanalysts, have resisted the application of principles drawn from the study of group dynamics to group psychotherapy on certain theoretical grounds (Locke, 1961; Lowrey, 1944; Wolf & Schwartz, 1962), while others, also on theoretical grounds, urge such application (Bach, 1966; Goldstein, Heller, &

Sechrest, 1966; Hunt, 1964; Lorr, 1963; Schneider, 1955). Small-group dynamics and group psychotherapy are the "twain" that have never really met; the group psychotherapist and the group dynamist have not been reading each other's literature. In self-actualization and interpersonal-growth laboratories, the two fields converge in a natural way. But the literature on sensitivity training, even though it has grown from an education- and social psychology-oriented background, still does not make sufficient use of group behavioral principles. An attempt is made to apply these principles in the following pages, but it is only a beginning. One hope is that interpersonal-growth experiences with normals, using principles drawn from individual and group psychotherapy, social psychology, and group dynamics, will produce research data which will help clear the confusion about psychotherapy with the disturbed.

A Theory of Method.   Rioch (1951) points out that most theories of psychotherapeutic process are really theories of method, not formulations of the nature of the process. The same could be said about most theories dealing with the process involved in sensitivity, growth, or basic-encounter groups. While the present study is ad-mittedly a theory of method, throughout it there are glimpses of an underlying formulation of the nature of the growth process. Any attempt to provide a rationale for including certain interactional variables, such as self-disclosure and confrontation, would have to make assumptions about the processes involved in interpersonal growth.

Other Contract Groups.   The idea of growth through contract is not widespread. In the field of psychotherapy, both Mainord (1968) and Mowrer (1968) exact contracts from prospective patients for the group growth experiences that each conducts. Mowrer's con-tract contains three provisions: the prospective group member must agree (1) to be completely open about himself to the group with respect to both past and current behavior, (2) to take re-sponsibility for himself once he enters the group (not to blame others for his predicament), and (3) to get involved with the other members of the group. Mainord's contract is somewhat similar to Mowrer's. What is most noteworthy is that these are some of the first attempts to introduce a high degree of visibility into the psy-chotherapeutic experience itself. In the area of sensitivity training, Bach (1966) has formulated a kind of contract for a marathon group experience. These "Ten Marathon Commandments" form a contract designed to make the marathon experience, which Bach describes as an "intensification and acceleration of transparency and genuine encounter by a deliberate instigation of group pressure focused on behavioral change [p. 995]," even more intense. Bach's contract will be discussed in the chapter on confrontation.

The Question of Training Trainers

The question of training effective trainers for laboratory groups, and especially for sensitivity groups, parallels a problem in the field of psychotherapy discussed by Schofield (1964). Schofield claims that many of the people flocking to mental-health professionals do not suffer from traditional forms of mental disturbance (such as those delineated in the American Psychiatric Association's diagnostic manual), but rather from what he calls "philosophical neuroses," characterized not by specifically neurotic complaints but by an "absence of faith, of commitment, of meaning, of the need to search out personal, ultimate values, or of the need to live comfortably and meaningfully each day in the face of final uncertainty [p. 150]." The philosophically neurotic, frequently because they can afford to, monopolize too much of the time of mental-health professionals. Therefore, Schofield calls for a way of increasing "the number of persons who are adequately skilled and appropriately competent to converse therapeutically [p. 3]."

Rioch, Elkes, Flint, Usdansky, Newman, and Silber (1963) took a step in this direction by training housewives as "mental health counselors." Their theory is that extensive academic training and formal degrees are not necessary to produce effective counselors, especially when these counselors are supervised by professionals. A follow-up note (Anonymous, 1967) indicates that all of Rioch's trainees (except one who dropped out because of illness) are working successfully in individual therapy, counseling, or group therapy. Three have gone on to advanced study in psychology or social work. The same note indicates that other centers (e.g., Johns Hopkins) are presently training nonprofessionals for work as therapists.

The whole question of who should be doing therapy (and, by implication, conducting laboratories in interpersonal relations) is a thorny one:

In the field of psychotherapy, evidence suggests that the most important determinant of the therapist's effectiveness lies in his personality, his capacity to empathize with the patient and to a much lesser extent his actual experience working directly with patients (Truax & Carkhuff, 1964). It seems that the preclinical experience such as medical school, Ph.D., School of Social Work, and other intensive educational procedures are largely irrelevant in this sphere as currently practiced (Schofield, 1964). What is even more devastating, according to an informal study conducted by Meehl, a significant number of practicing psychotherapists, despite the most intensive training, are judged by their colleagues as incompetent or ineffectual. Thus, we must assume that in the field of psychotherapy (perhaps excluding behavior therapy), the relevant sphere of knowledge is largely located in the area of *common* rather than *scientific* knowledge. This assumption is further buttressed by the fact that various studies suggest that people without the background of mental health professionals can, after a short period of clinical experience, achieve a facility in certain kinds of psychotherapy (taking account of the difficulty of making such evaluations) equal to that of someone with as tortuous and expensive an educational background as the psychiatrist (Rioch et al., 1963; Poser, 1966) [Werry, 1968, p. 7].

In my experience, the socially intelligent person, the person with a "feel" for his fellow human beings, makes the best trainer.

I would like to see programs similar to training programs for lay therapists instituted for training trainers for sensitivity work. Sensitivity-training groups seem to be excellent forums in which the problems of the philosophically neurotic can be resolved. Therefore, such programs would relieve some of the pressures under which mental-health professionals are now working. While few universities have set up programs for training trainers for laboratory work in general, and sensitivity training in particular, such university centers would fill a serious lacuna in the clinical sector of the behavioral science field. Not only could institutes be set up to train, and perhaps to certify, trainers (many groups looking for competent sensitivity trainers have no way of verifying the credentials of prospective trainers), but desperately needed research programs could also be established in these centers. Entrance into such programs should be controlled; not those who are competent only academically, but rather those who possess both academic *and* social competence, would be accepted for training. Such programs could become excellent ways of making "increased use of 'peripheral' resources such as teachers, clergy, and others [Schofield, 1964, p. 169]."

The Audience to Which
This Study Is Addressed

At present, no book deals directly and exclusively with sensitivity training in the sense in which it has been defined here (a laboratory experience centering around personal and interpersonal concerns). Although the present study does outline a specific approach to a laboratory in human relations, it deals principally with those variables (self-disclosure, expression of feeling, support, confrontation, and self-exploration as a response to responsible confrontation) found in any group experience in which self-actualization and interpersonal growth are goals. In a preliminary form, this study has been used as a text in a laboratory course in human relations and as an adjunctive text in courses in counseling and psychotherapy. It should be of interest to anyone who has already participated in, or is about to participate in, a laboratory experience with any kind of sensitivity orientation. Finally, anyone interested in interpersonal growth might find a stimulus for both reflection and action here, for much of what is discussed can be used outside laboratory and group settings.

Chapter Two:
The
Contract

Groups as Natural
and Groups
as Contractual

The Varieties of Groups. The field of group dynamics is very broad. There are many kinds of groups and many attempts have been made to classify them:

Over the years, many different classificatory schemes have been proposed. A common procedure has been to select a few properties and to define "types" of groups on the basis of whether these properties are present or absent. Among the properties most often employed are: size (number of members), amount of physical interaction among members, degree of intimacy, level of solidarity, locus of control of group activities, extent of formalization of rules governing relations among members, and tendency of members to react to one another as individual persons or as occupants of roles. Although it would be possible to construct a large number of types of groups by combining these properties in various ways, usually only dichotomies have resulted: formal-informal, primary-secondary, small-large, Gemeinschaft-Gesellschaft, autonomous-dependent, temporary-permanent, consensual-symbiotic. Sometimes a rather different procedure has been advocated in which groups are classified according to their objectives or social settings. Accordingly, there are said to be work groups, therapy groups, committees, clubs, gangs, teams, coordinating groups, religious groups, and the like [Cartwright & Zander, 1968, p. 24].

There is an extensive literature dealing with the interactions within groups and between groups, but, as Cartwright and Zander note, "only beginnings have been made [p. 25]."

The Conversation Group. In many small groups, the participants come together to talk with one another; conversation (social interaction) is either the principal goal of the group or one of the principal means of achieving some other goal. Conversation groups that meet by design come together for a variety of purposes—to negotiate a labor contract, to discuss community problems, to enjoy one another's company, to engage in group psychotherapy, to engage in a laboratory course in group dynamics. These conversation groups may have a highly structured purpose (for instance, to work out a labor contract) or a deliberately vague one (for instance, to learn about small groups by actually *being* a small group). The goals of the group are achieved principally through face-to-face conversation: decisions are reached, people get to know one another, and personal problems are handled. This study deals with the small, face-to-face conversation group interested in personal and interpersonal growth.

Contracts in Conversation Groups. In all small, face-to-face conversation groups that come together by design, there is at least a vague, implicit, and minimal contract—a series of rules—that makes the group operative and gives it direction. The members, either explicitly or implicitly, agree to follow these rules in order to achieve the purpose of the group. First, the participants agree to come to the group gatherings. Secondly, they usually agree to engage in or at least listen to the conversation in the group. Sometimes they agree to talk about something quite specific—for instance, the provisions of a labor contract. At other times, there is a more vague contractual specificity; for instance, those who agree to participate in group psychotherapy sessions realize that they are agreeing to talk about their problems or themselves with some degree of openness. At other times, members of a group agree to engage in unstructured conversation—for example, in academic laboratories in group dynamics and in sensitivity-training laboratories.

Ordinarily, in laboratory-training situations, there is no predetermined topic of conversation. The point, however, is this: these groups run according to a certain set of rules. The rules might well change as the group moves forward, but at any stage of the development of the group, a set of rules is operative. This is the *contract* which governs the group. Implicit in any group contract are the goals or purposes of the group and the means the group uses in order to achieve these goals.

Leader and Member Contracts in Small Groups. If the small group has a leader, there are at least two kinds of contract operative in the group: the leader contract and the member contract. The leader himself may be working under two different but related contracts: a commercial contract and a process contract. For instance, in a group psychotherapy situation, the commercial contract stipulates that the leader be paid, either by the patients or by a sponsoring agency, for using his professional skills to guide the participants to better levels of adjustment. The commercial contract usually assumes his professional competence and allows him to run the group as he sees fit. But the therapist himself usually has a specific approach to the therapeutic situation; he has goals in mind and some idea of the means he will employ in order to reach these goals. Thus, the therapist operates within a therapy-process contract which he himself has devised. This contract is usually quite flexible and it changes as he grows in experience. However, if the therapist is also involved in a research project, he might be operating under a therapy-process contract not entirely his own. It may have been devised by a research team of therapists and, once designed, imposed on all therapists working on the same project. Such a contract serves to standardize the therapeutic process for the sake of research.

The provisions of a member contract specify the ways in which the members are expected to act during the small-group experience. For most small, face-to-face conversation groups, the member contract is minimal and vague. For instance, when the faculty members of a high school meet to discuss the issues facing the institution, they operate under some kind of minimal contract, but the contract is practically never articulated. It is assumed that they know the reason for the meeting and what they are to do. In most laboratory-training situations, including laboratories in self-actualization and interpersonal relations, the member contract remains similarly unarticulated. The participants realize that they are a group of "non-patients" (Henden, Gaylin, & Carr, 1965) or of "nondiseased" (Burton, 1965) individuals pursuing personal or interpersonal growth through the group process. They realize they constitute a growth group, but they have only the vaguest idea of how they should act in such a group. A similar statement could be made about patients or clients entering psychotherapy; they realize that they are patients, but they usually have only a vague idea of what is expected of them during the therapy sessions.

The contract group differs from other kinds of laboratory-training or growth groups in that both the leader contract (the process rather than the commercial contract) and the member contract are spelled out in some detail *before* the group experience begins. Because both contracts are understood by all the participants from the beginning, the group is said to have high visibility, or comparatively low ambiguity. It should be emphasized that the use of an explicit contract is only one approach to growth-group experiences.

"Natural" Interactions versus "Contractual" Interactions in Small Groups. A distinction can be made between two kinds of small-group interaction (a distinction which I have not seen elsewhere, but which is important in understanding the nature of contract groups)—the distinction between N-interactions and C-interactions. *N-interactions* (for "natural") take place in small, face-to-face groups precisely *because* they are small, face-to-face groups, pursuing a goal principally through group conversation. In a sense, group-dynamics studies such as those of Hare, Borgatta, and Bales (1962) and Cartwright and Zander (1968) are attempts to identify and summarize the laws operative in such groups. These studies deal with such group-related topics as pressures toward uniformity, cohesiveness, power and influence, communication networks, equilibrium, role differentiation, leadership, motivational processes, and other variables operative merely because a number of people have come together for a purpose. *C-interactions* ("contractual"), on the other hand, take place because of the purpose of the group; that is, they arise from the contract to which the group participants have subscribed. A couple of examples will help clarify the difference between N-interactions and C-interactions.

The first example refers to group psychotherapy. A person in group psychotherapy might reveal something about himself, such as a personal problem, in order to please the therapist and his fellow group members. In this case, engaging in self-disclosure is a C-interaction, because talking about oneself and one's problems is vaguely implied in the member contract to which the patients subscribe when they enter the group. Self-disclosure is one of the means leading to the goal of constructive personality change. The implicit contract includes both the goals of the group and the means necessary to achieve these goals. The contract, then, determines what kinds of interactions are appropriate in the group and these are called C-interactions. However, the patient in question engaged in self-disclosure in order to please the therapist and his fellow group members. In small groups, low-status persons tend to engage in interactions that will please the leader and others who are considered higher in status (Collins & Guetzkow, 1964, pp. 166–187). The patient's interaction, therefore, is both a contractual interaction and a natural (dependency) interaction; that is, he did the right thing, but his motivation for doing so was most likely a reflection of his sense of inadequacy rather than his desire to grow. Given the status and power variables operative even in small groups, dependency and counterdependency interactions constitute a part of the group process.

Another example might illustrate the separability of N- and C-interactions. Let us say that a group of executives have met to air their feelings about a proposed merger with another company. No final decision is to be made at the meeting. The purpose of the meeting is to clear the air, and the implicit contract calls for the group members to be as honest as possible in expressing feelings about the merger. The members begin to speak. Mr. X waits until Mr. D, his immediate superior, speaks. Then Mr. X, instead of saying just what he feels, colors his own remarks with what he has heard from Mr. D. His N-interaction is a dependency interaction. But he has violated the member contract. He has not said what he really thinks. There is no C-interaction in this case; there is only the anti-C-interaction of dependency. If Mr. X had said what he really felt, even though he realized that this differed from what others, including his immediate superior, were saying, he would have been performing a C-interaction—open expression of feeling to the group. If he expressed his feelings *in reaction to* Mr. D, then his C-interaction would also have been an N-interaction, namely, counterdependency. But if he expressed his feelings because this was called for by the member contract, and if the contract also warranted responsible confrontation, then his interaction would have been a C-interaction on two counts: honest expression of feeling and confrontation of the opinions of others. But if the implied member contract calls for open expression of feeling, but does not allow a subordinate to confront a superior, then the contract itself is deficient and needs more explicit definition.

Dearth of C-interaction Literature. There is an extensive literature dealing with group dynamics. Much of it deals with the verbal and emotional interactions in the small, face-to-face conversation groups of interest in this study (e.g., Bales, 1950, in press; Bion, 1961; Borgatta & Crowther, 1965; Bradford, Gibb, & Benne, 1964; Cartwright & Zander, 1968; Hare, Borgatta, & Bales, 1962; Homan, 1950; Mann, 1967; Mills, 1964; Stock & Thelen, 1958; Whitaker & Lieberman, 1964). However, since none of this literature deals explicitly with the contracts underlying group membership and group behavior, it says little or nothing about C-interactions. As noted above, it studies groups principally as natural rather than as contractual. Slater (1966), for instance, with extensive experience in academic group-dynamics laboratories, speaks of such things as the "theme of group murder," the "theme of autonomy," the "theme of cannibalism," and the "theme of the sacred king." He talks about the revolts against the leader that take place naturally in groups, but he does not discuss ways of controlling or avoiding such revolts so that the group might be freer to pursue conscious and explicit goals more effectively. Bion (1961) talks of the "fight-flight group," the "pairing group," and the "dependent group," but he does not discuss ways of relating such group cultures to the overall purposes of the group. The point is this: sometimes N-interactions facilitate the work and progress of the group, while at other times they stand in the way of such progress. If a group has a solid understanding (a) of the group's goals and the means to the fulfillment of these goals and (b) of the N-interactions that facilitate or impede the attaining of these goals, then such a group becomes master of its destiny in a way unknown to groups that fail to differentiate between C-interactions and N-interactions.

An Hypothesis Concerning C- and N-interactions. The hypothesis is this: the more explicit both the member contract and the leader process contract are in any face-to-face group and the deeper the commitment of the participants to these contracts, the less crucial N-interactions become. If the member contract is vague and implicit, then variables such as pairing, fight-flight, and dependency naturally multiply and occupy a disproportionate amount of the group's time and energy. However, if the member contract and the leader contract are clear and, furthermore, if they are accepted by the members of the group as a condition of entry, then N-variables become less important. Rather, those N-interactions that are identified with or facilitate C-interactions will multiply, while nonfacilitative N-interactions will decrease. Explicit and universally accepted contracts do not eliminate nonfacilitative N-interactions (e.g., preoccupation with status within the group), but they do bring them out into the open where they can be dealt with more effectively.

Obviously, there has to be a prior decision as to whether the elimination or minimization of N-interactions in the group is a value. If the purpose of the group is to study N-variables through the group process (as it is in academic laboratories in group dynamics), then their prior elimination or minimization would defeat that purpose. However, if increased C-interactions is the goal of the group, and if a condition for their increase is a strong member contract and a strong leader process contract, then the minimization of nonfacilitative N-phenomena is a positive value.

In many laboratory-training situations, one of the precise goals of the group (though it may not be articulated to the participants beforehand) is to discover experientially and become enmeshed in both nonfacilitative and facilitative N-interactions, in order to get a real feeling for what makes groups move forward and what makes them grind to a halt. However, since the focus of this study is a contract approach to sensitivity-training or interpersonal-growth groups, ways of minimizing N-phenomena that impede C-interactions constitute an object of primary concern.

Operationalizing the Group

The Goal as Defining Group Process. The goals of a group give specificity to group interaction. Certain kinds of interaction move the group toward its goals while other kinds hinder goal fulfillment. The overriding goal of sensitivity training (or at least of the kind of contract group that is the focus of this study) is interpersonal growth. Therefore, the problem is to provide a group experience that will facilitate interpersonal growth. Other goals, such as learning how groups work, are not excluded from the total goal structure of the contract group, but they are secondary. Clear and explicit leader contracts and member contracts can help create a group climate conducive to interpersonal growth. The provisions of such contracts should be as detailed as is necessary to help achieve the goal of interpersonal growth.

Operationality. March and Simon (1958) distinguish between operational and nonoperational goals in group process. A nonoperational goal is one that is quite general in itself (e.g., to raise the cultural level of the community) and is not realized by a particular sequence of group activities. Therefore, the function of the member contract and the leader process contract is to break the general group goal—interpersonal growth—into more specific goals and to provide specific group activities designed to realize these goals.

Cartwright and Zander (1960) classify hypothesized determinants of group effectiveness under one or more of the following headings:

1. the extent to which a clear goal is present
2. the degree to which the group goal mobilizes energies of group members behind group activities
3. the degree to which there is conflict among members concerning which one of several possible goals should control the activities of the group
4. the degree to which there is conflict among members concerning means that the group should employ in reaching its goals
5. the degree to which the activities of different members are coordinated in a manner required by the group's tasks
6. the availability to the group of needed resources, whether they be economic, material, legal, intellectual, or other [p. 345].

Contracts can do much to provide these determinants of group effectiveness, for the following reasons: (1) The member-contract specifies both the main goal (interpersonal growth) and subordinate goals (self-disclosure, expression of feeling, confrontation, self-exploration, support) which, when taken together, constitute an operational definition of interpersonal growth. (2) Participants choose to enter sensitivity-training experiences because they want to grow interpersonally. The contract focuses or mobilizes the energies of the group by delineating the kinds of interaction that lead to interpersonal growth. (3) The contract does not eliminate conflict from the group (conflict, too, can be growthful), but it does tend to eliminate useless contract talk. Many participants find it much easier to argue about what the group should do than to engage in specific kinds of group interaction. The contract sets up an experiment in interpersonal growth and invites the participants to engage in the experiment rather than argue about its merits. (4) The contract also specifies the means to be used in the experiment in order to achieve the goal of interpersonal growth. For instance, the contract suggests that such activities as responsible, self-involving confrontation lead to interpersonal growth. The participants are asked to engage in or experiment with such activities (without prejudging the experience) in order to discover whether such activities do deepen their ability to involve themselves with others. (5) The leader is present in the contract group both as a coordinator and as a resource person. He both explains and models contractual behavior and encourages the other participants to engage in the experiment. The member contract stipulates that there will be a leader and it spells out his functions in the group. (6) Most of the resources needed for interpersonal growth lie within the members of the group themselves. The leader brings with him such resources as professional knowledge of group dynamics and experience as a member of groups. He places these resources at the service of the group. Ideally, his skills will become diffused among the members of the group.

Raven and Rietsema (1957) found that members with a clear picture of the group goal and the paths to it had a closer involvement with the group goal, more sympathy with group emotions, and a greater readiness to accept influence from the group than those who were unclear about goals and the paths to them. Apparently, the contract will help increase the members' involvement, sympathy, and openness to change.

The member contract is established, then, in order to introduce a high degree of operationality in the group from the very beginning. It is an effort to make the group be, from the start, what Bion (1961) calls a sophisticated or work group.

Eliminating Wasteful Design.   Wasteful design is not new to the behavioral sciences. The duplication of staff effort in arriving at a useless diagnosis and a treatment program that is frequently ignored anyway is all too common in many mental-health settings. It is my impression that too much wasteful design is found in sensitivity-training laboratories. For instance, a great deal of time in such laboratories is spent hammering out a viable contract to govern the interactions of the members. Sometimes almost the whole time is spent in formulating and reworking this contract. Undoubtedly, the participants learn much about themselves and one another during such an experience and a good deal of interpersonal growth takes place. But, often, the members of such groups leave with a great deal of frustration, because there is no time to implement the contract that has been hammered out. Both the member contract and the leader process contract eliminate a good deal of wasteful design from the contract-interpersonal-growth experience. The prospective member realizes what kind of experience it is and what is expected of him if he chooses to enter. The time usually spent in the elaboration of the contract is spent, instead, in the pursuit of the goals specified by the contract.

Psychological versus Mere Formal Membership in the Group

Being Involved in the Group Experience. The initial acceptance of the member contract by those choosing to participate in the group experience goes far in solving the critical problem of differentiating between what Golembiewski (1962) calls "formal membership" and "psychological membership [p. 67]." It is a common experience in sensitivity groups to herald the "coming out" of a member. "John has finally joined the group" is a recognition that he has passed from just formal to psychological membership. Or perhaps it is rather that John has finally given some concrete sign that he is (and has been) a psychological member. Obviously, the group operates more effectively if all of its members are psychological members from the start. Otherwise, instead of real group process, there is what Golembiewski (1962) calls "the behavior of individuals in an interpersonal situation [p. 67]." The contract, especially if it is freely chosen by the participants from the beginning, does much to elicit psychological participation from the outset of the group. No contract can assure psychological membership, but it can facilitate it. In this study, it is assumed that the members engage in the sensitivity-training experience because they want to and that they could stay away without recrimination. The behavior of those who are forced to take part in some kind of laboratory experience (House [1967] discusses the ethics of such an arrangement) is in a category by itself and is not the focus of this study.

In the contract group, the ordinary criterion used to determine psychological membership is fulfillment or nonfulfillment of the contract. Given the nature of the contract as described in this paper, it would be difficult, if not impossible, for a participant to "fake" psychological membership. The contract demands too much.

Participation in the Common Good. Any group which is more than a group of individuals in a social situation is so because, in some way, the group gives birth to a common good in which all of the members participate. Each member achieves his own individual good by participation in the common good. This common-good aspect of groups is one of the factors that make a group more than a collection of individuals. Slater (1966), however, claims that a group (in context he seems to be referring directly to academic groups engaged in a laboratory in group dynamics) is also *less* than a group of individuals, since only a portion of each individual is present. In the contract group, however, the member contract not only gives greater definition to the common good of the group, but entry by contract, it is assumed, increases the size of the portion of each individual present.

Ambiguity versus Clarity in Growth Experiences

Ambiguity. Over the years writers have sympathized with the person who feels that he must seek help in the form of psychotherapy. Curran (1944), for instance, describes such a person's confusion: "A confused person is likely to approach the first interview feeling a minimum of responsibility for himself and a maximum of fear, insecurity and defensiveness [p. 189]." Not only does the person feel confused as he approaches the psychotherapeutic situation; his confusion often persists because the therapist fails to provide any meaningful structuring: "The patient may at first feel that his task is unorganized and formless and that there are no rules. Then he experiences a strange feeling of helplessness and dissatisfaction. It is as though the therapist did not care what he talked about or how he spoke of it [Ingham & Love, 1954, p. 81]." The problem of the therapist's failure to provide constructive structuring persists, however. Hoehn-Saric and his associates (1965), for example, believe that the problem needs further attention:

Because of the diversity and ambiguities of public conceptions of mental illness and psychotherapy, psychiatric patients reach the psychiatrist's office with a wide variety of attitudes and expectations. Only the most sophisticated are perfectly clear about why they are there and what to expect. Less sophisticated patients may have unrealistic expectations for improvement: they may not understand their role in the therapeutic process and may be bewildered by a procedure that differs not only from usual medical treatment but from customary social interactions [p. 267].

To add to the confusion, even the sophisticated might find it difficult to say why they are sitting in the waiting room of a psychiatrist rather than that of some nonmedical therapist.

Some evidence indicates that patients and therapists have different views of the same therapeutic experience. Truax and Carkhuff (1967) summarize some of this evidence:

Among the plethora of studies concluding, in effect, that therapists prefer "better" patients, that is, those less sick and more sensitive, intelligent, and willing to talk about themselves and their problems, were a few studies showing the discrepant expectations of therapist and patient particularly with regard to the length of treatment (Garfield & Wolpin, 1963): the therapist thinks in longer terms and the patient in shorter terms of treatment. Feifel and Eells (1963), using an open-ended questionnaire to get at differential assessments of therapy, found that therapists tended to stress changes in symptomatic relief and improvement in social relationships, whereas patients stressed self-understanding and self-confidence. In addition, the patients focused on the opportunity to talk over problems and emphasized the "human" characteristics of the therapist, while the therapist focused on therapeutic technique [p. 377].

It is no wonder, then, that failure to structure the therapeutic relationship leads to deleterious consequences, including premature termination. Sherman (1945) found that leaving the client too much on his own resources early in the process of therapy resulted in strong resistance. Levitt (1966) found that patients enter therapy expecting some kind of therapist participation. The failure of the therapist to conform to this preconception reduces the probability that the experience will affect the client. Failure to let the client know the rationale that underlies therapy and to give him some idea of expected therapist and client behavior tends to make the therapeutic experience more manipulative than it should be. (Ambiguity can also be a difficult factor for normals in a task-oriented situation to handle. Mann and Mann (1959) made a study of indefiniteness in a classroom situation. Classroom groups, meeting four times a week for one hour over a three-week period, were organized as task-oriented study groups to discuss assigned reading lists *or* as free discussion groups. Ratings of the members' desirability as friends increased in the former groups and decreased in the latter, where, according to observers, the subjects were frustrated and angered by the indefiniteness of their situation.)

Goldstein, Heller, and Sechrest (1966) express a certain degree of amazement that many therapists fail to tell their clients much about the therapeutic process:

For whatever reasons, few therapists would seem to be anywhere near as explicit as the behavior therapists, either about the theories they hold or about the techniques they employ. But it is unclear whether patients are kept uninformed because (1) it is not believed that informing them would be of any value, (2) desirable results are obtained only when the learning is by self-discovery, or (3) it is believed that the value of the technique and treatment would be impaired by the knowledge of the patient. We would call into question the second assumption and refer the reader to the cogent arguments given by Ausubel (1963) in refutation of the idea that really meaningful learning must come through self-discovery [p. 246].

It would be less than honest to imply that no one sees ambiguity as a value in the therapeutic process. Rogers' (1951, 1961) approach to therapy involves a good deal of ambiguity, which he apparently sees as facilitative and Frank (1961) suggests that ambiguity tends to arouse unpleasant emotions, such as anxiety and resentment, which heighten the patient's desire for relief, thereby increasing his susceptibility to influence. Goldstein, Heller, and Sechrest (1966), however, comment on Rogers' position:

"Reflection of feeling" as a technique in therapy is assuredly manipulative and intended to have some purpose. Even Rogers has admitted that all psychotherapists are in the business of influencing and controlling behavior (Rogers & Skinner, 1956). . . . If the therapist told them (the patients) truthfully that by reflecting the feelings, rather than the content, of the patients' statements he hoped to have them come to a better understanding of their feelings and themselves, it seems much less likely that any resistance at all would be aroused. Whether such a straightforward statement would decrease the effectiveness of reflection as a technique (assuming that it has some) is an empirical matter [p. 247].

Frank's statement sounds too baldly manipulative. However, it is doubtful that either Rogers' or Frank's opinion is what it was in 1961. In fact, Frank is one of the coauthors of the Hoehn-Saric (1965) article previously mentioned, which urges "systematic preparation of patients for psychotherapy."

There is, then, growing dissatisfaction with the kind of ambiguity or secretiveness that characterizes approaches to the growth experience called psychotherapy. Sensitivity-training experiences or laboratories in interpersonal relationships are also growth experiences, though it would be unfair to liken the participants in such experiences to patients or clients entering psychotherapy. The ambiguity that characterizes the goals and processes of most sensitivity-training laboratories might well stimulate growthful activities (e.g., setting goals or formulating a contract). Still, evidence of deleterious effects of ambiguity in psychotherapy suggests that ambiguity need not characterize *all* growth experiences and that structuring a laboratory in interpersonal relations by means of a contract could prove beneficial. There is no need, however, to become embroiled in meaningless arguments: laboratory experiences high in ambiguity and laboratory experiences high in clarity or visibility are different experiences, each with positive and negative characteristics.

Clarity. Since the contract-group is characterized by high visibility, something should be said about the potential advantages of such visibility. Goldstein, Heller, and Sechrest (1966) have reviewed a number of areas of psychological research, such as the psychology of learning, and a number of areas of social psychology, with a view to applying the fruits of this research to the area of psychotherapy. One of the hypotheses established by them is the following:

Hypothesis 5.4a: Giving patients prior information about the nature of psychotherapy, the theories underlying it, and the techniques to be used will facilitate progress in psychotherapy.

We find it remarkable that psychotherapists have apparently been unwilling to impart to their patients more than a little of the process of psychotherapy. Some writers have made general suggestions about "structuring" of psychotherapy (e.g., Fromm-Reichmann, 1950; Holland, 1965; Rotter, 1954; Wolberg, 1954), but such suggestions have been rudimentary and sometimes even evasive. Many, perhaps even most, other writers have ignored the whole question of just what patients should be told about psychotherapy. We believe that in many cases a fuller explication would be quite desirable [p. 245].

In truth, a number of authors *have* discussed the value of structuring the psychotherapeutic encounter; the problem seems to be (though data is lacking) that few therapists have seen fit to introduce formal structuring techniques into their psychotherapeutic approach, especially to the extent that Goldstein, Heller, and Sechrest deem advisable. As early as 1949, Bixler reviewed the literature on structuring, but did so in terms of "the setting of limits." Ingham and Love (1954), on the other hand, take a more positive attitude toward structuring. They suggest six basic process values (all of them really patient variables) which should be communicated to the client both in structuring remarks and through basic attitudes: (1) that it is good for men to investigate themselves, (2) that it is better to investigate than to blame, (3) that emotion is to be regarded as a real and important thing, (4) that there must be relatively complete freedom of expression in the therapeutic situation, (5) that investigating the past may be useful in understanding the present, and (6) that values centering around the client's present view of his world are important for the therapeutic process. More recently, Hoehn-Saric and his associates (1965) have used the Role Induction Interview (RII) "to arouse or strengthen in the patient certain appropriate anticipations of the psychotherapeutic process, particularly with respect to patient and therapist roles [p. 270]." The RII, based on the Anticipatory Socialization Interview of Orne (reported in preparation for publication by Hoehn-Saric and his associates), consists of four components: "(1) a general exposition of psychotherapy; (2) a description and explanation of the expected behavior of a patient and of a therapist; (3) a preparation for certain typical phenomena in the course of therapy (e.g., resistance); and (4) the induction of realistic expectation for improvement within four months of treatment [p. 270]." The research conclusion was that "the RII had a favorable effect on certain aspects of patients' therapy behavior and improvement and, properly used, could be a valuable tool in psychotherapy [p. 280]."

Truax and Carkhuff (1967) refer to a rather interesting way in which initial structuring in therapy might take place:

Vicarious therapy pre-training (VTP) . . . may be employed in either group or individual psychotherapy. It simply involves presentation to prospective patients of a 30-minute tape recording of excerpts of "good" patient therapy behavior. The tape itself illustrates in a very concrete manner how clients often explore themselves and their feelings: it thus provides cognitive and experiential structuring of "how to be a good patient." In short, it allows for a vicarious experiencing of deep psychotherapy prior to the initiation of the psychotherapeutic or counseling relationship. Recent research (Truax & Carkhuff, 1964) completed using VTP in group psychotherapy with both mental hospital and juvenile delinquent patients provides both clinical and research confirmation of its facilitative effect. It was found that early psychotherapy sessions from groups receiving VTP showed significantly higher levels of self-exploration than non-VTP groups having the same number of sessions. Further, VTP resulted in significantly more successful outcomes in time-limited therapy as judged by a variety of objective outcome criteria [p. 373].

The authors mention only patient behavior, but it seems only reasonable to hope that VTP would also give the patient some idea of what to expect from a good therapist.

The Contract as Structuring the Sensitivity-Training Experience. Since psychotherapy deals with human growth, it is my conviction that we should search through the literature on psychotherapy and borrow whatever seems to be beneficial for a sensitivity-training experience. In the contract group, the contract to which the participants subscribe serves to structure the laboratory experience. Since, at least in this study, each of the provisions of the contract is thoroughly explained, the participant knows not only *what* he should do but also *why*. The idea of VTP is a most intriguing one. Even in laboratory groups that subscribe to a contract, there is much initial fumbling around trying to get started. Some groups, even late in the laboratory, take flight by claiming that they still do not understand what they are supposed to be doing. I would like to incorporate a videotape version of VTP as part of the structuring process at the beginning of a laboratory in interpersonal relations. The participants would first preread the contract and get some idea of what is expected of them (and of the leader) in the actual group situation. Then they would watch one or two videotapes of good group sessions—that is, sessions in which all of the major elements of contract behavior were illustrated. This would help make the contract much more concrete and eliminate some of the useless contract talk of early sessions. Objectors might say that viewing a good session would frighten some of the participants who might think that they are not capable of such intensive interaction. On the other hand, however, it might show the participants that intensive interaction can be quite engaging and growthful and not destructive.

These remarks deal with the problem of how much one should know about a growth experience—psychotherapy or a laboratory in interpersonal relationships—before entering the experience. A preference for high visibility in all kinds of growth experiences is stated, or, at least, it is suggested that high-visibility approaches are just as valid as ambiguous approaches. These remarks, however, do not touch on the question of the therapeutic or nontherapeutic nature of self-knowledge. Is it better for a man to know himself completely or is such knowledge, at least in certain cases, potentially destructive? This question is dealt with in the chapter on self-disclosure (chapter 7).

Minimizing Manipulation

A number of authors have discussed the humanistic and ethical problems of deception and manipulation in psychological experimentation (e.g., Aronson & Carlsmith, 1968; Jourard, 1967; Kelman, 1967). Jourard, for instance, sees psychologists as too manipulating in their experimentation. He makes a plea for greater openness on the part of psychologists, even in the area of experimentation, where deception and manipulation have been traditionally seen as both acceptable and necessary. "E" and "S," he says, should get to know each other on a more human level. Aronson and Carlsmith (1968), however, while encouraging a more humane treatment of experimental subjects, point out that it is not always possible to avoid subject distress:

Many questions in social psychology can be answered only by designing experiments which cause subjects some psychological discomfort, such as anxiety, embarrassment, annoyance, insecurity, etc. One simply cannot investigate the effects of anxiety except in situations where people are being caused anxiety [p. 29].

Manipulation and deception are even more suspect as values in therapeutic and other growth situations (e.g., sensitivity-training laboratories) in which the enhancing of responsible self-determination is a traditional goal. In the usual approach to sensitivity training, in which ambiguity is a value, the trainer, justly or not, is sometimes seen as manipulative. After all, he has been through many such experiences and at least *he* knows what is happening and, in a sense, what is going to happen. Even his silence is seen, at times, as manipulative, for he watches as the participants "dance." Even the word "trainer" sounds ominous to some, for, in their experience, only animals have trainers. This is not to say that ambiguity should not be a factor in sensitivity-training experiences. It does mean, however, that trainers should be aware of the impact that ambiguity can have on some participants and that ambiguity should never be used to manipulate. If there is ambiguity in the contract group, it does not stem from hidden dimensions of the experience itself. Individual participants may not be clear as to how to put the contract to work in their own interactions, but this is akin to the "beneficial uncertainty" which Beier (1966) sees as growthful in therapeutic situations. It is hypothesized that both the member contract and the leader contract will serve as safeguards against deception and manipulation.

Group Participants as "Therapists" to One Another

Patterson (1966) has discovered that one characteristic that unites therapists of widely differing approaches is commitment to a particular theory or method. The failure or inability of the therapist to commit himself to a definite approach apparently limits his effectiveness. This does not mean that a person has to identify himself definitively with a particular school of therapy—to be a Freudian, a Jungian, or a follower of Rogers—but he should have a philosophy of therapy that can be translated into therapeutic interaction. Steinzor (1967), when asked to what school he belongs, inevitably replies "Steinzorian." He explains himself:

I hasten to add that I'm not about to establish still another organization, but that it is my whole being, in all my lived and dreamed-of lives —my "voices of experience"—which infuses my interpretations, advice, actions, hopes and confrontations. If pressed far enough, I could add that my allegiance is American; my values are to some an amalgam of my working-class background and my present economic level; my idea of progress is affected by the Judaeo-Christian spirit of Western culture; my choice as the most significant person in modern psychotherapy is Freud; the teacher who has inspired me most is Carl Rogers; my latest enthusiasm and applause for authors in my field are directed to Jerome Frank and Thomas Szasz—and so on [pp. 1–2].

Yet, though Steinzor eschews specific systems, he does have a very vital philosophy of therapy, which he translates into therapeutic interaction. He maintains that therapy takes place when people meet and respond, that healing grows from trust and affection. These are the conditions, not just of therapy, but of human growth itself. It is the purpose of the contract to help put people into growthful contact with one another. Each member becomes a "therapist" to the others—that is, one concerned with the being and the growth of the others. The member contract and the leader process contract provide the therapist-members a definite theory or method to be used in the helping relationship. Acceptance of the contract is the commitment that makes for such "therapist" efficacy.

Some Objections to Growth by Contract

A discussion of objections must deal with two questions: (1) Is the factor objected to really undesirable? (2) Does the contract group foster the factor in question? Obviously, the second question cannot be answered aprioristically; actual experience with contract groups is necessary.

Objection: The contract makes what is usually a "cool" medium "hot." McLuhan (1964) makes an intriguing distinction between "hot" and "cool" communications media. Hot media are characterized by "high definition," a state of being well filled with data. The radio, he claims, is a high-definition medium, while communication by telephone is low in definition. Low-definition media are cool, for the participants have to "fill in the gaps" more and thus become more involved in the communication process. Listening to a tape playback of a group session is hot, for there is high definition and experience would seem to indicate that involvement is difficult. On the other hand, watching (and listening to) a videotape playback of a group session is quite cool. The viewers are flooded with a new communication dimension. They must interpret more (e.g., all the nonverbal communication taking place within the group); there are more gaps to be filled in. Involvement runs high.

Small groups are usually quite cool; that is, they are low in definition and thus deeply involve the participants. Sensitivity training and other forms of small group process have even been called "seductive." It is objected that a contract would make a group higher in definition and thus render a cool experience tepid, if not hot. However, if a group is very low in definition, that is, if it is almost completely without structure, it tends to die. The failure of a group to elaborate for itself some kind of viable contract leads to the "death" of the group. The members can no longer tolerate ambiguity and aimlessness. Ennui sets in; involvement disappears. Nothing is more agonizing than sitting through sessions of a group that has already died. The question is not whether the contract introduces structure; it is, rather, whether the degree of definition introduced by the contract is too high. Obviously, the answer is a function of the particular kind of contract introduced. The contract must be facilitating rather than restrictive. The contention in this study is that the kind of contract to be described in the following chapters is facilitating, that it introduces an optimal degree of definition, that it allows plenty of room for member movement, that it increases rather than decreases member participation, that it focuses the group on issues that in themselves exact participant involvement. The group filled with irrelevant interaction is high in definition, clogged with useless data.

Objection: The contract eliminates spontaneity, induces rigidity. In the contract group, group life is not as unprogrammed as in other forms of training or growth groups. The plaintive "what-are-we-supposed-to-be-doing?" is not heard, or at least not with the same intensity and frequency as in other groups. Slater (1966) claims that because the group is unprogrammed, the members face "questions dealing with the central dilemma of life itself." However, even the detailed contract to be presented leaves the group unprogrammed to a great extent. The leader, while he does try to see that the contract is fulfilled, does not tell the members *how* they are to fulfill it. He does not tell them in what modalities they must engage. If the members of the group confront one another when they engage in flight activity, their action could be looked upon as induced rigidity, but then the term "rigidity" begins to be equivocal. The contract still leaves many choices to be made by the participants, but these choices, because of the contract, are focused on much more central issues. The contract group is much more likely to deal with the key issues of life than is the group which must first hammer out its own contract. The contract provides structure, clarity, or definition, but with plasticity. Definition with plasticity seems to be an ideal condition for a group.

Objection: The contract antecedently limits the freedom of group members. Perhaps "guilty" is the best answer to this charge, but then it is necessary to ask whether such limitation is unfortunate. Maritain (1951), in discussing world states, objects to the concept of sovereignty. The body politic, he says, has a right to autonomy, both internal and external. But sovereignty adds another note to autonomy: the transcendentally supreme character of independence and power. If nations are to work together for the common good of the world, he claims, they must, while retaining their autonomy, surrender their sovereignty. The member contract in the growth group may be looked upon, analogously, as a surrender of sovereignty. Effective interpersonal involvement demands a surrender of sovereignty. Freedom is curtailed, if such a word should be used, in the name of an experience designed to make the group participants more free in their interpersonal living.

Objection: Entry by contract introduces a limiting selectivity factor in the group experience. Some kind of selectivity factor is always at work in both therapeutic and laboratory-training situations. Therapists often limit themselves to those who are considered good candidates (Truax & Carkhuff, 1967, p. 377). Candidates for therapy select themselves according to a number of criteria: for example, the ability to afford time off work, the desire to change, financial considerations, degree of psychic pain, and the desire to please others. Analogous self-selection criteria are operative in all groups. The objection is that the contract introduces an added selectivity factor, so that, for example, a person interested in sensitivity training might not attempt a contract experience. The contract might attract an elite. On the other hand, it might attract those who are desperately trying to improve the quality of their interpersonal living.

In order to discuss this question reasonably, it would be necessary to have the kind of hard data that simply are not available. It will certainly be interesting to see what kind of clientele the contract group draws. However, a desire for interpersonal growth seems to characterize both the interpersonal "haves" and the interpersonal "have-nots." It is hypothesized that those interested in sensitivity training would also be interested in a contract-group experience. In my own experience over the past two and a half years, no one has refused to enter a sensitivity-training laboratory because of the contract.

It is also hypothesized that those who actually engage in some kind of sensitivity-training experience and find it valuable would like to move on to a contract-group-growth experience.

Bugental and Tannenbaum (1965) describe the experience of a group of people who, having found an initial sensitivity-training experience fruitful, wanted to engage in a more high-powered "festival of growth." The participants chosen for the experience were an elite, that is, people who had moved beyond stagnated involvement with D-needs and M-needs. However, they found the experience somewhat disappointing. Either they could not recapture the spirit of their previous experience or the second experience was too much like the first. One view of their plight (though it is not suggested by the authors) might be this: they were eager, they were open, but they were without a feasible contract. New contractual provisions had not been built into the second experience, and therefore it resembled the first too closely. Those who sponsored the second experience could have designed a laboratory with different or more intensive features and these features could have become the provisions of a structuring contract. It is difficult to say whether such an approach would have worked, but it seems that a high-powered contract experience would have been ideal for such a group.

Objection: A contract makes the risk of failure greater. This might well be true, but greater risk of failure is not seen here as a negative factor. "Failure" is an equivocal term when used to describe both physical and psychic healing. If a physical agent is used to try to stem the spread of gangrene, failure means something quite specific. The battle is lost and the foot or leg must be amputated. Failure in psychotherapy is much more nebulous, because the criteria for success and failure are not clear. In one sense, psychotherapy does not fail, but is terminated. One reason that therapy cannot be said to fail is the low operationality of the goals of therapy. But, while low operationality prevents clearly defined failure experiences, especially in the mind of the patient, it also seems to stand in the way of effective therapy. The contract introduces a much higher degree of operationality than is usually found either in therapy or in other kinds of growth experiences. In a contract group, it is almost impossible for a person to say to himself or to the group that he is "getting something out of it" if he is not. He is not getting out of it what he should if he is not fulfilling the contract. And it is quite evident whether he is fulfilling the contract or not. If he tries to rationalize away his failure, his attempts ("These contract things don't work," "It was too contrived to get anything done," "We really didn't have the freedom to move," etc.) should be more transparent and hollow because of the contract. Ordinarily, then, such a person has to take responsibility for the failure himself, for it was *he* who did not engage in the modalities contracted for, it was *he* who fled group process. Because the contract was clear, he can see exactly *how* he fled the group experience. Even his failure is diagnostic. The contract group, because it more clearly defines success and outlines the activities of a successful experience, also heightens the risk of failure. This is good, for it is good to know *that* one has failed and *why* one has failed.

Objection: The contract reduces productive anxiety. There are those who are concerned about the anxiety factor in laboratory experiences:

Can the candidate tolerate the anxiety involved in the T-Group process? Most T-Group participants are adults, already settled in their ways, who have gone through adjustment processes involved in adolescence and early adulthood. They have well-established behavior patterns, habits, responses, values, emotional reactions and defense mechanisms— all of which have now become meaningful to them, and which allow them to operate in their own environment.

The T-Group is a very soul-searching process. It requires the individual to introspect, to look at his own values and his own emotions, to ask himself whether and why he likes them, and whether he wishes to live the way he has. After a person is established in his way of life, two things must be considered: a) Does he have the general ability to tolerate the anxiety involved in this kind of soul-searching? and b) Is he at this time going through some other stress experience such as adjusting to the change of life on the part of himself or other members of his family, or meeting difficult financial obligations?

To prevent avoidable emotional disturbances, admission to T-Groups should be based on a careful screening process designed to ensure that participants are able to withstand and profit from the anxiety induced in the T-Group process [House, 1967, pp. 25–26].

These concerns are very real, especially in the context in which House reviews the literature on laboratory training. He is talking about the application of T-group methods in business and other organizational settings. Sometimes entire organizations or entire departments are subjected to laboratory training without being asked and without being given the freedom to attend or not attend.

But, in the present study, it is assumed that the individual freely chooses to engage in the laboratory experience and in some way reflects upon his ability to profit from it. Indeed, in a contract situation, the prospective participant can make a more intelligent decision as to whether to attend because the contract clearly delineates the nature of the experience.

Participation in growth-group experiences is an approach-avoidance situation. Group process is both seductive and anxiety-arousing. It offers a fresh source of relatedness, but it demands a certain degree of self-immolation. There is the lure of fusion and the terror of it, the hope of greater individuation and the despair of it. Usually, the anxiety aroused as one approaches or begins a group experience is considered to be "anxiety at the service of the ego [Kris, 1952]." It is intimately associated with the pursuit of self-identity, which implies both separateness and relatedness.

Schofield (1964) claims that our society has tended to over-dramatize anxiety:

If this is the Age of Anxiety it is not so simply as a function of absolute increase in the things about which man is fearful. Rather it is so because *we have taught man to be anxious about his anxiety*. We have created a distorted image of anxiety. We have attributed to anxiety and to the efforts to escape anxiety all of man's neurotic ills. We have sensitized ourselves to recognize the signs of anxiety, and we have been encouraged to the fallacious value of a total avoidance of anxiety as a goal of life; we have been led to believe that a complete freedom from anxiety would be the distinguishing characteristic of an adjusted life [p. 152].

Anxiety is part of life. It is up to man to control and use it. Schachter (1959) showed that a state of anxiety leads to the arousal of affiliative tendencies. Man seeks out his fellow man when he is afraid. Need the resultant contact be any less growthful because it was sought in order to reduce anxiety?

The Yerkes-Dodson Law (Yerkes & Dodson, 1908) states that the relationship between fear or anxiety and learning is curvilinear. The level of anxiety or drive which stimulates optimal performance lies somewhere in the middle: the anxiety level must be neither too high nor too low. There has been some confirmation of this law by more recent studies (e.g., Matarazzo, Ulett, & Saslow, 1955; Stennett, 1957). It is assumed that this law is also operative in growth or therapeutic experiences. The ambiguous group situation that initiates sensitivity-training experiences produces relatively high levels of drive. The laboratory is designed to produce anxiety drive.

It is also assumed that there are optimal levels of anxiety for effective group process in contract-interpersonal-growth groups. The member contract does not eliminate anxiety; it is, rather, one of the sources of it. However, since the contract gives a fairly clear picture of the kind of group experience the members are entering, ambiguity and the unknown in general are not the primary sources of anxiety. Anxiety arises from the provisions of the contract and the question of one's ability to fulfill the contract. The contract calls for self-disclosure, confrontation, and a willingness to express human feeling. These seem to be more authentic sources of anxiety than ambiguity; they are more related to real-life concerns. Or, rather, the ambiguity that arises in a person when he views the contract is related to real-life concerns: how open can I be? what will I do when challenged? how can I start expressing my feelings now?

Anxiety in the contract group does not just happen. It is part of the contract. It is explained to prospective participants that in accepting the contract, they are subscribing to a certain amount of anxiety. It is explained that anxiety can be debilitating or it can be an energizer. This more rational approach does not eliminate anxiety. But it does prepare the participant to expect anxiety, to recognize it for what it is, and to use it to energize group activity.

There are relatively great individual differences in both state (situational, transient) and trait (part of the personality make-up, relatively permanent) anxiety (see Levitt, 1966). Participants come to sensitivity-training laboratories, then, with varying degrees of anxiety. It is very important for the trainer or leader to be aware of this. For instance, while certain exercises might have little impact on one participant, they might tend to immobilize another, because the latter is highly anxious. The function of the laboratory is not directly to make people anxious, but to use the anxiety that does arise as a drive. Sometimes, however, it is quite difficult to determine which participants are relatively calm, which are anxious, and which are too anxious. The contract calls for openness on the part of the participants, and disclosure of one's state of anxiety (especially if the participant feels that it is excessive or debilitating) should take place relatively early in the group. Therefore, while the contract itself might well be a potent source of anxiety, it also demands the kind of openness that allows anxiety to surface and be dealt with in the interaction of the group. The contract, then, can both elicit and help to control anxiety. The contract both provides a structure which increases the psychological safety of the experience (e.g., by building support into the experience, by demanding growthful rather than punitive confrontation, etc.) and acts as a stimulus to taking growthful risks (e.g., self-disclosure, expression of feeling, etc.) in the group.

A Variety of Contracts

This study will delineate one general kind of contract experience. But there is an almost endless variety of such experiences. Once the goals of a group are determined, the means can be elaborated. Finally, both goals and means can be made part of the contract. The use of a variety of contract groups in various kinds of experimentation seems to be one of the most promising features of these groups. The variables of the group experience can be spelled out in detail, and fulfillment or nonfulfillment of contract is relatively easy to determine.

Any contract can be purposefully rigid or flexible. In experimental situations, a certain rigidity of contract is called for. The purpose of the experiment is to see what effects *this* contract has. So the fulfillment or nonfulfillment of *this* contract is important. In growth experiences, on the other hand, it is possible to allow for the reworking or reformulation of the contract. In such groups, the goals are more important than the contract itself. If the contract has to be changed in order to provide a more profitable group experience, then it should be changed. However, the reformulation of a contract is a relatively drastic step. Blaming the contract for group or personal failure can be a type of flight from group process. Responsible contract reformulation can be undertaken only after responsible efforts have been made to fulfill the provisions of the contract.

Both in contract experiences and in laboratories characterized by planned ambiguity and goallessness, it is possible to introduce focused contracts in the form of exercises. In a sense, all exercises introduced to the group are contractual; that is, the exercise is generally imposed on the group and the participants are usually expected to follow the rules laid down for the exercise. For instance, in a contract group in which self-disclosure is one of the contractual variables, it is possible to define the topic of disclosure by means of a focused contract. There should be some reason for specifying the topic or area of disclosure and the participants should be willing to have such a subcontract imposed on them.

Lest the term "contract" remain too abstract, a sample contract for a laboratory in interpersonal relations is given below. However concise or extended a contract might be, it should provide a chance for prospective members to get some kind of "feel" for the group experience they are about to enter. Therefore, all of the major variables that will, ultimately, give definition to the kinds of interaction expected in the group should be spelled out adequately. The provisions for the contract below have been chosen because these are the major variables that belong in and take place in sensitivity-training laboratories and in other kinds of groups in which self-actualization and interpersonal growth are the superordinate goals.

A Contract
for a Laboratory
in Interpersonal Growth

This laboratory in interpersonal relations will be conducted according to a contract. The purpose of the contract is to provide a facilitating structure for the group experience and to let you know the nature of the experience you are about to enter. Please read the following contract carefully and then decide whether you would like to participate or not in the kind of experience described in the contract. If you want to participate in the group, you must subscribe to the contract.

The Goals of the Group. The overriding goal of the group is, of course, interpersonal growth. Interpersonal growth involves discovering new ways of being present to others. Personal growth, too, is a goal of the group, but it is assumed that all that is good in personal growth (e.g., reduction of anxiety, enhanced feelings of self-worth, a keen sense of self-identity) must be placed at the service of interpersonal relationships. Man is a relational being and the height of his growth lies in his relationships with others.

Leadership in the Group. The group will have a leader, but since he is not a leader in the traditional sense of that term, he is sometimes referred to by different titles, such as "trainer" or "facilitator." The name is not important, but his function is. He is skilled in group dynamics and has had a good deal of experience participating in and working with groups. However, he is in the group because he, too, is interested in growing interpersonally. Therefore, he subscribes to the same contract that you do; that is, he is a leader-member. As leader, his function is to put his knowledge of groups and his experience in groups at the service of your group. He is a resource person, not a super-member. He is someone like you, interested in increasing his interpersonal effectiveness by involving himself with you. If certain provisions of the contract are not clear, he will explain them to you, but he is not in the group as teacher, at least in the traditional sense. In fact, a good teacher is one who likes to get together with others in order to learn.

The ideal is that the leadership qualities he demonstrates become diffused among the members of the group so that, in a sense, the group might act as its own leader. He will work for that diffusion. What are some of the specific things he will do? He will tell you about some of the difficulties that face most beginning laboratory groups. For instance, some groups spend a good deal of time dealing with the leader; that is, they make him a father figure and try to work out authority problems with him. However, in this group, the leader is not meant to be an authority figure. It is not that the participants may not work through authority problems, but there are other ways of doing this besides focusing on the group leader. If too much time is spent dealing with the leader, this can prove detrimental to the overriding goal of the group. In this group, interpersonal growth means that the members are to spend a good deal of time involving themselves with one another (including the leader-member).

From the beginning, the leader-member will model the kinds of behavior called for by the contract. Again, he does so not because he is completely self-actualized in the area of interpersonal relating, but because the sooner the group begins to engage in contractual behavior, the better.

The Laboratory Nature of the Group Experience. The experience you are about to enter is called a laboratory for a number of reasons. Part of the contract is to accept the experience as a laboratory. This is what a laboratory entails:

(1) *Learning by doing.* You will learn how to relate to others more effectively by actually relating. You will see yourself in action and you will talk about the ways in which you relate to the other members of the group.

(2) *A climate of experimentation.* The term "laboratory" implies experimentation. You will experiment with your own behavior, attempting to relate to others in new ways. This does not mean that the group will invent new ways of acting. Rather, you will try to deal with others in ways that you do not ordinarily use in your day-to-day contacts. For instance, if you are usually quiet and reserved, you may experiment with speaking up in the group. For you, this is a new way of being present to others.

(3) *No prejudging the experiment.* The person who comes to the laboratory convinced that the experiment will not work usually leaves it feeling quite self-satisfied. His prophecy has been self-fulfilling. You are asked not to prejudge the experience but, rather, to reserve your judgment. The only way you will ever know whether the experiment works or not is to give yourself to it as completely as possible.

(4) *Feedback.* Your own behavior is the major input in the laboratory. But trying new ways of behaving is somewhat useless unless it is possible to determine how this behavior strikes others. Therefore, you are asked not only to react to others but to tell others how their behavior strikes you. You, too, will receive feedback from the other participants. By means of such feedback, you should come to a better understanding of your own interpersonal abilities and limitations.

Try to get a feeling for your ability to involve yourself with others. All of us have strong points and all of us have areas of deficit in our interpersonal living. Use the group to get a feeling for both.

Rules of Immediacy. If the laboratory experience is to be intensive, it must be as immediate as possible. Certain rules facilitate a climate of immediacy in the group.

(1) *The here and now.* Deal with the here and now rather than the there and then. Your interactions with one another are the most important part of the laboratory. When you do talk about things that have happened or are happening outside the group, do so in such a way as to make them relevant to what is happening in the group. If you keep talking about things outside the group, people and situations unfamiliar to the other participants, you will lose their interest. Make the outside and the past somehow present to your fellow group members. Talking about people and things outside the group is sometimes a way of fleeing from more intensive group interaction.

(2) *Cooperation.* Your goals can be reached only if you cooperate

with one another. This does not mean at all that there will not be disagreements, but interpersonal growth is much more likely to take place in an atmosphere of cooperation than in one of competition or conspiracy. This does not mean that you have to be "nice" for the sake of being nice; a cooperative group structure does not exclude strong feeling and confrontation. But there is little immediacy unless you move toward the other person in an effort to involve yourself with him. The contract provides a structure for cooperation. If you are fulfilling the provisions of the contract, you can be sure that you are cooperating with the other participants.

(3) *Avoid generalities.* When you speak, try to be concrete and specific. For instance, when speaking about yourself, use "*I.*" Do not use "you" when you mean "I." In fact, try to avoid using general words to refer to people, such as "you," "one," "people," "men," "they," "we," and the like. Do not say: "There are some people in the group with whom I get along better," but rather: "I seem to get along better with John and Mary than with any of the other members of the group." Finally, do not make speeches to the whole group; even if you want to address the whole group, try to address the group through another member. For instance, say: "John, you were not really listening to me this morning; in fact, this seems to be a group problem: we don't really listen to one another." If you address yourself always to the whole group, the other members will often sit there and listen respectfully to you, but no one will respond to you. Speeches addressed to everybody tend to be addressed to nobody. In summary, use "I" when you mean "I"; be concrete, avoiding vagueness and generalities; try to address individuals in the group, even when you are addressing the entire group (in a way, you are always addressing the entire group whenever you speak).

(4) *Do not "siphon off" issues of concern to the group.* Sometimes group members get together in twos and threes and work through issues that have arisen within the group. There is nothing wrong with this *provided* you summarize to the group what has taken place. If the issues come up within the group, then, in some sense, they belong to it. If these issues, then, are settled outside, some of the life of the group is "siphoned off," and the group becomes somewhat anemic because of it; that is, it loses a degree of immediacy.

The Elements of Dialogue: Emotion, Language, and the Fusion of the Two. You will contact one another principally by talking to one another. Language, then, and the expression of feeling are crucial factors for this experiment.

(1) *Emotion.* Try to let reality have an emotional impact on you, especially the reality of the other members of the group. Let yourself feel various emotions; feel what it is like to experience these emotions. Secondly, let yourself react as constructively as possible to what you experience. Do not try to hide the emotional dimensions of yourself. Do not be overly intellectual: ideas are certainly important, but in laboratories in interpersonal relations, emotions are equally important. Tell others, then, not just how you think about things, but how you feel about them. Sometimes our ideas and our emotions do not coincide. It is good to be able to recognize this division within yourself.

(2) *Human language.* Get a new feeling for the power of human language. How do you translate yourself into language? Find out whether your language gives expression to the deep you or only to the superficial you. If you tend to use lifeless language in your day-to-day contacts, experiment with a more forceful use of language in the group. Try to avoid clichés; use words that have more power than the words you ordinarily use. Language can be a form of contact or it can be a barrier between you and the others; try to make your language as contact-producing as possible. If you speak in clichés and generalities, this might well reflect an unwillingness on your part to make deeper contacts with others.

(3) *Poetry: welding feeling to language and language to feeling.* Try to let your feelings find expression in language and let your language be colored by feeling. Some of us experience things deeply, but we cannot translate our experience into language. The laboratory is an opportunity to make attempts to do just that. When you succeed, your language will be, in one of the deepest senses, poetry, for it will be an integrated expression of the person you are.

The Core Interactions. The heart of this contract and, therefore, of the group experience itself is the interaction in which you will engage. You are asked to experiment with the kinds of interaction listed below. They are ways of contacting others, of involving yourself with others and, therefore, offer possibilities of growing with others. You are asked, then, to engage in the following kinds of activity in the group:

(1) *Self-disclosure.* You are asked to be open about yourself. This means that you are to talk about yourself in such a way as to

get the real you (rather than a facade) across to others. In one sense, facts about yourself are not important in themselves; the fact that through them you translate yourself to others in the group is important. You are not asked to reveal your past life or your darkest secrets. *You* are important, not your secrets. What you say about yourself should encourage others to "come in"; that is, self-disclosure should constitute a kind of invitation to others to involve themselves with you.

It is up to you to determine how you will talk about yourself and what you will say. This sounds very abstract right now, and it will be easier to determine in the give and take of the group interaction. There are various levels of self-disclosure: the more personal something is, the deeper it is. The general level of self-revelation is determined by the group itself and depends on a number of factors —for instance, the willingness of individuals to take risks and the level of trust in the group. The point is that the group members, and not the contract, determine the level at which they will work. You will, undoubtedly, reveal yourself at a level at which you feel comfortable, or perhaps a little beyond (that is, you will "risk" talking about yourself). A moderate degree of anxiety in the group is generally a sign that you are working at least a little beyond the level of comfort, and such anxiety, if controlled, can be a help rather than a hindrance. Self-disclosure, if it is authentic, if it is really a translation of yourself, tends to create intimacy. If you have difficulty talking about yourself, if you become too anxious, it might well be that you fear rejection, but it is also possible that you are afraid of the intimacy to which self-revelation leads.

Self-disclosure must be in keeping with the here and now rule. If you talk about your past, you should do so because it tells something about the kind of person you are here and now in this group. If you talk about how you are outside the group, this, too, should be made relevant to the you that is in the group. That is, self-disclosure should stimulate interaction with others. Never just talk on about yourself to a passive audience. In keeping with the here and now rule, one area of self-disclosure is most important: You should talk about what is happening to you in the group. For instance, if you are anxious, let others know that you are anxious: others want to deal with you as you are, but this is impossible if you hide your feelings. If you are bored, let others know immediately. It is deadly to wait an hour and then tell others that you *have been* bored. In a sense, you are responsible for your own boredom if you do not speak up.

Finally, although it was said above that you do not have to talk about your deepest secrets, you may speak as deeply about yourself as you wish. The point is that you will not be forced to do so. Sometimes, if someone else speaks rather personally about himself, you will find it easier to talk about yourself (but you should remember that this works the other way around also).

(2) *The manner of expressing feeling.* Above, you were encouraged to let emotion be part of the group experience. Too often, we swallow our feelings (for instance, our anger) only to let them filter out in rather unproductive ways (we become cold or uncooperative, we make snide remarks or remain silent, etc.). There is another possibility, however: speak frankly about your emotion-laden contacts with one another. For instance, if you are angry, instead of just blowing up or swallowing your anger, let the other know that you are angry and would like to work it through: "John, I'm really angry with what you said, but I'd like to tell you why and get some response from you. If possible, I want to work this out with you here." Perhaps such frankness, coupled with a desire to work things through, would constitute for you a new way of being present to another.

(3) *Listening.* It is amazing to discover how poorly we listen to others. The contract asks you to examine your ability to listen. Listening does not mean just hearing words and sentences and understanding their meaning; rather, it means reaching out for what another has to say; it means listening to persons rather than just ideas. Learning to pick up *all* the cues that others emit, both verbal and nonverbal, is part of listening. Facial expressions, gestures, a shrug of the shoulders, bodily positions—all of these are sources of communication. Often, too, when we communicate with one another, we embed surplus messages in our overt communications by the way we say things. You are asked to become sensitive to the surplus-message aspects of communication also.

(4) *Support.* It is difficult for people to "put themselves on the line," that is, to engage in meaningful self-disclosure and to express feelings responsibly. When you and the other members of the group do make sincere attempts to fulfill the contract, then you need support. It is assumed that you are basically supportive, that is, that you have some kind of basic acceptance of others simply because they *are;* otherwise you would not want to engage in an experience for interpersonal growth. Still, you can accept others sincerely without always approving of everything they do. It may be, for instance, that you reveal things about yourself which you yourself do not

approve. Obviously, then, though you would expect others to support you in your self-disclosure, you would hardly expect them to approve of the things that you disapprove of in yourself.

Support has two phases. The antecedent phase consists in encouraging others to fulfill the contract. For instance, one of the best ways of encouraging others to fulfill the contract is to fulfill it yourself. The leader-member will try to do just this by modeling the behavior called for by the contract. The second phase refers to your support of those who do engage in contractual interaction. Others will reveal themselves; they will express their feelings. Support then means giving some kind of recognition that the other has fulfilled the contract, that he has done a good thing. Support means being responsive to the behavior of others. Again, engaging in contractual behavior is an excellent way of giving phase-2 support. For instance, if one of the members engages in responsible self-disclosure, you may give him a good deal of support by revealing something about yourself in the same area, something that responds to his concern.

Although support is absolutely necessary for effective group operation, it is also perhaps one of the most difficult of the contractual provisions. When someone "invites you in" by being open about himself, you may feel gauche and find it difficult to respond to him. When someone speaks feelingly about himself, it is too easy to ignore his feelings (for this may be an uncomfortable aspect of his communication) and to try to deal with him on an intellectual level —for instance, by asking him a lot of questions. Because of our discomfort, we try to intellectualize the whole process. However, if you are made uncomfortable by what another says, if you are unable to respond in what you think would be a meaningful way, do not pretend that you can. Counterfeit support, expressed in such clichés as "I understand," and "I know how you feel," deadens group process. Perhaps your best response is to admit that you are uncomfortable, that you are at a loss for a response. This can be supportive in itself, because it is honest. Do not try to show conventional sympathy to others merely because you think that you should say something. Support is the gift of one's person and not the fulfillment of a convention. Learning to be present to others in meaningful support is one of the most important tasks of the group experience.

(5) *Confronting others.* Sometimes you will find it impossible to agree with what another person is saying or doing. If this is true, tell him so as honestly as you can, and tell him why. This is con-

frontation. Confrontation is, basically, an invitation to another to examine or reflect upon his behavior "in community," that is, in the context of the group. For instance, perhaps another person in the group is simply not fulfilling the provisions of the contract at all (if he is silent all the time, he could not be). If you tell him this and ask him to examine his behavior, then you are confronting him. The *way* you confront, however, is very important: the cardinal rule is that you should confront another because you are concerned about him and want to involve yourself with him. Confrontation is not just irresponsible "telling a person off." Responsible confrontation is an invitation to self-examination, not an act of punishment. If you are merely punishing another, you might find some relief (for instance, from your anger), but you are doing little to set up interpersonal contact between yourself and the other. Undeniably, confrontation will almost always have some kind of punitive side effects (none of us likes to be challenged because of allegedly negative forms of behavior), but punishment cannot constitute the rationale of confrontation. Sometimes it is difficult to confront without making punishment the primary purpose of the act. Confrontation, then, is something you must experiment with in the group.

(6) *Responding to confrontation.* If confrontation is responsible, that is, if it really is an invitation to self-examination, then obviously the best response *is* self-examination. However, when we are confronted, even by someone who is concerned for us and wants to involve himself with us, our instinctive response is often twofold: to defend ourselves and to attack the confronter. That is, we respond to the punitive side effects of confrontation instead of to the confrontation itself. Therefore, try to listen to what the one confronting is saying and not just to the feelings he is evoking in you. If what he says is true and if, in addition, he wants to involve himself with you, then it is to your advantage to listen, to examine yourself, and to respond to him. This is difficult, but frequently rewarding.

Self-disclosure, expression of feeling, listening, support, confrontation, and response to confrontation—these, then, are the forms of interpersonal behavior with which you are asked to experiment. The ability to engage freely and responsibly in such behaviors *is* interpersonal growth.

A Stance against Flight. Engaging in the kinds of interactions described above is not easy, and therefore we find ways of running away from group process. We tend to run away because we are anxious, because we prefer not to know the truth about ourselves, because it is painful, perhaps, to be the object of another's concern. You are asked, then, to take a stance against all the different forms of flight from intimate group interaction: calling upon humor whenever things get too serious, keeping one's feelings to oneself, spending a good deal of time on intellectualized interpretations of the behavior of others. You must become sensitive to the ways you flee group process and to the different ways in which the group as a whole tends to flee (e.g., by tacitly deciding not to talk about certain subjects). Confronting modes of flight in yourself and in the group is essential to the life of the group. One mode of flight is extremely destructive: cynicism about the experience even before one enters into it. The person who comes to the group believing that he will get nothing from it will leave having fulfilled his own prophecy. Try not to flee from your anxiety by employing defenses. Rather, handle your anxiety by dealing with it in the group. It is obvious, by now, that the contract demands that you be active in the group. Silence and withdrawal are types of flight. Perhaps, in other groups, the nonactive member profits, even though he adds little more than his presence. This cannot be the case in the contract group.

Freedom. This contract is not meant to constrain you; it is meant to help you channel your freedom. It says, for instance, that self-disclosure is a value in this group, but it does not say what you must talk about, nor does it dictate the level of disclosure. This is something that you must work out yourself in the give and take of group interaction. You must choose the kinds of interaction most meaningful to you. Some of the experiments you engage in in the group will be successes and some failures, but this is a reflection of life itself. Try not to expect either too much or too little from the group. The only way you can really learn about the possibilities of the group experience is by giving yourself to it.

The elements in the above contract are found in any sensitivity-training group with the goal of interpersonal growth. The contract provides a certain degree of what Boy and Pine (1963) call "structured permissiveness"; it is both a stimulus and a safeguard: it moves the participants toward intensive interaction, but it lays down certain ground rules to insure that this interaction will be growthful.

It facilitates the formation of a "cultural island" in which the participants are given a good deal of "cultural permission" to investigate the possibilities of intimacy with one another; risk taking is not eliminated but it is controlled.

The Focused Contract

Contracts can be comprehensive—covering all the major facets of the group experience—or they can be focused—referring to specific facets of the training experience. For instance, the focused contract can be introduced as an exercise in the group. It may be that the participants have made a tacit decision not to talk about sex, even though it is an issue of major concern and the failure to deal with it in any way is "muddying" the interaction. The trainer, under the circumstances, might introduce a focused contract which will enable the participants to deal with the issue under relatively low-risk conditions. A sample contract might read something like this:

1. The general topic of the next meeting will be sex.
2. The purpose of the meeting is not to have individual participants disclose their sex lives but to examine the reasons why this group has completely avoided the topic of sex.
3. What are some of the fears you personally would have in discussing sexual issues here?
4. What are some of the advantages that would accrue to you personally from a more open discussion of sexual issues?
5. If you do talk about yourself, feel free to "bracket" any areas you find too uncomfortable to discuss.

Such a focused contract gives the participants a certain degree of cultural permission to deal with sexual issues. It stimulates but does not force. It is admittedly contrived, but so is the entire laboratory experience. Its advantage lies in the fact that it uses structure to rescind a possibly nongrowthful tacit decision; it gives the group the freedom to face an issue or to decide openly to bracket an area in future discussions. The variety of such focused contracts is limited only by the imaginative resources of the group.

The Imposed versus the
Freely Chosen Contract

It has been suggested above that the contract be given to prospective participants before the training experience begins so that they may decide whether or not they want to participate in such a laboratory. If this is done, then the contract can be pursued with a good deal of vehemence (see Bach, 1966), but even then, it should be remembered that the contract exists for the sake of the participants and not vice versa and intensive pursuit of a contract should exclude mechanical rigidity and inflexibility.

However, the more usual case is that the participants enter a laboratory experience with only general ideas about the nature of the experience. The question is: Can a contract be imposed on such participants? The answer, I believe, is yes. The participants come expecting some kind of experiment in interpersonal intimacy. The contract merely gives form to the experience. It does not exist in order to manipulate the participants in an inhuman way; it is there to channel their energies. I have imposed both general and focused contracts on groups with good effect. On occasion, there has been too much talk about the contract and its provisions during the inter-action, but this relatively mild form of flight is easily handled. It would be another question were a leader to impose a sensitivity-training contract on a discussion group. Since the participants had not opted for such an experience, even in a general way, to impose such a contract would be to impose on their freedom. Finally, if imposition of contract rather than entry by contract characterizes a laboratory-training group, the interaction will tend to be somewhat less intense.

Cautions in Contractual Approaches

The Myth of the Ideal Contract. The contract delineated in this chapter, while it does include many of the factors relevant to all interpersonal-growth-oriented laboratory, counseling, and thera-peutic experiences, is not necessarily an ideal that should be imitated. As noted above, the contract, if it is used at all, should be fitted to the needs and the goals of the participants; it is not a goal in itself. Furthermore, while the contract may both stimulate and channel the energies of the group, it has no magic in itself nor is it a substitute for work. Dozens of different contracts, both comprehen-sive and focused, could be elaborated, but they are valuable only if they serve the needs of the group. If they do not, they should be discarded. However, they should not be discarded before they are given a fair trial, for this would merely condone the flight tendencies of the group.

The Myth of the Ideal Participant. The contract is an ideal in at least two senses. First, it is an abstraction that becomes concrete only in the lives of the participants. If it is to be meaningful, it must be adapted to the needs of the individual participant. Since individual participants differ greatly, the contract is not to be rigidly applied to all participants in a univocal way. The contract (for instance, the contract outlined in this chapter) calls for experimentation with certain kinds of behavior (self-disclosure, confrontation, etc.), but the individual himself, in the context of the give and take of the group interaction, must determine what behaviors are most meaningful to him and the degree to which he thinks that he should engage in them. He may be asked to experiment with self-disclosure, but he is not asked to engage in as much self-disclosure as participant A nor as little as participant B, nor does he have to discuss the same areas that participant C does. In order to become more deeply himself, the participant has to make choices, but his choices should be based on his own interpersonal-growth needs rather than arbitrary ideals, whether these ideals are set forth in a contract or elaborated by the group itself. While the individual participant should become as aware as possible of his own resistance to growth and come to realize that this resistance can manifest itself in his inventing reasons that he should not engage in contractual behavior, still he should retain his autonomy throughout the group experience and not allow the group merely to carry him along. The hypothesis is that if he fails both to take risks and to make choices, the group experience will not benefit him.

The contract is an ideal in a second sense. The contractual behaviors outlined in the contract above and explained in the following chapters are not easy to engage in, and success is not measured by the participants' ability to engage in every one of them perfectly. The contract is primarily a stimulus and a guide for behavior, not an absolute measure of growth or a device by which one participant may be compared with another. The contract is an ideal in the sense that it sets goals, but it does not (and cannot) delineate idiosyncratic pursuit and possession of such goals. Growth is direction: in one sense of the term it means moving forward, but it also encompasses such notions as regressions, plateaus, and limits. The contract-group participant is expected to move forward, with the contract as a stimulus and a guide, but, since each participant has his own interpersonal potential and his own starting point, "success" in contract fulfillment must be defined idiosyncratically. As Bunker (1965) puts it, there is "no standard learning outcome and no

stereotyped ideal toward which conformity is induced [p. 42]."
Boyd and Elliss (1962), too, argue that no particular pattern can
be regarded as typical training outcome. The entire laboratory experience, including the contract, is at the service of the individual.

Fulfilling the Contract. There is, then, no perfect way of fulfilling the contract. One person's approach might be global; that is, he
gets some idea of the spirit underlying the provisions of the contract
and tries to experiment in a global way with contractual behaviors
that seem meaningful to him. Another person's approach might be
more studied; that is, he might carefully consider each contractual
provision and try to see what each means for his interpersonal
behavior. Neither of these extremes or anything in between is *the*
way of implementing the contract. It is certainly assumed that every
participant will violate the contract in one way or another from time
to time, but he can learn as much about himself through recognized
violations as through strict observance.

The Contract as Contrived. Some might say that contracts are
too rational, that life runs on a mixture of the rational and the irrational, and that people cannot be expected to do violence to their
life style in order to follow the provisions of a contract. A training
laboratory is a place where people come in order to examine their
life styles. If a person's life is governed too closely by reason, the
contract gives him an opportunity to experiment with the affective
dimensions of life; if a person's emotional life is too labile, the contract gives him an opportunity to experiment with growthful controls. The question is not whether the laboratory is contrived but
whether it has a growthful impact on the participant's real life. The
laboratory is not real life nor a substitute for it, but it can enrich life.

The Contract and
Research Possibilities

Research with training laboratories, especially laboratories in
interpersonal relations, is minimal. The purpose of this short section
is not to indicate what research should be done (Campbell and
Dunnette [1968, pp. 99–101] do point out major areas of needed
research), but to suggest what contributions contract approaches
might make to research in this area. They seem to be principally
two: control and provocation.

Control. Golembiewski (1962) divides small groups into three designations for the purpose of research. Designation I means that the group:

1. consists of a small number of individuals in more or less inter-dependent status and role relations who
2. have an indigenous set of values or norms which regulate the behavior of members, at least in matters of concern to the group [p. 35].

He quotes Bales (1950) in defining Designation II: "any number of persons engaged in a single face-to-face meeting or series of meetings in which each member receives some impression of the others as a distinct person even though it was only to recall that the other was present [Bales, 1950, p. 33]." Designation III refers to groups in a simple aggregative sense: "Thus one study dealt with a 'relatively stable group of college students.' 'Stable' was defined as lack of newcomers or dropouts. The group was a formal one of forty-two girls taking the same course of study [Golembiewski, 1962, p. 36]." Golembiewski complains that it is difficult to determine whether the experimental collectivities in any laboratory situation are really small groups in the sense of Designation I. And yet, he says, this question becomes crucial in the analysis of experimental results with such groups. The contract group offers a possible answer to the problem of membership (psychological rather than just formal). It is certainly a group in the sense of Designation I. Research with contract groups seems to be quite feasible, for the contract not only gives greater assurance of the kind of membership involved, but, through its provisions, it also eliminates a number of uncontrolled variables (e.g., it reduces the number of goals in the minds of group members) and provides a definite set of variables amenable to statistical analysis.

Truax and Carkhuff (1967) recommend, as a research model for psychotherapy, the general linear equation. The outcome desired is constructive personality change (CPC). The variables which lead to this outcome and which are to be placed in the linear equation are therapist variables (e.g., nonpossessive warmth), patient variables (e.g., self-exploration), situational or contextual variables (e.g., vicarious therapy pretraining), and interaction or process variables (e.g., the therapist's approach to hostile responses on the part of the client). The same linear model is applicable to laboratory-training situations also. The contract controls the variables that go into the training situation: leader variables, participant variables, situation variables, and interaction variables. Since the researcher can also determine whether the contract has been fulfilled or not, he can more easily relate training variables to outcomes.

Provocation. Weick (1968) defines the observational method in research as "the selection, *provocation,* recording, and encoding of that set of behaviors and settings concerning organisms 'in situ' which is consistent with empirical aims [p. 360]." With respect to provocation he says:

For the moment it is sufficient to note that settings and behaviors are robust and that interventions do not necessarily affect the ways in which they unfold. As was pointed out, it is "provocation" which tends, more than any other term, to blur the distinction between experimental and naturalistic methodology. We contend that such blurring is beneficial [p. 361].

He talks of "the use of directed settings" and of "evoking a behavior": "Careful choice and/or modification of a situation can enable observers to evoke behaviors that are of interest [p. 377]." The contract, then, is used to provoke or stimulate behaviors of interest. It is assumed here that training situations are robust, that is, that the addition of the contract does not radically alter the nature of the training group. The laboratory itself is contrived and it would seem that the contrived nature of the contract is not antithetical to the nature or purposes of the laboratory.

Scoring Systems. There are many different ways in which interactions in face-to-face groups can be scored (see Holsti, 1968 and Weick, 1968). They go from relatively simple methods to that of Katz (1964), which has 56 categories. In the contract group, the contract itself provides the scoring categories. For instance, I have used a rather simple scoring system in some informal research. The scoring unit used was the remark (Snoek, 1962): a series of phrases or sentences, uttered without interruption, about a single topic. Remarks are scored (+) if they were contractual, (−) if they were noncontractual, and (×) if they merely sustained the interaction without adding to it in a contractual way. The (+)'s and the (−)'s were also rated on a three-point scale to give some indication of how good or how poor the remark was. Participant profiles began to emerge. For instance, one young man's profile consisted almost entirely of $(\times)$'s; that is, he had become a kind of leader in his own right, but not a leader-member, for he contributed little in the way of contractual behavior. Remarks can also be broken down into other categories. For instance, $(+)$'s can be scored according to the kind of contractual behavior engaged in (self-disclosure, responsible confrontation, self-exploration as a response to confrontation, etc.). In the same way, $(-)$'s can be scored in such a way as to indicate the kind of flight involved (defensiveness, counterattack, pedestrian or merely factual self-disclosure, punitive confrontation, etc.). Such scoring leads to more elaborate and more useful profiles.

Concluding Remarks

How Detailed a Contract? How detailed a contract should be given to participants in a contract training laboratory? Only research can answer that question. One hypothesis is that the relationship between the definition (detailed nature) of the contract and group productivity is curvilinear: contracts either too high or too low in definition will result in low productivity, while a contract of moderate definition, indicating clear goals and flexible means, will result in high productivity. In high-definition conditions, the participants become too embroiled in the technicalities of the contract itself; in low-definition conditions, ambiguity is high and many energies remain unchanneled.

Maintenance versus Effective Synergy. Cattell (1951) calls the sum total of the energy that any group can command and expend "synergy." "Maintenance synergy" is the energy used up in the machinery that keeps the group in existence, and "effective synergy" is the residual energy available to carry out the explicit purposes for which the group exists. One of the primary functions of the contract is to cut down on maintenance synergy and maximize effective synergy. If the group has pre-established goals, then the contract can do just that. For groups whose primary goal is to create their goals, it is another question.

The Chapters That Follow. The rest of the book is a study in some depth of the provisions of the contract outlined in this chapter. Since the contract variables suggested are those associated with sensitivity-training experiences and other kinds of small-group activities designed to stimulate interpersonal growth, the following chapters probe the anatomy of such experiences.

Chapter Three:
Group
Goals

Introduction

Campbell and Dunnette (1968), in a review article, summarize some of the goals of laboratory training:

1. Increased self-insight or self-awareness concerning one's own behavior and its meaning in a social context. . . .

2. Increased sensitivity to the behavior of others. . . . It refers first, to the development of an increased awareness of the full range of communicative stimuli emitted by other persons . . . and second, to the development of the ability to infer accurately the emotional or noncognitive bases for interpersonal communications. . . .

3. Increased awareness and understanding of the types of processes that facilitate or inhibit group functioning and the interactions between different groups—specifically, why do some members participate actively while others retire to the background? Why do subgroups form and wage war against each other? . . .

4. Heightened diagnostic skill in social, interpersonal, and intergroup situations. . . .

5. Increased action skill. . . . It . . . refers to a person's ability to intervene successfully so as to increase member satisfactions, effectiveness, or output. The total of increased action skill is toward intervention at the interpersonal rather than simply the technological level.

6. Learning how to learn. This does not refer to an individual's cognitive approach to the world, but rather his ability to analyze continually his own interpersonal behavior for the purpose of helping himself and others achieve more effective and satisfying interpersonal relationships.

Differential emphasis among the above objectives constitutes one of the most important dimensions for distinguishing among variations in T groups [p. 75].

The overall emphasis depends principally on the unit of society that is the focus of the laboratory. Laboratories may focus on individuals, groups, or organizations or on any combination of the three. A key question in any laboratory is whether the participants have a clear idea, at the beginning of the laboratory, of its purpose.

Developmental Sequence in Training Groups. Another way of getting a feeling for the general goals of training groups is to see what actually takes place in such groups. Tuckman (1965), in reviewing developmental sequence in small groups in general, distinguishes between the *interpersonal stages* of group development and *task behaviors* manifested in the group. He calls the pattern of interpersonal relationships the group structure, while the content of interaction as related to the task at hand is called the task activity. This distinction is somewhat difficult to maintain in therapy groups, however, since the task is a personal and interpersonal one: "the group exists to help the individuals deal with themselves and others [p. 385]." The proposed developmental sequence in training groups is as follows:

Stage 1. Group Structure: Testing and Dependence. In this initial stage there is a good deal of testing and dependency behavior, the latter being predominant. Participants express strong dependency needs toward the trainer. There is a tendency toward quick acceptance of structure and arbitrary norms.

Stage 1. Task Activity: Orientation. There is a good deal of talk about what is to be accomplished (goals) and how (means).

Stage 2. Group Structure: Intragroup Conflict. Polarization takes place in the group. For instance, those who favor a more active, less defensive approach vie with those who remain defensive and who try to find safety in structure. Anxiety, threat, and resistance characterize this stage. There are also struggles for leadership.

Stage 2. Task Activity: Emotional Response to Task Demands. Members express themselves freely in experimental aggressiveness and hostility. The task is to remove blocks to learning about themselves, to reduce anxiety, and to express real reactions to one another.

Stage 3. Group Structure: Development of Group Cohesion. "All the relevant T-group development studies see the stage of conflict and polarization as being followed by a stage characterized by the reduction of conflict, resolution of the polarized issues, and establishment of group harmony in the place of disruption. It is a 'patching-up' phase in which group norms and values emerge [Tuckman, 1965, p. 392]."

Stage 3. Task Activity: Discussing Oneself and Others. "While the social function of the third stage is to cause a unique and cohesive group structure to emerge, the task function is to attempt to use this new structure as a vehicle for discovering personal relations and emotions by communicating heretofore private feelings [p. 392]."

Stage 4. Group Structure: Functional Role-Relatedness. The members coalesce into a work organization which has strong but flexible norms; members provide one another with support and mutual acceptance.

Stage 4. Task Activity: Insight. The participants discover things about themselves and provide one another with growthful feedback.

If, then, the development sequence of a training group gives any indication of the sequence of desirable goals, the following goal pattern emerges: (1) The expression of dependency needs and the need for structure; (2) discussion of goals and means; (3) experimentation with aggressiveness and hostility; (4) declaring where one stands with respect to proposed goals; (5) attempts to reduce defensiveness and anxiety; (6) reduction of conflict, increased cohesion; (7) open discussion of self and others; (8) working to maintain an organization of support and mutual acceptance; (9) deepening of communication, intimacy, responsible feedback.

Ambiguity versus
Clarity of Goals
in Laboratory Training

Confusion in Face-to-Face Groups. In most small, face-to-face groups, whatever their nature—laboratories in group dynamics, T-groups, psychotherapy groups—the members undergo a good deal of initial confusion, anxiety, and discomfort because they have no clear knowledge of group goals. Obviously, their knowledge of the means to achieve nebulous goals is even less distinct. For instance, the patient in a group-psychotherapy setting realizes that he is in the group to get better, and he either has a vague idea himself, or he is told, that getting better is contingent upon his talking about his problems in the group. But the patient often wonders why he is being cured in a group. Many patients see the group—and often this is a true perception of what is actually happening—as a place where a number of individual therapy sessions are conducted at the same time.

The novice T-group member is traditionally at sea during the early sessions of the group. He may be told of the general contract that exists between trainer and group, but both the contract and the goals implied in it, if remembered at all, remain vague. Benne (1964), for example, tells his groups that he is a resource person who is there to help them learn about groups and membership in groups. He indicates that there are two sources of data for learning about groups: (1) the knowledge that members already have because of membership in other groups, and (2) the observation and clarification of behavioral events and the relationships that emerge in the T-group itself as the members interact with one another. Bennis (1964) spells out the goals of a human-relations laboratory:

There are two major goals of the T-Group which can be indivisible in operation: (1) that group members become more aware of the enabling and disabling factors in decision-making in groups and of their own behavior and feelings in groups; (2) that group members utilize the group as a crucible for increasing their own repertoire of skills in managing group processes and their own behavior in groups [p. 272].

But, despite these adumbrations of some kind of operational goals, early-session confusion is almost universal:

> If we were to interview members of a T-Group during its early sessions concerning the then current goal of the group, we would find two modal perceptions. One is the perception of goallessness. . . . The other is that the group goal is what "I" (that is, the group leader) and a few other members have stated it should be and that most of the other members are aimlessly (or willfully) wandering from this goal [Benne, 1964, p. 217].

Such ambiguity, goallessness, and division are beneficial in laboratories in which the participants are to learn "group formative processes" (Benne, 1964) by immersing themselves in group process. Bennis (1964) sees this initial groping for goals not primarily as a search for a viable goal-structure, but rather as a dependency plea: "The group's pretense of a fruitless search for goals is a plea for him (the leader) to tell the group what to do [p. 254]." The leader is presumed to know what the goals are or ought to be. But, according to Bennis, initial dependency gives way to something more solid: "Without any particular structure or clear-cut goals to begin with, the group must develop its own muscles and structure; and this demands sophistication about the group formative processes, as well as sensitivity to the self as a result of this maturation process [pp. 274–275]." The group *must* start goalless because one of the principal goals or functions of the group is to *create* its own goals. The interactions involved in this creative process contribute also to the personal and interpersonal growth of the participants. Gibb (1964) distinguishes between natural groups and T-groups precisely in terms of goals; T-groups are forced by the nature of the social contract to both create and scrutinize goals.

In groups in which the participants must create their own goals, there is bound to be a good deal of frustration and division. French (1941) showed that the attractiveness of a group is lessened when the members disagree over the way to solve a group problem (e.g., the establishment of goals). He notes that withdrawal is most likely to occur when the members disagree on the method they should use in solving the problem. Indeed, in a residential laboratory, there is usually a good deal of talk about "getting out of here" because of the disorder, confusion, and hostility that characterize the goal-setting phase of the laboratory. However, since it *is* a laboratory and since goal setting is part of the experiment, few if any participants actually do leave (many more would probably leave if this were a real-life situation). Undoubtedly, there is much to be learned from such a process. The group both feels and, later, reflects on the frustrations and divisions that go into a group decision-making process. The individual, because of the behavior he emits and the feedback he gets, learns a great deal about himself on an interpersonal level. There are undoubtedly other advantages in engaging in such goal-creating activity. For instance, Lorge and his associates (1958) note increased productivity on the part of groups which have had a hand in setting goals for themselves.

In the typical T-group, the members come with such a variety of personal goals that the trainer must be oriented toward a "meta-goal," namely, "establishing the group conditions which are necessary for maximally meeting the needs of the various members who enter with discrepant individual goals (Horwitz, 1964, pp. 365–366)." Therefore, in the early sessions at least, even though group leaders or trainers have a panoramic view of the group process and where it is going, the members remain confused. But, again, this is understandable if one of the principal reasons for their being there is the creation of their own goals. One problem is that group members sense that the leader has some idea of what goals will be formulated and of the developmental sequence that will take place. A plausible hypothesis would be that such differential knowledge in trainer and participants would stimulate or emphasize the authority- or leader-problem in the group.

In academic laboratories in which students get together with a leader-teacher to study the formation and processes of small groups, the goals again are purposefully vague. The members are supposed to experience periods of ennui and drifting, to have "hang-ups" with the leader and to rise up against him in revolt, to experience group inertia with respect to the formulation and execution of goals—for these are some of the most effective ways to study the nature of small groups (Slater, 1966).

Not all of the confusion concerning goals, however, stems from the practical necessity of creating goals for the group. Much of the goal disturbance found in groups is a cover-up for anxiety. The implication of goal confusion is: "If I knew the goals of this group, if the leader would not insist on hiding them, then I would pursue them." Actually such statements as "I don't know what the goals are" can often be translated: "I am afraid," "I don't want to move too fast," "I want in, but I am not sure that I can pay the price," or "I have decided not to invest myself yet; it is too early for me."

Goallessness as a Value. The danger is to assume that the purposeful goallessness that characterizes so many different kinds of groups—whether by design or by accident—is a value in itself, a value that must characterize all kinds of laboratory-training groups, a value so central that other group values must be subordinated to it. It is undeniable that group participants learn much about group dynamics as they participate in the often agonizing process of working out a viable contract for the group. Too often, however, grinding out the contract becomes a goal in itself, an absolute value, because it engenders a kind and degree of learning about group process impossible to duplicate in a didactic classroom situation. The formulation of the contract becomes the absolute value; or rather, learning about group process is the absolute value and such learning is achieved by working out a contract. This absolute value is surrounded by satellite values such as the members' working through their feelings about one another and becoming more aware of their own interpersonal strengths and limitations. If it is undeniable, however, that there are groups in which the creation of goals or the formulation of an operational contract are the prime values, it is also true that such groups often end with just that—a formulated contract which cannot be implemented because time has run out. In such groups, frustration often runs high, no matter how much has been learned about group formative processes.

Goals in the Contract Group. Although goallessness and planned ambiguity characterize most of the sensitivity-training paradigms to be found in the literature and are assumed by Tuckman (1965) in elaborating his developmental-sequence model for training groups, this need not be the case. In fact, the widespread acceptance of goallessness as a value is almost unwarranted, for there is no empirical evidence demonstrating the superiority of a goallessness approach in all training groups. While the value of goallessness and planned ambiguity in many training situations is not denied, clear-cut goals and high visibility may also be values in certain training situations. Ambiguity and goallessness are of especial value in situations in which learning about group formative processes is a primary goal. This is not the case in the contract group. The primary goal of the contract group is interpersonal growth. The contract, then, provides structures which enable the participants to make intimate contact with one another as quickly as possible. The contract delineates specific goals in order to make the group more operational from the beginning. Goallessness, ambiguity concerning goals, differential knowledge of goals in the leader (panoramic vision of developmental sequence) and in group members (goal confusion), creation of principal goals, contract talk, formulation of contract, goal disturbance, and similar factors need not be values in all training groups and are not values in groups that use a contract approach. While the benefits of working through goal conflicts may be lost in contract groups, other benefits take their place—for instance, there is more time for intimate interpersonal contact. Contract fulfillment takes the place of contract formulation. This does not mean that such factors as goal conflict and ambiguity do not occur in contract groups, for the group remains natural even while it is contractual. These variables, however, are minimized. When a member, despite the contract, is uncertain about group goals, his uncertainty is diagnostic and must be worked through in the group. This is a far cry, however, from developmental goallessness and ambiguity. Finally, even though interpersonal growth is the overriding goal of the contract groups described in these pages, this is not to say that little is learned in such groups about group process. Indeed, much is learned about group process, even though such learning is secondary.

Varieties of Goals
in Group Process

Research has shown that goals become operational to the degree that they are clear and to the degree that the steps or means leading to goal achievement are made clear (March & Simon, 1958; Raven & Rietsema, 1957). In laboratory experiences, then, one of the first objectives is to establish and clarify goals and goal-facilitating structures. The members of a contract group, however, should have a clear understanding of goals from the start so that energy can be channeled into pursuing instead of clarifying goals.

An Example. The following example will be used to illustrate different kinds of group goals. Let us say that a group member makes the following statement: "You know, at home my wife and I don't really talk to each other very much any more; that is, there is little or no serious talk. And lately I have been finding excuses to stay late at work so that when I come home the kids are already in bed. I am withdrawing from them. It seems that I have a need *not* to be with people, at least in any very close way. And I know that it has been affecting my participation here. I speak only when it's safe. I haven't really put myself on the line with you. I feel alone right here in the group, as if I were not a part of the whole operation."

This example illustrates different kinds of goals found in the contract group:

Contract Goals. This is a generic term and refers to all of the provisions of the contract. In the kind of contract group under discussion, interpersonal growth is the superordinate or overriding goal. This is the key contract goal and, hypothetically, all other contract goals are subordinate to and subserve this goal. For instance, in the example cited above, the participant is engaging in self-disclosure. Self-disclosure is a contract goal, for it is seen as one of the ways of establishing the kind of intimacy that is at the heart of interpersonal growth. By engaging in responsible self-disclosure (a means), the participant is pursuing the superordinate goal of interpersonal growth. He reveals the kind of person he is, both within and outside the group, and through this revelation makes contact with his fellow participants. All of the provisions of the contract are contract goals.

Interaction Goals. The contract specifies certain kinds of inter-action—specifically, self-disclosure, expression of feeling, support, responsible confrontation, and self-exploration as a response to responsible confrontation. In the example above, self-disclosure is the predominant interaction. The contract also forbids certain kinds of interaction—for instance, long-winded, intellectualized inter-pretations of the behavior of others and defensive, self-excusing behavior. In the example above, the participant reveals an area of deficit factually without trying to rationalize or excuse it. This re-fusal to involve himself in defensive behavior is, in a negative sense, also an interaction goal. Interaction goals are the heart of the contract experience.

Process Goals. Since *group* process is involved, one set of goals indicates the kinds of activities necessary in order to establish effective group process. These goals are essential to any group desiring to handle its business as a group rather than as a collection of individuals in a social setting. One of the process goals illustrated in the example above is dealing with the here and now. Whatever a group member talks about must be made relevant to *these* people (his fellow group members) in *this* situation (the give and take of group interaction). The participant quoted above does just that: while he talks about an interpersonal problem that he has at home, he realizes that this problem in some way defines an aspect of his personality makeup and influences the quality of his participation in the group experience. He deals with the here-and-now relevance of a there-and-then problem. In doing so, he makes contact with, or engages, the group. Process goals are a species of contract goals. Their purpose is to make the group run more efficiently and with greater immediacy.

Content Goals. Content refers to the specific subjects or topics discussed by group members. A contract may or may not specify the topics to be discussed by group members (the contract described in these pages does not). If the contract does specify areas of discussion, then content goals become contract goals. This may be the case with focused contracts that take place within the laboratory experience. For instance, the leader may suggest an exercise that involves discussing a specific topic (for example, one's relation to authority). In the example above, the participant talks about his tendency to withdraw from people. However, *he,* not the contract, specifies the area of self-revelation. While authentic self-disclosure is specified by the contract, talking about alienation is not. The participant himself chooses the subject matter of his act of self-disclosure.

Need Goals. Each participant enters the group with a variety of personal needs and a tendency to use the group to achieve these needs. Horwitz (1964) indicates possible conflicts between personal needs and group goals:

Although certainly there are unstructured features of a T Group, the T Group does generate a group goal which, however, will ordinarily differ from the individual goals with which trainees enter the group. Frustration arises from the goal's being difficult to define and exceedingly difficult to attain.

The trainee may be oriented toward reaching a more or less specific goal—X', e.g., to deal more effectively with persons in authority. A second trainee may be oriented toward reaching a specific goal—X", e.g., to work better with subordinates. By contrast, the trainer is oriented toward what might be called the meta-goal—X, namely, establishing the group conditions which are necessary for maximally meeting the needs of the various members who enter the group with discrepant individual goals. This goal is enforced upon members by the particular characteristics of T-Group interaction.

The underlying task of the T Group is to develop a social system which enables maximal satisfaction for each of its members [pp. 365–366].

In the contract group, too, need goals must be integrated with contract goals. Certain needs may be antithetical to the goals of the group, such as the need to withdraw, the need to dominate others, or the need to monopolize conversation, while other needs, such as the need for affiliation, may be more readily integrated with contract goals. In a sense, the chief concern is not *whether* individual need goals are satisfied, but *how* they are satisfied. In the example mentioned, the participant is acting counter to his need to withdraw; if he finds affiliation safe, growthful, and rewarding, his need to flee may be reduced or eliminated. At any rate, his first attempt to deal with this need is to reveal it, to get it into community where it can be dealt with more effectively.

If the group is to run smoothly, there must be some kind of goal harmony. Since goal harmony and goal clarity are considered very important in the contract group, each kind of goal will now be taken up separately in detail.

Contract Goals

Contract goals include not only the overriding goal of the group—interpersonal growth—but also those interaction, process, and sometimes content goals that are seen as means of achieving interpersonal growth. Interaction, process, and content goals will be dealt with separately. In this section, the emphasis is on the superordinate goal of the contract group—interpersonal growth.

Interpersonal Growth as the Overriding or Superordinate Goal. "Interpersonal growth" as a superordinate goal is too general and must be defined operationally. Interpersonal growth is defined operationally as the sum of process and interaction goals. More concretely, one who engages in authentic self-disclosure, responsible expression of feeling, concerned confrontation, nondefensive self-exploration, and realistic support (all of these are described in the following chapters) and does so by effectively contributing to and using group resources (process goals) *is*, by hypothesis, growing interpersonally. Operationally, these activities *constitute* interpersonal growth.

Growth in interpersonal effectiveness is considered to take place through practice in establishing a responsible and viable dialogue of words and feeling among the members of the group. The participant is expected to learn and put into practice new ways of being present to the other and new ways of allowing the other to be present to him. If a participant is shy and his shyness keeps him from interacting with others, he is considered to be irresponsibly out of community. He must try new ways of getting into community; he must risk embarrassment, discomfort, and anxiety in involving himself with the other participants. If, on the other hand, a participant is a manipulator, then he is considered to be irresponsibly in community. He, too, has to learn new ways of being present to the other members of the group. The interactional provisions of the contract—that is, interactions such as self-disclosure, confronting others responsibly, accepting confrontation, giving effective support, all of which are called for by the contract—present general guidelines for formulating new ways of being present to others. If a participant usually does not talk about himself, if he never lets others know what he is like inside, what kind of person he is—then self-disclosure will be for him a new way of being present to others.

Interpersonal Rather than Personal Growth. While it would be fruitless to introduce here a meaningless dichotomy between personal and interpersonal growth, the goal of the group is stated as interpersonal rather than personal growth. Ego-centered and other-centered goals are thought of as a dynamically interrelated system. A healthy egocentricity (loving oneself) even has a kind of existential priority over involvement with others (loving others). Fromm-Reichmann (1950) believed that any display of lack of self-respect was inevitably accompanied by a reduction of one's respect for others. Sullivan (1940), too, found that one respects others only to the extent that he respects himself. Erikson (1959) sees true engagement with others as both the result and the test of firm self-delineation. According to Erikson, when a person who has not achieved a sense of self-identity attempts to engage in interpersonal relations, he experiences a "tense inner reservation, a caution in commitment [1959, p. 125]." Such a person engages in only stereotyped interpersonal relations. He does not really encounter the other, but deals in desperate attempts at clarifying what Erikson calls the "fuzzy outlines" of his own identity. The other is not the "other," but a kind of narcissistic mirror. His relationships with others, then, involve fusion rather than growthful involvement and result in a loss of identity.

Lynd (1958) emphasizes the relatedness of personal and interpersonal growth:

Openness to relatedness with other persons and the search for self-identity are not two problems but one dialectical process; as one finds more relatedness to other persons one discovers more of oneself; as the sense of one's own identity becomes clearer and more firmly rooted one can more completely go out to others. It is not a loss of oneself, an "impoverishment," but a way of finding more of oneself when one means most to others whom one has chosen. *Nor must complete finding of oneself, as Fromm and others sometimes seem to imply, precede finding oneself in and through other persons.* Identity is never wholly realized. Love is never perfect. Strength to apprehend love that is beyond anxiety, beyond the need to use other persons for one's own security, beyond desire for power over others is never complete, but may grow throughout life. Like identity and mutuality with others it is a lifetime process of discovery [p. 241, emphasis added].

This is true and some kind of understanding of this idea is cardinal to psychological growth. Nevertheless, it is also true that interpersonal effectiveness is a preeminent goal of human living and, as such, superordinate to individualistic or ego-centered goals, such as personal psychic comfort. While self-identity has its antecedent priority in human living, responsible interpersonal involvement has a subsequent or ultimate priority. That is, ultimate self-actualization can take place only through effective in-community involvement, and self-actualization in community becomes the composite goal of human living. These, at any rate, are the assumptions underlying the present delineation of group goals.

The contract group is to serve as a means of getting its members more effectively into community. This can mean dyadic community, the community of the small group, or the wider community. If

Buber (1937) is right and a person does not effectively become an authentic "I" until he has worked at transforming another from object to "Thou," then it is also true that a person is not fully a social or societal or community "I" until the community or communities to which he belongs become "Thous" in his life. Studies (Jacob, 1957; Allport, 1961) describe the average American college student as quite conformist and quite disinterested in wider community concerns. Jacob's study showed the average student to be "gloriously contented" and "unabashedly self-centered." Though they discharge the obligations demanded of them by the government, they will not voluntarily contribute to public welfare. Nor do they particularly desire an influential voice in public policy. They vote, but otherwise they abdicate the citizen's role in the political process. Though they predict another war, international problems are the least of their concerns. Although pouring one's energies into various forms of concern for the wider community may be a way of avoiding intimacy on a more personal level, disinterest in the larger community can also reflect a general disinterest in others.

It is true that these studies are dated and that it is quite evident that more students are becoming actively interested in social issues, including the issue of their own education. However, in the absence of hard data, I would still assume that the percentage of students actively involved in social and political life is, absolutely speaking, rather low even today. There is a revolution afoot. I am not sure how deeply it penetrates into the masses.

The reason for making something of the distinction between personal and interpersonal growth is this. It is amazing how many people come to group experiences—and this seems to be especially (if obviously) true of psychotherapy groups—"to get something out of it for myself." The contention here is that many people enter groups intending to grow in some way, but without any realization that the *condition* of growing is coming together. Too many fail to realize that the experience is taking place in a group, not just because others have something to contribute to one's own personal growth, but because the culmination of personal growth lies in the ability to involve oneself growthfully with others. In the contract group, the members come together in order to grow together.

Berne (1966) doubts that authentic intimacy, as described here, can take place in groups. At least in psychotherapy groups, all that can be expected is a kind of pseudo-intimacy. "Affective expression is encouraged without careful assessment of its authenticity.... The affective expression is largely socially (externally) programmed, and it is usually part of a game in which the patient compliantly participates [pp. 231–232]." I disagree. The "game" structure that is evident in Berne's psychotherapeutic method seems, at least partially, to be imposed upon the psychotherapeutic situation rather than to grow out of it. As Coles (1967) points out, "the cynicism, the cult of self, the lack of any philosophical, historical or religious perspective" found in Berne are "thoroughly contemporary, thoroughly American, and awful [p. 17]." The contract group is anti-game, even while admitting that many do engage in games in order to avoid intimacy.

Interaction Goals

Little more will be said here about interaction goals because these are studied in some depth in Chapters 6, 7, 8, and 9. They constitute, however, the heart of the contract. The participant agrees to experiment with:

(1) *The Elements of Dialogue:* freer experiencing and responsible expression of emotions; the value of language as a means of translating oneself to others; the recognition and use of nonverbal channels of communication.

(2) *Self-Disclosure:* revealing to the other members, in some way, the "person inside";

(3) *Support:* listening effectively to others; encouraging others to fulfill the provisions of the contract; giving others recognition and help when they do engage in contractual behavior; reacting responsibly when others present themselves emotionally in the group;

(4) *Confrontation:* inviting others to fulfill the contract, if they are not doing so; inviting others to examine aspects of their behavior which, it seems, they have not sufficiently examined;

(5) *Accepting Confrontation:* responding to responsible confrontation, not by defensiveness and attack, but by self-exploration;

(6) *Taking a Stance against Flight:* refusing to engage in interactions antithetical to the interactions listed above; refusing to withdraw from the interaction; trying to minimize flight in oneself and in others.

Process Goals

Process goals refer to the *way* in which any group goal is pursued. Their purpose is to regulate and give definition to the interactional process itself. They provide cautions and structures that make the group a more efficient and effective organization. In the contract group, these pragmatic goals are also contract goals.

The Distinction between Self-oriented and Altruistic Goals. The entire discussion of goals might become a bit clearer if some attention is first paid to a distinction that Cartwright and Zander (1960) draw between selfish and altruistic goals in group process. In the schematization shown in Figure 1, process goals—that is, the ways in which the group is used in the pursuit of other goals—have a kind of primacy over other goals. Examples of interactions il-

	Process goals: The ways in which any other goal is pursued in the group	
	selfishly	altruistically
Other Goals: selfish	A	B
contract, content, altruistic	C	D
need		

Figure 1. Process Goals.

lustrating each quadrant of the diagram will help make the distinction between goals, especially the distinction between process goals and other goals, clearer.

Quadrant A: Selfish goals (contract, content, need) pursued selfishly. This means that a group member pursues a contract, content, or need goal that redounds to his own benefit (a selfish or self-oriented goal) in a way that is inimical to the interests of the group. That is, the way in which he pursues his goal tends to destroy the efficiency and the cohesiveness of the group. Mr. A finds that his anxiety is running very high in the group. He has learned from experience that he can reduce his anxiety by monopolizing the conversation (this might not be a completely conscious realization). This keeps him occupied and it also keeps disturbing stimuli at bay. He proceeds to do this, and his anxiety is lowered. He has pursued a selfish goal (the need goal of reducing personal anxiety), and he has done so in a selfish way (by monopolizing the conversation in the group, by keeping the group from being an *interacting* group).

Quadrant B: Selfish goals pursued altruistically. This means that a group participant pursues a goal (need, contract, content) that redounds to his own personal benefit, but he does so in a way that is designed to promote inter-member engagement and group cohesiveness. For instance, Mr. B, too, is quite anxious, and he feels the same need that Mr. A felt, namely, to reduce his anxiety. But, instead of dodging the issue, he confesses to the group that he is anxious and that his anxiety is affecting the quality of his participation. He wonders if other participants are anxious, too. He tells the group that he would like to know what it is about the group and about himself in the group that causes such anxiety. He has pursued an ego-centered goal (the reduction of personal anxiety) in an altruistic way (by bringing his concern before the group, by eliciting the feelings of other members, by engaging the other members of the group). He has also fulfilled a contract goal—self-disclosure.

Quadrant C: Altruistic goals pursued selfishly. This means that a participant pursues a goal that is intended to benefit some other member or the group itself, but he does so in such a way as to hinder desirable group-process variables. For instance, Mr. C decides that the group should talk about sex. He realizes that a discussion of sex will make him quite uncomfortable, but he thinks that it is an issue that this particular group should handle for its own good. He brings the subject up a few times and even gets the group to discuss the fact that it had been avoiding this area of discussion. However, the group as a whole is not ready to pursue the subject; sex is not yet a viable topic for the group. Still, Mr. C, at every opportunity, brings up the subject and tries to get the group to engage in a serious, perhaps self-revealing, discussion of it. He is pursuing an altruistic content goal (though it is hardly denied that other more basic need goals are operative); that is, he sincerely believes that a comparatively open discussion of sex will benefit everyone. He pursues the goal, however, in a way designed to disrupt group process. He wants what well might be good, but he wants to obtain it in his own way. He cannot trust the group to handle the problem.

Quadrant D: Altruistic goals pursued altruistically. This means that a participant pursues a goal (contract, content, need) that is of benefit either to another member or to the group as a whole, and he does so through the group process, by engaging the other members of the group. For instance, Miss D says: "I don't want to hurt or embarrass you, Mr. Y, but you have been rather quiet in the group. It just seems to me that you have been reneging on our contract, and I don't think that that is fair to the group or to you. I think we have been remiss in not trying to involve ourselves with you sooner." She pursues an altruistic goal (it is a contract goal, for she confronts another to join the group both for his own sake and for that of the group, and she confronts the group—including herself —for being remiss), and she does so in a way designed not to alienate either Mr. Y or the other members. Her confrontation is not an act of punishment, it is not primarily an expression of her own frustration; rather, it is an attempt to get the group members—including herself—to involve themselves more completely with one another.

Given these distinctions, it is clear that a certain degree of group altruism is essential if the *group* itself is to become the vehicle of problem-solving and growth.

Some Key Group-Process Goals. Group-process goals are also contract goals; that is, the participants agree to use these goals as standards for their manner of participation. These goals or standards set the interactional tone of the group. The following group-process goals are considered essential to the effective running of the group:

(1) *All concerns made group concerns.* Another way of stating this is: whatever is done is to be done through group process. The examples above make it clear that it is not important to multiply contract goals nor is it important that the content and need goals pursued be altruistic. What is important is that *all* goals—contract, content, need—be pursued through the group process. The members of the contract group not only agree to pursue interpersonal growth as the superordinate contract goal, but they contract to pursue both personal and altruistic subgoals in such a way as to involve themselves more deeply with the other members of the group. This is the cardinal group-process goal: to submit everything to the group. The group should never become just a group of onlookers, while only two of the members interact. It is not against the better interests of the group for two members to discuss their relationship, whether it be one of concern or of antagonism, but they should do so in such a way as not to exclude the other group members. If Mr. A and Mrs. Q show a great deal of antagonism toward each other and finally discuss it in the group, the other group members are free to comment on the relationship and how it affects them

and the entire group, and should be encouraged to do so. This is often difficult. Other group members do not want to "butt in." They feel that it is "none of their business." Often the other members are afraid of the emotions involved in the interchange; they are afraid to engage themselves.

One of the violations of the everything-through-the-group standard, at least in residential sensitivity-training laboratories, is siphoning. Two or more members get together outside the group in order to work out their relationship. They return to the group changed, and this interrupts the rhythm of the group. Or worse, one member will pair with another member outside the group in order to discuss and work out feelings toward a third member. This dilutes group process and manifests negative feelings toward and mistrust of the group. It is only natural that a certain amount of pairing take place outside the group, but whatever significant interactions this involves should be made public to the group. Pairing may be encouraged or planned, however, if it helps make the group sessions more meaningful. For instance, one of the group members might find it quite difficult to engage in self-disclosure. So, outside the group, he tells what he thinks is important to another group member. This breaks the ice for him and enables him to be open in the group. Mowrer (1968) will interview a patient before he enters the integrity group. The patient unburdens himself here first and then it is usually easier for him to tell his story to the entire group.

Participants in various kinds of face-to-face groups often fail to participate, it is true, because they are selfishly preoccupied with their own concerns. They neither engage other members nor want to be engaged by others. When they speak, they do so in a rather solipsistic manner, or they look to the leader for a solution to their problem. But there are also participants in these groups who realize that a group has been assembled precisely because some problems are handled more effectively through group interaction. Cattell (1953) even defines the entity "group" in terms of the interreliance of the members:

The definition which seems most essential is that a group is a collection of organisms in which the existence of all (in their given relationships) is necessary to the satisfaction of certain individual needs in each. That is to say, the group is an instrument toward the satisfaction of needs in the individual. Individuals belong to the group only because they achieve certain satisfactions made possible by its organization which would not be so readily possible (or which did not happen to occur) for them through any other device [p. 20].

No one or two individuals should be allowed to act as if the other members of the group did not exist. Many participants are too polite or too timid to interrupt noninvolving group action (or dyadic action, as the case might be), to intrude themselves. Everyone should feel free to speak on every issue and actually take advantage of this freedom.

Fouriezos, Hutt, and Guetzkow (1950) showed that groups primarily concerned with self-oriented needs are relatively ineffective. After observation of 72 decision-making conferences, they concluded that groups with the highest scores on self-oriented needs rated themselves lowest on satisfaction measures. They were less satisfied with the meeting in general, with the decisions reached, with the manner in which the group reached its decisions, and with the chairing of the meeting. Groups with high scores on selfish or self-oriented behavior completed fewer items on the agenda, but they held longer meetings. The contract for the interpersonal-growth contract group calls for altruistic process goals, not just because they seem to be more fully human, but also because they are more economic. Such goals assure that further contract goals will be pursued more quickly and more efficiently.

(2) *Acceptance of the laboratory nature of the group experience.* The laboratory nature of the group experience is explained in some detail in the Introduction and the chapter on the laboratory method itself. The contract-group participant is asked to assume a laboratory set. The experience he is entering is, in a sense, contrived; it is different from day-to-day experience. It focuses on many of the molecular aspects of human interaction. It demands that the participants experiment with new forms of behavior—that is, potentially growthful ways of involving themselves with one another that are not presently part of their interpersonal life style. Since the laboratory is an experiment, the participant is asked to reserve judgment; he is asked not to prejudge the experience, not to determine beforehand that it is going to be completely successful or unsuccessful.

(3) *Cooperation.* Israel (1956) found that groups that establish a cooperative goal structure are more effective than groups that establish a competitive goal structure. In the contract group, the assumption is that cooperation is essential to the work of the group,

and therefore the participants are asked to adopt a cooperative set. Since cooperation is so important, it will be considered here at some length.

(a) *Cooperation and personality.* In disturbed relationships, working against tends to take the place of working with. Horney (1945) describes the interpersonally disturbed as (1) moving toward people in a compliant way that is both an expression of helplessness and a call for support, (2) moving against people in an aggressive way, competing with others in order to surpass and defeat them, with the ultimate purpose of becoming strong enough to disregard the possible counter-hostility of others, and (3) moving away from people, avoiding all the threats and risks involved in any kind of close interpersonal relating. Such actions tend to give rise to N-interactions that can hamper the efficient running of the group. They certainly stand in the way of establishing a cooperative goal structure and working pattern in the group.

On the other hand, Dreikurs (1967) insists that effective human relationships are characterized by cooperation. Cooperation, according to Dreikurs, demands four attitudes together with a stance against their antitheses: (1) social interest versus hostility, (2) confidence in others versus distrust and suspicion, (3) self-confidence versus inferiority feelings, and (4) courage versus fear. Interest, trust, a feeling of self-worth, and courage are all essential to optimal performance in the training group.

(b) *Cooperation in therapeutic situations.* Individual therapy is being seen more and more as a cooperative venture in which therapist and client become involved with each other (Schofield, 1964; Steinzor, 1967); it is a route taken by both therapist and client (Stern, 1966). In a study by Fiedler (1950), the good therapeutic relationship was described by a variety of therapists as one in which the therapist saw the patient as co-worker on a common problem. In my own experience, group therapy progresses most steadily when the members realize that they are not just recipients of help, but that their involvement with one another is the condition for growth. When patients cease being patients in therapy and become agents instead, then there is cause for hope. In the contract group, neither leader nor members are finished products in the area of interpersonal maturity. All the members have much to offer one another if they are willing to drop some of their defensiveness and become involved with one another.

(c) *Cooperation as a process goal in training groups.* In the natural developmental sequence suggested by Tuckman (1965) for training groups, a period of initial dependency and confusion is followed by a period of antagonism and turmoil in which personal differences and differences in goal orientation are worked through. This is followed by a period of cohesion and cooperation. Such a sequence seems natural to a group situation characterized by initial goallessness and planned ambiguity. Group participants may gain some value from working through the problems associated with the first two stages; however, a group experience in which the first two stages are eliminated, or at least shortened and in other respects attenuated, has its own peculiar value. Though group members may learn a good deal about the value of cooperation by both engaging in and becoming the victims of noncooperation, there is also a value in forestalling and minimizing noncooperation. Cooperation, after all, must be some kind of ultimate goal in all training groups, for productivity, no matter how it is defined, is impossible without co-operation.

Cooperation, then, is one of the process goals to which the members of the contract group subscribe. The empirical evidence supports the value of cooperation for smoother performance and increased productivity in a variety of group situations (e.g., Cartwright & Zander, 1968; Deutsch, 1949; Grossack, 1954). There is also a good deal of evidence that cohesiveness in groups is enhanced if members work together for common, rather than mutually exclusive and individual, ends (see Lott & Lott, 1965 for a review of the evidence). Cooperation in the kind of enterprise called for by the contract is not an easy thing. As Goffman (1967) notes, "Joint involvement appears to be a fragile thing, with standard points of weakness and decay, a precarious unsteady state that is likely at any time to lead the individual into some form of alienation [p. 117]." The hypothesis in the contract group is that if the participants enter the group with a set toward cooperation, decay is a good deal less likely. Deutsch (1958) found that prior cooperative orientation increased cooperation on a task that ordinarily evoked relatively low levels of cooperation; Oskamp and Perlman (1965) found that public commitment to cooperation had the same effect. Making cooperation one of the process goals of the contract group is similar to Deutsch's cooperative orientation, and the participant who agrees to the contract makes a form of public commitment to cooperation.

(d) *The nature of cooperation in the contract group.* In the contract group, cooperation means getting into community as quickly as possible. It means that members have come together not to compete but to grow. A cooperative style of group interaction will produce a distinctive type of interpersonal movement in the group. Three types of interpersonal movement may be indicated as follows:

Type A.　　　self ⟵――――― other
Type B.　　　self ―――――⟶ other
Type C.　　　self ――⟶⟵― other

In Type A, one member remains entrenched in himself and makes the other capitulate or move out toward him. In Type B, which is the opposite of Type A, one "leaves" himself in a movement that entails giving in to the other. In Type C, which is characteristic of cooperative group movement, both participants venture out of themselves and each encourages the other to venture forth. In the contract group, the participants subscribe to Type C movement. This does not mean that types A and B will not occur. For instance, if a group member remains silent long enough, other group members will finally remark on his silence and make efforts to get him to move out into the group. The silent person is engaging in Type A movement (or lack of movement), while those who finally pursue him are engaged in Type B movement. The silent member should be confronted. However, were he engaged in pursuing the provisions of the contract with others who were doing the same, then all would be engaged in Type C movement. Type C is the ideal, though this hardly lessens the value or necessity of Type B.

At first it would seem that confrontation, one of the interaction goals of the contract, would automatically and necessarily involve a combination of Type A and B movements. However, if the group is characterized by cooperative effort, this will not be the case at all. At least in an ideal confrontational situation, Mr. X, the object of confrontation, first gives the group some cues that he is open to confrontation. By his verbal exchanges he moves into the group in various ways. When he is confronted, then, he is already in the group in some sense. There are a variety of ways in which a participant can move into the group, and once he does so, he becomes available for a variety of interactions.

(e) *Cooperation and complementarity of contractual roles.* The members of the group enter it by accepting the stipulations of the group contract; that is, they say that they want the kind of experience described by the contract. One way of interpreting this is that the participants willingly assume, or try to assume, certain roles in the group. The contract is set up to induce within the group a complementarity of roles. Thus, because of the contract and the role complementarity that it induces, fewer decisions are required about certain aspects of group activity, energy is conserved for more important activities, and the group process proceeds more smoothly. For instance, the contract calls for responsible confrontation; but it also calls for self-examination, rather than defensiveness, attack, or other forms of counter-behavior, as the response to such confrontation. The role of the confronter and the role of the self-examining confrontee are complementary. If the contractual roles are learned and accepted, group process moves along vigorously, meaningfully, and comparatively smoothly.

Spiegel (1957) points out various causes for failures in role complementarity. Such failures are deleterious to group cooperation and disruptive of effective group process. Some of the causes for complementarity failures are relevant to the discussion on cooperation. First, *cognitive discrepancy* takes place when one or more parties are not familiar with the roles they are expected to assume and therefore miss their cues. However, if the participants in the contract group understand the provisions of the contract and are willing to take a cooperative stance, the possibility of cognitive discrepancy is lessened. In the group, "missing cues" usually has some other meaning than failure to understand the contract. *Allocative discrepancy* refers to nonacceptance of roles. If the participants really subscribe to the provisions of the contract, allocative discrepancy should also be minimized. The problem arises when a group member, after agreeing to the contract, reneges on his agreement. In situations in which the contract is imposed, allocative discrepancy arises from the fact that some members do not really accept the contract or some of its provisions. Complementarity also suffers when one or more members simply *are incapable of assuming the roles* called for by the contract. For instance, a particular member might always see even the most responsible confrontation as attack. He cannot assume the role of one who explores himself upon confrontation, because his self-identity is too weak to sustain confrontation. He might be almost completely lacking in the capacity to lay aside his defenses and engage in the self-examination called for by confrontation.

(f) *Cooperation, dependency, and conformity.* One might object that this demand for a cooperative goal structure is an unrealistic attempt to banish difference of opinion and disagreement—part of the warp and woof of interpersonal relating—from the group interaction. Nothing of the kind is meant. The kind of cooperative effort suggested here is not meant to eliminate difference of opinion and disagreement, but to have them take place as growthfully as possible. The contract states that the members are present not to compete but to become involved with one another. Becoming involved with one another will, obviously, entail conflict and difference of opinion. For instance, when A confronts B on B's mode of acting, ideally B will respond—if A's confrontation has been responsible—by exploring his own behavior. After B, in the give and take of the group interaction, has examined himself and his behavior, he may well reply to A that he disagrees with him. A comes to realize that there are modes of living that differ from his own, but by involving himself, within the structure of the group, with others who live and think and feel differently from the way he does, he can broaden the base of his experience. A certain degree of heterogeneity in the makeup of the group would seem to be in order precisely for this reason.

Nor can the cooperation called for by the contract be identified with conformity or dependency. Tuckman (1965) says that initially there is a period of dependency in the training room. The members look to the trainer for goals and direction. Cooperation, however, means that the members assume corporate responsibility for the group from the start rather than assigning this function to the leader. The early sessions of groups are always filled with anxiety, and anxious people tend to surrender blindly to the security of authority (Fromm, 1955; Getzels, 1957; Maslow, 1959; Riesman, 1950). But this tendency to polarize into leader and members must be counteracted by leader and members alike, for it militates against cooperative effort and involves working through problems that are not the focus of the group. Darley (1966) found that fear causes increased conformity and that the increase is greatest if the conformity pressures come from people toward whom the subject feels affiliative. Anxiety in the contract group should be handled as openly as possible so that dependency and conformity can be minimized. The only conformity looked for in the contract group is fulfillment of contract, and the purpose of the contract is to facilitate the development of responsible autonomy and relatedness.

(g) *Cooperation and the deviant member.* Since failure in cooperation and role complementarity involve the notion of deviancy, a word might be said about the deviant member. The problem of deviancy is minimal in groups in which entry by contract is the norm, but it is a more serious problem for imposition-of-contract groups. Many members may be deviant in the sense that they renege on certain provisions of the contract while fulfilling others. If such deviancy does not become too widespread, then the group can still function adequately. It is a different matter if a particular member refuses, on a wholesale scale, to give himself to the group interaction. For a period of time, his deviancy becomes the focus of group interaction; and in the end, he is usually rejected, strongly so if the group is a highly cohesive one (Schachter, 1951). Once he is rejected, he hangs albatross-like around the neck of the group. If the deviate simply refuses to engage in contractual behavior and does not leave the group, then the group members should deal briefly with how such a member should be handled. If the deviate actually disrupts group interaction, then the question of expulsion arises. Groups are very reluctant to expel a deviate because the members are usually concerned about him and expulsion is tantamount to admitting failure on their part.

(4) *The here and now.* This is one of the most important process goals in both contract groups and other kinds of training experiences. It involves what might be called the space-time dimension of the group. The group is a group only when the members are actually together. Therefore, the principal focus of the group is the present, the here and now. The content of the interactions in the group must in some way lose their space-time distance. A participant's search for identity may be complicated by the fact that his father made him an appendage, denied him the freedom to grow as an individual. What is important to the group, however, is the member's *present* being in the world as appendage, his present feelings of identity diffusion, and how this mode of being influences his action in *this* group. The member may well talk about the past, but the past has to be made relevant to the present. He may well talk about what has happened or is happening outside the group, but the "there" must also be made "here." For instance, a participant's mode of being present to his co-workers at his place of employment can be transported by comparing it to his mode of being present to the other members of the group. "At work I'm a mouse. Here it's still the same. I'm still a mouse." Or—"At work and at home I can hardly contain my hostility, but I don't feel hostile here at all, even when I'm confronted. Maybe you have accepted me. Or maybe I have accepted you more than I have the others. Anyway, there's a big difference." If a past or future concern can be

made relevant to the activity within the group, then it loses its space-time distance.

The problem with the past is that it (coupled with other factors associated with it that will be discussed below, e.g., the quality of a person's self-disclosure) engenders ennui. If group members spend a good deal of time discussing problems outside the group, the group members lose contact with one another. There is, as noted above, such a thing as healthy egocentricity. A person must be a person first, before he can involve this "person" in various activities. There is also such a thing as healthy group egocentricity. The group cannot survive, much less operate effectively, unless certain of its needs are fulfilled. Prolonged dealing with concerns that are too distant is like cutting off the oxygen supply of the group. A kind of suffocation takes place. Therefore, group members have to search out ways of rendering their then-and-there concerns present to the group. These concerns, if they are real concerns and not just dodges that insulate the participant from interacting meaningfully with the other members of the group, in some way define him. They color him and his activity, including his activity in the group. The group leader can be very helpful here, by modeling ways of transporting then-and-there concerns so that they become relevant to this group. It seems to me that one of the principal defects of psychotherapy groups is the inability to deal with the here and now. Members keep talking about the problems that they have at home and outside the group in general. They fail to see that these various problems are defining their manner of participation in the group. The members fail to see the group as a laboratory for the examination of these problems. The inept group psychotherapist falls back on the expedient of using the group as a locus for multiple individual therapy.

If a member finds it difficult to overcome the space-time dimensions of his concerns, then this difficulty should become a concern for him and for the group. His inability to overcome distance partially defines his mode of presence in the group. The fact that he cannot overcome distance is diagnostic in the best sense of the word. If he recognizes his group behavior for what it is, he will gain some practical insight into his interpersonal life style. His discussion of the then and there might be a flight from group process. Or the concerns that he verbalizes might not be his real concerns but only diversions, ways of keeping him from thinking about issues that are really pertinent to his style of interpersonal living.

This concern for the here and now is also rooted in a theory concerning the usefulness (or uselessness) of investigating past behavior in order to change the present.

This is not to deny the significance of the past in indirectly affecting behavior. However, even though the past can create a certain condition which carries over into the present, it is, nevertheless, the *present* condition that is influential in the present. Strictly considered, linking behavior with a past event is an extremely difficult undertaking; it presupposes that one knows sufficiently how the past event affected the psychological field at that time, and whether or not in the meantime other events have again modified the field [Deutsch, 1954, p. 186].

Rogers (1951) applies such thinking to the therapeutic situation:

It should also be mentioned that in this concept of motivation all the effective elements exist in the present. Behavior is not "caused" by something which occurred in the past. Present tensions and present needs are the only ones which the organism endeavors to reduce or satisfy. While it is true that the past experience has certainly served to modify the meaning which will be perceived in present experiences, yet there is no behavior except to meet a present need [p. 492].

Too often, in training-group situations, participants become pre-occupied with there-and-then concerns not because they are more meaningful but because they are safer. If they are really meaningful, they should be translated into here-and-now concerns and become vehicles of involvement rather than modes of flight.

(5) *The Rules of Immediacy.* It is difficult to listen to conversations filled with vagueness and generalities. It is difficult because it is boring. Truax and Carkhuff (1964) have suggested that concreteness in therapeutic conversation might well be a variable worth exploring. They define concreteness as follows:

A *low* level of concreteness or specificity is when there is a discussion of anonymous generalities; when the discussion is on an abstract intellectual level. This includes discussions of "real" feelings that are expressed on an abstract level. A *high* level of concreteness or specificity is when specific feelings and experiences are expressed—"I hated my mother!" or "... then he would blow up and start throwing things"; when expressions deal with specific situations, events, or feelings, regardless of emotional content [p. 266].

Such concreteness is definitely a value in the contract group and forms part of the rules of immediacy—ways of making the interaction more immediate and personal. The rules are:

(a) *The use of "I."* When the participant is speaking of himself he must use "I" and not some substitute such as "we," "one," "you," "people," or some impersonal expression such as "it happens." Any substitute for "I" entails a loss of immediacy, puts distance between the speaker and the state or action he is discussing.

(b) *Concreteness.* The speaker should avoid vagueness, abstractions, and generalities. If he does talk about something abstract, such as a principle, he should illustrate what he means by a concrete example, preferably from his own experience. In general, he should talk about his own experience. If he talks about the experience of others, he should talk about the impact that the others' experience has on him.

(c) *Speak to a particular person.* The participant should, in general, address specific people in the group rather than the entire group. The participant who always speaks to everyone often speaks to no one. It is more immediate to address the whole group through a specific member. For instance, someone might say: "I think that there is a lot of flight behavior in the group. John, you tend to talk about the there and then all the time. Bill, when confronted, you are always very defensive. You seldom open up and examine the issue at all. In the morning session I said nothing at all." The person who addresses the whole group tends to talk about generalities and to give speeches. Both are deadly to group interaction.

(d) *Questions.* The participants should not ask too many questions, especially the question "why?" Pointed questions that demand concrete answers help keep the interaction concrete. The question "why?" usually demands an interpretation on the part of the respondent. Interpretations tend to become vague, highly intellectualized, and hypothetical and, therefore, are antithetical to the immediacy desired in the interaction. "Did you hit him?" gets at the facts of the respondent's behavior. "Why did you hit him?" can lead anywhere and thus nowhere.

Content Goals

In most kinds of group interaction in which personal and interpersonal growth are the overriding goals, the content of the interaction is not predetermined. It is believed that this would unnecessarily limit the scope of group interaction (Grinker, MacGregor, Selan, Klein, & Kohrman, 1961). Goals, they say (and, I would add, specifically *content* goals), depend on and develop from the transactional experience of the group. Any human concern is grist for the mill. If the growth experience is taken seriously, the content of the interaction will be pitched at a deep personal level; that is, group members will tend to treat of subjects that touch their persons.

Although content freedom is also the goal in the contract group, still, as was indicated above, it is possible to include certain focused contracts in which the content of the discussion is specified. This is especially true if the participants are trying to avoid certain areas of human concern. Focused content contracts may also be used to stimulate interaction.

An Example of a Focused Content Contract. A group might contract to discuss nongrowthful conformism in day to day living. If the members are to discuss such a subject concretely and intelligently, they should be prepared in some way to do so. Although some topics need little preparation, this one needs a great deal. The participants could be given the following remarks on conformism for preparation or stimulation.

By "conformism" is meant the tendency to follow fixed patterns and conform to certain standards in situations in which conformity is not a value at all, and to do so from nongrowthful motives, such as fear, laziness, or lack of motivation. Munroe (1955) contends that the "triviality and the magnificence of human devotion to social goals represent the folly and the grandeur of our species [p. 116]." Doubtless all of us are wedded to certain social conventions that are meaningless and perhaps even detrimental to interpersonal living, but they usually go unchallenged in our lives. Henry (1963), for instance, denounces our conformity in the area of advertising in America. Advertising, he says, preys upon unhealthy conformist tendencies. He sees it as a means used by an irrational economy to imbue the subjects of the economy with "pecuniary logic"—that is, money counts more than almost anything else. If Americans could wrest themselves from their conformist tendencies and pursue a more realistic logic, such an economy, he claims, could not survive. This is the paradox: if Americans are to exist economically as they are, they must work at remaining a herd of sheep. Erikson (1964) sees no reason that a technological world, as such, need weaken man's inner resources of adaptation and produce a "nation of sheep." Still, subscribing without reflection to the values of a technocratic society, leaving one's creative potential untapped because it thrives on socially unacceptable divergent thinking, submitting without criticism to the host of unexamined conventions imposed by the societies and organizations to which one belongs, accepting the common rituals that govern interpersonal living because they provide an escape from intimacy (Berne, 1957, 1964, 1966), submitting to personal suppression built into the American system of education (Friedenberg, 1963; Keniston, 1965)—all of these forms of conformism are prevalent and some of them affect us. Such conformism undoubtedly, either directly or indirectly, gives a certain definition to our persons and affects the quality of our human relationships. We may welcome conformism because it saves us from the agonies of decision and intimacy. Convention and ritual undoubtedly have their value in human living, but when do they obstruct and deaden human relating instead of channeling it?

Residential sensitivity-training laboratories seem to stimulate the nonconformist tendencies of its participants. Whitman (1964) seems to be a bit wary of the kind of regression or adolescent culture that springs up in these situations, although he calls it a "healthy and understandable thing [p. 314]." He claims that some regression is necessary for learning, but sees problems with those who regress either too little or too much in laboratory settings. However, it seems possible to interpret the adolescent-culture phenomenon in terms other than regression. During adolescence, a person evidences a certain number of quite engaging qualities. The adolescent is often quite spontaneous, clever, humorous, adventuresome. There is a pleasing unpredictability about him, for he is striving to get a feel for himself as an independent being, a person in his own right rather than an appendage of home, school, church, or society. His speech is often quite refreshing, because there are few filters between what he thinks and what he says. He is open, honest, candid, frank. The qualities of the creative person—*fluency,* or the ability to put out a large number of responses to a situation rather than focusing on just one; *flexibility,* or the ability to change one's thinking and to change the meaning, interpretation, or use of something; and *originality,* or a flair for the unusual, the novel, the farfetched, the remote, the clever (Guilford, 1962)—these qualities are often much more in evidence in the "immature" adolescent than in the "mature" adult. Maturing is often a process of controlling such adolescent behavior in the face of the conventions of society and its organizations. In the residential sensitivity laboratory, the need to conform is minimized, conventional conformism disappears, and many of the more admirable qualities of adolescence reappear. This is hardly regression. It is progress.

The purpose of the above discussion of conformism is not to induce an intellectual discussion of this phenomenon but to serve as a basis for self-exploration by the members of the group. The discussion should be a concrete, personal one: the conformism of *these people* and the way it affects their relationships to one another here and now. If the participants adhere to the process and interaction goals of the contract, the conversation will not become intellectualized, abstract, and apersonal.

Need Goals

The group is not only a contractual group, but also a natural group. Each member has his own psychological makeup and his own constellation of needs. One of the reasons a member joins the group is that he feels a need for a more effective interpersonal life. The group itself helps to fulfill this need. In one sense, all needs are ego-centered, yet it is logical to divide needs into ego-centered needs (e.g., a need to reduce personal anxiety) and altruistic needs (e.g., a need to improve one's neighborhood). Most needs, however, are not pure; they are multi-determined. A person's altruistic need to serve his community also satisfies ego-centered needs for recognition and belongingness.

Within the context of the contract group, conflicts will arise between need goals and contract goals. A need to dominate will, obviously, conflict with the kind of cooperation called for by the contract. Therefore, the contract-group experience should prove diagnostic with respect to the strength of certain needs. Often it is only within the context of a group experience that a person begins to realize how strong is his need to withdraw. The group experience also gives its participants an opportunity to test their ability to control their needs—that is, those needs that conflict with the contract. Again, conflict will not be eliminated and contract violations will occur; but, because of the contract, conflicts should be highlighted in such a way as to render them more manageable.

The Overriding Goal— Interpersonal Growth— Revisited

Interpersonal growth is defined operationally as the sum of the interaction goals (pursued according to process goals); that is, the person who experiments with and engages in responsible forms of self-disclosure, expression of feeling, support, confrontation, and self-exploration as a response to confrontation is, at least by assumption, growing interpersonally. This definition admittedly introduces a kind of circularity in the training process. As Campbell and Dunnette (1968) note: "It appears that some of the interpersonal skills most important for accomplishing the T-group's objectives are also the very skills constituting the major learning goals of the method [p. 77]." The assumption, however, is that the participants have the basic ability to engage in these behaviors, but because of personal, group, and cultural circumstances, they have had inadequate practice in 'them. The group, as a cultural island, allows the members to actualize these behaviors rather quickly. The participants learn principally in the sense of converting to action what already exists in potency.

The sensitivity-training experience does not provide a major personality overhaul. The person who leaves the group with the intention of going back home to demonstrate to family, co-workers, and friends how different he is is a horror to behold. The average participant, upon leaving the laboratory, finds that growthful behaviors that became relatively easy to engage in in the laboratory situation are difficult to manage in his real-life situation. He realizes that he experienced something quite valuable in the laboratory, but now he is faced with the very difficult task of integrating the laboratory experience with life. A certain modesty with respect to the ultimate goal of the laboratory is in order. I would say this: if the interactions that take place in the laboratory induce in the participant a healthy form of *diagnosis* which leads to *attitude change* which, ultimately, leads to growthful *behavioral change,* then the training experience is a success. A word about healthy diagnosis and attitude change is in order.

Dynamic Diagnosis: The Cybernetic Function of the Group. Experimentation with the kinds of behavior described in the contract should serve a diagnostic function. It is an opportunity to challenge what Frank (1961) calls one's "assumptive world" (see pp. 18–34), especially in the area of interpersonal relations. Some people say that it would be a waste of time for them to participate in a sensitivity-training experience; they are adjusted both personally and interpersonally, they experience deep relationships with others, they are productive. They see the group experience as a refuge for those who cannot make it interpersonally, a kind of substitute for real interpersonal living. However, the assumption is not that a person enters such a group because there is something radically wrong with the quality of his interpersonal life. It is, rather, that all human relationships can be improved; the group offers opportunities to experiment with new ways of being present to others. The group is not meant to be a flight from real life or a substitute for it. Those who come to it thinking that it is usually suffer quite a bit.

For some, diagnosis has become a dirty word in psychology. It is assumed that, as a process separate from treatment, it is relatively useless or at least uneconomic; that is, the fruits of a separated diagnosis are not sufficient to warrant pretreatment expenditure of time and energy, which in many mental health systems is reduplicated time and energy. Erikson (1964) even sees the diagnostic process as potentially dangerous:

Hospitalized patients, having been committed, are often ready to commit themselves. They expect "to go to work," both on themselves and on whatever task they may be asked to do. But too often they are met with a laborious process of diagnosis and initiation which emphasizes the absolute distance of patienthood from active life. Thus literally "insult is added to injury" in that the uprooted one, already considered expendable or abnormal by his previous group or affiliation, finds himself categorized and judged by those who were expected to show him the way through a meaningful moratorium. Many a man acquires the irreversible identity of being a lifelong patient and client not on the basis of what he "is," but on the basis of what is first done about him [p. 97].

However, diagnosis, freed from its pejorative connotations (and perhaps from a too strict association with the medical model of emotional disorder), is a human value. Plato, in the *Apology*, claims that the unexamined life is not worth living. The fact is that we tend to drift to maintenance levels of interpersonal relating. In the contract group, the member gets a sense of or feeling for his own areas of competence, his own areas of promise, and his own areas of deficit in interpersonal relating. In the matrix of the group experience, disturbances in human communication (Ruesch, 1957) come to the surface. The participant develops a feel for his present interpersonal limits (and this is usually quite painful) and perhaps even for his absolute interpersonal limits (and this is even more painful). He comes to a realization of failed potential in interpersonal living, but this implies that he gets a deeper insight into this potential. Thus, the diagnostic aspect of the group experience is a starting point—dynamic, hormic, motivational.

Diagnosis here is contextual and cybernetic. It is contextual in that it develops in the context of actual interrelating. It is cybernetic in this sense: The participant emits interpersonal behavior in the group. He receives feedback about that behavior from the other members. Finally, he uses this feedback as a corrective device or as a stimulus to try different modes of behavior in the group. For instance, Miss G constantly introduces new topics of discussion in the group, often in the middle of ongoing discussions. The other members confront her with this fact, first by a rather cool reception of the new topics and then by more direct forms of confrontation. Miss G begins to realize that she never really listens to what others have to say. Or she realizes that there are areas or topics discussed that arouse too much anxiety in her. Or she begins to realize that she is not happy in the group unless she is the center of attention. Because of the feedback she receives, she can try new forms of behavior in the group: "I always change the subject when you discuss sex, because it makes me afraid."

The group is not miraculous. It does not create capacity when none exists. But, if Maslow (1968) and a host of others are right, none of us comes close to using a very significant amount of his human potential, interpersonal capacities included. Diagnosed patterns of unsatisfactory interpersonal behavior may be amenable to modification, to learning and relearning. Finally, diagnosis, in the sense explained here, is not easy, especially for those with high levels of anxiety. Studies show that the highly anxious do not show a great deal of interest in exploring new areas and having new experiences (McReynolds, Acker, & Pietila, 1961; Penney, 1964, 1965).

Attitude Change. It is suggested that effective diagnosis in the training group will lead to attitude change (that is, if such change is warranted). Although attitude change seems to be a natural goal of laboratory learning, it is not mentioned with any frequency in either the theory or research literature: "Turning to another type of internal criterion, the authors were surprised to find relatively few studies relating T-group experiences to attitude changes. ... The scarcity of research relating laboratory education to attitude change is disappointing and rather hard to understand [Campbell & Dunnette, 1968, pp. 92, 95]." Attitude change is a modest and realistic goal. For instance, a participant who has difficulty responding to even responsible confrontation by self-examination finally realizes that he is very defensive, that he usually sees even helpful and well-meant confrontation as attack. Gradually, his attitude toward confrontation changes. Although even responsible confrontation has punitive side effects, it is possible to ignore or endure these for the sake of the benefit to be obtained. After the laboratory is over, the participant may still react adversely to honest criticism (he has not changed overnight), but his attitude has changed and this is the seed of behavioral change. Research, then, should show attitude changes by the end of the laboratory experience and behavioral changes in follow-up studies.

Behavioral Change. The ultimate goal of the laboratory is behavioral change. Experimentation with behavior in the laboratory is the first step in the process of effecting change. The laboratory offers no magic and works no miracles. Behavioral change demands work, both during the laboratory and, especially, after it. The person who sees little value in working at bettering his interpersonal relationships is ill-advised to enter a sensitivity-training experience.

Chapter Four:
The
Laboratory
Method

Introduction

Although a summary of the fundamental aspects of the laboratory method is given in the first chapter, an indication of how these factors apply to interpersonal-growth experiences in general and to the contract group in particular is in order.

Diversities in Laboratory Experiences. It would be unrealistic to try to catalog here all the differences among the various kinds of laboratory experiences. It is much more feasible to discuss some of the sources of these differences. Two factors that account for many of them are the size of the social unit in focus in the laboratory and the purpose of the laboratory. For instance, a laboratory might be oriented primarily toward (1) the community, (2) the organization, (3) the group, or (4) the individual. In each instance, a variety of goals might be contemplated.

(1) *The community.* Klein (1965) describes the use of labora-

tory experiences in community-development programs. The purposes of such programs are quite broad:

For the purposes of the program which this chapter describes, community development has been considered to encompass work with community groups and entire communities for the purpose of assisting in the development of leadership skills, of fostering effective citizen participation in meeting economic, social, and civic needs, and of enabling optimal utilization of state and national resources from both government and voluntary bodies while strengthening local community initiative and autonomy [Klein, 1965, p. 185].

In laboratories, goals such as the following are set for the participants:

1. Increasing their sense of community, by which [is] meant the readiness to view community events in terms of interacting forces and processes within a coherent whole.
2. Enlarging their definition of citizenship ... an increased ability to identify and respond to opportunities for effective participation in community events.
3. Enhancing their sensitivities and skills as citizen participants within groups and organizations.
4. Developing more sophistication and objectivity in their attempts to diagnose the forces and processes contributing to community problems.
5. Helping them to function more effectively as agents of change in situations where collaborative planning and effort is needed [Klein, 1965, pp. 185–186].

In some cases, community teams, composed of a number of workers from the same community agency or representatives from a variety of community agencies, come as units to the laboratory. Teams of trainers or community consultants also go into the community itself and work toward a variety of goals with community leaders *in situ*.

(2) *The organization.* An example of a laboratory experience that focuses on a single organization is found in *The Managerial Grid* (Blake & Mouton, 1964; see also Blake & Mouton, 1965). The grid deals with managerial styles and emphasizes the two major dimensions of managerial skill: human relations and productivity. The grid itself is depicted in Figure 2. An entire laboratory program with a large organization may require from three to five

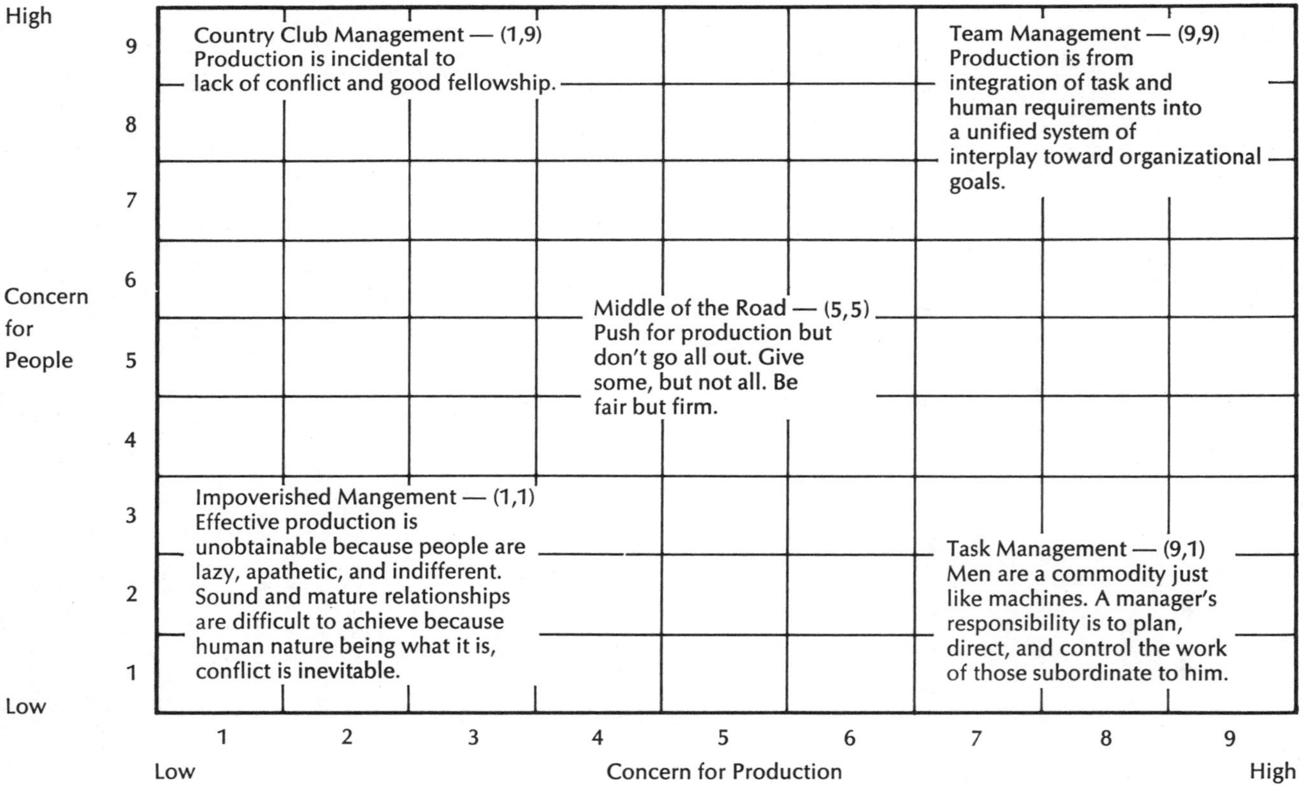
High
Concern
for
People
Low
9
8
7
6
5
4
3
2
1
Country Club Management — (1,9)
Production is incidental to
lack of conflict and good fellowship.
Team Management — (9,9)
Production is from
integration of task and
human requirements into
a unified system of
interplay toward organizational
goals.
Middle of the Road — (5,5)
Push for production but
don't go all out. Give
some, but not all. Be
fair but firm.
Impoverished Mangement — (1,1)
Effective production is
unobtainable because people are
lazy, apathetic, and indifferent.
Sound and mature relationships
are difficult to achieve because
human nature being what it is,
conflict is inevitable.
Task Management — (9,1)
Men are a commodity just
like machines. A manager's
responsibility is to plan,
direct, and control the work
of those subordinate to him.
1
2
3
4
5
6
7
8
9
Low
Concern for Production
High

Figure 2. The Managerial Grid.

years to complete. A six-phase approach to organization improvement is suggested (Blake & Mouton, 1965). Phase I is learning to apply, in a human laboratory, the behavorial-science theory of solving work problems. "The aim is for managers to study and to understand behavioral science theory and research findings sufficiently well, and in such a concrete and personal way, that intuitive assumptions underlying habitual behavior can be replaced by sound managerial approaches for getting work done in a manner that arouses mutual confidence and respect [p. 172]."

The laboratory is structured so that line personnel, rather than academic behavioral scientists, serve as the faculty for each of the laboratory sessions. This makes them better teachers (one assumption is that a good manager is an effective teacher) and also makes them feel more responsible for the implementation of what is taught. The participants engage in various exercises designed to reveal to them their own managerial styles and to improve managerial skills with respect to both human relations and productivity. The ideal, according to the grid, is a 9,9 style of management (see Figure 2).

The other phases of the program involve team training, inter-team cooperation, setting organization improvement goals, implementing planned change, and stabilizing and replanning. Even though the managerial-grid laboratory is a highly structured, organization-oriented experience, the participant learns much about himself personally and interpersonally in the give and take of group interaction.

(3) *The group.* "Group" here means the small, face-to-face group. Obviously, small, face-to-face groups are used in both community and organization laboratories, but there are also training experiences in which the principal focus is on the small group itself. For instance, some courses in group dynamics are taught in a laboratory fashion. The participants (the students) learn about the small group by actually being one (or becoming one) for the duration of the course. The leader (usually the teacher) establishes his position as leader (usually by merely being the teacher), but otherwise offers little direction, much to the frustration of the participants. The members of such a group, in an even more basic way than the members of a goalless sensitivity-training group, must determine the goals of the group and work out viable ways of dealing with one another. This is often a tortuous process during which they tend to take out their frustrations on the leader by symbolically expelling, symbolically killing, or usurping the position of the leader (Slater,

1966). From time to time the members use the sessions to explore themselves and one another, so that the meetings sound like group psychotherapy sessions. Therefore, though the direct goal is to learn about small groups by becoming one, the participants engage in a good deal of behavior similar to that found in growth experiences of various kinds.

Laboratories are also designed to study the potentialities of small groups—for instance, group versus individual ability in problem-solving and decision-making situations. Small groups may be given different types of problems to work out or asked to make managerial decisions. With the help of a trainer, such groups reflect upon themselves and the processes they engage in to solve problems and make decisions. The participants become more aware, not only of group problem-solving and decision-making processes, but also of the human-relations problems involved in group processes. According to Collins and Guetzkow (1964), inability to handle the interpersonal dimensions of task situations is one of the greatest sources of task failure.

> Meeting interpersonal obstacles contributes as much toward group productivity as meeting problems posed by task-environmental obstacles; in fact, because group members have a tendency to ignore interpersonal issues, interpersonal obstacles may be the major barrier to task effectiveness in many groups [p. 88].

The principal focus of a laboratory, then, may be the small group itself—how it is formed, how a group of unrelated individuals becomes a cohesive unity, problem-solving processes in groups, group decision making, and group characteristics such as norms, climate, structure, and power factors.

(4) *The individual.* The contract group is a laboratory in which intrapsychic and, especially, interpersonal issues are the direct focus of the group experience. A small group provides a unique opportunity for handling such issues: the participant can experiment with a wide variety of interpersonal behaviors and can benefit from the comparatively wide spectrum of feedback he receives from his fellow participants. Stoller (1968) refers to such experimentation as "stretching accustomed modes of behavior." The group forms a kind of culture in miniature within which new constructs may be tried, not just in an intellectual but in a behavioral way. Hampden-Turner (1966), in formulating an existential learning theory ap-

plicable to training situations, suggests that part of the growth cycle involves a person's periodically letting go and risking a portion of his experienced competence in order to bridge the distance between himself and the other. The participant ventures out into the group, experiments with new behavior, receives feedback, and ends with a new synthesis, including broadened knowledge and a clearer sense of his identity.

A Different Kind of Learning. In all laboratories, including the contract laboratory, theory is subordinated and emphasis is placed on impact through involvement. The whole purpose of a laboratory is to translate theory into action. Very often, the participants are not ready for this kind of learning; the emphases are unaccustomed ones: "The learning of concepts, the setting of goals, the clarification of values, and even the achievement of insight into self, are sometimes far ahead of the development of the performance skills necessary to expression in actual social transactions [Benne, Bradford, & Lippitt, 1964, p. 17]." One of the principal modes of flight used by groups is to regress to an abstract discussion of concepts and values. But the group demands interpersonal performance rather than discussion: "Laboratory method starts with a different overall view of learning as a transaction between learner and environment in which neither learner nor environment is regarded as fixed and in which both undergo modification [Benne, Bradford, & Lippitt, 1964, p. 24]." Even if the laboratory is an academic course, books are absent or secondary. If there are lectures they are very short. The participants are not asked to repeat what they have learned and the general authoritarian structure associated with learning is laid aside. In fact, almost all the cues that traditionally enable a learner to identify a learning situation are absent. This disturbs some people. Some think that no learning, or an inferior kind of learning, is taking place. After the experience is over, the participant finds it difficult to categorize, in traditional terms, what he has learned. This at times embarrasses him and confuses those with whom he discusses his experience.

Kelly (1955a, 1955b) is interested in man in evolution. He claims that man is best understood in the perspective of history and that, by reflecting on himself, he can discover ways of restructuring his life. The patterns man uses to view or construe the world he is in are called constructs. Whether these constructs are right or wrong, they exist: "What he perceives may not exist, but his perception does [1955a, p. 8]." Even though a person tries to improve his constructs by increasing his repertory of experience, his general construct system is resistant to change. Thus, two factors hinder him from bettering his construct system: (a) fear and the resultant need to hang on to the old and (b) the lack of a laboratory in which he could experiment with new constructs in a relatively controlled and safe way. The training laboratory is precisely the place where the search for new constructs is secure. It is much easier in the laboratory to let go of the old, for letting go is both permitted and encouraged by the group culture. Perhaps one of the reasons for the almost phenomenal growth of sensitivity-training laboratories and encounter groups is the need to have a relatively safe place in which to rethink one's construct system.

Cultural Permission. Residential laboratories are sometimes referred to as cultural islands, both because they are cut off or insulated from the highly routinized culture in the back-home situation and because they develop their own culture in miniature. But whether the laboratory is residential or not, it affords the participants cultural permission, not found in the back-home situation, to engage in certain activities. Cultural permission is one of the keys to the success of laboratory training; it allows the laboratory situation to be different from day-to-day living so that it might make a difference in such living. Laboratory, then, means the establishment of a climate of freedom. If it is to succeed, there must exist in it a kind of freedom that is lacking outside the group. The contract is not just a structure; it is a stimulus to a certain behavioral freedom. It serves as a guideline to the kinds of experimentation that are encouraged and even demanded. Even contract laboratories, then, are freer than ordinary life, for they declare a moratorium on certain inhibitory conventions.

What are some of the cultural permissions afforded by the laboratory? It allows comparative strangers to talk with one another at comparatively deep levels: the cultural prerequisites for friendship and intimacy are laid aside and the participants deal with one another at some depth, not because they are longtime acquaintances, but merely because they are fellow human beings. Confrontation is another important area of cultural permission. We seldom tell one another what impact we have on one another. In our culture, it seems much more permissible to tell a third party our impressions about another that we would not dare tell the other. Such conversations abound, and while they may satisfy a need to ventilate one's frustrations in interpersonal living, there is little in them that could be called growthful. A laboratory contract, in a sense, is a list of the cultural permissions given the participants in their interactions with one another: they may disclose themselves, express their feelings, tell others what they like about them, challenge their behavior or attitudes, lay aside those forms of politeness that are really no more than interpersonal constrictions, and do anything else that appears to be both interpersonally responsible and growthful. There is some complaint that some laboratories go too far, that they permit or even encourage too much, so that the cultural and even ethical sensibilities of the participants are offended. In view of the sensitivity-training explosion taking place on the American scene, this may well be true. However, the contract group encourages responsible cultural permissiveness without subscribing to cultural or ethical license. The person who participates in a contract group not only learns the operational provisions of the contract but also learns why the contractual variables have been chosen. In the contract, wide cultural permissions are extended, but it is the participant who must determine what he is going to allow himself.

The Assumptions of Training Technology

Campbell and Dunnette (1968) outline the implicit and explicit assumptions of T-group methodology. These assumptions will be listed here, with some indication of how they apply to the contract group.

Feedback. "A substantial number of group members, when confronted with others' behaviors and feelings in an atmosphere of psychological safety, can produce articulate and constructive feedback [p. 77]." The entire contract is designed to facilitate this kind of feedback. The inactive and the irresponsibly confronting participants are not fulfilling the contract, and they become themselves the object of group confrontation. Perhaps few of us feel comfortable revealing to another the impact his behavior has on us, but the contract provides a stimulus to do just that.

Agreement on Feedback. "A significant number of the group members can agree on the major aspects of a particular individual's behavior exhibited in the group situation. Certainly a complete consensus is not to be expected, but neither must the feedback go off in all directions [p. 77]." If the participant goes off in all directions, then the feedback should reflect precisely this; that is, the contradictions in his behavior should become apparent. Also, a person must reveal enough about himself to give a definite impression if he expects consistency of feedback from the group. If he gives little of himself, then the feedback will be scattered, for each other member will *interpret* the participant's behavior in his own way, and there is no guarantee that there will be consistency of interpretation. If the participant wants to get some consistent picture of himself from the other members of the group, he must assume an active role in the group, he must generate sufficient data as the raw material for feedback. If the participant is active, then the feedback will be consistent; this certainly is the assumption in the contract group, though it still awaits empirical verification.

Completeness of Feedback. "Feedback is relatively complete and deals with significant aspects of the individual's behavior [p. 77]." If the members are actively pursuing the contract, then feedback will be as complete as the participant receiving the feedback will allow. A participant will not receive feedback on those dimensions of his person that he chooses not to reveal. But even if the participant is quite defensive in certain areas, feedback will be complete in the sense that others will tell him how defensive he appears. Again this assumption depends upon whether the members of the group assume an active role in the group, especially with respect to the significant aspects of one another's behavior. The contract, because it encourages both self-disclosure and responsible confrontation, is a stimulus to deal with the significant.

Representative Behavior. "The behavior emitted in the group is sufficiently representative of behavior outside the group so that learning occurring within the group will carry over or transfer [p. 77]." There are really two assumptions here: (1) that the behavior in the group is a sample of behavior outside the group and (2) that changes in the sample behavior will transfer to behavior outside the group.

If a group not only permits but demands that its participants be themselves, then behavior in the group will be representative of behavior outside the group. A case comes to mind. A young lady in a weekend laboratory experience was all sweetness, light, and clichés. She was immediately supportive of everyone and thus·ingratiated herself with everyone. However, I did not believe that her behavior in the group was "sufficiently representative of behavior outside the group"; she seemed less than real. I confronted her with my misgivings several times. She finally got quite angry and manifested a completely different side of her personality. After that incident, her feedback to others became more realistic. A group has a way of dealing with facades; facades prevent person-to-person contact, and thus inhibit the growth of the group. It is not that there is any particular sense of accomplishment in stripping away the facade of another; it is rather than in the give and take of the group it is too frustrating to try to communicate with a facade. The contract demands a variety of significant behaviors. If a person does not engage in a particular kind of contractual behavior, this in itself is revealing. For instance, if a person simply never confronts anyone else in the group, this can mean several things. It may mean that he is afraid of others or overly sensitive. It may mean that if he were to confront someone, people would see a side of him that he does not want to reveal. In any case, he should be faced with his refusal to confront; he should be faced with the fact that his behavior in the group does not seem to be representative.

Psychological Safety. "Psychological safety can be achieved relatively quickly in the group (in the matter of a few hours) among either complete strangers or among associates who have had varying types and degrees of interpersonal interaction [p. 77]." The contract increases psychological safety in a number of ways: it adds high visibility to the training experience and is thus anti-manipulative; it helps create a common group culture, so that the risks taken by the participant take place against the background of a shared culture; it demands growthful forms of behavior (e.g., concerned rather than punitive confrontation); the leader models contractual behavior and serves as a kind of guardian of the contract. Some would probably object that the contract makes the training situation too safe. I would rather hope that the participants would see in the contract a pledge of response and support no matter what they risked.

Interpersonal Incompetence. "Almost everyone initially lacks interpersonal competence; that is, individuals tend to have distorted self-images, faulty perceptions, and poor communication skills [p. 77]." This assumption is overstated. Most people have areas of competence, areas of promise, and areas of deficit in the interpersonal dimensions of their lives. The laboratory, however, should never be considered as just remedial. The laboratory gives its participants an opportunity to examine their interpersonal styles, including their areas of promise. A person, even though he feels that he is adequate in relating to others, might discover that he is even more comfortable or stimulated when he approaches others in ways different from those he is used to. The participant, then, is asked to share his areas of competence, explore and experiment with his areas of promise, and discover and experiment with changes in his areas of deficit.

Anxiety and Learning. "Anxiety facilitates new learning [p. 77]." The place of anxiety in the training situation was dealt with earlier.

Transfer Learning. "Finally, transfer or training occurs between the cultural island and the 'back home' situation [p. 77]." While there is much anecdotal evidence that such transfer does take place, there has been relatively little empirical corroboration. Bunker and Knowles (1967), using questionnaires sent to those who knew the laboratory participants in the back-home situation, found evidence indicating that transfer of training does take place. As suggested above, perhaps the immediate fruit of training experiences lies in the area of attitude change, which hopefully underlies subsequent behavioral change.

Most experimental findings are useless unless they can be applied somewhat generally. Interpersonal-growth laboratories are failures if the participants do not transfer their learning to other social groups. One way of facilitating transfer is for each participant to consider his wider social environment as part of the laboratory. I have been in groups in which college students, once having experimented with openness with their peers, widened the scope of their experimentation to include parents and siblings. A number of them reported rather dramatic improvement of relationships, while a few said that people outside the group thought that they were "putting them on." However successful or unsuccessful these experiments outside the group might be, they enhance the group experience itself, especially to the degree that what takes place outside the group is transformed into the here and now. "I talked to my dad, and I tried to be open, but I don't think that he had the slightest idea what I was talking about. I'm not sure whether it's him or me. Do I talk and say nothing here? I just wonder whether I am as vague as he makes me think I am." It is not just a question of trying out laboratory gimmicks on one's friends. Such childish manipulation would merely reflect the immaturity of the participant. But if the laboratory experience generalizes to include some of the significant others in the lives of at least some of the participants, then it is having the impact that it is meant to have, and this dialogue with others outside the group can add a new dimension to the total group experience itself.

Experimental Controls

The laboratory, as such, is not an experiment in the strict sense (unless it is also the object of research, but then such research stands apart from the actual laboratory). Still, the notions of laboratory and experimentation, even in their widest sense, imply some concept of experimental controls. The contract adds a degree of control to the laboratory. Goals are clearly defined and an attempt is made to eliminate all variables except contractual ones. Even when noncontractual behavior arises (e.g., the intrusion of need-goal behavior that is antithetical to contract goals), it is rather readily identified and controlled. The contract also offers a structural schema that facilitates the elaboration of different training designs.

Suspension of Judgment

On the one hand, the laboratory offers the participant a climate of interpersonal freedom that is available in few other social contexts; on the other, it demands of him a suspension of judgment with respect to the design of the laboratory. In the contract group, this design is quite visible and might seem, at least at first glance, to involve a number of artificialities (these are discussed below). There is a natural tendency to prejudge the entire experience or at least some aspects of it. The participants, however, contract to suspend judgment as much as possible, to experience the laboratory and its exercises before evaluating them. Both traditional sensitivity-training laboratories and contract experiences involve a certain amount of psychological risk. In the former, the participants are not sure what lies ahead; in the latter, the members know what lies ahead and are apprehensive about it. In both experiences, the participant might find out that he is not as interpersonally effective as he thinks he is. Risk engenders anxiety, and anxiety engenders defensiveness. This defensiveness can well take the form of attacking as meaningless an experience that well might highlight interpersonal inadequacies, both to oneself and to others. If the participants are forewarned about the elements of risk and anxiety and the tendency to attack what might prove to be painful, it is likely that they will approach the laboratory experience with a greater sense of openness. An ideal attitude would be something like this: "In general, I want the kind of experience described in the contract. I realize that it involves a certain amount of risk and anxiety. I also realize that I am not entirely convinced as to the meaningfulness of all provisions of the contract, and I will probably have some reservations concerning the communication exercises that will be proposed. Still, I prefer not to prejudge any particular aspects of the laboratory, insofar as this is possible. I am going to try to enter into everything with an open mind." If antecedent suspension of judgment is a value, so is consequent evaluation of laboratory and exercises. Again, if the laboratory itself, or some particular aspect of it, reveals certain areas of deficit in interpersonal capability, there will be a natural tendency to attack the source of this knowledge. Still, laboratory designs will grow in effectiveness only if the laboratory experience is realistically criticized by the participants.

What a Laboratory in Interpersonal Relations Is Not

The laboratory is not an assemblage of guinea pigs who are being manipulated either by the leader from within or by researchers from without. Jourard (1967) strongly questions the kind of research in which the human person becomes an object to be manipulated:

A humanistic psychologist, like his less humanistic colleague, is concerned to identify the factors that affect man's experience and action, but his aim is not to render man predictable to, and controlled by, someone else. Rather, his aim is to understand how determining variables function, in order that man might be liberated from their impact as he pursues his own free projects [p. 109].

Jourard goes on to suggest that the experimenter-subject relationship be one of dialogue rather than manipulation. Rome and Rome (1967), who have been developing a unique method of studying the organization and government of large social organizations, report successful research in which subjects are seen as collaborators in the enterprise rather than as objects of manipulation. Milgram (1963) conducted a study in which obedience to the experimenter meant that the subject had to administer what he believed were extremely painful shocks to another subject. Twenty-six out of forty subjects "administered" the highest shocks on the "generator" (the subject at the receiving end was a stooge and was not receiving any shocks at all). It is chilling to think what a subject will do for a man of science. Milgram's subjects were given a kind of scientific permission to do what they would ordinarily consider inhuman. It would be ironic if the leader were to engage in any kind of large-scale manipulation, for one of the purposes of the laboratory is to have the participants learn to involve themselves with one another in nonmanipulative ways.

Artificiality-Reality Dimensions of Laboratory Life

The Sources of Artificiality. At first glance it would seem that a laboratory in interpersonal relations labors under a relatively high degree of artificiality. In a sense this is true; laboratories are contrived, and their artificiality would make little sense unless it had an impact on day-to-day living. The sources of artificiality in the contract group, for instance, are at least three.

(1) *Laboratory artificiality.* The laboratory itself is artificial. The people who comprise the various groups in the laboratory situation do not come together naturally; that is, they do not choose to be with other members of the group because they are attracted to them. In most instances, the participants find themselves in stranger groups; that is, most of the participants are relatively unknown to one another. Or, if they do know one another, it is not in the dimensions emphasized by the laboratory. And yet they are expected to achieve quickly a certain degree of intimacy in the give and take of group interaction. The artificiality of being with the members of *this* group is often emphasized if the laboratory is composed of a number of groups. After a while, certain members begin to feel the "distant-fields" urge, and they begin saying to themselves "I wish I were in *that* group."

(2) *Contract artificiality*. The second source of artificiality is the contract itself. Not only are the participants expected to achieve a certain degree of intimacy, but the contract (at least the one described here) specifies, to a great extent, the nature of this intimacy. For instance, the participant is expected to reveal to others the kind of person he is, at least in some degree. He is expected to confront others and be confronted by them. Not only are strangers thrown together in a kind of intimacy, but the dimensions of this intimacy are imposed.

(3) *Exercise artificiality*. The laboratory usually entails certain stimuli to communication in the form of laboratory exercises. These will be considered in greater detail elsewhere, but at least one example must be treated here, because exercises do constitute a third source of artificiality. For instance, there is the snake exercise—a somewhat ominous term, arising innocently enough, however, from the physical arrangement of the participants. The members of the laboratory divide into two groups, arranging themselves in two lines a couple of feet apart, so that each member is directly opposite another member. Then each member merely looks silently into the eyes of the person standing opposite him for fifteen or twenty seconds. Each row circles around (the snake undulates) until every member has gazed into the eyes of every other member. This part of the exercise is entirely nonverbal. Then the members of the group sit down and discuss how they felt, what emotions or reactions arose, during the exercise. There are other exercises, both verbal and nonverbal, most of which are designed to stimulate different modes of communication among members or to dissolve communication blocks that arise in the group. Whatever their purpose, however, they are still artificial; they are ways of interpersonal acting that are not current in even the relatively intimate associations of ordinary life.

The Reality of Laboratory Life.   One of the assumptions underlying the laboratory experience is that it must be different from day-to-day living if it is to make a difference, if it is to have an impact on such living. But the laboratory experience is not designed just to be different; it is not a question of pursuing a game artificially. Artificial experiences are countenanced only to the degree that they are considered useful in changing interpersonal attitudes and behaviors in the direction of fuller interpersonal living. Perhaps a better way of putting it is this: the artificialities of the human-relations laboratory are valuable to the degree that they highlight overlooked realities in day-to-day interpersonal living. Much of what takes place in a laboratory is artificial only in the sense that it is not what is usually done in interpersonal relationships, not in the sense that it is false or inauthentic. Training groups, then, are something more and something less than real life. They are certainly more meaningful than most of the ritualistic and cliché interrelating that goes on in everyday life, but they are less meaningful than the natural, spontaneous, growthful contacts that take place between those who choose one another as friends at the deepest levels.

(1) *Laboratory reality.* The members come together because they want to grow interpersonally. The participant is expected to involve himself with this group of strangers precisely because they are human beings. They involve themselves with one another; they work out their likes and dislikes, and they do so in the context of *this* group. The laboratory demands that each member face *this* set of interpersonal relationships.

One of the realities of ordinary human living is that people are locked into relationships with other individuals or groups of individuals. In the laboratory, interpersonal problems cannot be solved by ignoring them, by moving to a different group of persons, or by using other modes of interpersonal flight. The pressure for involvement with this particular set of people, while artificial in one sense, highlights the unproductive modes of involvement or noninvolvement with the people in the participant's normal life situation. Moreover, dealing with the stranger in the laboratory group can bring home to the participant, in a dramatic way, his failure to deal with the stranger element in those with whom he is intimate in real life. The laboratory does not allow the opportunities of flight from intimacy that day-to-day living often does. Therefore, part of its impact arises from its being *more* rather than less real than ordinary interpersonal living.

(2) *Contract reality.* The laboratory itself makes it impossible for the participant to take flight from *these* people, *this* set of interpersonal relations. The contract, insofar as it defines the general ways in which each is to involve himself with the others, prevents group members from avoiding certain important modalities of interpersonal relating. The member is forced to engage in interpersonal activities that may not be part of his interpersonal life style. Not only is he engaged with these particular people, but he cannot avoid the qualitative realities of this engagement that are

called for by the contract. A member, in his ordinary life, might manage to avoid letting others know something about the "person within"; he may court peace at any price and thus avoid confrontation and the self-examination it involves. But in the group, the pressures of the contract tend to force him to face, at least to some degree, these realities of interpersonal living. Therefore, the contract, too, for all its artificiality, exacts an engagement with interpersonal realities, which are too often avoided in real life.

(3) *Exercise reality.* Exercises usually focus on smaller elements of the communication experience. The snake exercise, for instance, does this. When two people communicate, they usually look at each other from time to time, and they are aware that they are present to each other. The snake exercise isolates this aspect of communication. It is artificial in its isolation of certain elements of communication, in its protractedness, and in its completely nonverbal character. But eye contact and mutual nonverbal presence are human realities, although they usually go unnoted in human interrelating. Exercises focus on molecular aspects of relating in order to make them more real in molar living, just as some artists exaggerate various forms in their painting in order to make the observer look at a form that has never really lived in the observer's eye or to revive a feeling that once may have lived but now is dead. Exercises are the "zoom lens" of the laboratory experience. If they are used judiciously, they can make certain aspects of interpersonal relating come alive in dramatically new ways.

Aronson and Carlsmith (1968), in discussing experimentation in social psychology, refer to both experimental and mundane realism.

> In one sense, an experiment is realistic if the situation is realistic to the subject, if it involves him, if he is forced to take it seriously, if it has impact on him. This kind of realism we call *experimental realism.* The term "realism" can also be used to refer to the extent to which events occurring in the laboratory setting are likely to occur in the "real world." We call this type of realism *mundane realism* [p. 22].

If this terminology is adapted to laboratories in interpersonal relations, it may be said that such laboratories are high in both experimental and mundane realism. The participant can become as deeply engaged as he desires in the interaction of the group. The intimacy that develops within the group should reflect, in some way, the intimacy of the participant's real world, and thus become diagnostic, if not motivational.

Conclusion

Laboratories as Centers for Study of the Normal. The inter-personal-growth laboratory provides an opportunity to study some of the deepest reactions of man in an atmosphere of relative security. The environment has realism and yet it is controlled. There is no reason why growthful training experiences and research cannot take place at the same time.

Laboratories as Centers for the Therapy of the Normal. Schofield (1964) expresses concern about the number of people with philosophical neuroses who take up the time of clinical professionals with more important or pressing work to do. According to him, the philosophically diseased

suffer a freedom of complaint. The absence of conflicts, frustrations, and symptoms brings a painful awareness of absence—the absence of faith, of commitment, of meaning, of the need to search out personal ultimate values, or the need to live comfortably and meaningfully in the face of final uncertainty. For increasing numbers of rational, educated, and thoughtful men the central struggle becomes one of finding and keeping an emotional and psychological balance between the pain of doubt and the luxury of faith. A distaste for this struggle, or an insistence on its resolution as a necessary condition for continued existence is at the heart of the *philosophical neurosis* [p. 150].

Encounter groups, led by those with drastically less formal training than professional therapists, seem almost ideal in handling such problems. The participants are suffering and therefore the group is serious business to them. But one of their chief complaints is that, in their day-to-day lives, they are out of meaningful community. The small group is a meaningful community, but it is not meant to take the place of more realistic forms of community involvement. Rather, it is a center where the participants learn to involve themselves more effectively with others, with the wider community, and with the problems that face the country in general.

Schofield is also concerned with the need for trained people to work with the emotionally disturbed. He favors recruiting and using nonprofessionals as mental health counselors (see Rioch, Elkes, Flint, Usdansky, Newman, & Silber, 1963). Contract groups, under the direction of professionals, could be used quite effectively to train such mental health counselors.

The Present Culture. Growth through groups has caught on in America. Although there have been diatribes against and spirited defenses of sensitivity training, encounter groups, residential laboratories, and other facets of human-relations training, any wholesale approval or condemnation of these phenomena is meaningless. Sensitivity training is simply not a unitary phenomenon. There are good laboratory experiences, poor ones, and even dangerous ones. We should now see to it that a wholesome laboratory culture takes roots in our social system. It seems that there is even a humanistic-laboratory orientation to life. If I am laboratory-oriented, this means that I am always somewhat aware of my areas of deficit and promise and that I can experiment with ways of reducing dissonance in my life and actualizing interpersonal possibilities. It means that I am willing to take risks in order to grow. It means that I realize that others have resources, even for my own growth, which I do not possess myself, but which I can tap in a very human and growthful way.

Chapter Five:
Leadership

Introduction

The question of leadership is a complex one. Gibb (1950) studied two sets of ten-man leaderless groups (one group of college students and one of army officer candidates). He had outside observers rate the group members on leadership qualities, and the members of the groups themselves rated one another on three sociometric questions. The group members were to choose (1) those with whom they would like to spend leisure time, (2) those with whom they would like to work, and (3) the person whose removal from the group would bring about the largest group change. The results showed that sociometric choice on the third criterion (removal and group change) had, by far, the highest correlation with observer ratings of leadership. It is difficult, then, to point out in any general way what makes a good leader, for leadership criteria can change from situation to situation. As Lindzey and Byrne (1968) point out, "it appears that the nature of the relationship between sociometric status and leadership is dependent on the demands of the situation and the characteristics of the individuals composing the group [p. 485]."

Mann (1959) summarizes some of the problems associated with evaluating leadership.

Viewed historically, the study of leadership has stimulated more than its share of controversy. The trait approach to leadership, the view that leadership is an attribute of the individual, has received the harshest treatment throughout the years. To have spoken of an individual as possessing a measurable quantity of leadership was perhaps an unfortunate choice of words. The clear implication of such a statement is that since leadership is specific to the individual, it will remain constant for the individual regardless of the situation in which he finds himself. Investigations of the actual consistency with which an individual maintains leadership status in different groups and under varying conditions have yielded results sufficiently equivocal to permit a new bifurcation of the field. On the one hand, the trait approach has been modified to imply that an individual's achieved leadership status is a function of his personality. On the other hand, sufficient evidence has been accumulated to give impetus to the situational approach to leadership, which maintains that leadership is an emergent phenomenon, created through the interaction of individuals (leaders and followers), and that selection and stability of any leadership pattern is a function of the task, composition, and culture of the group. From all this work has emerged some such summary formulation as that an individual's leadership status in groups is a joint function of his personality and the particular group setting [pp. 246–247].

With these cautions, Mann goes on to indicate those personality qualities that the empirical literature shows as associated with effective leadership in small groups.

The positive relationships of intelligence, adjustment, and extroversion to leadership are highly significant. In addition, dominance, masculinity, and interpersonal sensitivity are found to be positively related, while conservatism is found to be negatively related to leadership [p. 252].

It is difficult to specify leadership qualities in as restricted an area as laboratory training, for little research has been done on leadership in such groups and leadership styles vary greatly from leader to leader and from situation to situation. According to Whitman (1964), the trainer in a T-group should have experience in two areas: (1) his own inner life, and (2) group dynamics. Both of these qualities seem essential for a trainer in a contract group.

The Trainer
as Leader-Member

Leader-Member. In the contract group the leader is also a member; that is, he subscribes to the same member contract that the other participants do. In most sensitivity-training groups, part of the planned ambiguity revolves around the role of the trainer in the group. For a while, he seems to be neither leader nor member, for he gives the group little direction and in general interacts little with the individual members. Again, it is difficult to generalize about what trainers do or do not do in groups, because of the great variability in trainer styles. In the contract groups, however, the function of the leader is explicit. What he should do as member is spelled out in the member contract. What he should do as leader is spelled out in this chapter. What follows, then, constitutes a kind of leader contract.

The Leader-Member and Interpersonal Effectiveness. Mann (1959) indicated that an effective leader is an adjusted one. Rogers (1967) has found that the congruent therapist is more effective, and describes such a person as one who "responds as the real person he actually is," who "employs no artificial front and does not have to hide or fear his real reactions [p. 10]." The trainer in the contract group should also be adjusted and congruent, but this does not place him in a separate category in the group. It is not essential that he be the best adjusted or the most congruent. The leader-member is in the group because he is interested in interpersonal growth, his own included. He is not there because he has "made it" in the area of interpersonal relations, but because he thinks that interpersonal growth is important. Because of his experience, he may be more aware of his own interpersonal strengths and his areas of deficit, and it is this awareness that enables him to make contact with others. Ideally, the leader-member is a person of high social intelligence; that is, he has a feeling for people and knows how to get in contact with them without manipulating them. His social intelligence is seen partly in his ability to become a sincere member of the group, even though he is the leader or trainer. If the leader-member is not congruent and not socially intelligent in other respects, then his presence in the group will be disturbing rather than growthful, and the participants will have to spend a good deal of energy in learning how to deal with him.

The Functions of
the Leader-Member

Initial Structuring.   The leader should be familiar, both theoretically and experientially, with the contract under which the group will be working. If the contract is given to prospective members *before* they enter the group, then the leader need say little about the contract once the group begins. However, if the contract is imposed, there may be more contract disturbance during the first few meetings, and some minimal discussion of the contract itself will be in order. Under no condition, however, should the leader allow the contract to become the object of continual discussion; one of the reasons for the contract is to avoid such contract talk. The leader should avoid answering a multiplicity of abstract questions about the contract, even when the contract is brief and therefore open to some misinterpretation. The best time to answer a question concerning the contract is when the particular contract problem arises during the group interaction itself. Many areas within the contract can be cleared up effectively only within the context of group action.

Whitman (1964) sees the initial remarks made by the trainer in a T-group as extremely important in defining the subsequent character of the group (see Redl, 1942). The situation in the contract group, however, is quite different in that the contract itself bears a good deal of the weight of the initial structuring. What is important in the contract group is the immediate affective impact that the leader has on the group. There is no reason why he should not be warm and accepting from the very beginning, rather than aloof and ambiguous.

If the emotional attitudes he expresses arouse the resistance of the participants, then the group will have to spend time dealing with this resistance rather than proceeding to the immediate concerns of the contract. Working through such resistance may well be a fruitful experience in itself, but it is not part of the explicit design of the contract-group experience. In the contract group, a poor beginning due to a clumsy leader is simply uneconomic, for it is a time-consuming undertaking to try to correct mistakes in group process once they have been made.

Putting His Knowledge and Experience at the Service of the Group. According to Whitaker and Lieberman (1964), one of the sources of the group therapist's power comes from the unique position from which he sees the group focal conflict, which consists of two elements: a disturbing motive—that is, a wish on the part of one or more participants—and a reactive motive—that is, the fear or fears aroused by the disturbing motive. The therapist, because of his experience and training and because he stands apart from the group, has a vision of the group that none of the participants has. This is one of the factors that make him a powerful figure. In training laboratories, any leader who has a high degree of social intelligence, who has a solid knowledge of group dynamics, and who has had experience in groups is a powerful figure indeed. However, the way in which the trainer in the contract group uses his power differs from the way in which a therapist traditionally uses his in group psychotherapy. It also differs from the way in which another trainer, in a more traditional sensitivity-training group, would use his power. This is to be expected, since the goals (or at least the means) differ in these three situations. The primary function of the leader in the contract group is to place all of his resources at the service of the group *as directly and as unambiguously as possible.* He is there both to fulfill the contract and to help the other members to fulfill it. He is a kind of social engineer, who is interested in the development of the conditions of the interpersonal setting. The statement of these conditions is taken care of by the contract, but it is up to the trainer to see that these conditions develop in such a way as to lead to the fulfillment of the contract goals. His leadership does not place him outside the group, nor does it give him any special position in the group with respect to the member contract. He is not even different from the other members in that he is to *serve* the group, since it is the function of all the participants to serve the group. However, because of his knowledge, experience, and skills, he has a special ability to serve the group.

Because of his knowledge of group dynamics (groups as natural) and because of his experience (including his experience with groups as contractual), he knows, even before the group begins, the kinds of problems that will most likely arise naturally and impede the progress of the group. He therefore uses this knowledge of groups as natural to forestall the kinds of group process that do not contribute to the goals of the group, no matter how profitable such activity would be in another context. For instance, he prevents the participants from entering into a long, intellectualized discussion of the merits of the contract or of sensitivity training in general. Such discussions, no matter how intellectually profitable they may be, do not contribute to the goals of the contract and therefore are considered by definition (or rather by contract) to be forms of flight behavior. If the group wants to pursue goals other than those outlined in the contract, the members should come to a consensus, abandon the contract, and subscribe to a different process.

Dealing with the Major Problems of Groups as Natural. N-interactions (see chapter 2) can be disruptive, neutral, or facilitative with respect to the goals set by the contract. The contract trainer ignores the neutral, confronts the disruptive, and encourages the facilitative. For instance, Lott and Lott (1965), in a review of the literature on group cohesiveness, found that increased contact or interaction on the part of group members heightens the cohesiveness of the group. The trainer, then, encourages the members of the group to interact with one another as much as possible, and he discourages or confronts behavior that limits interaction (e.g., speeches, monologues, psychological withdrawal, excessive silence). There are, in groups, some usually unavoidable natural problems that are so important that, at least in the contract group, they should be explained in some way from the very beginning. If these problems, which are productive of disruptive N-interactions, are explained in the contract itself, then the leader need not explain but should merely comment on them (and confront when necessary) when they do arise. However they are explained and handled, it should be *before* they interfere with an economic pursual of group goals. In other kinds of group experiences, these same problems arise, but often they are handled only after they disrupt the group. Such an approach is used purposely. For instance, a group might become entangled in long, intellectualized discussions of psychodynamics. During the course of these discussions, many members become bored and withdraw psychologically from the group. Finally, after the participants have experienced the deadening effect of this particular kind of nongrowthful N-interaction, the trainer may ask the group to reflect on what is happening. The participants learn, painfully but profitably, that they have really been avoiding more intimate contact with one another. However, learning the anatomy of disruptive or nongrowthful N-interactions by actually experiencing them is not one of the primary goals of the contract group.

Perhaps the central natural problems that will face the group should be included in the contract or discussed by the leader from the very beginning. Later, as less crucial natural problems arise, the leader can interpret them in the context of the group interaction. Some N-interactions are more disruptive than others, and it is also possible that different kinds of N-interactions will prove disruptive (or facilitative) to groups with different kinds of contracts. The problems discussed below are considered important enough to the contract group to warrant attention before the group begins:

(1) *The problem of handling the leader.* Almost everyone who discusses the question of leadership in small groups deals with the problems arising from the polarization between leader and members (e.g., Bennis, 1956, 1964; Bion, 1961; Tuckman, 1965; Whitman, 1964). Tuckman (1965) suggests that the initial stage of training groups is marked by a degree of member-leader disturbance. Bennis (1964) divides participants into three categories during this initial stage: the dependents, those who look to the trainer for cues; the counterdependents, those who solve their dependency needs by opposing the leader; and the independents, those who are "not threatened by the prospect of intimacy [p. 264]." Nor is it certain that such polarization is confined to the initial stage of the group. Bennis (1956) hypothesized that the group would deal first with the problem of authority (evidenced by power struggles and by preoccupation with relationships with the trainer) and then with the problem of intimacy (evidenced by such concerns as how much self-revelation there could be). The results of his study, however, showed a continuous dealing with both these issues. Perhaps Slater (1966) is the one who deals most intensively with such natural phenomena as dependency, counterdependency, revolt, and exclusion of the leader. Mann (1967) has developed a rather extensive member-leader analysis system in which all feelings of member toward leader are scored. The system includes such categories as moving against, resisting, withdrawing, guilt inducing (e.g., blaming, accusing, feeling misunderstood), identifying, moving toward, showing dependency, and showing self-esteem (e.g., showing the leader the ability to be open and honest).

As intriguing as such variables are and as focal as they are in a variety of group experiences, in the contract group an attempt is made to render them relatively inconsequential. The overriding goal of the contract group demands that the participants become as deeply involved as possible with one another. However, if the group spends the initial stage dealing primarily with member-leader phenomena (Tuckman, 1965) or deals continuously with such problems (Bennis, 1956), time and energy are diverted from more important goals. Therefore, the leader "blows his cover," as it were: he tells the group about member-leader phenomena, he indicates the kinds of N-interactions (e.g., dependency, counterdependency behavior) that arise in face-to-face groups because of member-leader polarization. He abdicates his "fatherhood" and his "divinity" from the beginning. If members are to have difficulty with him, he wants it to be because he is another group member and not because he is the leader. This does not mean that dependency and counterdependency phenomena will not arise in the group, but it is hypothesized that they will not arise with the same frequency and intensity as they would in groups not made aware of such phenomena from the beginning. That a particular member refuses to allow the leader to abdicate his fatherhood or his omnipotence is quite significant. Authority problems do exist, and they will be stronger in some participants than in others. Member-leader polarization stages or cultures are to be avoided, but not the individual N-interactions that arise from very deep needs in individual cases. No contract can legislate individual authority or dependency problems out of existence. In fact, individual problems in these areas will be highlighted in the contract group because they will not appear merely as a part of a stage or a culture.

According to Whitaker and Lieberman (1964), part of the therapist's power in group therapy comes "from the frequency with which the patients impute to the therapist the power of gratification, threat, and magical solutions. On this basis, the therapist becomes an object of impulses involved in the group focal conflict and a source of solutions [pp. 197–198]." It is precisely this power that the leader, insofar as possible, abdicates. The contract-group leader differs from both therapist (at least as traditionally conceived) and trainer in that he makes himself quite visible. He tries to avoid, rather than use, ambiguity. Unlike the trainer as Whitman (1964) conceives him, he is not concerned with a middle road between "absence of visibility" and "complete visibility [p. 312]." His cards are on the table. He does not feel constrained to withhold information from the group because they cannot tolerate it. Both member contract and leader contract are group property. It is hypothesized that such openness will facilitate communication within the group and make the leader less of a problem.

Finally, the trainer in the contract group does not conceive of the members' relationships to him and his to them in terms of transference and countertransference. While there is no need to look upon transference as "a devil conjured up only to be sent back to his usual habitat with much expenditure of time and energy [Eysenck, 1959, p. 74]," it is not considered a crucial issue in the contract group. Those who conceive of resistance to growth in terms of transference (e.g., Bernstein, 1965) might argue that an attempt to eliminate problems of member-leader polarization by increasing the visibility of the phenomenon merely makes the problem of transference less visible and thus more acute. On the other hand, many therapists work without the concept of transference, or at least conceive of it in other than psychoanalytic terms. For instance, May (1958) suggests that "the neurotic is one who in certain areas never developed beyond the limited and restricted forms of experience characteristic of the infant. Hence in later years he perceives wife or therapist through the same restricted, distorted 'spectacles' as he perceived father or mother [p. 79]." It is not a question of transferring feelings, but of persistently perceiving relationships in maladaptive ways.

(2) *Preventing tacit understandings.* Whitman (1964) refers to the different levels on which a group operates simultaneously. He says that "for practical purposes, two levels is a useful division. Overt and covert, or manifest and latent, are ways of describing these levels [p. 318]." Both Bennis and his associates (1957) and Lieberman (1958) found that norms of member behavior were established early in the group sessions and tended to persist throughout the life of the group.

Groups naturally make decisions; that is, they make N-interaction decisions, and not just C-interaction decisions, about all sorts of things: procedure, topics to be discussed, limits to be set, etc. Some of these decisions are overt, some are covert. For instance, sex might come up in the course of the group discussion, but somehow or other it is sidetracked. It comes up again later, but again it is sidetracked. Finally, even though it is not openly discussed, group members realize that "we do not talk about sex in this group." This is what Slater (1966) calls a "tacit understanding." A covert decision has been reached in the group. The group of tacit understandings that is currently operative, gives direction to the group, and sets limits for group interactions may be called the group mentality or the group culture. Bion (1959), Slater (1966), and Whitaker and Lieberman (1964) all deal with this phenomenon.

Tacit understandings can sabotage group process. The trouble with covert decisions is that once they are made, they are very difficult to change.

The group forms its own history and constructs its own standards and modes of behavior and, once fixed, they are extremely difficult to alter. . . . They have almost the binding effect of laws; for the social punishment when they are broken (such as disapproval, ostracism, and hostility) is as severe as its equivalent prison sentence in Western society [Whitman, 1964, p. 315].

Groups can die from stumbling over their tacit culture.

Since covert decisions impede rather than facilitate group process in the contract group, the leader discusses the notions of tacit understandings and group culture with the participants. He not only blows his own cover, but he also blows the cover of the group. The ideal is that decisions in the group be made overtly and not covertly. Explaining the concept of tacit understanding at the beginning of group process certainly does not eliminate the natural tendency of the group to operate this way. The leader must confront the group in the process of coming to a tacit understanding. For instance, if the leader witnessed the sidetracking of the sex issue mentioned above, he would confront the group. "The sex issue has been brought up a number of times and each time it has been sidetracked. It seems that we are on the verge of entering into a tacit understanding not to talk about sex. If we really want to avoid the sex issue, let's first talk about it and then make a decision aboveboard." Crucial (and thus anxiety-provoking) issues are often sidetracked through this covert decision-making process.

Any kind of hidden agenda in the group muddies communication and should be avoided as far as possible. Both individuals and groups can develop a hidden agenda. For example, A might be attracted to B and would like to see the attraction become mutual. Therefore A, in any number of indirect ways, acts to elicit B's attention and favor: for instance, he might pair with B in a variety of ways, to show B that they think and feel alike. Or a group may conspire, indirectly, to "get" a punitive trainer. The participants become apathetic and bored, or they sabotage exercises suggested by the trainer and, in general, see to it that the trainer fails in his task. Since pursuit of a hidden agenda ultimately works counter to the declared goals of the contract group, it should be dealt with in the same way as tacit understandings.

(3) *Lowest-common-denominatorism.* When even one person in a group displays indifference toward the goals of the group, the efficacy of the group is lowered. Whitman (1964) claims that the T-group can move along only as rapidly as the slowest member.

The problem of the lagging, delinquent, or deviant member is one that arises naturally in groups. An effective contract can help control deviancy by eliminating the unmotivated (especially if the contract is freely chosen and not just imposed) and by eliminating the kinds of vagueness and ambiguity in group process that often engender the indifference or apathy of the deviant member. However, there is no ultimate way of ensuring the interest and cooperation of all members. The problem of lack of motivation is one of the most difficult to handle in all kinds of growth experiences. Rogers (1966) believes that it is more difficult to deal with than psychosis:

From our own experience in working with unmotivated schizophrenic individuals and a small matched group of unmotivated normal individuals I have come to a conclusion which you may regard as startling. It is my present conviction that working with a lack of conscious motivation in the individual is more difficult than working with the problem of psychosis. This is of course a subjective opinion, based in part on our general lack of success in trying to form a facilitative relationship with unmotivated "normals" of low socioeducational status. Insofar as the two elements are separable, I believe the absence of conscious desire for help presents a greater challenge to the therapist than the presence of psychosis [p. 8].

The leader, then, should discuss the possibility of the group's ultimately having to deal with an unmotivated or deviant member. If the possibility is discussed, it is hypothesized that the delinquent member will have a less retarding effect on the group. Whether such a member should be expelled or encouraged to remove himself from the group is a moot question. The natural tendency of groups that lose a member for one reason or another is to spend a good deal of time dealing with their own feelings of guilt and loss. Whatever is done, the contract group should not allow a deviant member to absorb its energies.

The Leader as Guardian
of the Contract

Stock (1964) suggests that a trainer may be sensitive to missing functions in the group and may either deliberately try or unconsciously tend to supply the missing element. In the contract group, the elements of the group experience are more clearly delineated and it is therefore much easier for the leader (and the other members) to see what is missing. The trainer, then, should consciously try to stimulate the group to add the missing element. In a sense, therefore, the leader-member is, at least initially, the guardian of the contract. He is in the service of the group members principally to see that the contract is fulfilled. The individual participants benefit to the degree that they share in the common good of the group, and it is the function of the leader to see that this common good, as defined by the superordinate, interaction, and process goals of the group, is pursued. He fulfills this function by encouraging and modeling contract behavior and by confronting those who do not engage in such behavior or who engage in anticontractual behavior. He has every right to encourage and confront directly, for his being a stimulus is part of the contract to which the members agree. He does not have to apologize for upholding the contract. However, the way in which he fulfills his function as guardian is quite important. If he is a watchdog, an authoritarian figure who confronts in alienating ways, then he will induce a nongrowth polarization between himself and the other participants. An important way of encouraging contractual behavior is to have the participants reflect on their own behavior. The leader has them stand back and evaluate, or process, the ways in which they are pursuing or avoiding the goals of the contract. Such self-criticism is less ego-deflating, and often more direct and incisive, than that of an observer. There is perhaps a curvilinear relationship between the degree of guardian behavior and productivity in the group. Productivity will be low if the leader-member is either too cautious or too eager to confront a delinquent group. Optimal productivity will correlate with forceful but tempered confrontation. This is a difficult task; again, there is no substitute for social competency in the leader.

The Leader as Model

There are various ways in which the leader can promote the contract: he can encourage, stimulate, confront, process, and in general act from the outside. But since, in the contract group, he is a leader-member, he promotes the contract perhaps principally by modeling the behavior called for by the contract: he accepts, encourages, engages in self-disclosure, invites others to self-examination, responds to confrontation by examining his own activity, expresses his feelings, cooperates with others, sticks to the here and now, tries to involve himself with others, encourages others to involve themselves with him, and generally searches for new ways of being present to others. Campbell and Dunnette (1968) suggest that such modeling characterizes trainer behavior in all kinds of sensitivity-training experiences:

The role of the trainer also constitutes a dominant technological element bearing on the group's effectiveness for giving feedback and promoting psychological support. The trainer serves as a model for the participants to imitate; that is, he absorbs feelings of hostility and frustration without becoming defensive, provides feedback for others, expresses his own feelings openly and honestly, and is strongly supportive of the expression of feelings of others. In short, he exhibits for consideration the very process deemed necessary for maximum learning to occur [pp. 76–77].

Modeling, however, demands a good deal of tact. For instance, if the trainer engages in self-disclosure, he does not rush in with a degree of self-revelation that would shock and inhibit rather than challenge and encourage. Dramatic self-disclosure would then be the leader's way of deciding for the group at what level of disclosure they should operate. To set this level is a function of the group as a whole and should not be usurped by any single individual. Similar cautions apply to other interaction goals, such as confrontation.

The Diffusion of Leadership

Whatever might be the most current thinking on leadership in training or therapy groups, the function of the leader in the contract group is to become less and less a leader and more and more a member. That is, all of the functions which have been listed as leader functions should become dispersed among the members of the group. Leadership, according to Collins and Guetzkow (1964), "is a scattered activity—one member being influential at one time because of a particular combination of environmental demands and personal characteristics, and another being influential at another time because of a different congruence of demand and trait [pp. 214–215]." As Cattell (1951) suggests, leadership is measured by impact on group. If an appointed leader has no real impact on the work of the group, then his leadership is merely nominal. Leadership, then, is really a shared function; it is something fluid in the group. Having a leader-member in the contract group is a contrived state of affairs in the same sense that the entire laboratory is contrived. He is the leader in the beginning because of his experience, knowledge, and skills. But the whole function of the group is to enable the participants to grow in precisely the same skills. As the members begin to engage in contractual behavior, there is less and less need for the leader-member to stimulate such behavior. Whenever any participant engages in contractual behavior, at that moment he becomes a leader in the sense that he promotes the work of the group. Status in the contract group, if such a term is even applicable, is identified with contract fulfillment.

If leadership is to be diffused in the group, then the leader must be willing to relinquish his favored position. If he is overinvested in being a "parent," it will be difficult for him to recognize, and reinforce through support, the increasing skills of the participants. If he hangs on too tightly, not only his level or depth of intervention, but even his manner of intervention is likely to become the standard of the group (Blake, 1964). Such behavior, however, runs completely counter to the purposes of the group.

There are analogues to the above conception of leadership in certain therapy groups. Bach (1966) describes a marathon group in which "every member is a cotherapist responsible for the relative success or failure of any given marathon meeting [p. 997]." The professional cotherapists in the group, "if and when they feel like it," participate as patients rather than consultants. Structure is provided by the "Ten Commandments" of the marathon, which provide a kind of contractual foundation for the group experience. The staff in Mowrer's (1968) integrity groups are there as participants rather than therapists or observers. They are leaders in the sense that they go ahead and fulfill the contract.

If the trainer in the contract group models effectively and monitors the contract judiciously, trying to see that C-interactions increase while disruptive N-interactions decrease, if he teaches the group to confront itself according to the provisions of the contract, then his skills will be disseminated throughout the group and the group will be leaderless, paradoxically, by being full of leaders.

Leaderless Groups

Research is currently being carried on with unled training and psychotherapy groups. Leaderless groups are not new, for Gibb (1964) and others have been experimenting with them for a number of years:

Our many years of experience with "leaderless" groups in various settings lead us to feel that maximum participative behavior is attained more readily in training groups without trainers than with trainers. The groups are perhaps more aptly described as "leaderful," in that what occurs is not an abolition of leadership but a distribution of leadership roles in the group. It is perhaps even more accurate to describe the participative groups as "trainerless." Members learn to observe and experiment upon their own behavior in increasingly creative ways. They learn that it is less adaptive to take a "trainer stance," that is, advise, "help," teach, change, or persuade others [pp. 298–299].

Harrow and his associates (1967) found that unled groups tended to be warmer and more supportive. Salzberg (1967), in studying the verbal behavior of therapy groups, found that unled groups produced fewer problem-relevant responses, but were more spontaneous. Berzon and Solomon (1966) not only found leaderless group therapy to be feasible, but found that one kind of interaction —confrontation—increased in unled groups. The authors do not say, but I presume that the confrontation was considered therapeutic. In experimenting with unled sessions in group marital counseling (I observed the interaction through a one-way mirror), I found that not only were the groups more spontaneous (that is, there was much more self-initiated interaction), but also there was a high degree of problem-relevant interaction. The latter (although contrary to Salzberg's findings) was most likely due to the fact that the group was working under a contract. Once they had learned the contractual process ("how therapy goes"), they could have profitable sessions without me.

Not all the evidence in this area is completely positive. Truax and Carkhuff (1964) found that although some of the deepest levels of therapeutic process took place with juvenile-delinquent groups during unled sessions (sessions were alternately led and unled), the alternately unled groups showed no greater progress on a variety of outcome criteria than did continually led groups. In unled groups, then, there is the possibility of greater patient process without greater outcome. However, the saving of manpower seems significant in itself; nor is there any reason to suppose that the cautions suggested by Truax and Carkhuff need apply in any way to laboratory training groups with normal populations.

Instrumented Laboratories. The National Training Laboratories have been experimenting for some years now with "instrumented" training laboratories (Blake & Mouton, 1962; also see Benne, 1964).

There is no trainer in the instrumented group; whatever staff there is usually works outside the group. In place of the trainer, a series of self-administered evaluation forms, or instruments, are introduced. These instruments are used throughout the laboratory to provide its participants with feedback. Group action is interrupted from time to time, and, through feedback, the participants learn to see themselves better. In a trainer-directed group, feedback takes place through his interventions. In the instrumented group, wall charts and graphs indicate the characteristics of both group and personal action during each meeting. In instrumented laboratories, the staff engages in a variety of activities: they provide the instruments of action research, train members to use the data gathered, give general sessions in modeling and in setting standards for giving and receiving feedback, arrange for intergroup competition and collaboration among development groups. Although their activity may provide a good deal of structure for the laboratory, they do not sit in the groups and control them. The information that is fed back into the groups from the data collected is used as the members see fit.

The instrumented laboratory has been used in industrial, university, and hospital settings, both with normals and with psychiatric patients. Johnson and his associates (1965), in a follow-up study of an instrumented laboratory with psychiatric patients, found that the improvement-cure record of the instrumented groups equalled or surpassed that of the regular therapy groups.

The contract group begins with a leader in order that it may become effectively leaderless in as short a time as possible. If the leader is warm and skillful in engaging in contractual behavior, then "behavioral contagion" (Lippitt, Polansky, Redl, & Rosen, 1952) will take place and the group will be quickly on its way to a creative interpersonal experience.

Semi-led Training Groups. Although, as indicated above, it is not uncommon for psychotherapists to experiment with alternate led and unled group-therapy sessions, and although completely unled training groups are common (Gibb, 1964), there is no mention in the literature of training groups with alternate led and unled sessions. I have experimented with such a procedure in a laboratory course in interpersonal relations. When I was in the group, I was there as leader-member, but obviously it was much more difficult to become a full member. One member even commented: "Since you were on the outside of the group, we did not have to work through the whole problem of your leadership." Even though such part-time leader-membership is hardly ideal, it is workable, especially if it is made clear from the beginning that this is part of the contract.

Conclusion

The style of the contract-group trainer differs, at least theoretically, from that of the trainer in more traditional T-groups. Campbell and Dunnette (1968) say that in a traditional training experience, "a trainer is usually present, but he does not accept, in fact he overtly rejects any leadership role [p. 75]." He may overtly reject leadership in some sense of the term, but he is still present in the group as leader in some sense. If, as Campbell and Dunnette suggest, his modeling of growthful behavior does give direction to the group, then he is a leader. In the contract group, he overtly accepts his role as leader, but he makes it clear that one of his primary goals is the diffusion of leadership among the participants. There is evidence (Fleishman & Harris, 1962; Halpin, 1957; Oaklander & Fleishman, 1964; Rush, 1957) that high-consideration, high-structure behavior is frequently associated with effective and successful leadership for widely different populations. If this is true, then a warm and accepting trainer working within the structure of a viable contract should be successful, even though success is ultimately defined as the diffusion of his leadership qualities. It is not structure per se which is offensive, but constricting, controlling, non-facilitative structure.

The Leader as "Anti-entropic." Entropy has been described by Rosenblith (1967) as the "tendency of a closed system to deteriorate and run downhill by going from a highly differentiated and less probable state to the more probable, undifferentiated, and chaotic state [p. 274]." The group can be considered analogous to such a system. Left to its own devices, the group tends naturally to run downhill. The leader is an anti-entropic force in the system. He keeps the communication system open. The group system closes when the individual members seal themselves off from one another. When the members are fulfilling the contract, they are engaging in nonprobable interpersonal behavior that is assumed to lead to growth. The system, then, is open. The leader helps keep the communication system open by his knowledge of groups as nature and by fulfilling his function as monitor of the contract. When members close in upon themselves, they become undifferentiated; that is, the group resembles, analogously, the run-down state of the system in entropy (see Wiener, 1950). The ideal is that each member become an anti-entropic agent in the group.

Leadership and Individual Style. The demands of leadership in the contract group still allow the leader to be himself, to possess his own style. Any particular leader may be more effective in, or put more stress on, one set of contract variables than another. The leader should be himself just as he allows (or encourages) others to be themselves. The contract-group leader will also become a member of the group in his own individual way. Perhaps he will always remain differentiated from the group in some way (Slater [1966] claims that the image of the leader as differentiated from the group serves as a point of orientation in turmoil), but he should stand off from the group as little as possible. The contract itself is a point of orientation.

At times he may be the victim of what Goffman (1967) calls "interaction consciousness"; that is, he becomes preoccupied with his special responsibility to see that the interaction goes well. The leader who becomes too preoccupied both fails to "give himself to his own party" and forgets that the responsibility for effective interaction is a corporate one. Finally, although the leader should be a fairly well integrated person, there is no reason that he must be the best group member. Different participants will excel in different interpersonal skills, with each learning, in some way, from each of the others.

Chapter Six:
Total
Human Expression:
The Elements of
Human Dialogue:
Pathos, Logos, Poiesis

Introduction

Needless to say, the members of a face-to-face sensitivity-training group are in the group in order to communicate with one another. Since, in the contract group, the members agree to experiment with their interpersonal behavior, they must experiment with the process of communication. Communication, however, is both an ambiguous word and a complex task. The purpose of this chapter, then, is to consider the elements of communication insofar as they relate to a laboratory in interpersonal relations.

Total human expression refers to a man's ability to communicate himself fully—that is, on both an intellective and an emotional level. This ability will be examined in terms of three dimensions of dialogue: *pathos, logos,* and *poiesis. Pathos* refers to all the elements, passive and active, that constitute the experience of feeling and emotion. *Logos* is a large concept; it refers to man's ability to communicate himself to others, both in words and through nonverbal behavior. *Logos* also refers to the ability to use all channels of interpersonal communication in the translation of oneself, intellectually and emotionally, to the other. These channels, according to Wiener and Mehrabian (1968), include (1) language in its most straightforward sense—that is, "verbal content, e.g., word meaning and syntax"; (2) the *way* in which the verbal message is delivered—that is, the "extralinguistic phenomena of communication (Mahl & Schultz, 1964), e.g., variations in tonal qualities, patterns of stress, pitch, and pauses which are not dictated by the required linguistic form"; and (3) all the forms of nonverbal behavior that enter into the communication process—that is, "motoric or bodily phenomena . . . , e.g., facial expressions, gestures, postures, and proxemics [p. 51]." *Poiesis* refers to the ability of man to be "poetic" in his communication—that is, the ability to integrate verbal, nonverbal, and emotional expression in dialogue. Negatively, it is the refusal to strip words of their human feeling together with a refusal to allow emotions to become irrational.

The logic of the following discussion of these three elements is not the logic of human living; elements discussed separately (and therefore somewhat abstractively) here are, in actual living, woven into idiosyncratic patterns in the transactions of any particular individual. However, if this dissection leads to the kind of awareness that underlies behavioral change, then it is justified. It is obvious that these elements of dialogue are important in everyday life. It is just as obvious, then, that they are important in any kind of sensitivity-training experience. The contract group, however, is explicit in requiring its participants to focus their attention on their emotions, especially those arising from the interaction within the group, on their ability (or inability) to translate themselves into language, on their nonverbal communications, and on the difficulties involved in allowing emotion to give color and character to one's verbalizations.

Men, by their inability or unwillingness to communicate deeply with one another, seem to foist upon themselves a state analogous to social deprivation. It would seem that such self-inflicted deprivation might well have effects analogous to those observed in studies on social deprivation. Studies by Mullin (1960), Nardini (1962), and Rohrer (1961) indicate that variables such as monotony of environment and absence of sources of emotional gratification can cause intellectual inertia, impaired memory and concentration, insomnia, headaches, low-grade depression, and greatly increased appetite (with resultant weight gain). An interesting hypothesis is that similar symptoms found among relatively normal populations of our society reflect self-imposed estrangement from others, although such a macro-hypothesis would be difficult to verify. The contract group is a laboratory in which the participants come together to determine whether or not they themselves are victims of any form of self-inflicted social deprivation, and, if this is the case, to find ways of remedying such a situation by in-community activity.

**Pathos: Man as the
Subject of Feelings
and Emotions**

The Flight from Emotion

There is growing concern—and perhaps it may also be said that there is growing evidence, though it is the fruit of observation rather than experimentation—over the inability of some people to engage in a free and constructive expression of emotion. The hypothesis might be stated: many men in our society, especially those in the middle and upper classes, are constricted in their ability to experience emotion and to give expression to their emotions; for one reason or another, they have not faced up to their possibilities in these areas. Even in sensitivity laboratories, where it is expected that a selectivity factor would engage a population somewhat more free than the average in the area of emotional experiencing and expression, participants have to be reminded again and again to give expression, not just to what they think, but to what they feel.

Formal education is overloaded in the area of intellect, impoverished in the area of emotion. As Neill (1968) notes:

Today our schools educate the head and leave the emotions to the crowd-compellers—the press, the radio, the TV, the churches, the commercial exploiters with their lying advertisements. Our pop heroes and film stars have become our leading schoolmasters dealing with real emotions. . . . The danger today is underdeveloped emotion, perverted emotion, infantile emotion [p. 37].

Paperback novels, movies, and the ubiquitous television set all constitute a two-edged sword in the emotional life of man. If used with imagination and discretion, they can complement a person's emotional life, enhance and enrich it by broadening his emotional experience, and provide the beginnings of some kind of insight or vision into a wide variety of human experiences. But too many people misuse these media, with the result that the media are not complements to emotional living but rather substitutes for it; and, for many, this vicarious emotional living is sufficient.

Fromm (1941) decries the general tendency of society to discourage emotion, and the resulting "cheap and insincere sentimentality with which movies and popular songs feed millions of emotion-starved customers [p. 271]." He sees the child developing a "pseudo character," not because he has to learn to control his feelings, but because he must deny that he even experiences them. Lynd (1958) notes the same trends: "In our society 'emotional' is frequently used as a derogatory term. Developing emotional maturity is more often conceived in terms of training a child in what he should *not* feel and in controlling the expression of his feelings than in extending the range and depth of his emotions and their expression [p. 236]." Fromm goes so far as to suggest that bad dreams result from the fact that people force their true feelings out of consciousness because these feelings do not fit in with the social self.

In a recent book, Schutz (1967) describes the joy that he experienced watching his newborn son being totally absorbed in the experience, both happy and unhappy, of growing. He describes what he sees as unbounded joy, but also begins to wonder: "But will something happen to Ethan as it does to us all? Where will his joy go? In most of us it becomes depleted, distorted, contorted. Guilt and fear begin to defile it. Somehow the joy of Ethan goes, never to fully return [p. 10]." The rest of the book is an engaging essay on some ways and means of winning back the joy that too many men forfeit as the price of security, socialization, and productivity.

Keniston's Hypothesis. One way of looking at the emotional parasitism of society—men become parasites to television, movies, and the other things mentioned above—is that it is an essential or at least unavoidable phenomenon in a technocratic society such as ours. Keniston (1965) suggests that two phenomena of our society converge to create an emotional dilemma for the working man. First of all, many men find little emotional satisfaction in the work they do to earn a living. Work, instead of satisfying emotional needs, intensifies them. Breadwinners come home, then, hungering for emotional satisfaction and expecting to find it with their families.

But today's family—and this is the second phenomenon—is a smaller unit than yesterday's. Family no longer means a complex of grandparents, aunts, uncles, and children living in the same at least relatively circumscribed geographical area. Family today means wife and two or three children, too geographically or psychologically separated from close relatives to constitute an interactional unit with any direct emotional meaning or impact. Keniston claims that, given the emotional constriction or frustration of the breadwinner at work, the family, especially so small a family, cannot satisfy his intensified or exaggerated emotional needs at home. Obviously, the wife faces analogous emotional frustrations, and then husband's and wife's intensified emotional needs become interactive.

There are no ready-made solutions for these emotional binds. Ideally, husband and wife, without abandoning their obligations to work and children, will move out into the community, into such things as church and civic activities, thus broadening the bases of emotional fulfillment. However, other less responsible solutions tend to destroy the equilibrium of the family: tension and fighting in the home, extramarital adventures, emotional constriction and insulation, and the vicarious emotional living mentioned above, made easy, for instance, by the proliferation of engaging but undemanding sports events on television.

Man's struggle for freedom has been the theme of much of his literature from the very beginning of recorded history. While this freedom is conceived of in more or less political terms, there has been a concomitant or parallel struggle for more interior forms of freedom such as emotional freedom. Today, even if men have been freed from the emotion-constricting slavery of Jansenism, Puritanism, and Victorianism (and certainly not all have), many have managed to shackle themselves with new bonds. While the prior slavery was enjoined in the name of morality and religion, the new slavery is imposed in the name of technocracy, progress, and production. Many have been duped into thinking that they are emotionally free, when all that has happened has been a change in the facade of their bondage. It is as if men were afraid to allow men to experience either themselves or their environment in an unfettered way and to institute communication with one another based on this experiencing. Rather, this is the unknown, the unknown is dangerous, the dangerous is to be feared, and the feared is to be resisted.

Some men are relieved when they are told that "feelings get in the way," for it justifies an already determined mode of interpersonal acting. Men who are guarded in their feelings toward others do not particularly want to become aware of these feelings. They would also prefer that others not feel strongly about them. It is thought uncivil, rude, unconventional, unwarranted, and even obscene to express feelings toward others. Emotional insulation parades under such euphemisms as "respect for others" and the "dignity of privacy." Sometimes the mentally ill are feared, not because they express too little but because they express too much. Men who are afraid of feelings and emotions to begin with are utterly terrified when these are expressed without restraint. Perhaps the best symbol of man as emotional today is the polyethylene bag. Nothing gets in. Nothing gets out. He remains encased in interpersonal asepsis.

Normal Alienation from Experience. Laing (1967) conceptualizes what is assumed here to be a fairly widespread flight from fuller emotional living as man's "normal alienation from experience":

As adults, we have forgotten most of our childhood, not only its contents but its flavor; as men of the world, we hardly know of the existence of the inner world . . . as for our bodies, we retain just sufficient proprioceptive sensations to coordinate our movements and to ensure the minimal requirements of biosocial survival—to register fatigue, signals for food, sex, defecation, sleep; beyond that little or nothing. . . . our capacity even to see, hear, touch, taste and smell is so shrouded in veils of mystification that an intensive discipline of unlearning is necessary for *anyone* before one can begin to experience the world afresh, with innocence, truth and love [pp. 10–11].

For Laing, psychotherapy is the process of getting back into contact with one's experiencing through affective contact with another:

The psychotherapeutic relationship is therefore a re-search. A search, constantly reasserted and reconstituted, for what we have all lost and whose loss some can perhaps endure a little more easily than others, as some people can stand lack of oxygen better than others, and *this research is validated by the shared experience of experience regained in and through the therapeutic relationship in the here and now* [p. 34].

The contract group, or any growth experience for normals, is also an emotional re-search project. Emotional alienation might be more easily endured by the normal, but if the psychopathology of the average or man's normal alienation from experience is as serious a problem for society as it is assumed to be here, then, while the individual might be able to endure his emotional constriction, society cannot.

The evidence is in. It would be a simple, but rather useless, task to go on cataloging the evidence of man's sins against the emotional dimensions of his humanity. However clinical and anecdotal such evidence is, it is still compelling; but one need not prove what is self-evident. The growing popularity of organizations such as the Esalen Institute, the National Training Laboratories, and the Western Behavioral Sciences Institute, and of sensitivity laboratories in general dramatizes the plight of a people seeking deliverance from emotional bondage. Whether this deliverance takes place in responsible ways depends, at least partly, on the willingness of behavioral scientists to channel some of their talents into creative thinking and experimentation in this area. The growing laboratory-learning culture in our society offers any number of possibilities for such work. Perhaps a new era is dawning in the field of mental health, an era in which concern with prevention of illness is absorbed into larger concerns, such as self-actualization and community potential for human growth.

Emotional Life and the Function of the Contract Group. Sensitivity groups have the potential of developing an intense intragroup emotional life. Since one of the process goals of the group as a whole and of members individually is diagnosis, the group provides ample opportunity for the participants not only to deal with one another on an emotional level but to examine the quality of their emotional living. The members should experiment with all the phases of the *pathos* experience outlined below; they should try to feel and express emotions and nuances of emotion that do not constitute their ordinary patterns of emotional living. This does not mean that the participants should manufacture emotions, for probably most of them already spend too much time expressing emotions that they do not really feel. Rather, they should try to interact as intimately as possible with one another, and allow themselves to feel the whole range of emotions that arise from such interaction. Only then will they be able to evaluate, both within themselves and in dialogue with one another, their emotional successes and failures. The members of the contract group are told explicitly that the group is to serve as a laboratory in which the quality of one's emotional living can be evaluated and, hopefully, enriched. The participants contract (1) to examine their ability to face up to the emotional realities of personal and interpersonal living, and (2) to experiment with different aspects of emotional living. The analysis of the *pathos* experience below will help operationalize these provisions of the contract and serve as a guide as to what to look for both in individual emotional experiences and in the corporate emotional life of the group.

The Phases of
Emotional Experiencing

The *pathos* experience, dealt with at a level of abstraction that is meaningful for sensitivity experiences, has four phases: awareness, impact, reaction, and expression. It is possible to short-circuit *pathos* at any one of these phases, the result being a truncated emotional experience.

Awareness. As Arnold (1960) notes, emotion is preceded by a cognitive element, in which the individual first evaluates the situation in which he finds himself. If he evaluates it as immediately dangerous, fear arises. Thus, the quality of a person's emotional life is dependent on the quality of his awareness. If, by either nature or nurture, a person's ability to be aware of what is happening around him is constricted, then his emotional life will be constricted. On the other hand, if a person wants to grow emotionally, he must improve his awareness of himself and of his environment, especially his interpersonal environment.

The refusal or inability to be aware of self and others is characteristic of the emotionally disturbed. In fact, it may be hypothesized that the more disturbed a person is, the greater his tendency to cut off the *pathos* process or experience at an earlier stage. The most severely disturbed, then, would sabotage emotional experience at the level of awareness. I have been in group-therapy experiences in which the most severely disturbed have been challenged merely to repeat the gist of what another had revealed in an emotionally charged disclosure. An "I-didn't-hear-what-he-said" typified the poverty of awareness that characterized these patients. This inner numbness or preoccupation with self effectively fended off any kind of affective contact with others.

In a parallel way, this lack of awareness of self and others characterizes the more severe forms of the psychopathology of the average. In the contract group, it is assumed that the unfettered ability to experience oneself and one's environment is a relatively rare phenomenon. Awareness can be cut off in a variety of ways: men can be "too busy" to notice emotion-generating stimuli in themselves or coming from without; emotional involvement "gets in the way" and cuts down on productivity, and this is treason in a technocratic society. Recently, however, industry itself has realized that closing one's eyes to the emotional realities of life is literally unprofitable. Programs have been set up for alcoholics because merely dismissing them meant a loss of valuable personnel and decreased morale. Men in managerial positions have been sent to human-relations laboratories in order to become more aware of the emotional realities of interpersonal relating on the job. Ignored emotion leads to ineffective communication; ineffective communication leads to decreased productivity. Managerial involvement in human-relations laboratories is growing because it is profitable in terms of dollars and cents. It would be a sad commentary on the human condition if industry's newfound interest in the emotional climate of the work situation because it is both humanly and financially profitable were not paralleled by a renewed interest in emotional variables on the part of private individuals simply because it is profitable in terms of human growth.

Denial is not the only mechanism used to fend off emotion-provoking stimuli. Festinger (1957) suggests that men distort their perceptions—that is, the quality of their awareness—so that reality may seem to be concordant with preformed attitudes or prechosen forms of behavior. For instance, A might be angry with B and express his anger in a variety of ways, and yet B, because he does not want to deal with emotional realities of the situation, distorts the cues emitted by A. He sees A's anger as A's "not feeling well," because "not feeling well" is not a factor that would force B to become involved with A on an emotional level. Or a person might not want to be in contact even with himself, because it would force him to come to grips with his emotions. For instance, a person might somatize his anxiety: his colon is in an uproar, but he tries to ignore the painful stimuli or if he does advert to them, he interprets them as signaling poor eating habits rather than anxiety. He cannot experience himself reflexively as anxious, for this would have behavioral consequences that he prefers not to face.

The contract calls for a willingness to become aware of one's self and one's environment. The first step, then, in the *pathos* process is, broadly speaking, a cognitive one. Awareness is not merely passive, however; a person has to make himself aware, he has to reach out into his environment. Instead of defending himself from input—especially input that will start the emotional process—he has to court such input. Schutz (1967) makes much of what he calls the "creative process." The first aspect of this process is called "freeing, or acquisition": "Before one is able to use his experience in unusual, productive, and satisfying . . . ways, he must acquire a repertoire of experience. He must be open to experience, able to perceive and sense his environment, and be aware of his own internal feelings [p. 55]." In developing one's emotional potential, the element of perception or awareness seems to have at least a logical priority.

Another reason awareness must be a dynamic, active process is that emotionally tinged or charged stimuli in interpersonal transactions are often ambiguous. Fiedler (1960) sees distortions in interpersonal perception as so common as to provide a means of attitude measurement:

It has become a psychological truism that a person's behavior is influenced not by some objectively definable reality but rather by the individual's perception of reality. Ambiguous stimuli increase the likelihood that perceptual distortions will occur, and we assume that these distortions reflect in part the inner needs, emotional states and attitudes of the perceiver. Among the most ambiguous of our everyday stimuli, as Festinger (1957) and others have pointed out, are the feelings and attitudes of others. Moreover, it is frequently difficult, and often socially taboo, to discuss one's feelings towards others openly with them. As a result, distortions in interpersonal perception are frequent, and they provide an important avenue for the measurement of attitudes, and hence also, of the individual's interpersonal relations with these others [p. 587].

Sensitivity laboratories do not operate under the social taboos to which Fiedler refers. For instance, in the contract group, the participants are encouraged not only to scrutinize the quality of their own awareness, ferreting out tendencies to misinterpret and distort stimuli received from others, but also to be active in having others clarify the ambiguous stimuli that they emit.

Impact. Even if a person does not short-circuit the *pathos* experience at its very roots—that is, at the level of awareness—he can do so at the level of impact. It is true that at times feelings and emotions take us by storm; willy-nilly, we are flooded with fear, anger, sexual desire, or some other emotion. But even though a person remains more or less open to emotional stimuli at the level of awareness, he can still *learn* how to cut off the affective impact of that of which he is aware. While he realizes, in a rather detached, intellectual way, that he is encountering an emotionally evocative stimulus, and can even correctly identify the emotion or emotions that the stimulus is geared to evoke, he has learned how to neutralize the affect-evoking dimension of the stimulus. He has learned not to allow himself to react at all, or to react in such an attenuated way that there is no proportion between the stimulus and the strength (or weakness) of the reaction.

Laing (1960) describes a number of syndromes in which the "logical" defense is to strip one's environment, especially one's interpersonal environment, of its emotional impact. First of all, there are those with such a poor sense of self-possession or identity that they see interpersonal encounter as potentially engulfing. The best defense in the face of the engulfing presence of another is isolation. Since it is impossible always to manage absolute physical isolation, the next best thing is to preserve emotional isolation. The other is allowed to be present physically, but not emotionally. Secondly, there are those who feel so empty that they fear the implosion of reality. If reality, especially affective reality, were to rush in upon them, this would mean their destruction, for they *are* their emptiness. In order to get away from the impingement of reality, the sufferer learns how to cut off the affective dimensions of his contacts. In a third syndrome, the sufferer, rightly or wrongly, perceives himself as being treated by others as an "it" rather than as a person with feelings; he feels that he is being "petrified." In order to counteract this process of depersonalization, he petrifies others first; he refuses to run the risk of experiencing the others as free agents. Interpersonal transactions, therefore, when they do take place, become stereotyped "business contacts" with no emotional overtones.

Laing depicts extremes, but perhaps most of us, at one time or another, are victims of milder forms of the syndromes described. He observes, with respect to implosion, that all of us are literally just a few degrees Fahrenheit away from such an experience, for when we are suffering from even a slight fever, the world can become quite threatening and impinging.

Whatever the reasons underlying the tendency to eliminate or minimize the emotional impact of reality, and whatever different idiosyncratic patterns or syndromes this process might take, the participants in the contract group contract to determine the extent to which they are victims of such a process. To put things more positively, the group is a laboratory in which the participants try to allow affective reality to have as full and as constructive an impact as possible.

Rogers (1967), in dealing with a psychiatric population, discovered, with respect to the client's in-therapy behavior, that the major variable was "the degree of immediacy of the client's experiencing—that degree to which he is 'in' his experience or remote from it [p. 74]." This refers to the degree to which the client is open to his feelings, able to "own" them and to explore them in search of their personal meaning. Rogers goes on to suggest that the neurotic may be one who looks away from the felt process of experiencing as it goes on within him. The degree to which a person can be present to his own experiencing indicates the degree to which he is disturbed or self-actualized:

At one end the individual's psychological functioning is rigid, static, undifferentiated, impersonal. Constructs are fixed. He exhibits feelings but does not own them. He is remote from the experiencing going on within him. He is unable to relate. He is unable to communicate himself. He sees himself either as having no problems, or being in no way responsible for the problems which do exist. At the other end of the continuum the individual is functioning in a fluid, changing way, responsive to the ever-changing experiencing which is going on within himself, and responsive to the events going on outside himself. Feelings are experienced with immediacy, are owned, may be expressed when appropriate. The individual is close to his experiencing and refers to it in guiding his behavior. Experience is construed tentatively, and new meanings are drawn from new experience [Rogers, 1966, p. 5].

Hobbs (1962) sees the neurotic as one who cannot be intimate even with himself; he is unable to let himself feel how he actually feels about himself and others. Others (McReynolds, Acker, and Pietila, 1961; Penney, 1965; Zuckerman, Kolin, Price, and Zoob, 1964) have found that the anxious tend to avoid sensation-seeking. They restrict their interest in the sensual, in excitement, in the new, in the strange, in the unpredictable. If this is the case, then the neurotic has problems with both the awareness and the impact levels of the *pathos* experience.

Contract-group members are asked to check tendencies to look away from their experience or to flee the intimacy with self that develops from full emotional openness. Yet, if McReynolds and the rest are right, the laboratory should not be so anxiety-provoking that it causes or encourages the very process of constriction that it is supposed to combat.

Most of us are readily aware of the impact of the "heavy" emotions such as anger, fear, sexual desire, and depression, especially when they are strong and make us aware of their existence; but we are not as aware of or as open to their more attenuated or subtle forms, or to more subtly shaded emotions such as wonder, surprise, curiosity, ennui, and caution, to name just a few. The English language is filled with words referring directly or indirectly to these more subtle forms of feeling and emotion, but, though this might give some witness to the reality of such emotions, the reality does not seem to play the role it should in our interpersonal lives. For instance, when one person meets another for the first few times, he might "like" the other, but "like" merely summarizes a whole group of emotion-laden variables. Part of this liking is a rather wholesome and pleasing curiosity. He is attracted to the other and finds a certain delight in psychologically exploring the other or in engaging in mutual exploration. Again, the contract group is a laboratory for learning how to become aware of, experience, and enjoy the whole range of these more subtle emotions. Therefore, the laboratory must provide an atmosphere in which such subtle emotions are viable. Perhaps too often, sensitivity laboratories are rather heavy-footed, providing opportunities only for the more dramatic emotions.

Many laboratories use various exercises to stimulate awareness of some of the emotional dimensions of life. Participants are asked to relax, to be quiet and become aware of themselves as body (to become conscious of their own breathing, to listen to the beating of their hearts), to experiment with the "forgotten" senses of taste, touch, and smell. Gunther (1968) considers the process of socialization, at least in part, as one of "desensitization" in a pejorative sense:

Children by nature are sensitive, involved in sense play and exploration ... Social and formal education stress the cognitive and motor functions of the organism without regard for sensory development. We teach them non-sense. This lack of sensitivity creates desensitization: an imbalance in being; a loss of feeling; senseless: inhibition-alienation-depression-anxiety-deadness [p. 20].

He has devised many exercises or games to enable people to regain contact with the physical realities within and around them. One group exercise in tasting, the "bread ceremony," seems even to reach back deeply into the religious history of man:

Sit in a circle *surrounding* a loaf of unsliced bread. After sitting quietly, looking at the bread, pass it around the circle. Allow each person to feel its weight and smell its flavor. As the loaf is passed from one person to another, look into each other's eyes. One person slowly (just a fraction of an inch at a time) breaks the bread open. The group watches. The two halves are passed around the circle, each person looking at the inner exposed half and breaking off a piece no bigger than he can chew comfortably. After each person has taken his piece of bread, he closes his eyes. He puts the bread in his mouth and slowly chews, not swallowing until the bread is completely liquefied. Afterward open your eyes and see all of the group [p. 179].

Such exercises may or may not form part of the contract-group culture. However, if exercises and games are to be used for emotional awareness and contact, then the participants should know this from the beginning.

Nonverbal Reaction: The Passive Element. There are those who, although they are quite aware of the emotion-provoking stimuli in their environment and even allow these stimuli to have their impact, still short-circuit the *pathos* experience at the level of expression, even of nonverbal expression, if possible. They have learned to control the emission of nonverbal cues that would give others some insight into their interior lives. They seem unemotional, but this does not really mean that they are devoid of emotion—frequently they are just the opposite—but rather that they have learned to control its expression. Actually they are over-controlled. All of us, at one time or another and for one reason or another, engage in such control, but over-control becomes a problem only when it is resorted to frequently or becomes part of a person's life style. The contract laboratory provides an opportunity for its participants to examine the positive and negative aspects of the emotional control they exercise from day to day.

Rogers (e.g., 1961, 1967) has long insisted on what he calls "congruence" in the therapeutic relationship:

. . . each of us knows individuals whom we somehow trust because we sense that they are being what they are, that we are dealing with the person himself, not with a polite or professional front. It is this quality of congruence which we sense which research has found to be associated with successful therapy. The more genuine and congruent the therapist in the relationship, the more probability there is that change in personality in the client will occur [1961, pp. 61–62].

At least part of this congruence is emotional. If the therapist hides his emotions from the client behind a professional facade, then he lacks emotional congruence and is not as effective as he might be. It would seem, however, that lack of congruence is nontherapeutic for the same reason that most kinds of behavior are termed nontherapeutic: It is nonreal; that is, it falls short of being fully human behavior.

Some men choose to be emotionally incongruent; they look upon natural, nonverbal emotional reactions as too dangerous, too self-revealing, too intrusive, or too disruptive. And so they opt for a rather drab, expressionless, "archaic-smile" emotional style (or rather lack of style), in appearance and gesture, as being both proper and safe. The problem is that such emotional asepsis is less than human. Rogers says that such incongruence is nontherapeutic, not because it falls short of some medical or professional standard, but because it falls short of being fully human behavior.

Nonverbal Emotional Expression: The Active Element. The term "expression" here does not refer to using language to give expression to what one feels. This interpenetration of feeling and language will be considered below under *poiesis.* "Expression" here refers to the *active* use of *nonverbal* forms of emotional expression as part of one's communication style. As Murphy (1964) notes, nonverbal communication of emotions has not been sufficiently tapped as a source of knowledge about man:

If communication theory is conceived of only in terms of bits of verbal information received, it can miss its most fundamental role; for the world of blushing, blanching, sighing, hinting, and averting the eyes leads into a rich communication world that can be treated as communications and which we can teach our recorders, and magnetic tapes, and our computers to understand and use. We need to understand the whole communication process. The inner structure of man will then be seen more fully in its relation both to the social environment he encounters and the social environment which he is forever creating [p. 101].

Smith (1966) acknowledges this argument and explains that speech is only a small part of the communication process:

... people interact not only through words but also through spatial relations ... through temporal relations ... and people interact through gesture and touch and many other media. They not only send and receive information in these many different ways; they use each of these ways for participating in a communal dialogue, for reciprocating and mediating one another's meanings. Communication is far more comprehensive than language [p. 3].

However, some people—even though they are aware of emotional stimuli, allow these stimuli to have their impact, and react in the sense that they allow their emotions to appear in public in their facial expressions and gestures—still truncate the *pathos* experience to a certain degree by failing to make *active* use of these nonverbal forms of affective communication. It is the difference between merely allowing oneself to react and being involved in one's reactions, even taking delight in them, to the extent that they become part of one's active communication style. One can become active, in communication, even in such involuntary reactions as blushing, if, sensing one's reaction, one puts oneself "in" one's reaction in such a way as to say, nonverbally, by such actions as smiling, eye contact, a shrug of the shoulders or other gestures: "You have caught me, you have hit upon a vulnerable area, a point of shame."

All laboratory training and, especially, all sensitivity-training laboratories deal with the problems and potential of feeling and expressing emotion. The contract laboratory is not only a place where one can experience all the dimensions of the *pathos* experience, including authentic emotional response from others, but a place where the feedback potential of the group provides a unique opportunity for the objective appraisal of the role of emotion in human life.

The Sensitivity Laboratory as Stimulator of Feelings and Emotions

Lieberman, Lakin, and Whitaker (1968) have found that an important capacity of a therapy group is to "induce and release powerful feelings." In a group

individuals may be carried away, may experience feelings which they later believe are uncharacteristic of themselves, and may act on feelings without displaying their typical controls.... An individual may experience previously-denied feelings not with enduring terror but with growth —the corrective emotional experience of finding that the feelings are not overwhelming or that the feared consequences do not occur. . . .

In group therapy, participation in group-generated affect may allow the patient to by-pass defenses so that the feared affect may be experienced first, thus rendering the resistance less necessary. . . .

The patient in individual therapy who intimates his innermost feelings to a benign professional person undoubtedly risks far less than the group therapy patient, who may undergo feelings of extreme exhilaration or fear as he reveals himself "in public."

The managing of group affect becomes one of the essential skills of the therapist. This skill involves tamping down contagion where necessary, protecting individuals who need to be exempted from participation in group affect, breaking up group resistance in order for affect to emerge, sensing when to let the affect run on and develop and when to introduce cognitive reflection about the affect [p. 32].

Sensitivity groups, too, generate a good deal of emotion, and perhaps experimentation with emotional expression can be more intense in them than in therapy groups because of the greater initial psychological integration of the participants. The cautions that Lieberman notes, while they should be taken into consideration, refer specifically to psychiatric populations. Moreover, the safeguards built into the contract experience, such as the emphasis on supportive behavior, go far in making experimentation with emotion as safe as possible.

Emotion-Evoking Exercises. In sensitivity groups, not only are emotions allowed to arise naturally from the verbal interaction of the participants, but occasionally, at the discretion of the trainer, exercises are introduced to further stimulate the arousal and expression of emotions. These exercises may be verbal or nonverbal, and they may or may not involve physical contact. Exercises involving some form of touch are usually powerful emotional stimulants both in themselves and because we as a people generally refrain from touch as a mode of communication. Tactile communication, according to Frank (1957), is one of the more important forms of nonverbal communication: "Tactile experiences considered as messages and responses are exceedingly diverse and capable of an amazing variety of transformations in human communication, where, as in language, we must recognize both the cultural patterning and the idiosyncratic deviations and elaborations [p. 209]."

Perhaps tactile contact is too immediately related to sexuality in our society, and therefore we are afraid to explore its communication potential. Be that as it may, it is not suggested here that the kind of contact that takes place during certain laboratory exercises become a way of life. But such contact, insofar as it stimulates a variety of feelings and emotions, can be diagnostic in the very best sense. Frequently it reveals—sometimes dramatically—to a person how hesitant he is to make human contact, how far away from others he really is, or how little or how ineffectually he makes use of emotion in his attempts to relate to others.

Manufacturing Emotion. It may be objected that the participants in sensitivity laboratories are called to "manufacture" feelings and emotions (feelings by contract). Rather, they are asked not to suppress, at any stage, the feelings and emotions that arise naturally in the group and to give themselves to exercises designed to stimulate emotion. Berne (1966) claims that expression of real feeling rarely takes place in therapy groups and that the feelings expressed are actually socialized feelings. Whether this is true or not of therapy groups (and even if it is true, I do not believe that it need be), it is my experience that there is a good deal of authentic emotion in sensitivity groups—enough to dramatize to most participants their areas of strength and areas of deficit in emotional living.

Emotion as a Dimension of Laboratory Interaction. Emotion has been discussed here somewhat abstractively, but in the laboratory the participants do not express emotions abstractly. They do so in the context of the interactions of the meeting. This can be done in several ways. First of all, and this is the usual case, emotion is expressed as a dimension of the variety of interactions in which the participant engages. For instance, when someone engages in self-disclosure, he does so with some (and perhaps a good deal of) emotion. Likewise emotion can be (and in some sense should be) a dimension of other kinds of interaction, such as support, confrontation, and self-exploration. Second, a person might talk about his emotions directly. He might say, for instance, that he is very angry. However, if a person merely talks about his emotions without giving expression to them in some way, he usually appears too cold and controlled, and the others wonder whether he really owns his emotions. Finally, emotion can be expressed nonverbally. A person may cry or throw his arms around another person or stalk off from the group. The laboratory encourages the expression of emotion if it is really felt, but does not demand emotion for the sake of emotion.

**Logos: Man's Translation
of Himself
into Language**

Introduction

The contract group places emphasis on *logos,* effective interpersonal communication through human language. It has been assumed above that a great number of men suffer from emasculation in their emotional life. Now it is also assumed that many men suffer a concomitant emasculation in the quality of their verbal communication, in their ability to use language as a mode of interpersonal contact.

Logos, when used as a generic term, refers to man's interaction with man in terms of human language, the way a man translates himself into language. Both philosophers and behavioral scientists have theorized about the phenomenon of language as a form of what Lorenz (1955) calls "expressive behavior"—that is, as a reflection of the structure of personality (e.g. Buhler, 1934; Cassirer, 1953; Hodges, 1952; Honigfeld, Platz, & Gillis, 1964; Moscovici, 1967; Piaget, 1952; Stout, 1902; Von Hartmann, 1884; Wittgenstein, 1922). There have always been people interested in the language differences between psychiatric and normal populations (e.g., Forrest, 1965; Glauber, 1944; Gottschalk, 1961; Lorenz, 1955; Newman & Mather, 1938; Sanford, 1942; Spiegel, 1959; Wender, 1967), and more or less molecular psychological studies are increasing man's understanding of the phenomenon of language and verbal behavior (e.g., Cofer & Musgrave, 1963; Dixon & Horton, 1968; Kansler, 1966; Mehrabian, 1966; Salzinger, 1967; Wiener & Mehrabian, 1968). Still, little of this theorizing and research has been translated in such a way as to be useful in dealing with people, either normal or abnormal, on a clinical or applied level. More attention must be given to such molar dimensions of language as the quality of man's verbal expression in his interpersonal contacts.

As Wiener and Mehrabian (1968) note, it is too fruitful an area of interpersonal discovery to ignore:

Anyone who listens carefully to the way people say things quickly learns that the particular words a speaker uses to describe an event or experience can be a rich source of information about his feelings and attitudes. The bases for making these kinds of inferences are not usually explicit, although members of a communication group appear to respond regularly to these subtle variations in word usage [p. 1].

Laboratory learning situations seem to provide excellent opportunities for research on this subject and for the application of research findings. What follows is a brief indication of the aspects of language that might be profitably considered and experimented with in a sensitivity laboratory. The laboratory experience is an opportunity for the participants to examine man as one who speaks by subjecting their own verbal interactions to the scrutiny of the group.

The Problems and Potential of Language

Problems. There are various ways in which people underuse or abuse language in interpersonal situations and many reasons why they do so. Some language problems stem directly from, and reflect varying degrees of, psychopathology. Bettelheim (1967) discusses children who have surrendered the use of language because of parental disapproval, their mutism being an indication that they have given up any hope of influencing their world. This surrender of speech closes a vicious circle:

Once the child has even stopped communicating with others, his self becomes impoverished, the more so the longer his mutism lasts, and the more so the longer his personality remains underdeveloped at the time of the onset of withdrawal [p. 56].

If this [mutism] happens before he has fully learned to manipulate symbolic forms, before the age of three or four, then the child also fails to develop the higher intellectual processes [p. 57].

Erikson (1954) discovered that one of the outcomes of traumatic war experiences was a distrust and devaluation of language. Meerloo (1956) found neurosis manifested in language-use disturbances: "The insecure neurotic shrinks from free word-play; he tries to manipulate words mechanically, like machinery. He fears the adventure of communication [p. 87]." Ruesch (1957) sees the origin of communication problems in parents' inability to adapt themselves to the maturation level of their children. According to Ruesch, three types of language are learned in succession: somatic, action, and verbal. If parents do not adapt their language to the developmental stage of their children, while at the same time offering encouragement to improve verbal-language proficiency, then communication disturbances may arise in their children.

Language problems arise from and reflect not only psychopathology in the strict sense; they reflect also the psychopathology of the average. Many normal men fear the communication process because of more or less normal fears of involving themselves deeply with others. They neither pour themselves into their language in interpersonal situations nor expect others to do so. Language must remain on a safe level. They habitually put filters between what they really think and feel and what they say. This results in exsanguinated or muddied, but safe, communication. Some men engage in language that is overly precise—they ask too much of language—while others engage in language that is too vague—that is, they ask too little of language. Both extremes are usually defensive measures, ways of keeping interpersonal contacts at acceptable levels of intensity. Some men are victims of poor education in language. They have lived in families or in societies that are afraid of open communication, with the result that patterns of language are not available to them to express what they would like to express. This conversational or language anemia is recognized by the novel writer:

Even in modern-novel dialogue the most real is not the most conformable to actual current speech. One has only to read a transcribed tape of actual conversation to realize that it is, in the literary context, not very real. Novel dialogue is a form of shorthand, an impression of what people actually say; and besides that, it has to perform other functions—to keep the narrative moving (which real conversation rarely does), to reveal character (real conversation often hides it), and so on [Fowles, 1968, p. 89].

Men read novels not only for vicarious *pathos* but also for vicarious *logos*, the meaningful talk that is missing from their lives.

In societies that subtly discourage or limit conversational freedom and deeper interpersonal contact through language, some men abandon language (at least in a relative sense) either because it is useless as an instrument of deep human communication or because the patterns of language allowed are identified with the establishment that is being rejected. In the case of the present "hippie" culture, this flight from language involves both (1) the creation of an argot reflecting a break from the values of society seen as useless or oppressive, while emphasizing the values of the subculture and (2) an often irresponsible immersion in the *pathos* dimensions of living. A counter language evolves, and a counter *pathos* society is established, parallel to or outside the confines of the society being rejected.

Potentialities. Despite the problems involved in using exsanguinated language and communication, language is still one of the most dramatic ways in which man differs from other animals. Stout (1902) sees language as an instrument by means of which man examines the world around him. If he is afraid of this world, his language will be anemic and feeble, but if he loves the world and is challenged by it, his language will be strong and searching. To adapt a phrase from Wittgenstein (1922), the limits of a person's language are the limits of his world. Cioran (1968) sees silence as unbearable and says he would find it easier to renounce bread than speech. He claims that one cannot withdraw one's confidence from words "without setting one's foot in the abyss." Language exposes, reveals both individuals and societies: "Words, at least in traditional societies, often express far more than feelings or ideas. The way words are used—in tales, riddles, proverbs, and typical modes of address and conversation—can reveal a great deal about the structure and values of a society [Abrahams, 1968, p. 62]."

Novelists and writers frequently have, if not deeper insights, at least more striking, distinctive, and challenging insights into the nature and force of human language than do behavioral scientists. Writers continually try to enlarge the possibilities of language. D. H. Lawrence, Virginia Woolf, and James Joyce never hesitated to experiment with verbal symbols that would most fully convey what they experienced. As Burgess (1968) notes: "Language, of its very nature, resists tautology; it wants to launch out, risk lies, say the thing which is not."

Brian Friel's entire play *Philadelphia Here I Come* is based on the distinction between what the leading character really thinks, feels, and would like to say and what he actually says. In the play, there are two levels of conversation—the vague, hesitant, compliant, failed bravado of the son about to leave his father in Ireland to seek a new way of life in the United States, and the vigorous speech of the son's "inner core" (played by a separate character). The pity of it all is that, although the audience is electrified by what the "inner man" says, it knows that his speech really dies (and in a sense the son dies with it) because it is never spoken. The man who chains his language chains himself.

The contract group is a laboratory in which the participants can experiment with the potential of language. The purpose of what is said here is not to apotheosize language, for, as Lynd (1958) notes, language is sometimes a sensitive instrument and sometimes a clumsy tool of communication. But when a man enlarges the possibilities of his language, he enlarges his own possibilities. The laboratory gives him the opportunity to extend the range of language in order to contact himself and others at deeper levels. In the safety of the laboratory, he can run risks in his use of language that he could not take in everyday life. The following discussion of language might serve as a basis for experimentation.

Different Kinds of Language

In keeping with the consideration of language from a molar, interactional point of view, the following distinctions—again, despite the fact that they are somewhat abstractive—might give direction to the discussion that follows.

Logos. *Logos,* in the strict or restricted sense, refers to man's ability to translate his real self into language. *Logos* is language filled with the person who is speaking, and therefore refers to his ability to use speech to express his identity. It also refers to the use man makes of speech in order to establish some kind of growthful interpersonal contact. Negatively, it is the refusal to use speech merely to fill interactional space and time or as a smoke screen or shield behind which to hide.

Just as there are different kinds of truly human contact and various degrees or levels of such contact, so there are different kinds of *logos.* If a man talks meaningfully about his political or religious beliefs, this is *logos.* *Logos* need not be self-disclosure in the sense discussed in chapter 7, but, in that it is meaningful speech, it will always provide some insight into the identity of the speaker. Meaningful speech with an intimate friend will be on a different level from meaningful speech with one's fellow workers. The special ability to allow one's language to express not only one's thoughts but also the feelings and the emotions that surround these thoughts is a special kind of *logos* called *poiesis*. *Poiesis* will be treated separately.

Logos must be clearly differentiated from the ability to speak fluently and elegantly, for both fluency and elegance are at times used to camouflage, rather than reveal, one's identity. It also seems necessary to distinguish *logos* from the ability to speak with insight about oneself. This ability has traditionally been seen as a favorable condition, if not a prerequisite, for effective participation in psychotherapy—an hypothesis that is being seriously challenged today (Carkhuff & Berenson, 1967; London, 1964). *Logos* here means translating oneself, or handing oneself over to others, through the medium of speech, whatever the esthetic value of the language used.

Logos implies a respect for language as a form of communication and contact. It implies dialogue, and, as Matson and Montagu (1967) point out, for certain contemporary existentialist thinkers, authentic existence *is* communication, life *is* dialogue. Dialogue is certainly the life of the contract group. That is why the group member, by contract, is expected to examine his use of speech. If he is to develop new ways of being present to the members of the group, he must discover new ways of speaking and perhaps develop a new respect for language.

Dialogue, in the sense in which it is used here, is opposed to "game" communication. Dialogue is game-free, or at least an attempt to make communication game-free. Rapoport (1964) and Wiener (1950), both of whom have made significant contributions to the mathematical theory of games, caution against the use of game theory as a basis for human communication. Rapoport finds dialogue with the "strategist" impossible, for the basic question in the strategist's mind is: In a conflict, how can I gain an advantage over my opponent? Rapoport thinks that the much more basically human question is: If I can gain an advantage over another, *what sort of person* will I become? The "cybernetic" man is basically monological, not dialogical, and for him, communication is intimately wedded to control—the control of the other.

Berne (1966) uses "game" in a somewhat different sense. The "games people play" are ways of avoiding intimacy in human relationships. The game prevents dialogue. Berne goes so far as to say that the most that one can expect in a psychotherapeutic group is the discovery and analysis of the games played there. Real intimacy, he says, is almost never found in such group situations. It is the contention of this book that the members of a contract inter-personal-growth group can establish dialogue, can free themselves, to a great extent, from a game approach to one another, and can establish not just the social imitation of intimacy that Berne speaks of, but real human intimacy.

Commercial Speech. "Commercial speech" refers to the lan-guage of the marketplace, the use of language in the commercial transactions of men. Such language is lean, utilitarian, pragmatic; it deals with objects rather than persons, for it is a medium of ex-change rather than of interpersonal contact. Much of such language today is left to computers. It would be of no interest to us here were it not for the fact that there are people who use commercial speech as their principal mode of speech in interpersonal transactions. They see people as objects to be manipulated, rather than persons to be contacted, and this is reflected in the quality of their speech.

If speech is principally commercial, then, as McLuhan (1964) suggests, it can be dispensed with: "Electric technology does not need words any more than the digital computer needs numbers [p. 80]." However, the utopia he envisions, characterized by a "speechlessness that could confer a perpetuity of collective harmony and peace" arising from a "collective awareness that may have been the preverbal condition of man [p. 80]," is antithetical to man him-self. Speech defines man. It is just strange that he makes such poor use of it in his effort to humanize himself.

Cliché Talk. "Cliché talk" refers to anemic language, talk for the sake of talk, conversation without depth, language that neither makes contact with the other nor reveals the identity of the speaker (except negatively, in the sense that he is revealed as one who does not want to make contact or does not want to be known). Cliché talk fosters ritualistic, rather than fully human, contact ("Do you think that it is really going to rain?"—"The way they're playing, they'll be in first place by the first of September!"). Cliché talk fills interactional space and time without adding meaning, for it is super-ficial and comes without reflection. Perhaps it is the person who is overcommitted to maintenance functions (see Introduction), a person who is either unaware (because he lacks the requisite social intelligence) or afraid of possibilities for further interpersonal growth, whose speech will be predominantly cliché talk.

People usually listen politely to cliché talk, especially when it is pseudo-*logos*—that is, dressed up or doctored to sound important:

When a conversation fails to capture the spontaneous involvement of an individual who is obliged to participate in it, he is likely to contrive an appearance of being involved. This he must do to save the feelings of the other participants and their good opinion of him, regardless of his motives for wanting to effect this saving [Goffman, 1967, p. 126].

If the needs of the listener are such that he is willing to put up with the boredom of cliché talk in order to enjoy the safety that is found in ritual, then the circle is complete and the field is wide open for such conversation.

One of the most common forms of cliché talk in our culture (and perhaps this is a transcultural phenomenon) is "griping," a more or less superficial communication of dissatisfaction with persons, institutions, or things outside oneself. It is one of the few verbal expressions of feeling allowed in public, and it is probably allowed because it is a ritual and most rituals are safe. The trouble with chronic griping is that it is a fixative. As Ellis (1962) points out, a person's verbalizations to himself and others often stand in the way of change: "Forces outside me control me"; "I can do nothing to change."

Cliché talk is just words, while *logos* always connotes human contact. Some people speak endlessly about themselves and say nothing (if they were really disclosing themselves, others would not find it boring). They say nothing about themselves because they have no real feeling for themselves—they are deficient in the *pathos* dimension of life—and could hardly be expected to relate what they do not experience. Such people simply are not using speech as a mode of contact. For them, speech is solipsistic, self-centered, centripetal. It is monologue rather than dialogue.

Anti-logos. When language is actually used to destroy growthful interpersonal contact rather than to foster it, then it is *anti-logos*. There are a number of forms of speech that are really violations, rather than uses, of language. For instance, in the heat of anger, language can be used as a weapon, a tool of destruction rather than an instrument of growthful encounter. When a married couple stand shouting at each other (often saying things they do not really mean), language becomes completely swallowed up in emotion; it loses its identity as language. At such times it has more in common with a sledgehammer than with speech. Lying, too, can be a form of *anti-logos*, for deception cannot be the basis of growthful interpersonal contact. The speech of the psychopath, for example, is frequently, if not continually, *anti-logos*, for he uses speech to create situations, to manipulate others rather than to engage in growthful encounters with them. Finally, the language of the psychotic, while it might have its own peculiar logic (and without discounting the possibility that a psychosis may be a desperate form of revolt against a sick family or society—see Laing, 1967), is frequently *anti-logos*. The psychotic, at least at times, appears to use language to drive others away. He fears human contact so deeply that he reverses the function of language, making it a barrier instead of a bridge.

Another way of conceptualizing *anti-logos* is to see it as the kind of expression that stems from high deficiency functioning (see Introduction). The stronger the influence of deficiency needs in a person's life, the more likely he is to engage in some form of *anti-logos*.

Most men engage in all four kinds of speech at one time or another. They not only use commercial speech in strictly commercial transactions, but also allow it to slip occasionally into interpersonal encounters. Indeed, life without some cliché talk would be intolerably intense for most men. It is a question, however, of proportion, and most men need to find ways of increasing the amount of *logos* (in the restricted sense) in their lives. The sensitivity laboratory affords an opportunity of discovering ways to do that.

Language: Content, Invitation, and Self-Expression

That Buhler's (1934) analysis of the functions of language strikes at a phenomenological core is evidenced by the number of writers who use his analysis as a basis for further discussion of the nature and use of language. Language, according to Buhler, (1) has *content*, (2) is an *invitation*, and (3) involves *self-disclosure* or *self-expression*.

First of all, language has content; that is, it signifies or represents something; the speaker communicates, explains, or verifies something. Insofar as speech merely imparts information, it is functioning at its lowest, most impersonal level. And yet many people have difficulty even at this point; that is, they have difficulty in making language a clear conveyer of their ideas. It is extremely important, however, for a person to know whether what he says comes across with enough clarity. If the content of a person's language during group sessions is not clear, it does not help for others to be "polite" and pretend to understand a muddled message. Some people, in affective situations, defend themselves by dealing in unclear content. In this case, it takes courage, but is a sign of interest in the other, for a listener to say: "I don't know about the others, but I really didn't understand what you just said." It is amazing how often group members allow muddled or unintelligible communications to go by without any kind of responsible challenge. On the other hand, there are those who habitually strip language of other than utilitarian content functions. They take pains to see that the content of their communications is clear, but for them speech is nothing more than commercial speech. Even these attempts to restrict the function of language, however, are disclosures of the personalities of the speakers.

Second, speech is always some kind of invitation, challenge, or summons. It is, at the very least, a request to be heard, even when it is used as a means of driving others away. When a person speaks, he does so in order to be heard; his speech is a call for a response. The response is expected to be proportioned to the nature of the invitation or challenge: a command requires obedience, a petition hopes for a concession, a promise expects trust, an explanation demands attention, testimony looks for faith, and so forth. Therefore, speech not only has explicit content, but it also contains implicit messages for the listener: it tells him to come close or go away, to take a particular stance, to become active or remain passive, and so forth. It is not just the ability to understand the explicit content of language that makes a person a good listener, but rather a sensitivity to the other messages embedded in language. In the contract group, the participants are asked to reflect on their use of language in terms of the invitations or challenges that it implies. A participant's language might be an invitation to affective contact, or it might be a command to stand clear. It is important for participants to come to some understanding of the habitual invitations, summonses, and challenges characterizing their speech.

Finally, speech always involves some degree of self-revelation, even when the speaker uses it as a means of hiding himself ("Even thy speech betrays thee"), for he then reveals himself as one who is afraid of the intimacy of dialogue. But speech, for the nondefensive person or for the person who is attempting a responsible relaxing of his defenses, becomes self-expression in a most positive way, even though he is not speaking directly about himself. When a person becomes less defensive, two things happen with respect to his use of language: he puts more of himself into his speech, and he initiates a truer communication with the other by aiming directly at the other as a person. If the other responds in a nondefensive way, then dialogue becomes a reciprocal opening up, a mutual revelation. But, if this is to happen, both the speaker and the one addressed must respect one another in the mysteriousness of their personalities, and there must be both mutual trust and mutual availability. Only under these conditions does language lose its fetters and take on the strength and color of the personalities of those who use it. Much will be said about self-disclosure in the contract group; but the participants are encouraged to examine their use of language in order to discover how much of themselves they really disclose through their use of language. It may well be that, by the way they express themselves, they are disclosing precisely what they think they must hide.

The Function of Language in Organizing Reality

Sapir (Mandelbaum, 1949) and Whorf (Carroll, 1956) suggested one more function for language in a proposition that has been called the Sapir-Whorf hypothesis, which states that language functions not simply as a means of reporting and communicating experience but also as a way of defining experience (see Wiener & Mehrabian, 1968, pp. 5–10). Language is an instrument that actually shapes perception to some degree. Lynd (1958) also recognizes the ability of language to influence perception:

In his study of "Memory and Childhood Amnesia" Schachtel (1947) gives a particularly illuminating account of the way in which language inevitably reflects the dominant preoccupations and the limitations of a society. By such reflection it restricts perception and experience unless refreshed by innovation. Certain kinds of experience may be buried or lost because the culture provides no language through which they can be expressed [p. 247].

Schachtel (1947) discusses the ability of socialized language to turn experience into a cliché: "The capacity to see and feel what is there gives way to the tendency to see and feel what one expects to see and feel, which, in turn, is what one is *expected* to see and feel because everybody does. Experience increasingly assumes the form of the cliché... [pp. 12–13]." But Lynd admits that language is a two-edged sword, that although acquiring a language frequently means a dulling and conventionalizing of perception, it is also possible "for the use of words to quicken, not to deaden, awareness [p. 171]." Though language hardly creates reality, it is one of the organizers of perceived reality and, as such, can perhaps reveal a good deal about the inner organization of the speaker. Therefore, the participant who is aware of his use of language has found another diagnostic tool by which to gauge his personal and interpersonal life.

Translating Messages into Logos

When two or more people are talking, there are usually at least two levels of communication: (1) what is conveyed by the verbal interchange (the content mentioned above) and (2) a variety of other messages that are transmitted in a number of different ways—for example, the qualities of the verbal exchange itself such as speed, tone, inflection, intensity, and emotional color, and nonverbal cues such as eye contact, bodily stance, facial expressions, and gestures. These messages are similar to what Ruesch (1963; see also Ruesch and Bateson, 1951) refers to as "metacommunicative processes," the purpose of which is to interpret or classify the content of the verbal message or to send a parallel message more or less unrelated to verbal content. These metacommunications can even negate or deny the explicit meaning of the verbal message (for instance, it is a rather common occurrence to hear "no" on an explicit verbal level and at the same time to experience "yes" on a metacommunicative level, the latter being the real message). As Berne (1966) notes, the metacommunicative message might even substitute for some kind of tactile stimulus:

Game analysis is grounded in the principle that the human organism can accept, up to a point, visual, auditory, and symbolic recognition signals as a substitute for direct tactile stimulation of corresponding quality. This is the biological advantage derived from playing games. Thus soft looks and a smiling face may have partial effects similar to those resulting from physical caresses, a fact heavily exploited by female players. Verbal teasing may have partial effects similar to those of physical prodding or tickling [pp. 281–282].

Whether one accepts Berne's underlying theoretical formulations or not (e.g., his intimations concerning the primacy of touch and the substitutive nature of language), the tactile-like effects of both verbal and nontactile nonverbal communication that he suggests do seem to be an important part of the communicative process. If one wanted to look at the same phenomenon from the point of view of words rather than touch, however, one should note that words are reinforcing agents, and, even though their values are acquired, they are frequently more powerful as satisfiers than the original non-verbal stimuli (see Rotter, 1954).

Sometimes entire encounters take place in which the explicit verbal level is relatively meaningless, for it is only a sterile carrier for an exchange of metacommunicative messages. Language becomes a pastime, something to do while the reality of the encounter takes place at a different level. It would be an interesting experiment to have groups of two or more talk to one another for a half hour and then have each individual write down three or four of the more important nonverbalized messages that he thought, on reflection, he had communicated to the others and three or four of the messages that he, again on reflection, thought that each of the others in the group had sent out on a nonverbal or metacommunicative level. The hypothesis would be that there would always be some correspondence between messages believed sent and messages believed received (that is, people would "read" one another, if asked to do so, on a metacommunicative level, even though they might seldom verbalize the fact that they have either sent or received such messages). Still, people would differ in their sensitivity to metacommunicative messages and in the number and kinds of messages sent out over nonverbal rather than verbal routes.

One of the functions of the contract group is to become aware of the metacommunicative dimensions of language and then, as opportunities arise in the give and take of group interaction, to attempt to translate metacommunications into *logos*. This means, first of all, becoming aware of oneself as transmitter of such messages and translating them into verbal language and, second, becoming aware of the messages of others and confronting them with translations. Obviously, this does not mean that one should be on the watch for and attempt to translate all metacommunications, for this would make the communication process intolerable. The metacommunication process is a kind of communication shorthand and, if used correctly, it facilitates the communication process. However, both vague and never-translated metacommunicative messages can clog or muddy interpersonal contact. Excessive reliance on metacommunication might also manifest an implicit distrust of language. At any rate, *all* interpersonal communications problems are fair game for the training laboratories.

**Language and
Self-Identity**

One of the messages of G. B. Shaw's *Pygmalion* is that, in some fashion, language makes the person. Not only do differences in the use of language reflect class differences in society, but language actually helps create and maintain the differences in values that separate one class from another. For instance, a person from a lower class might speak quite freely about sexual matters and do so in public, while a member of an upper class might not feel free to speak about sexuality at all. Language, then, is an instrument of reinforcement regarding the different approaches to sexuality that exist in the two classes. What is true with respect to social identity is also true in the area of self-identity. Self-identity is one of those heuristic "impact-concepts" that are just beginning to be translated into operational terms and subjected to controlled investigation (e.g., Bronson, 1959; Hess, 1963). Language not only reveals a person's identity, who he is, but in some way it makes him the person he is. The literary dictum, *Le style c'est l'homme même*, can also be applied to a person's style of speaking: *La parole c'est l'homme même*. If a person's language is weak, insipid, cliché-ridden, and consistently ritualistic in social situations, this says much about the person's ability *and* willingness to relate both to himself and to others. Language not only reflects his encapsulation but becomes one of the instruments of his self-imprisonment.

Erikson (1956) sees the relationship between language and self-identity as developing early in the maturational process:

... A child ... learning to speak ... is acquiring one of the prime functions supporting a sense of individual autonomy and one of the prime techniques for expanding the radius of give-and-take. ... Speech ... defines him as one responded to by those around him with changed diction and attention ... A spoken word is a pact: there is an irrevocably committing aspect to an utterance remembered by others. . . . The child may come to develop, in use of voice and word, a particular combination of whining or singing, judging or arguing, as part of a new element of the future identity, namely, the element "one who speaks and is spoken to in such-and-such a way . . . [p. 115]."

Erikson (1963) also discusses the case of a man who wanted to bury his past, to break with certain aspects of his self-identity. One of the things he did was to pursue graduate studies in a foreign language. Erikson suggests that this new language, in terms of a new career, a new medium of expression, and a new culture, may well have offered his client an opportunity to establish a different self-picture.

It is hypothesized, then, that language reveals certain dimensions of a person's life style and also creates and serves to maintain certain patterns of living and interacting. Ryle (1952), for instance, suggests that personality differences exist between those who use dispositional verbs such as *believe, wonder, suppose,* and *aspire,* which signify ability, tendency, and proneness-to, and those who deal principally in modal verbs such as *does, can,* and *must.* The person who constantly *believes, wonders,* and *supposes* is seen to be differently oriented toward reality from the person who disposes of reality in terms of what *does, can,* or *must* happen.

Identity crises (Erikson, 1956, 1963, 1964), too, are reflected in the use of language. The adolescent, who, according to Erikson, goes through a kind of natural period of identity diffusion and a moratorium in which society allows him to experiment with a number of different roles, speaks the specialized language of his subculture. Language becomes one of the ways in which he declares that he is not just an appendage of parents, church, school, and society in general, but a person in his own right.

The training group, then, is a laboratory in which the participants have the opportunity to reflect on the implications of the propositions: "My language is me," and "In some way I use language to make myself what I am." It is an opportunity to examine the ways in which they use *logos,* commercial speech, cliché talk, and *anti-logos* to fashion a communication life style.

Logos in the Contract Group

The contract group, obviously, calls for *logos* rather than any form of commercial speech, cliché talk, or *anti-logos.* Moreover, the contract specifies the kind of *logos* that is acceptable during group sessions. Therefore, with respect to the contract group, *logos* can be divided into both contractual and a-contractual *logos*. For instance, if a participant begins seriously to spell out his views on the current political situation, but in no way relates what he is doing to contractual goals (e.g., rendering the there and then here and now), given the ordinary sensitivity contract, he would probably be engaging in a-contractual *logos*. Engaging in a-contractual *logos* is frequently a fairly sophisticated form of flight from group process, for while a-contractual *logos* might well be meaningful in itself, it is not so in the context of the contract group. It is one thing if a member speaks about values, another if he speaks meaningfully and feelingly about *his* values. The latter is contractual, while the former is a-contractual *logos*. Group members often hesitate to challenge the member engaged in a-contractual *logos* because they feel that they would be keeping him from doing something that is good in itself.

The general rule is that *logos* in the group stimulates *logos*. If a person uses language powerfully in the group, others will tend to follow his lead. Therefore, one of the functions of the leader-member is to model *logos*. However, he must do so intelligently; that is, he must proportion his manner of speaking to the ability of others to listen. His language must be a spur rather than a club. Goffman (1967) suggests that this might well mean, at least in the first sessions of the group, scaling down one's expressions in the service of dialogue:

These two tendencies, that of the speaker to scale down his expressions and that of the listeners to scale up their interests, each in the light of the other's capacities and demands, form the bridge that people build to one another, allowing them to meet for a moment of talk in a communion of reciprocally sustained involvement [pp. 116–117].

However, this line of reasoning should not be used as an excuse to keep talk on a "safe" level.

In my own experience, I have seen ill-timed and ill-controlled *logos* (which then really becomes *anti-logos*) inhibit and even destroy group process. Once one group member, tired of the anemic communication that characterized the first couple of meetings, spoke with such dramatic force about himself as problem-laden and the group as anemic that he frightened the other members into shutting off communication rather than upgrading it. Instead of challenging the group from the start, he allowed his frustration to build up until it burst forth in language that could not be handled by the group. On the other hand, I frequently (but not frequently enough) find myself stimulated by the strong talk of a number of my friends. Their *logos* awakens *logos* within me, and I find myself thinking thoughts, feeling emotions and giving expression to both with a depth that surprises me. It is as if the third thing, dialogue, is greater than its parts, which are my thoughts and feelings and those of my friends taken separately. This kind of mutual stimulation is the goal of the contract group.

The Extra-Linguistic
Dimensions of Speech

Much can be learned about a person, not only from the verbal content of his communications (the content can be strong, cliché-ridden, ambiguous, weak, etc.), but also from the quality of the voice in delivery, or as Wiener and Mehrabian (1968) put it, from "variations in tonal qualities, patterns of stress, pitch, and pauses which are not dictated by the required linguistic form [p. 51]." For example, a person may claim that he is not anxious but betray his anxiety quite openly in the tone, pitch, and timbre of his voice: "An insecure person...may speak in complex, involved or even unfinished sentences, with poor pitch and volume control, and with frequent nervous mannerisms [Mahl & Schulze, 1964, p. 51]." Voice quality, rhythm, continuity, speech rate, and verbal output all communicate something to the listener, or, from a more active point of view, the speaker has all of these extralinguistic factors at his disposal, to use, as he sees fit, to increase the effectiveness of his communication. In a sense, there are two kinds of extralinguistic phenomena: (1) those related to speech itself (e.g., pitch, tone, etc.) and (2) those forms of behavior which, although they communicate, are more or less separable from speech in the strict sense. Such nonverbal behavior, as it is called, is a subject of intense interest and debate in sensitivity-training laboratories and, as such, deserves separate consideration.

Logos: Nonverbal
Communication
in the Laboratory

The Scientific Study of Nonverbal Communication. Although it is a truism that nonverbal behavior plays an extremely important part in the entire communication process, some have suggested that its scientific study is not worth pursuing. La Barre (1964) takes strong exception to such a suggestion:

It is easy to ridicule kinesiology as an abstruse, pedantic, and unimportant study by pure scientists. But I believe that kinesiology is, on the contrary, one of the most important avenues for better understanding internationally. Consider, as one small example, how Chinese hate to be touched, slapped on the back, or even to shake hands; how easily an American could avoid offense by merely omitting these intended gestures of friendliness! Misunderstanding of nonverbal communication of an unconscious kind is one of the most vexing and unnecessary sources of international friction. (Consider, for example, the hands-over-the-head self-handshake of Khrushchev, which Americans interpreted as an arrogant gesture of triumph, as of a victorious prize-fighter, whereas Khrushchev seems to have intended it as a friendly gesture of international brotherhood.) [p. 218].

Birdwhistell (1952, 1961, 1963a, 1963b) and Hall (1959, 1963a, 1963b, 1964, 1966) have both elaborated categories which relate body movements, including gestures and facial expressions, to the process of communication. Davitz (1964) has reviewed the literature on the interpretation of emotions from facial expressions, and researchers such as Ekman (1965) and Ekman and Friesen (1967) continue to do research in this area. Dittmann (1963) is another who studies the relation of bodily movement to communication. La Barre (1964) discusses (not without humor) a wide variety of nonverbal communicative behavior—greetings, kissing, sticking out the tongue (in China "a quick, minimal tongue-protrusion and -retraction signifies embarrassment and self-castigation [p. 200]"), gestures of contempt ("Neapolitans click the right thumbnail off the right canine in a downward arc [p. 201]"), gestures of *politesse* ("a Shan may bend over and snuff the sleeve of the benefactor's coat [p. 202]"), conventionalized motor acts (e.g., in both Oriental and Occidental acting), and conversational gestures (e.g., "the shaken right forefinger of accusation, sharp criticism, and threat [p. 203]")—on a cross-cultural basis. On the other hand, while there is a good deal of talk about the nonverbal dimensions of sensitivity training, and even though many laboratories use nonverbal exercises in group interaction, I know of no systematic study of this phenomenon. Perhaps many of the studies mentioned above could begin to lay a theoretical foundation for their use.

Nonverbal communication is always present in the sensitivity-training group, but in varying ways. The following division might help the reader to conceptualize the presence of such behavior in training groups:

(1) *Inadvertent nonverbal communication.* First of all, since the participants are physically present in the group, they are continually giving communication cues by their facial expressions and bodily posture, both as a complement to their verbalizations and when they are silent. They grimace, sit on the edge of their chairs, yawn, cough, bury their hands in their faces, cast their eyes down, wring their hands, scratch their heads, cry, and engage in a whole host of communicative nonverbal acts. Very often such acts give some evidence about how they are feeling at the moment, but at other times these acts seem ambiguous, out of place, or even contradict the verbal portion of the participant's message. For instance, I once videotaped the last session of a laboratory course in interpersonal relations. One of the participants engaged in a fairly lengthy remark on how much he had liked the experience and how interesting and worthwhile it had been. However, his voice was flat and without affect, he could hardly be heard by the other members, he was slouched down in his chair, and he made no eye contact with any of the other members. In fact, his entire tone and posture belied what he was saying, a fact that was not lost on him during the replay of the tape.

(2) *Advertent nonverbal communication without physical contact.* A participant may intentionally emit some form of nonverbal behavior in order to make psychological contact with another participant or with the group as a whole. He may groan, wink, smile, and engage in a variety of other noncontactive acts in order to transmit some message. The person who scratches his head might unwittingly be saying something about his perplexity or anxiety, while the participant who winks at another is actively using a nonverbal channel in order to communicate (e.g., he may be flirting or he may be engaging in a form of nonverbal support).

(3) *Advertent nonverbal communication with physical contact.* A third category, and this kind of nonverbal behavior is the object of most of the controversy and discussion, involves actual physical contact—touching, holding, hugging, kissing, pushing, swinging, "passing." Sometimes such nonverbal behavior takes place naturally within the group. For example, one participant, after disclosing himself at a rather deep level, begins to cry, and a second participant puts his arm around him to give him support. Other forms of physical contact can take place through exercises designed to have

the participant feel the effects of physical contact. Some exercises involve dyads. For instance, Gunther (1968) suggests an exercise called "back talk":

The couple stands back to back with eyes closed, and through movement get to know each other's backs. Have a nonverbal conversation with your backs. (One person rubs; the other listens; take turns.) Have a back argument. Make up. Be very gentle, playful. Move up and down at various speeds. Eventually stand quietly back to back and slowly separate. Experience your back—how you feel. Turn around, open your eyes and see your partner [p. 118].

Other exercises may involve the whole group—for example, "under the sheets":

Each person goes under a sheet and stays quiet for 5 minutes. They are allowed to do anything they want to, except to move around the room. Then move about the room, contact/encounter other people or groups as long as each stays under his own sheet. Be open to your desires and let whatever action-reaction that wants to happen occur. No talking during the experience. When it is over, experience how you feel; come out from under the sheet [Gunther, 1968, pp. 174–175].

Such exercises are frequently quite diagnostic: they quickly reveal areas of emotional constriction. For example, during a processing session that took place immediately after a few simple nonverbal exercises involving physical contact, one of the participants, who had been obviously rigid during the exercises, made a statement something like this: "I really feel somewhat disturbed, not by the exercises but by my reaction to them. Over the past couple of years I have become much more at home with myself and with others. I felt that I was more or less in possession of myself both on the personal and interpersonal level. These exercises this morning disturbed me because I experienced residues of rigidity in myself, I saw dramatically that not everything has been worked out, I saw that I am still afraid of intimacy with perhaps both myself and others." Insofar as these exercises are diagnostic, they aid the process of communication in the sense that they put the participant in more effective (though sometimes painful) contact with himself. Such communication with self serves as a basis for more effective communication with others.

The Anxiety and the Value Inherent in Physical Contact.   Physical contact in our society is anxiety-arousing. First of all, it is an expression of intimacy, and many of us are afraid of intimacy. Secondly, physical contact in our society seems to be over-identified with sexuality; it is not seen as a universal mode of contact and communication. Anxiety runs very high when the exercise is so structured that the dyads are of the same sex, especially if both are male. "I would feel a lot better if my partner were a girl" says a number of things: "I live in a culture in which physical contact of male with male is more or less taboo"; "physical contact is, of its very nature, sexual"; "I consider intimacy as something intersexual." However, the laboratory is a cultural island; that is, it attempts to develop its own human culture apart from the cultural rigidities that exist outside the laboratory. In the case of exercises involving physical contact, the laboratory culture says this: "Physical contact is another channel of human communication. It can be so restricted as to communicate only certain dimensions of interpersonal living such as hostility (in acts such as shoving, striking, etc.) and sexuality (in *any* physical act showing interest or concern). Here we experiment with physical contact as a channel of communication. Our purpose is to see how many different human realities we can express through physical contact or through a combination of physical contact, nonverbal behavior that does not involve physical contact, and verbal behavior. Our purpose here is to grow interpersonally by involving ourselves with one another. Physical contact is one of the modes of human involvement. Here in the laboratory there is cultural permission to deal with it more freely than we could in day-to-day living. It is hoped that we can take advantage of this permission."

Some of the Problems Associated with Physical Contact in the Laboratory.   Physical contact can arouse strong emotion, especially strong anxiety. In my own experience, I have found that the way in which exercises are introduced to the group is of paramount importance. For example, in the first residential laboratory I attended, we had generally avoided exercises, especially nonverbal exercises involving physical contact, during the first half of the laboratory. Around the midpoint, we were involved in a session in which communication had noticeably bogged down. It seemed that we just could not get in contact with one another. We were sitting outside on a patio, when suddenly the trainer said: "I'd like to do something. Let's go inside." The anxiety level in the group shot skyward. My imagination ran wild: we were going inside because we were going to do something that should not be seen by others. Once inside, we sat around for a while, saying nothing. The trainer remained in a very serious, brooding mood. Our anxiety continued to mount. Finally he said: "I would like a volunteer." Again my imagination ran riot: volunteers are called for (especially under the "battle" conditions under which we were operating) only when the mission is dangerous. We remained silent and frozen in our seats. The trainer made another plea for a volunteer. Finally, with obvious trepidation, one of the men in the group (certainly not me) said that he was tentatively willing to try to cooperate. The trainer said: "Hold out your palms, I'd like to feel your strength and let you feel mine." They pushed against each other for a while, but the volunteer's willingness faded and he withdrew from the exercise.

The exercise the trainer proposed was really a simple, fairly non-threatening exercise, but the way in which he introduced it created such anxiety that it practically immobilized the group. Communication had floundered. The trainer's purpose was to offer an exercise or two to stimulate contact and communication, but he completely defeated his own purpose. The leader can control the degree of anxiety (at least the general anxiety level of the group) by the way he introduces the group to such exercises. In the contract group, both the experimental nature of the laboratory experience and the reason for using nonverbal exercises are explained before the laboratory begins. Furthermore, if nonverbal exercises are first introduced as experimental games, they will arouse much less anxiety than if used as serious dynamite to get rid of communication blocks in the middle of group sessions. I often begin a laboratory with a "micro-lab," a kind of festival of communication games that involves many different kinds of exercises—verbal, nonverbal without physical contact, nonverbal with physical contact, and mixtures. This tends to make the participants less wary and thus more ready to experiment, later on in the laboratory, with communication through physical contact.

In the contract laboratory, the participants should not be forced or bullied into more serious exercises or exercises that take place at more serious times during the life of the group. Again, the way the exercise is proposed will often determine whether the participants will engage in it or not. For instance, if two people seem to be avoiding each other or if they have not been able to make contact on a verbal level, the trainer might reflect on this and then say:

"I wonder whether the two of you would like to engage in a little nonverbal experiment which may or may not facilitate communication between you. These exercises work no magic, there's nothing mystic about them, but they may help." Individuals differ quite a bit in their willingness to explore the nonverbal dimensions of communication. But if this dimension of laboratory life is made relatively nonthreatening (it will almost always arouse some anxiety), most of the participants will make use of it, and it can become a fruitful area of experimentation, complementing the verbal interaction of the group.

Choosing the Right Exercise. Exercises should not be used indiscriminately in laboratories, but should rather be integrated with the task at hand. If the overriding purpose of the laboratory is for the participants to become more aware of themselves and of others as body and as sensing, then the laboratory might be highly exercise-oriented, and many of the exercises suggested by Gunther (1968) might be used. If the purpose of the laboratory is interpersonal growth, many of the exercises suggested by Schutz (1967) could be integrated into the experience. But the choice and timing of an exercise is important. If the participants are already anxious and the exercise is seen principally as an instrument that will arouse more anxiety, there is a strong probability that it will not have a beneficial effect, for the participants will not be able to give themselves to it properly. In the contract laboratory, the exercise is not an end in itself. Even when it constitutes a form of communication in its own right, it is still there chiefly to complement and help stimulate verbal involvement. Some trainers mechanically substitute exercises for the give and take of verbal interaction, but this often merely reflects their own anxiety and their need to keep the interaction moving. There are certainly plenty of exercises of all kinds available. Besides those listed by Gunther, Schutz, and Malamud and Machover (1965), there is an endless supply in the fertile imaginations of those who conduct laboratories. An exercise created or modified to fit a specific situation that arises in a group will fare better than a borrowed exercise, which, although interesting, does not fit.

Exercises and Life. Exercises, like the laboratory itself, are contrived. They are not meant to be a way of life. If they make a participant pause and reflect on some dimension of his interpersonal life, if they show him some of his unused potentialities, if they enlarge his area of freedom with himself and others, then they have served their purpose well. However, even though a participant might not make a contrived exercise culture part of his day-to-day living, he may find that, because of his laboratory experiences, he interacts in somewhat different ways. For instance, he may show affection more readily in physical ways. The only caution is that he not inflict himself, in his newfound freedom, on others.

Poiesis: Words Made Flesh

When *pathos* finds expression in human language, when *logos* is suffused with human feeling and emotion, a new term is needed to describe the communication that takes place. The term used here is *poiesis*, which comes from the Greek verb meaning "to do, to make." The English word "poetry" comes from the same stem. When meaning and feeling become artfully one in language, the result is poetry. In human dialogue, when words are meaningfully filled with human emotion, when feelings and emotions find creative expression in human language, the result is *poiesis*. Forrest (1965) uses the same term with somewhat negative connotations. For him, *poiesis* is a "making" almost in the sense of "making up" or "contriving." The schizophrenic, for instance, uses language not just to describe or communicate something, but to "make" something. In the schizophrenic's language, wishes are not merely uttered but fulfilled. In fact, fulfillment of his wishes occurs only in the world of words. Be that as it may, in the present context, *poiesis* has only positive connotations. It is too rich a term to be wasted on pathology. *Poiesis* is word made flesh in human dialogue.

Men seem to feel safer when they compartmentalize their experiences. Feelings are all right, and language is all right, but they are to be kept apart, if possible. Lynch (1967) recognizes in movies a similar movement—that is, toward immediate, private, and wordless experience. He deplores such a movement: "Words and ideas have been given a hard time; they have been pushed into a polarized state, devoid of contact with images and things. They need to be allowed to re-enter the world and re-establish their relation to things and their own power as a human art [p. 79]." Meaningless words and unverbalized feelings both sin against human communication. Lynch suggests that even brutal language is better than either emasculated words or silences that hide hate and bitterness:

... The words in *Who's Afraid of Virginia Woolf* are, on the surface, ordinary human words that say something. On the second level they turn out to be words describing games being played at, unrealities, fictions. On the third and final take they have inflexibly human rules behind them and are the only forms of salvation and *contact*, cruel though they might be, between George and Martha [p. 83, emphasis added].

Language, then, can be strong medicine, if it is made strong by becoming the vehicle of the speaker's experience.

The members of the contract group are asked to experiment with *poiesis*. This does not mean that their language must be continually filled with emotion. First, there are degrees of *poiesis*, and second, we could not keep up the process of communication if all words were afire. What is demanded in the contract group is feeling *proportioned* to meaning and expressed with simplicity, in human language.

Experiencing, Expressing, Communicating. Men first experience something, then they express it, and, if their expression is successful —that is, if they actually contact another—they communicate their experience. Gendlin (1962) suggests that psychotherapy deals primarily with the first variable, experiencing. He suggests that psychotherapy is fundamentally concerned with the client's struggle with his directly felt experiencing and that the individual's inward data are more important than words. In sensitivity groups, however, it is rather a question of getting participants to verbalize the more or less integral *pathos* experiences they *do* have and *are* in contact with. But even in therapy, the impact of the therapist is determined, according to Patterson (1966), by the client's perception of the therapist. It is not sufficient for the therapist to have positive feelings toward his client, nor is it sufficient merely to express these feelings. Rather he must express them in such a way that they are actually picked up by the client; that is, he must *communicate* these feelings. Therefore, although helping a patient to get into contact with his own experience seems to be the first step in the therapeutic process, still, since integral functioning is ultimately defined by the quality of a person's interpersonal relationships, the ability to express and communicate oneself integrally are also essential goals of therapy. Patterson thus highlights one of the frequently forgotten dimensions of *poiesis*—that is, that feelings must be expressed through language in such a way that others actually do pick them up. This is work, hard work. This is why integral communication is called *poiesis*—a doing, a making. Therefore, when Salter (1949) recommends feeling talk—"we must forego premeditated utterances and say what we feel when we feel it [p. 99]"—it must be remembered that mere feeling-talk may not be sufficient. The expression of feeling must be suffused with *logos* so that it becomes an invitation to dialogue.

Failed Poiesis: Action Divorced from Language.   While perhaps the primary failure to achieve *poiesis* consists in an inability or a refusal to include emotion in verbal expression, there is also another, even more dramatic, form of failed *poiesis*. It involves what Bloch (1968) calls "an inability to substitute and utilize language for action and activity [p. 178]." When a married couple stand screaming at each other, a kind of communication through action is taking place, but the use of language is really incidental to the whole process. This dumping of raw emotion on each other is an action or an activity devoid of both *logos* and *poiesis*. But if a marriage begins primarily on the level of *pathos* so that, although each experiences the other, neither is capable of translating that experience into language, and if the marriage continues principally on the level of *pathos,* with commercial speech alone used in the necessary transactions between partners, then trouble is almost unavoidable. The couple turns up in some marital-counseling situation, and it is discovered that their problem is, predictably, a lack of communication. From the beginning, their feelings toward each other have been strong and turbulent, but strength and turbulence do not imply depth. They have never really questioned their feelings. They eschew *logos:* they never speak meaningfully about their core, their values, their goals, the interlaced meanings of all the phases of their lives. *Pathos,* therefore, is not modified, stimulated, and matured by effective *logos*. There has never been any "need" for words. When ephemeral feeling dies away, however, and the inevitable problems of living together arise, communication fails because it has never really been a part of the relationship. The *pathos* level on which the relationship has been based is not sufficient to handle the problems. When undiscussed problems mount too high, irresponsible *pathos* runs wild, with words becoming the lackeys of feeling. Then the conversation that does exist is nothing but a caricature of communication. The sooner a couple realize the potential of human language and make mature verbal interactional systems part of their relationship, the better prepared will they be to handle problems that arise, and, more important, the greater will be their potential for interpersonal growth.

The Expression
of Emotion

In human affairs there seem to be two highly prevalent, though probably not growthful, ways of handling strong feeling—both positive and negative feeling. Actually, both are ways of avoiding, rather than handling, emotion in transactional situations.

The Suppression of Feeling. The safest way of handling strong feeling is to suppress it. Perhaps "conceal" is a more accurate word than "suppress," for hidden emotion does make itself felt under a number of disguises. For instance, if a person suppresses or conceals his anger, it frequently comes out in a number of deceitful ways, such as coolness, unavailability, snide remarks, obstructionism, and other subtle forms of revenge. Feeling has not really been suppressed; rather, it has been translated into a number of nongrowthful activities that are difficult to deal with precisely because of their underground character.

Riecken (1952) describes a work camp in which, because of the philosophy and religious convictions of the members, the prevailing atmosphere was one of friendly and gentle interactions. Since the members disapproved of all kinds of aggression, both physical and verbal, a problem arose with respect to the handling of the minor antagonisms that arose daily and tended to interfere with the work to be done. Meetings were held, but problems were discussed in a most abstract and intellectualized way. Because of the failure to institute real emotional communication, the antagonisms persisted, much to the dissatisfaction of everyone. But an intellectual approach to a nonintellective situation was bound to fail.

Acting Out. The second way of handling strong feeling is to foist it on the other. Pent-up anger is allowed to explode, or pent-up affection is allowed to overwhelm the other. Such solutions are rationalized as forms of honesty, but, strangely enough, such honesty seldom results in growthful encounter. Acting out does satisfy immediate instinctual needs, but seldom serves the process of communication. Some people pride themselves on "blowing up" and getting it "out of their systems," claiming that this is more honest than concealment and the subtle leakage of negative feeling that ensues. This may well be true, but such pride should be tempered by the knowledge that there is a more human way.

Poiesis in Responsible Encounter. Let us suppose that once George has been angered by John, he says something like this: "John, I am really angry with you. I could try to swallow my anger or I could blow up, but I don't think that either of these would solve anything, because I think that in a way my anger is really *our* problem, yours and mine, and I'd like to talk it out with you. How about it?" Such a tack (especially if the stylized way in which it is presented here is overlooked for the moment) is rarely employed, for it demands too much honesty and one runs the risk either of refusal or of disquieting discoveries about oneself. It also demands dealing with feelings instead of relinquishing them in one way or another. George remains angry, but now his anger becomes a point of possible contact instead of just an abrasive force. Sometimes a person has to choose between the pain of talking out another's hostility toward him and the discomfort of being the victim of a dozen covert expressions of hostility so rationalized that it is impossible to get at them.

The Prevalence of Hostility

One of the first emotions that members of sensitivity groups tend to experiment with is hostility. For a number of people, hostility is a relatively inexpensive emotion (though there are those who find it almost unbearable either to express or to be the object of hostility), more or less readily available for use. Because it is readily available, some use it recklessly, and this serves to perpetuate the caricature of the sensitivity laboratory as a place where people "tell one another off."

The Responsible Expression of Hostility as a Form of Poiesis. Contract-group members are in no way discouraged from expressing anger or hostility, but they are asked to do so in as constructive a way as possible. Mann (1959), in reviewing the literature, discovered that the expression of positive feelings in group situations is positively correlated with intelligence and adjustment, while the expression of negative feelings such as anger, hostility, disagreement, tension, and antagonism is negatively correlated with these variables. But it seems that the mere expression of negative feelings is not the issue; it is rather *how* they are expressed. Negative feelings, too, are part of the human condition and are experienced by the intelligent and well-adjusted. The hypothesis here is that the intelligent and well-adjusted, when they do express negative feelings, would tend to do so in a positive way—that is, through some form of *poiesis*. The positive expression of negative feelings can be growthful. Therefore, the airing of negative feelings can be quite beneficial to contract-group interaction if it is done responsibly, but it should hardly be the major emotional preoccupation of the group.

Hostility that is expressed by some form of *anti-logos* rather than *poiesis* merely elicits more hostility. A study by Bandura, Lipsher, and Miller (1960) showed that hostile therapists encourage patient hostility. The study also indicated that therapists tend to avoid patients who direct hostility toward them. Finally, patients suppress or redirect hostility following avoidance reactions on the part of therapists. Thus, when hostility is a more or less buried variable in a transactional setting, it tends to evoke a manipulative, "game" culture that is hardly growthful. In the contract group, if anyone tries to engage in this "attack-immunity" game of Bandura's therapists, he should be challenged immediately.

The Meanings of Hostility. Hostility frequently expresses more than raw "againstness." Especially in group interaction, it can mean many things. (1) It may be a way of expressing one's individuality or showing strength in the group. This use of hostility, however, is relatively immature and usually characterizes only the earlier sessions of the life of the group. Real strength and individuality can be displayed in contractual ways. (2) For the person who feels threatened by the interaction of the group, hostility may be a defensive maneuver rather than a form of attack. (3) Planned hostility may be used as a dynamite technique to stimulate action during a boring session. (4) Hostility can also have a more subtle and constructive meaning: it may be an attempt to achieve some kind of interpersonal contact or intimacy. A number of authors (e.g., Burton & Whiting, 1961; Mills, 1964; Ogilvie, 1961; Slater, 1966) have suggested (and some have conducted research that supports the hypothesis) that identification tends to follow aggression. For instance, Slater states: "It is for this reason that aggression leads to identification: in fantasy the attack is a freeing of the desirable attributes from the hateful shell that prevents their acquisition [p. 146]." It would take rather ingenious empirical investigation to determine whether this is true, but it does seem to be a fact that sometimes after two people storm at each other, they tend to draw closer together. Perhaps the direct route to intimacy is too difficult, and the turmoil of the indirect route is all that is available.

Perhaps one of the best ways available to a participant in a sensitivity group to discover the meaning of hostility in his interpersonal relations is to express the hostility that wells up within him during group sessions.

The Problems and Potentialities of Poiesis

One of the problems of *poiesis* is that it is an anti-manipulative and anti-"game" form of communication in a manipulative and game-prone culture. Even therapy does not escape verbal manipulation, for, as Krasner (1963) has observed, the communication of therapeutic influence is a function of the therapist's verbal behavior. His studies indicate that the patient learns the rote that the therapist expects of him through verbal conditioning. And yet the hypothesis under which this book is being written is that the less manipulation there is in human interaction, the more growthful will the interaction be.

A second problem is that it is doubtful that our present culture is ready for a sharp rise in the amount of *poiesis* in interpersonal relating. The character Jerry in Albee's *The Zoo Story* is somewhat disconcerting to the average reader, for people are not accustomed to dealing verbally with reality on the level that he deals with it. Jerry is resented both because he feels too much and because he translates what he feels into language. Therefore, even those who are responsibly and intelligently "poetic" in their encounters must expect to experience a certain amount of rejection from those who cannot tolerate intimacy.

And yet, as Lynd (1958) sees it, men have a moral obligation to become artists in communication. This is difficult, for schisms within man, according to Maslow (1967)—for instance, splits within the personality due to the inward battle between impulse and control—cause splits in his communication: "To the extent that we are split, our expression and communications are split, partial, one-sided," but, on the other hand, to the extent that we are integrated and whole, our communications are "complete, unique, idiosyncratic, alive, and creative [p. 197]." The split between feeling and verbal language reflects the schizoid nature of the average man. His task is to overcome this split, because, if Lynd (1958) is right, too much will be lost if he does not:

It may be asked why, since the language of intimacy will always be to a large extent a language of gesture, facial expression, and touch, it should be important to enlarge the possibilities of verbal language for such communication. For at least three reasons: 1. Lack of a verbal means of communication of certain experiences may sometimes lead to atrophy or lack of awareness of the experiences themselves. 2. Ranges of mutual exploration may be cut off and unnecessary misunderstandings may arise if there is a feeling that words should not be used or an unwillingness to search for words to use as one medium of communication. 3. The creation of symbols in language is a characteristically human ability that can bring unconscious creative forces into relation with conscious effort, subject into relation with object, can give form to hitherto unknown things and hence make possible the apprehension of new truth [pp. 249–250].

Such integration of words and feeling is perhaps both a cause and a reflection of the general integration of the individual. If the participants of a contract laboratory come away with a deeper respect for honest emotion, honest language, and honest attempts to integrate the two, then the laboratory has been successful.

Chapter Seven:
Self-Disclosure

Introduction

One of the principal interaction goals in the contract group is self-disclosure. Since self-disclosure of some degree constitutes an integral part of almost any kind of laboratory experience and does so in a special way in laboratories in interpersonal relations, it needs special attention, especially in view of the fact that most of us fear self-revelation to a greater or lesser extent and therefore find it difficult to estimate its value in interpersonal living.

Since this chapter is comparatively long, a preview is in order. The following topics are dealt with: (1) *Dangers associated with concealment.* There is a growing literature pointing toward the potential pathogenic nature of concealment. The works of such people as Mowrer and Jourard are considered from this point of view. (2) *Our culture and self-disclosure.* The relationship between our culture and self-disclosure is placed in focus, for there seem to be a number of cultural bans against self-disclosure. This same society seems to extol privacy as an absolute value. Therefore the value of privacy and its relationship to interpersonal involvement are considered. (3) *Truth and honesty.* At least in practice, truth and honesty are not the precious commodities that they are made out to be. Some of the factors militating against a greater spirit of truth and openness in society and how these factors affect self-revelation among men are discussed.

(4) *Intra-individual resistance to disclosure.* Resistance to self-disclosure is not just a function of certain factors in society. There are also intra-individual factors which prevent a greater spirit of openness among men—for example, flight from self-knowledge, fear of intimacy, and a refusal to bear responsibility. (5) *Guilt and disclosure.* Guilt is an everyday human commodity that often is instrumental in keeping a person out of community in some way. It has many faces, and some of these are probed. (6) *The value of shame in human life.* Shame, too, is a common experience. Depending upon how it is approached, it can either enhance or prove detrimental to both personal and interpersonal living. How it differs from guilt and how it relates to communication with self and others are considered. (7) *Honesty in the group experience.* Possible areas of self-disclosure during the group experience itself are discussed. Of especial importance is the here-and-now honesty of what is happening to oneself and how one stands in relation to the other participants during the group interaction.

(8) *Self-disclosure: "story" and "history."* It is argued that humanistic self-disclosure is not a mere recital of actuarial data, no matter how intimate the data might be. (9) *The degree of disclosure in the group.* Different groups achieve different levels of self-disclosure. Some of the factors determining the depth of disclosure are reviewed. (10) *Labeling as a form of behavioral control.* It is hypothesized that self-disclosure can be used as an effective behavioral control device. It is then called "labeling," a term borrowed from Dollard and Miller (1950) to describe a process somewhat different from theirs. (11) *The dangers of self-disclosure.* Finally, some of the dangers of self-revelation, especially self-revelation in a group situation, are reviewed. However, it is suggested that these dangers can be minimized or even eliminated, so that the potential advantages of self-disclosure will outweigh its potential disadvantages. This is not to deny, however, that self-disclosure always entails a certain degree of risk.

Interaction Goals

In contrast to the T-group in which there is an "absence of any prearranged or externally assigned task [Benne, 1964a, p. 217]," the contract group imposes certain tasks on its members. The impact value of the traditional T-group lies in its members' search for viable goals and effective modes of interrelating. The impact of the contract group, on the other hand, lies in the specific kinds of interactions to which its members subscribe. The provisions of the contract dealt with so far—the concept of the contract itself, group goals, the laboratory nature of the group experience, leadership, and the elements of dialogue—have, to a large extent, specified attitudes that group members are expected to adopt and the structures of group process. Interaction goals, however, deal more specifically with the kinds of interaction that are expected to take place in the group. These interactions flow from the attitudes and the structures that have already been dealt with. The participants are expected to engage in self-disclosure, for this is one of the provisions of the contract. But the self-disclosure engaged in must be made relevant to the here and now, and it must be done in cooperation with (rather than opposition to) other members. That is, all the interactions to be discussed in this and the following chapters must reflect the attitudinal and structural aspects of the contract that have already been discussed. Self-disclosure, then, is one of the interactional means of "operationalizing" (March & Simon, 1958) the overriding goal of the group. If self-disclosure, as outlined in this chapter, is effectively engaged in, then it *is*, in part, interpersonal growth.

Self-Disclosure: A Basic Step toward Growth

All the participants in a laboratory in interpersonal relations must agree to engage in some degree of self-disclosure; they must make some efforts to reveal the person within to the other members of the group. Self-disclosure is cardinal in growth groups, pivotal in the sense that many of the good things that happen in such groups happen because of self-disclosure. In noncontract groups in which interpersonal or personal psychological growth is at least an implicit goal, a good deal of the group's activity, especially in earlier sessions, deals with formulating policy with respect to self-disclosure. "I'm not so sure how far I can go," "I am beginning to wonder whether we are starting a therapy group here," "Boy, that [some disclosure made by one of the participants] was a bomb; how are we going to handle that?"—these and similar statements are contract talk referring principally to self-disclosure. The prospect of revealing oneself is unsettling and must be approached gradually in such groups. The group must first decide whether self-disclosure is a value or not, at least for *this* group in *these* circumstances. Or, while many of the members of such groups might realize that it has a value in human living and even in this group, they need time to get used to the idea, or time to decide how to approach such a dangerous undertaking, or time, perhaps, to screw up the courage needed to talk about oneself. In the contract group, the person must make most of these decisions before he enters the group, or at least at the time that the contract is imposed.

Self-disclosure in the contract group *is* a value. The rest of this chapter is an attempt to explain why it is a value and how it may be approached in the group. Lynd (1958) says that "a person who cannot love cannot reveal himself [p. 241]." The converse also seems to be true: the person who cannot reveal himself cannot love. Thus, the question of self-disclosure is intimately associated with interpersonal growth. The assumption in this statement is that responsible self-disclosure is a kind of royal road to community. This sharing of the human condition—in its sublimity, banality, and deformity—pulls people together.

Deception and Concealment as Pathogenic or Growth-Stifling

Mowrer's position. In a series of publications (e.g., 1950a, 1950b, 1952a, 1952b, 1953a, 1953b, 1961, 1964, 1965, 1966a, 1966b, 1966c, 1966d, 1968a, 1968b), Mowrer has elaborated a theory concerning the etiology of emotional disturbance. Mowrer is constantly rethinking his position, so that what started out to be a theory of psychopathology is being modified, complemented, and expanded to such an extent that a coherent interpersonal theory of man is beginning to emerge. Much of what Mowrer says deals, directly or indirectly, with the problem of self-disclosure.

Mowrer (1968a) places himself in the camp of third-force psychology. Man is both free and responsible. To a large extent, he can fashion his own destiny, and need not be just a simple product of his heredity (force I) and his environment (force II). Or, from a different viewpoint, neither Freudian psychoanalytic theory (force I) nor Watsonian and Pavlovian behaviorism (force II), separately or in combination, provide an adequate working model of man. He sees Adler (Adler, 1964; Ansbacher, 1967; Dreikurs, 1950) as having "anticipated both aspects of contemporary Third-Force psychology: the emphasis on volition, individual choice and responsibility, and the emphasis on man's irrevocable need for community, that is, deep communion and identification with one's fellow men [Mowrer, 1968a, p. 9]."

Mowrer turns to Pratt and Tooley (1964, 1966) for a conceptual or structural model of man in community, man's interactions with himself and his fellows. For Pratt and Tooley, all social relations represent "contractual transactions." All of life is a patterning of contractual arrangements that men make with themselves and with others, so that contracts become the instrumentalities for both the creation and the exchange of values among men. "These contracts may be explicit or implicit, conscious or unconscious, unilateral or multilateral, voluntary or coercive. They constitute the warp and woof of personal and social life. Men *are* their contracts [Pratt & Tooley, 1966, p. 882]." Much of psychopathology, then, can be conceptualized in contractual terms: "Psychological and psycho-social disorders are conceptualized as personal-social, contract-system disorders, contract crises, contract conflicts, distorted or anti-social contracts, contract deficit, contract stress-and-strain, inadequate or immature contract system development [p. 882]." Self-actualization is also depicted as a contract function: "The ideal is authentic competence in the major contract spheres of living [1966, p. 882]."

The first step on the road to emotional disturbance, then, is some kind of mismanagement of contractual life. A man may overcommit himself, he may undercommit himself, he may miscommit himself, and he may cheat on the commitments that he has made (Mowrer, 1968a). The selfish person is someone who is overcommitted to himself and undercommitted to others. He is either irresponsibly out of community (e.g., the miserly recluse) or he is irresponsibly in community (e.g., the person who must always have his way when he is with others). A person may mismanage his contractual life in a seemingly endless variety of ways, and no man's life is entirely free of contractual failure. Emotional disturbance may be defined in terms of contractual failure itself. Thus the sociopath, either in a specific area of life or more generally, disregards the contractual structure of interpersonal living. He makes his own rules.

Contract mismanagement, then, is man's first mistake. The second mistake is, in a sense, worse than the first. If a man fails to fulfill a contract, but admits that he has failed, and tries to make restitution, he can usually avoid emotional trouble. This, however, is not the course that all men follow. Some men fail to live up to their contractual obligations and then try to *conceal* their failures, both from themselves and from others. Deception, then, becomes a way of life. Mowrer sees this refusal to face up to what is as pathogenic. It is a break with reality, and breaking with reality is the warp and woof of emotional disorder.

In his writings, Mowrer contends that this refusal to confess one's misbehavior, at least to the significant others in one's life, often leads to emotional disorder. He tentatively divides the usual symptoms associated with emotional disturbance into two types (Mowrer, 1967). Type I symptoms are the agonies usually associated with emotional disturbances of one kind or another: tension, anxiety, depression, loss of appetite, fatigue, loneliness, phobias, scrupulosity, sense of unreality, hypochondriasis. He sees these symptoms as discomforts arising from deviant behavior, contractual failures. These symptoms are usually involuntary, mediated by the autonomic nervous system. Yet they are potentially useful in that they aim at motivating the sufferer to change his life style, to get at and do something about the contract disorders underlying the symptoms.

Type II symptoms are the means, usually ineffectual, that the sufferer uses to try to handle Type I symptoms. They are attempts to escape the pain rather than attempts to get at its roots: withdrawal, suicide, rationalization, blaming others, self-pity, busy-ness, overeating, abuse of sex, daydreaming, intoxicants, tranquilizers. Type II symptoms are disabling, because they prevent the sufferer from moving in the right direction. They are "home remedies" of various types, either chosen by oneself or suggested by others. Though they may bring temporary relief, they do not get at the root of the problem. Since they are delaying tactics, they ultimately make things worse. Both Type I and Type II symptoms are muted confessions; they are signs of a person's inability or refusal to involve himself responsibly in his contractual obligations.

Type I symptoms are nature's response to the deviant person's attempt to conceal his deviancy. Refusal to admit one's deviancy to oneself and to others is keeping secret what should be told. Such secrets are pathogenic. Mowrer is not the first to recognize the pathogenic nature of such secrecy. In his writings (e.g., 1964, 1968b) he uses examples drawn from literature of the therapeutic value of confession. By doing this, I believe, he is intimating that much of his work is an attempt to give scientific conceptualization to a fact or a truth that is deeply embedded in man, though it is a truth that man is loath to face. Harper (1959) suggests that sometimes emotional disturbance loses its power when it loses its privacy. Mowrer probes further into the why of the pathogenic nature of such privacy.

In his earlier writings, Mowrer refers to the process he instituted to help those with emotional problems as "integrity therapy." Recently he has tended to drop the term "therapy" and substitute "training," for various reasons. First, the term "therapy" implies illness, but, generally, Mowrer does not see the emotionally disturbed as sick in the usual sense of the word. He does not reject biochemical approaches to psychopathology, but he is wary of their overextension:

We are not here holding that organic or biochemical anomalies do not reflect themselves in the sphere of human functioning; and in this sense and to this extent, the so-called medical model is highly adequate and relevant. The danger lies in possible over-extension of the model. . . . To the extent that mental and emotional suffering have a biochemical basis, their elimination or amelioration is a merciful boon to all humanity. But where suffering is the consequence of behavioral malfunctioning, it has motivational, educational work to do, and its chemical counteraction is clearly not indicated. We have yet to determine the dividing line between the organic and the functional, and the argument advanced in this paper is offered primarily as a means of conceptualizing emotional problems with a behavioral and interpersonal, rather than a strictly organic, biochemical basis [1968a, pp. 37–38].

Second, Mowrer's groups are actual training grounds for more effective interpersonal living. I had experience with these groups in Galesburg, Illinois—both at Galesburg State Research Hospital with Mowrer himself and in the community. These groups were run according to a simple contract, which was the basis for entry. The prospective participant was to agree (1) to tell his story— that is, to reveal the unconfessed deviant behavior that could possibly be at the root of his disturbance and to remain "confessionally current" as the group moved along; (2) to assume responsibility for himself—that is, to stop blaming others for his problems and to assume the direction of his own life; and (3) to become interested in and involved with the other members of the group. The group formed a small community, which became the vehicle of the reintegration of its members into the other communities from which they had come—family, neighborhood, church, job. Self-disclosure, however, was not the only, or even the most important, group variable. Once a person revealed himself, he was next expected to discuss with the group what kind of restitution he was to make and how to go about it. He was asked to review his contractual relationships with himself and with others, especially with the significant others in his life, and to start on a process of contractual readjustment, first within the group and then in the other groups to which he belonged.

The group produced some dramatic successes, but there were also failures. One of the sources of the failures, I believe, was a violation of the laws of groups spelled out in this paper. Too often, the groups became places where individual therapy or training took place in the presence of others. The members were not sufficiently encouraged to interact with one another. It was seldom that they dealt with their feelings toward one another. Too much of what was revealed dealt with the then and there, no attempts being made to make it relevant to *these* people in *this* group. All in all, the *theory* of the source of emotional disturbance became so central that other conditions for effective interpersonal involvement were overlooked. While Mowrer's natural feel for what kind of interaction should take place within a group made him an excellent group leader, I believe that he has underestimated the necessity of teaching effective group process in the training sessions. I also have some difficulty with a certain narrowness in Mowrer's initial formulations concerning the etiology of emotional disturbance, but this problem will be dealt with later.

Other Approaches to the Relationship between Openness and Growth. Mowrer is not alone in advocating complete openness in the therapeutic situation. Mainord (1968) describes what he calls "Therapy #52—The Truth." The prospective client must agree to a group contract which is much like Mowrer's: (1) The patient must agree to be completely open with the group. (2) He must agree to accept total responsibility for all of his behavior all of the time, twenty-four hours a day. Responsibility here means acting according to one's own ethical code. (3) Each patient must accept responsibility for every other patient in the program. Mainord says that the first two conditions are usually accepted, but with a lack of understanding of the behavioral demands that these conditions will entail. The third condition, he says, is usually bewildering to the patient. In Mainord's group, the therapist has absolute power. Once the patient has agreed to the contract, then the therapist can manipulate the reinforcements connected with hospital living, withholding rewards when the patient fails to live up to the contract. Mainord's groups are much more behaviorally oriented than Mowrer's:

> The group meetings are to be sources of new information, and an avenue for feedback, for manipulation of consequences, and even a place to learn skills in new modes of interaction, but the truly important social environment will never be some group sharing a similar plight with reinforcements manipulated for the patient's benefit. The appropriate social skills can never be completely demonstrated in the therapeutic group, and only a rigid adherence to the use of an external criterion makes it possible to expect much generalization.
>
> The group meeting should result in extracting new behaviors, but the crucial reinforcements can come only from the environment [p. 33].

Mowrer, too, was beginning to talk about a totally controlled hospital environment in which group work would be only a part of a total program.

Jourard on Concealment. Jourard (1964, 1968) has been investigating the implications of concealment and self-disclosure in a context that is much wider and perhaps more positive than Mowrer's. He, like Mowrer, believes that concealment can sicken a person. The person who finds his behavior unacceptable, in one way or another, both to himself and to others, must conceal his own identity. The energy that he pours into concealment adds to his stress and dulls his awareness of his own inner experience. Whatever contact he makes with others is through a facade; a kind of rigidity or stereotypy permeates his relationships with others. Loneliness and depression are inevitable as part of the price for concealment, for the concealer is separate, apart, out of community. The concealer thus increases the stress factors in his life and thus becomes susceptible to all sorts of sickness, both physical and psychological. But when Jourard talks like this, he is not describing just the neurotic or the emotionally disturbed. He sees this problem as the affliction of most men, at least in our own society. This lack of transparency is a major element in the "psychopathology of the average" that afflicts the so-called "normal" personality of our time. The more desperate the need to conceal, the greater the stress, and the more likely the occurrence of physical and psychological decompensation.

The Pathogenic Secret. Ellenberger (1966) discusses the concept of the "pathogenic secret." Like Mowrer, he believes that the content of this secret may be deviant behavior, but it is not limited to deviancy. For instance, the secret may deal with thwarted love, jealousy, or some physical infirmity. It does not always deal with guilt and shame, but it always has hopelessness connected with it, a "no-exit" aspect. Ellenberger claims that Moritz Benedikt (1835–1920), a Viennese physician, was the first to deal systematically with the pathogenic secret. Benedikt cites instances of hysterical women who were cured of their neurosis by confessing their pathogenic secrets and working out related problems.

Perhaps none of these men definitively proves that concealment in itself causes emotional disturbance and that self-revelation, even accompanied with restitution behavior in the case of deviancy, effects a cure. However, both Jourard (1964, 1968) and, especially, Mowrer (1968c) detail a large amount of empirical research concerning both the deleterious effects of guilt- and shame-provoked concealment and the salubrious and self-actualizing effects of self-revelation. It is also undoubtedly true that, in many well-documented clinical cases, deception and concealment have at least aggravated, if not caused, emotional anguish, and that confession or self-revelation, often coupled with restitution behavior, has led to dramatic improvement. Self-disclosure of guilt and failure is certainly one of the principal patient variables in the psychotherapeutic process, just as concealment, Jourard notes, is an undeniable facet of normal living. It is essential, then, to review the factors, within society and within the individual, that militate against greater openness. Evidence concerning the deleterious effects of concealment has always been with us; it is only recently that men have begun to point a scientific finger at this evidence. But why is self-disclosure in such disrepute?

Self-Disclosure and Cultural Taboo

There seem to be at least two forces in society that militate against greater self-disclosure among its members: (1) a kind of cultural ban against intimate self-disclosure, and (2) a society-wide cultivation of the "lie" as a way of life.

Self-Disclosure as Weakness. The person who exhibits strength by suffering in silence has become a cultural stereotype in our society. "Little boys don't cry" is an early version of the masculine ideal, and the woman who, in the fiction of radio, TV, or the novel, confesses that "I simply have to talk to someone" is thought to be really confessing, not a deep human need, but her own weakness, even though such weakness might be understandable and even excused in a woman. If self-disclosure is not weakness, then it is seen as exhibitionism, and, as such, a sign of illness rather than a desire for human communication. Very often, the adolescent, in his discovery of himself and the "other," engages in a good deal of self-disclosure. But this drive to exchange intimacies, even though it might have overtones, at times, of exhibitionism and other kinds of problem behavior, should be looked upon as the beginning of something that could be quite good—being at ease in discussing oneself with significant others at an intimate level (see White, 1964). Instead, it is often considered adolescent behavior, naive and immature. Such behavior, we think, will pass, just as the "natural neurosis" of adolescence passes. When the adult finds it necessary to communicate himself to a friend, he often feels that he needs an excuse for such action. "The person with a painful and perplexing personal problem is loath to ask a friend to share the knowledge of it, and his friend is loath to encourage him to talk it out [Schofield, 1964, p. 160]." It is difficult for both of them, for there is little cultural support for what they are doing. Lynd (1958) goes further and maintains that the ban refers not only to "revelations of the inmost self" but to the revelation of the "central dynamics of society [p. 231]." A racist community is loath to have the racial aspect of its culture discussed, and nominally nonracist communities sometimes engage in rather ludicrous startle and denial behavior when the unpondered and unconfessed racist elements of their culture are exposed and openly discussed.

Mowrer has received a good deal of criticism for his views on the therapeutic value of confession. While much of what he has written and, especially, the tone of his writing are not above criticism, it is still interesting to listen to the tone of his critics as they focus on the confessional aspects of his theories. It is difficult not to see an element of "Thou dost protest too much" in their spontaneous "this is nonsense" style of criticism. Much of this criticism, it seems, stems from unexamined cultural taboos against self-disclosure. The critic is speaking, ritually, the fears of his society, the central dynamics of which have been challenged.

The Medical Model and Cultural Permission. Even a society that is somewhat afraid of honesty cannot ban self-disclosure completely. One person's communicating himself intimately to another, especially in times of special stress, is such a basic need that even a relatively closed society must find ways of channeling such disclosure, must find cultural justification for it. Freud was a courageous man. He took a bold step forward when he declared that the revealing of intimacies about oneself was a medical act and, as such, was perfectly justified in any society. Society could hardly be accused of greeting Freud's thesis with wholehearted approval. Still, over the years, it has become quite acceptable to reveal oneself to a doctor or to a psychologist or counselor. Intimate self-disclosure became justifiable as a medical act, or at least as a paramedical act. Society's way of allowing self-revelation was also its way of containing it: it should take place between a client and a professional. Seeking therapy or counselling gives a person the cultural excuse he needs to establish a relationship in which he is free to tell anything about himself. But "therapy" implies illness, and even "counseling" implies problems, so that, to a large extent, self-disclosure is still associated with weakness, if not illness or emotional disturbance.

The professional has become the traditional one to listen to and deal with the intimate details of one's life because he is considered capable of understanding what is behind disturbing or uncontrolled behavior. At least, he is the one who can become the catalyst for understanding or insight, and insight has long been considered the key to the control of behavior. The problem is that we live in a day when both the medical model of emotional disturbance (Szasz, 1961; Werry, 1968; Sarbin, 1967) and the primacy of insight (London, 1964; Carkhuff & Berenson, 1967) are being challenged more and more. One of the problems is the word "problem," or at least the word "solution." It is true that men refer to disturbances in interpersonal living as "problems," and when they come to mental health professionals, they are looking for "solutions." Behavioral scientists have, more or less, followed this problem-solution paradigm in their approach to psychopathology. But, while this paradigm is obviously well suited to mathematics, it is not clear that it is generally applicable to human relationships. Too many people think that they have the problem and that the professional has the solution. But impasses in interpersonal relationships are more properly transcended than solved; that is, when two people change their attitudes and their ways of acting toward each other, when they communicate more freely with each other, areas of conflict dissipate or are transcended. The problem-solution paradigm is too neat and pat to fit the complexities of human interaction, especially the complexities of disturbed communication. The person suffering communication disturbances does not need a professional solution. He needs experiments in communication, not someone to give him an answer. The professional is a professional, not because he has answers, but because he is creative, because he can set up and evaluate these experiments in communication.

Group therapy widened the scope of the cultural permission to reveal oneself. One was now allowed to reveal himself to peers, provided that some professional presided over the group interaction. The present popularity of all kinds of sensitivity training is a further breach in the wall. People do not want to have to declare themselves ill in order to involve themselves in communication experiences analogous to those in group therapy, so they turn to sensitivity training as a kind of therapy for normals. The latest National Training Laboratories brochure asks prospective participants not to look upon the various laboratories as psychotherapy or as a substitute for psychotherapy; yet, for many, sensitivity training seems to afford a cultural permission to speak freely about themselves, not unlike the permission granted in group psychotherapy. It seems that there are several different brands of sensitivity training, and the question of therapy for normals in a laboratory setting is an issue that has not been settled, even within the National Training Laboratories (e.g., Weschler, Massarik, and Tannenbaum, 1962; Benne, 1964b; Frank, 1964). The contract group encourages its members to speak freely about themselves, even though these participants are not sick. As such, the contract group seems to take a position somewhere to the right of group psychotherapy and to the left of traditional sensitivity training.

Privacy: The Pros, but Especially the Cons. Much has been written on the value of, and the individual's right to, privacy (e.g., The Panel on Privacy and Behavioral Research, 1967). Much heat has been generated in discussions concerning the tendency of the behavioral scientist to overstep his bounds in this area. But the coin has two sides, and Bennett (1967) takes a rather refreshing look at the obverse side:

Privacy . . . is a graceful amenity, generally to be fostered, but with discriminating restraint and with due recognition of obligations as well as privilege. It is the writer's contention that the moral imperative is more often allied with the surrender of privacy than with its protection. . . . Secrecy within the community is incompatible with cooperation, inimical to the welfare and progress of the ingroup . . . Strictly speaking, of course, sex is not ordinarily a private experience, but a peculiarly delicate and intimate transaction between at least two people. I submit that even in this sensitive area, more serious problems stem from mismanaged communication about sex—partners who cannot discuss it, children who must not be told, and alienation of the deviate—than from mere breaches of privacy. . . . The confessional is also respected as a confidential relationship. It should be noted that this, too, is a communication; a revelation, in fact, of the most private secrets to at least one other person. . . . The reference, in many religions, is to public confession. The Protestant sinner must bear witness "before men" to achieve absolution. Indeed, it is recognized in Catholic circles that the traditional confessional, intent on making peace with God, leaves unresolved the problem of making peace with the community. . . . The readiness of people to discuss their personal problems with neighbors, and even strangers, makes one wonder, in fact, whether confidentiality is so necessary to the privacy of the patient as the comfort of the therapist. There are therapists who believe that the therapeutic process is facilitated in the presence of an audience. The popularity of group therapy reflects a similar assumption that patients find help in sharing personal problems—that confession is good for the psyche as well as the soul. . . . The contemporary concern over privacy parallels a pervasive need to communicate. . . . Our dilemma will not be resolved by hiding away from each other in separate caves, but through more and more interpersonal communication, better managed. . . . The critical problem we face is not how to keep secrets from each other but how to facilitate this readiness to communicate. The overriding question is how to maintain an atmosphere of trust and confidence which will enable us to talk about personal affairs . . . freely. . . . It is the writer's conviction that the importance of honest communication in our interdependent relationships outweighs the sanctity of privacy as a social value. . . . Anyone who undertakes to influence the lives of other people must accept an obligation to let them know where he stands, to reveal his motives, to share his purposes [pp. 371–376].

This entire article is worth reading. Undoubtedly, many would take exception to much of what Bennett has to say. It is a kind of confrontation that one might find difficult to respond to with honest self-examination and honest examination of the dynamics of society.

Jourard (1967) has already been mentioned as championing more openness, less secrecy, by means of a more honest experimenter-subject dialogue in behavorial research. Sidowski (1966, p. 22) discusses the "mutual distrust" between experimenter and subject that characterizes a good deal of behavioral research. Wiener (1950) approaches the problem of secrecy in the context of a different kind of research, but perhaps he, too, has hit on a principle that has wider application to the human enterprise than one might at first suspect. Wiener has strong reservations regarding the secrecy that surrounds research projects, specifically those involving government research. It is his contention that, in the long run, such secrecy is uneconomic. Lack of communication leads to duplication of effort. Thus, if the purpose of secrecy is, let us say, to gain time on an enemy in an area of research that will eventually yield its secrets anyway, then the price of secrecy is usually too high: the loss of progress that greater communication would lead to. It seems that Mowrer, Mainord, Jourard, Bennett, and Wiener are all saying, though from different points of view, that there is a tendency in society to look upon secrecy and privacy as values in themselves, even though in the long run they may be self-defeating. In many areas of life, the loss imagined to stem from revelation is imaginary. The energy expended in keeping the secret and encoding it—the neurotic may be considered to encode his secrets in his symptoms —is too costly and ill spent. It is much more costly than revelation. Just as secrecy is often considered a value in itself, so revelation is considered an evil in itself. We have learned to fear self-disclosure as self-destructive, so that few of us are ready to examine the possibility of its having constructive consequences.

Society and Truth

In a study by Kohn (1959) in which middle-class and working-class parents were asked to select the three characteristics most desirable in a ten- or eleven-year-old child, the top-rated choice was honesty. This may or may not point to some fundamental drive for truth and honesty—at least in these segments of the population— but whether it does or not, there is some question about both the availability and the social desirability of truth.

Psychoanalysis on the Availability of Truth. The widespread impact of psychoanalysis on society, or at least on some segments of society, is undeniable. Every educated man has some knowledge, however distorted, of psychoanalytic theory. Psychoanalysis has opened up (at least some would say so) whole new vistas in the domains of history (e.g., Erikson's *Young Man Luther*, 1958) and literature. Comedians find in it an almost limitless source of humor, their wit sometimes adding to the distortion of already distorted conceptions, and sometimes, though more rarely, laying bare the very marrow of some Freudian insight.

There is no intention here to mount an attack against psychoanalysis, but it does not seem out of place to suggest a hypothesis pertinent to the question of self-disclosure. One of the perhaps not too subtle messages of psychoanalysis—whether this be the fault of the theory or of those who exercise the right of private interpretation after inadequate exposures to the theory—is that truth is not readily available. Things, especially human things, are not what they seem to be. The "really real," to borrow a phrase from Plato, is a below-the-surface phenomenon; it is a source which is not easily tapped, however good the intentions of the searcher might be. The analyst demands free association rather than revelation of the intimate details of the patient's life, for the latter is not as significantly revealing as the former (Munroe, 1955, p. 38). Therefore, it would seem that psychoanalysis is one of the forces contributing to a kind of tacit understanding in society, that man is relatively incapable of telling the truth about himself, of revealing the deepest sources within himself.

Nor is such a view restricted to psychoanalysis. Thorne (1950) claims that the individual is never able or willing to reveal what is really important about himself. "Nothing should be taken at face value in eliciting facts concerning the life record [p. 116]." It seems to be something other than strong addiction to empiricism that leads him to say: "Actually, no statement or behavior pattern should be taken at face value, whether the person is normal or abnormal, except with confirmatory evidence from external sources [Thorne, 1950, p. 134]." Mowrer has been heavily criticized for his sharp attacks on psychoanalytic theory. However, I would suggest that at least part of Mowrer's intuitive distaste for psychoanalysis arises from the philosophical position of the theory that man is unable to tell the truth about himself. It is a definition of man that Mowrer finds intolerable. It is a philosophical position that affects man's appraisal of himself and his communication with others.

The Cultivation of the Lie. While it may be assumed that many men in society have become more or less convinced that the deepest truths about themselves are unavailable, many others find a need to distort the truths that are available. The fact that most men lie now and again is such a truism that, on a widely used personality inventory, a confession to this effect is part of a validity scale built into the test (Hathaway and McKinley, 1942; Hathaway & Meehl, 1951). The fact that most men lie now and then, however, is not the point here. It is rather that we live in a society that seems actually to cultivate the lie, and does so in ways unavailable to the generations that have preceded us. Perhaps Alexander the Great and Caesar lied about their campaigns to their subjects at home. That is a question that classicists and historians must settle. But it seems undeniable that a good deal of the uneasiness felt in the United States today stems from the suspicion that "they" are not really telling us the truth in many areas of national living. Some critics are quite outspoken in their condemnation of what they see as a lying generation.

... This new generation of the Left hated the authority because the authority lied. It lied through the teeth of corporation executives and Cabinet officials and police enforcement officers and newspaper editors and advertising agencies, and in its mass magazines, where the subtlest apologies for the disasters of authority (and the neatest deformations of the news) were grafted in the best possible style into the ever-open mind of the walking American lobotomy: the corporation office worker and his high-school son [Mailer, 1968, pp. 83–84].

Lying in diplomatic circles is frequent enough, well documented enough, and publicized enough to be considered axiomatic. It could be the cause of a good deal of hilarity were one not sober enough to interpret it in terms of devastating mistrust among individuals and communities. Henry's (1963) comments on the lack of passion for truth in our culture are certainly apropos: "Most people are not obsessive truth-seekers; they do not yearn to get to the bottom of things; they are willing to let absurd or merely ambiguous statements pass [p. 49]." One of the principal objects of his attack is the phenomenon of advertising:

The relaxed attitude toward veracity (or mendacity, depending on the point of view) and its complement, pecuniary philosophy, are important to the American economy, for they make possible an enormous amount of selling that could not take place otherwise [p. 49].

One of the discoveries of the 20th century is the enormous variety of ways of compelling language to lie. ... We pay intellectual talent a high price to amplify ambiguities, distort thought, and bury reality [p. 91].

How many men in our society are "outer-directed" (Riesman, 1950), their antennas high in the air in an attempt to pick up cues from society as to what they may and may not say? Fromm (1947) sees men as considering themselves, their personalities, as a commodity to be marketed in society, and one wonders how much deceit, falsification, and facade are indigenous to this marketing process.

The point of these remarks is not that psychoanalytic theory is without value (this would be absurd) or that twentieth-century western culture is necessarily more addicted to both the blatant and the subtle lie than other cultures, past and present. However, given the assumption that the kind of self-disclosure required in the contract group has some interpersonal-growth value, it is essential to face the fact that there are subtle and not-too-subtle forces within society that militate against this kind of self-disclosure. A deeper awareness of these forces, it is hoped, will help facilitate self-disclosure in laboratory groups.

Intra-Individual Sources of Resistance to Self-Disclosure

The Flight from Self-Knowledge. The problem-solution model of psychotherapy, which sees self-disclosure as a transmission of necessary information to the therapist so that he can work out a solution, is so obviously inadequate that it could be easily ignored, were it not for the fact that a certain percentage of clients, at least initially, subscribe to such a conception. Stockpiling information about oneself with another simply does not cure. Unless the client begins to listen to himself in such a way that he begins to get a feeling for himself, then he speaks on in vain. Self-disclosure is one of the principal ways, not only of communicating with others, but of communicating with oneself. Perhaps the latter is even logically prior. It is assumed here that many men flee self-revelation because they fear this closer contact with themselves. "The human organism seems capable of enduring anything in the universe except a clear, complete, fully conscious view of one's self as he actually is [Sherrill, 1945]." Self-disclosure both crystalizes and, in a sense, reifies aspects of the self that a person would rather live with silently—however painful the living—than face. At least in this one aspect, then, a group is only as threatening to a participant as he is to himself. Inevitably it is the individual participant who is his own severest judge. Jourard (1964) speaks out very strongly to this very point.

... When a man does not acknowledge to himself who, what, and how he is, he is out of touch with reality, and he will sicken and die; and no one can help him without access to the facts. And it seems to be another empirical fact that no man can come to know himself except as an outcome of disclosing himself to another person. This is the lesson we have learned in the field of psychotherapy. When a person has been able to disclose himself utterly to another person, he learns how to increase his contact with his real self, and he may then be better able to direct his destiny on the basis of knowledge of his real self [p. 5].

When I say that self-disclosure is a symptom of personality health, what I really mean is that a person who displays many of the other characteristics that betoken healthy personality . . . will also display the ability to make himself fully known to at least one other significant human being. . . . Neurotic and psychotic symptoms might be viewed as smoke screens interposed between the patient's real self and the gaze of the onlooker. We might call the symptoms "devices to avoid becoming known."

A self-alienated person—one who does not disclose himself truthfully and fully—can never love another person nor can he be loved by the other person [p. 25].

Much is being written about alienation and identity conflicts, with attempts being made to establish both the social conditions and the intrapersonal dynamics of these problems. Man's flight from himself is, in large part, a flight from communication with himself. Self-alienation is frightening, but any kind of intimate contact with the problem self is seen as even more frightening. Self-alienation, then, becomes self-reinforcing, its reward lying in its being, supposedly, less painful than its alternative. Even when a person gets out of contact with himself and with others to the degree that he flees to a mental hospital, this is still no guarantee that he is ready to face himself. Time and again in mental hospitals, when a patient is faced with the choice between the pain of alienation and the pain of therapy, he chooses the former, unable to find the courage to be. Since a similar dynamic is seen as operative in the psychopathology of the average, self-disclosure is stressed in the interpersonal-growth contract.

Fear of Intimacy. In dealing with patients in both individual and group psychotherapy, I discovered another block to self-disclosure. It is difficult to reveal oneself on a deep level to another without creating, by the very act of self-revelation, some degree of intimacy. In a group situation, for some reason, this intimacy has a special intensity. The participants in group psychotherapy and in other kinds of group growth experiences are aware of this, and even though they might have the courage to let others see the "mystery of iniquity" or even the "mystery of goodness" that they are, they cannot tolerate the intimacy that this act would create. They do not flee self-revelation as such. They flee intimacy. Meerloo (1956) believes that, for many persons, fear of human relations is greater than the fear of death. Berne's (1964) thesis seems apropos in our present culture. The all too real possibility of intimacy frightens many people. They prefer to skirt real self-revelation and to avoid real intimacy. They engage in sporadic acts of pseudo-self-revelation leading to pseudo-intimacy in a games approach to human relationships. Others merely eschew self-revelation. If it takes place by accident, they try to neutralize its effect. "Am I frightened? I suppose so. Most men are from time to time. It's quite normal." The obvious message here is "Don't probe." Failed intimacy is another major dimension of the psychopathology of the average.

Flight from Responsibility. In some cases, flight from self-disclosure is a flight from responsibility, a flight from the anxiety and work involved in constructive personal change. Self-disclosure leads to the revelation of areas of deficit and areas of aspiration in human living. It is relatively easy to avoid both these areas in day-to-day living. However, once these areas are reified, once a person declares what he finds unacceptable in himself and what goals he thinks he should be pursuing, he commits himself to change, and avoidance behavior becomes more painful. Self-disclosure commits one to conversion, to the process of restructuring one's life; it demands that a person leave the security of his own house and journey into a foreign land, and most men balk at that. If one senses that conversion is impossible, then he must avoid self-disclosure. So it is assumed that some men fear, or even deprecate, self-disclosure because of the behavorial consequences it entails. If the self-revelation takes place in a group, then the pressure to change is even greater than in a one-to-one situation, for there is the necessity of facing the pressures and demands of a community.

In the mental hospital, it is common to run into patients who would like to be cured, if the cure could be effected through some kind of magic. Popular forms of magic are: just being in the hospital, drugs, getting other people to change, getting the answer from the professionals, and the hope for spontaneous remission. In this sense, it seems not unfair to say that a certain percentage of mental patients actually choose their illness. Some will argue that it is the function of the therapist to motivate the patient, that if the patient does not want to participate in some therapeutic program, he should be taught to appreciate the program and its potential benefits. So much of psychotherapeutic theory and technique is predicated on the assumption that the patient wants to be cured. In the academic setting, plans and discussions can center on theory, method, technique. In the mental hospital, the question of motivation is more important. If a person "chooses" to be mentally ill, how much money and energy should society pour into convincing him that he really wants to be well and that he should decide to undertake an arduous program of psychotherapy? This problem is not as serious in private practice. First, the private patient most likely is actively seeking therapy. Second, there is the selection factor: the best candidates for therapy are often chosen, and part of the definition of "best" is "well-motivated." Psychotherapy and growth experiences in general can be proffered, in many different ways and repeatedly. Part of the proffering may even be a hospital ward behavioral reinforcement program (e.g., Ayllon & Ayllon, 1959; Ayllon & Haughton, 1962; Ayllon & Azrin, 1964), designed to help the regressed patient achieve, if possible, a state of integration and contact sufficient to elicit from the patient some kind of cues indicating that he wants to be cured. Beyond a certain point, however, the patient himself must opt for health and the work involved in striving for it.

Mowrer's (1968b) contract intimates that self-disclosure is part of the psychotherapeutic work, but that it is not enough. Self-disclosure is the prelude to behavioral change, especially self-initiated behavioral change. Mainord's (1968) contract implicitly demands a great deal of behavioral change, though he admits that the patient is somewhat unsuspecting when he agrees to contractual terms that do not appear to be excessively difficult. The contract group also demands behavioral change. The change directly contracted for is greater openness. But it is only fair to warn the person who intends to be open about himself that this has behavioral consequences beyond the group.

Anderson (1964) proposes the thesis that at least some of men's emotional problems have their root, not in guilt, but in grandiosity. Men, she says, are filled with feelings of entitlement. When they are frustrated, these feelings give way to resentment. Grandiosity also underlies feelings of helplessness. The helpless person is one who cannot reach a preconceived degree of perfection in some area or who cannot get others to behave as they should. The pride of such a person is subtle and insinuates itself into all areas of life.

Anderson's thesis is interesting and perhaps pertinent to flight from self-disclosure. There is in most men a rather deeply embedded desire to change first, if they think that they must change at all, and then present themselves as changed to others—in the case at point, to the group. Anderson would recognize this as false independence. Perhaps there are some changes that demand a group, a community of some kind. There are some things that either cannot be done outside of community or are done much more effectively in community. It takes humility, and not just a surrender to dependence, to admit this. Group experience is not an abdication of autonomy, but it is a potent vehicle of change. However, a man will reveal himself to the group only to the extent that he wants to change.

The Reverse Halo Effect.   Another source of fear of self-revelation could be termed the "reverse halo effect." The halo effect refers to the fact that a person judged to be competent or outstanding in a particular area is likely to be judged similarly competent in other areas. If A is an expert in psychology, his aura of expertise tends to spread to other areas and either he or others begin to look upon his pronouncements in theology or political science with the same awe. The reverse process sometimes stifles self-disclosure in growth groups. The group member fears self-disclosure because he usually thinks first in terms of disclosing the worst in himself. If he tells the other members about incompetence in one area of living, he feels that they will assume similar incompetence or irresponsibility in related or even unrelated areas. If a person admits problems in his private life, he fears that others will assume incompetence in his professional life. This is especially true if the person's profession is closely related to human living, as is, for example, psychology. There are several ways of handling such a problem in the group. The participant can try to give a balanced view of himself, speaking alternately of strengths and weaknesses. Or the group can take up the problem of the reverse halo effect and discuss it directly. The reverse halo effect is related to the problem of stereotyping and categorizing. No one likes to be dealt with as "problem," but there is a tendency in groups to identify the participants with their problems in living, for it is easier to deal with problems than with persons. Self-disclosure in the contract group should be dialogue disclosure; that is, the participants should reveal themselves gradually in dialogue with one another and not allow themselves to fix on one person, even though his problems differ from those of the rest of the group.

These, then, are some of the reasons people tend to avoid self-disclosure. As Shaffer and Shoben (1956) note: "One of the hindrances to successful counseling is that it depends on discussing the very things that the client is least inclined to discuss...[p. 529]." And yet, willingness to engage in self-exploration—which certainly involves self-revelation—is central to the growth process. Truax and Carkhuff (1967) review the evidence for such a statement:

A number of studies have explored what it is that successful patients do in therapy. There is a great deal of convergence upon the patient's intrapersonal or self-exploratory experiences. Using a variety of indices of constructive behavioral and personality change, Truax (1961) found significantly more depth of self-exploration ... in successful than in unsuccessful cases of hospitalized schizophrenics. Truax and Carkhuff (1963) reviewed results indicating relatively clear-cut findings that the greater the degree of patient engagement in the deep intrapersonal or self-exploratory process, the greater the degree of constructive personality changes in the patient. Further analysis indicated that even during initial stages of psychotherapy (the second interview), the level of patient self-exploration was significantly predictive of final outcome ... Wagstaff, Rice, and Butler (1960) report similar findings in a study of client-centered counseling. Their data indicated that patients with successful outcome tended to explore themselves more in the course of psychotherapy, whereas patients who could be classified as therapeutic failures showed little self-exploration and emotional involvement. In a more specific study of client-centered counseling, Braaten (1961) found that measures of self-reference and "private self" differentiated successful from unsuccessful cases. Tomlinson and Hart (1962), employing the Walker process scale to measure depth of patient experiencing, self-exploration and rigidity of concepts, found that the scale was able to differentiate successful from unsuccessful counseling cases [pp. 372–373].

It is hypothesized here that such openness will be of equal benefit to nonpsychiatric populations.

In a study by Talland and Clark (1954), clients judged the therapeutic value of fifteen topics discussed during counseling. There was general agreement on the relative value of the topics. Ratings showed a high correlation between the perceived helpfulness of a topic and its disturbing qualities. The topic called "shame and guilt" was experienced as extremely upsetting, but the discussion of this area of life during counseling sessions was considered to be very helpful. A group of psychologists also rated the same fifteen topics for their intimacy—that is, the degree of personal significance for the clients. There was a high correlation between what the psychologists deemed intimate and what the clients judged to be helpful. Guilt and shame are household items in human living. It would be impossible to deal adequately with self-disclosure without treating of them. They will be treated separately, guilt in this section, shame in the next.

The Many Faces of Guilt

The psychological literature, especially the literature dealing with theoretical formulations, is filled with references to guilt and guilt feelings (e.g., Cameron, 1963; Erikson, 1963; London & Rosenhan, 1968; Lynd, 1958; May, 1958). Guilt and anxiety are often related. For instance, Lowe's (1964) work with a guilt scale compiled from MMPI items indicates that anxiety and guilt are closely related phenomena. Levitt (1967) suggests that individuals with high anxiety proneness are given to stronger guilt feelings or to more easily provoked guilt feelings. He suggests that anxiety and guilt are really not separate constructs, but that guilt is simply another form of anxiety. Mowrer (1968b) suggests that poorly handled guilt leads inevitably to increased anxiety.

The problem is that guilt seems to be a genus with a number of species. Guilt as a genus implies violation of standard, whether the standard be real or imagined, and some kind of perception of this violation on the part of the violator, whether this perception be clear and distinct, vague, or even unconscious. The species of guilt differ, depending on the kind of standard violated and the kind of perception involved. The species of guilt that seem relevant to the discussion may be termed: moral, existential, pseudo- (or neurotic or psychological or fantastic), and pharisaical (or conventional). It is my contention that *hidden* guilt, of any kind, is a potential source of psychological trouble and that one of the most effective ways of handling guilt is self-disclosure. Self-disclosure is related, though in varying ways, to the therapy used for all species of guilt.

Moral Guilt. Moral guilt refers to a willful violation of some moral, ethical, or contractual standard that a person holds, either implicitly or explicitly. If A, realizing that it is a violation of his norms of conduct, steals money from B, then he becomes the subject of moral guilt. Ethical value systems differ from culture to culture, and even from individual to individual; that is, both individual and cultural subjectivity enter somewhat into the determination of a particular value system. Almost everyone, however, has some kind of value system or, from the viewpoint of Pratt and Tooley (1964, 1966), a network of contracts with self, others, and society at large. If the network itself is either nonexistent or deficient, one is considered "ill" in whatever sense the psychopathic or antisocial personality may be considered ill. It is not necessary for a person to reflect explicitly on the contractual nature of his relationships. By merely existing as a human being, by entering into relationships with others, and by living in society, one assumes contractual responsibilities. When a person, more or less knowingly and willfully, violates one or more of these contracts, he becomes the subject of moral guilt.

It is, of course, Mowrer's (1964, 1968a, 1968b) thesis that the complexus—contract-violation behavior, followed by concealment and failure in restitution behavior—is pathogenic. Confession, especially when coupled with restitution, seems, at least generally, to deprive contract violations of their potentially pathogenic power. Since value systems usually deal with social relationships, a violated value usually implies a break in human relationships. The guilty person is one who, by his behavior, has gotten out of community. Recognition and revelation of this behavior is a step toward getting back into community. Many people would say that this is good common sense; at least it seems to be a very good working hypothesis. However, attempts should be made to test this hypothesis in various ways, though it is evident that experimentation in this area would be quite difficult. There are apparent exceptions to the hypothesis. For instance, some people brag about exploits that others would consider to be contract violations. In defense of the hypothesis, however, such behavior might not be the exception that it at first seems to be, for (1) the deviant behavior is confessed—that is, it is externalized in the community, and (2) those who engage in such behavior might not see it as a violation of any contract. Different contractual systems exist at different levels of society. It is enough to know this fact without entering into the question of the relative merits of each contractual system. Therefore, what seems to be contractual unawareness might merely reflect cultural and individual variations, ignorance, or, if the deviation is significant, the illness of the antisocial personality.

Tournier (1962) calls moral guilt "value" guilt. It arises, he says, from a decision of the self against the self. Becker (1966) calls it "realistic, objective, or social" guilt. It is a falling short of the requirements of life with others. He, too, admits that cultural differences are important in the determination of such guilt. Others see the whole question of moral guilt as an unfortunate mixing of theology with psychology. Terms like "guilt," "self-disclosure," "confession," "restitution," "contract," and the like are considered too "moralistic" to be dealt with in a behavioral science. I would have to disagree with them. Secrets concerning past moral failure may well be contemporary determinants of behavior if they divert energy into the task of putting up a facade and keeping it in good repair. Undoubtedly, some of Mowrer's critics are unduly disturbed by the fact that he refers to man's moral life at all. However, one criticism of Mowrer does seem justified. It is disturbing that Mowrer, at least in his writings published to date, deals almost exclusively with moral guilt. At least this is often the tone of his writings. His position is reductionistic in that he tends to reduce most, if not all, neurotic guilt to moral guilt, and in the process ignores both existential and pharisaical guilt. Perhaps Mowrer says too little rather than too much.

Existential Guilt. It is also assumed here that self-revelation gets at another kind of guilt that is just as pervasive as moral guilt. Existential or ontological guilt deals with failed potentialities. From the very fact that we are human, there stand before us any number of possibilities in the organic process that we call human life and growth. It is quite obvious that a man cannot choose and fulfill all of the possibilities or potentialities in his life. But that he allows too many possibilities to slip by, that he chooses poorly among the possibilities that are at hand—this is the source of existential guilt. May (1958) follows Boss (1957) in his treatment of this species of guilt:

If, as Boss puts it, we "forget being"—by failing to bring ourselves to our entire being, by failing to be authentic, by slipping into the conformist anonymity of *das Man*—then we have in fact missed our being and are to that extent failures. "If you lock up potentialities, you are guilty against . . . what is given you in your origin, in your 'core' " [p. 53].

Failed potentiality can take a number of forms, both intrapersonal and interpersonal:

. . . We can be as guilty by refusing to accept the anal, genital, or any other corporeal aspects of life as the intellectual or spiritual aspects.

We have cited only one form of ontological guilt, namely, that arising from forfeiting one's own potentialities. There are other forms as well. Another, for example, is ontological guilt against one's fellows, arising from the fact that since each of us is an individual, he necessarily perceives his fellow man through his own limited and biased eyes. This means that he always to some extent does violence to the true picture of his fellow man and always to some extent fails fully to understand and meet the other's needs. This is not a question of moral failure or slackness—though it can indeed be greatly increased by lack of moral sensitivity. It is an inescapable result of the fact that each of us is a separate individuality and has no choice but to look at the world through his own eyes. This guilt, rooted in our existential structure, is one of the most potent sources of a sound humility and an unsentimental attitude of forgiveness toward one's fellow men [p. 54].

The lack of interpersonal sensitivity can be considered as forfeiting one's own potentialities, for it is a case of failed potentiality in the area of interpersonal living.

Clark (1967) makes a distinction between existential guilt and existential shame, but the notion of failed potentiality underlies both:

Buber has shown (1965, pp. 121–148) that existential guilt is the guilt of not having affirmed another, of not having answered another's plea for community, of not having entered an I-Thou relationship. Existential guilt, then, is clearly an important determinant in one's coming to value and create relation, for such guilt can often be expiated only by the establishment of relation in the here and now.

Existential shame, on the other hand, is the shame of not experiencing oneself as an actor, as a creator, as—to use Bugental's term (1965, pp. 203–208)—an "I-process." We experience existential shame as we are aware of having treated ourselves only as recipients of power and not also as expressers of it [p. 256].

Dealing with existential shame and guilt seems to be a function of a growth experience or therapy for normals. Thus, Clark sees sensitivity training as specifically designed to deal with them: "The kind of experience people in sensitivity training groups have is one which is designed better than any other I know of to allow for the experiencing of both existential guilt and existential shame, and both are manifestly important for man to experience [p. 256]."

What are the standards violated in existential guilt? They cannot be contractual standards, for violation of contract leads to moral guilt. In many of the contracts that define a person's life, some things must be done or not done, if the contract is to remain integral. Beyond that, however, lies the fullness of the contract. Scholastic philosophers make a distinction between *esse* (to be), the bare existence of something, and *bene esse* (to be well or fully), the perfection of its being. In marriage, for instance, the parties must not commit adultery, the husband usually must support his wife, and so forth. These contractual provisions belong to the *esse* of marriage. When the partners move beyond mere contract fulfillment, when the relationship deepens, putting them into more intimate contact with each other, with themselves, and with others (children, friends, etc.), then they are participating in the *bene esse* of marriage. Husband and wife both have a certain degree of potential with respect to the *bene esse* of marriage. Living out this potential seems to be related to a kind of quasi-contract that a person has with himself, to what he demands of himself with respect to the *bene esse* of the marriage. It is no longer a question of fulfillment or nonfulfillment, it is rather a question of degree. Existential guilt refers to the *bene esse* of living.

Men do experience existential guilt. Everyone carries the burden of failed potentiality—in the pursuit of a career, in interpersonal relationships, even in play and creative enjoyment. But few men discuss failed potentialities. The contract group and growth groups in general afford an excellent opportunity to reveal and discuss areas of failed potentiality. However, entering a sensitivity group, and especially a contract group, may increase the risk of adding to one's store of existential guilt. Once it becomes clear that the provisions of the contract, such as self-disclosure and expression of feeling, are possibilities for growth, then a refusal to participate in these experiences will only add to one's existential guilt. The group experience becomes just one more failed potentiality. Such failure can produce a real sense of diminishment.

Pseudo- or Neurotic Guilt. This guilt, which Tournier (1962) calls "functional," and which Becker (1966) refers to as "fantastic," is usually considered to be the domain of professionals dealing with emotional disturbances. This kind of guilt has a number of subspecies, or at least it can be expressed in quite different ways. Some psychotics think or feel that they have committed the unforgivable sin, when they have not done anything very reprehensible. Some neurotics think they are "rotten," though they do not speak of, or even know of, any particularly egregious contract violations in their lives. I prefer to refer to this kind of guilt as "pseudo-guilt" rather than "neurotic," for (1) its analog is also found in psychotic patients, and (2) "pseudo-" implies that either there has been no real violation of standard, no relevant instance of contract violation—although the "guilty" party insists or at least feels that there has been—or there has been some kind of contract violation, but the individual's reaction is out of proportion. Stern (1954) recounts a case in which a woman, after the death of her rather brutal husband, talked about having committed the unforgivable sin. It was finally learned that her guilt revolved around the fact that a friend of her husband's had made a "pass" at her some thirty years previously. She had not cooperated with the man, so that no real contract violation had occurred. Her reaction was simply not proportioned to the incident.

Stern summarizes the differences between moral and neurotic guilt (which, in Stern's sense, is a narrower concept than pseudo-guilt): moral guilt has the quality of proportion, can be assuaged by realistic restitution or atonement, does not necessarily depend on emotion, and refers to realized acts only; pseudo-guilt lacks proportion, cannot be "undone," is so inextricably interwoven with anxiety that at times only the anxiety is experienced subjectively, and refers to repressed drives rather than realized acts.

Sometimes pseudo-guilt takes the form of an exaggeration of existential guilt. A person feels, without reason, that his whole life has been meaningless, that his life, or rather he himself, is defined by failed potentiality. Some draw a distinction between guilt and guilt feelings. If there have been instances of contract violations or failed potentialities, then the individual feels guilty (and should). If, however, a person invents, exaggerates, or otherwise distorts normal guilt, either moral or existential, then he has guilt feelings. This terminology is abandoned here as being too ambiguous.

Another problem, more complex than that of classification and terminology, is the source of abnormal guilt. As indicated above, Mowrer (1964, 1968a, 1968b) has tended to think that neurotic guilt is the result of concealed and otherwise mismanaged moral guilt. There has been little room for pseudo-guilt in his system, though I have the feeling that he is moving away from what I consider to be an overly reductionistic position. Psychoanalytic theories, on the other hand, tend to see the origin of pseudo-guilt in such processes as repressed libidinal drives. A drive exists. The individual learns in some way that, at least for him here and now, it is prohibited. The drive is repressed. Since this process, in the main, takes place on the level of the unconscious, it remains unlabeled (Dollard and Miller, 1950). Even though the individual has never actually violated the standard in question, he feels as if he did, and because of repression he does not know why he feels guilty. This developmental guilt is explained somewhat differently by others. For instance, the significant adults in a child's life may reject him for one reason or another (e.g., he was not wanted in the first place, he is not attractive, they are too busy with other interests, etc.). The rejection may be open or subtle, but the point is that the child forms his self-image from the cues he receives. As Erikson (1964) puts it:

Hardly has one learned to recognize the familiar face (the original harbor of basic trust) when he becomes also frightfully aware of the unfamiliar, the strange face, the unresponsive, the averted, the darkened and the frowning face. And here begins ... that inexplicable tendency on man's part to feel that he has caused the face to turn away which happened to turn elsewhere [p. 102].

In the extreme case, the child learns to look upon himself as worthless. Guilt learned in this fashion becomes a mode of being. I have dealt with cases in which the patient who "learned" his worthlessness as a child and youth later acted out his worthlessness. " 'They' treated me rottenly, so now I will act rottenly" is the logic of such behavior. This renouncement of responsibility seems to be a contract-violation situation, however mitigated the person's guilt might be. These are cases of mixed guilt.

The point of this hurried, incomplete, and somewhat oversimplified consideration of the possible etiology of pseudo-guilt is to suggest that it, too, can be, and is, treated, at least in part, by one form or another of self-disclosure. The concealed is laid open, the repressed is labeled. If therapy is considered not just a question of insight but a "corrective emotional experience [Alexander, 1963]," it, too, demands self-revelation. The paradigm, perhaps oversimplified, is something like this: Patient: "I am worthless." Therapist: "Tell me about yourself, reveal to me the 'person inside.' " Then, perhaps slowly and painfully, the patient reveals himself. Therapist: "I have to be honest with you. I find the person you have revealed worthwhile. If you have really been listening to yourself, I think that you might have the same reaction."

But enough about pseudo-guilt. Perhaps the pseudo-guilt of everyday life can be handled in the contract group. However, the consideration of the etiology, nature, and treatment of its more serious manifestations belongs in works on psychopathology and psychotherapy. Laboratories in interpersonal relations are, by definition, made up of normals.

Pharisaical Guilt. Pharisaical guilt can arise if one feels overly conformed to certain nonessential standards of living. Some of the standards of conduct established in society refer to the more superficial, conventional, and ritualistic aspects of interpersonal relating and living in community. Ritual—religious or secular—is an essential part of human living. It is a deep human need and finds expression in any number of ways: in liturgical services, in guru-style meditation, in the stylized activities of fraternal organizations, in some stereotyped family activities (e.g., Sunday visiting of relatives can be deeply ritualistic). Indeed, this area of human behavior would be a fruitful area of more intensive sociological and psychological research.

The sick rituals of the obsessive-compulsive and of the psychotic are dealt with in detail in works on psychopathology, while normal ritual remains comparatively ignored. Berne (1964) sees much of ordinary human living as overly ritualistic, but his viewpoint is somewhat cynical (though often realistic), and he ignores the deeper rituals that bind men together. Why do people keep going to movies and watching television programs that are cast in the same mold, that follow the same pattern? Why do people read certain genres of literature such as spy, detective, and love stories? At least part of this behavior seems to be ritualistic, a search for sameness. Ritual, whether it centers on the deepest core of human living or on its more superficial aspects, connotes security, control, rhythm of living, a sense of well-being from knowing what is going to happen, a kind of securely encompassing knowledge. Ritual excludes the intrusive and the unexpected.

Ritual taps something deeper in man than does convention. The latter refers to the more superficial aspects, and even to the more humorous aspects, of what is done and what is not done in social intercourse. For instance, it is said that Mrs. Vanderbilt once asked Fritz Kreisler to play at a dinner party that she was giving for her exclusive set of friends. She asked him what he would charge. The violinist replied: "Thirteen thousand dollars." She agreed, but added: "Of course, you will not mingle with my guests." "In that case, Madame," Kreisler is said to have replied, "my fee is five hundred dollars." Day-to-day living is filled with conventions. The conventions of society usually call for a certain degree of conformity, and men readily respond. Technological societies are particularly demanding. Keniston (1965) suggests that, since so many of the positions offered by the corporations and organizations of our society demand on-the-job training, the primary value of a diploma and a degree is to give witness to the fact that one has been able to endure sixteen years of education. This is the proof that a technocracy requires to be assured that a prospective employee will become an obedient cog in an efficient organizational machine.

Allport (1962) suggests that the concept of social influence, as usually understood, does not explain the phenomenon of conformity noted in groups. The group is rather a theater of operations for the satisfaction of individual needs, a medium of self-expression. Norms arise from a kind of cyclic action within the group, rather than from the group acting upon the individual. The group is constituted by behaviors of seeking and recognition. The relationship, then, between the conduct prescribed by group norms and the cooperative activities of the group members is close and facilitating. The forces that Allport sees as operative in a group, then, seem to arise from a kind of benign, security-motivated utilitarianism.

Collins and Guetzkow (1964) see both advantages and disadvantages in the conformity behavior noted in groups. In general, "the social weighting given to the majority opinion (i.e., conformity) frequently causes the better alternatives to be chosen [p. 41]." But there are circumstances under which social influence is more likely to lower the quality of a group product:

(1) An expert may continue to receive the respect of an authority even though the topic is outside his own area of specialization. (2) A group member may conform merely for social approval. (3) Conformity and agreement can set in so soon that all opinions are not considered. (4) Finally, group members can become so much in the habit of depending on other persons for knowledge and information that they cannot make contributions on their own.

Useful as social knowledge may be, it must be used intelligently. It may be that we place too much emphasis on getting along with others and not enough on the content of communication in our culture [pp. 41–42].

In general, Collins and Guetzkow take a more moderate approach to the question of the "pressure to conform" in our society than does someone like Whyte (1956) in *The Organization Man.*

Ritual and convention do have a place in human living, and in this sense a certain degree of conformity or utilitarian patterning of behaviors is part of the social cement that binds men together. To reject ritual in personal and interpersonal living and to defy convention as conformism would obviously have a devastating effect on both the individual and society. To the extent that ritual and convention are necessary for the relationships between the individual and society, they belong to the sphere of contract obligations. However, ritual can become outmoded, and convention can prove stifling. Pharisaical or conventional guilt is the guilt that arises from violation of standards of ritual and convention that have lost their function. Personal growth and necessary change within society demand the ability to go beyond ritual and convention. Both the individual and society should feel free to experiment with bypassing certain conventions. The overritualized and the overconventionalized balk at this for such pruning and experimentation make them feel guilty. The flexible person knows when ritual and convention may and should be set aside. He feels not guilty, but free.

The training laboratory is a place where one might well explore his relationship to ritual and convention. Mutually shared self-revelation in this area has the potential to free the rigid and inhibited and to confront the insensitive.

An Example Illustrating the Four Species of Guilt

Perhaps an example in the area of sexuality might draw together some of the principal notions concerning guilt. (1) An outright misuse of sex such as adultery is a contract violation and leads to moral guilt. (2) If a couple have failed to integrate sexuality into their married life so that it becomes a means of deepening their love for one another—at once a symbol of their love and an expression of it—this can lead to a sense of failed potentiality and existential guilt. (3) Repressing one's sexuality, learning to fear this drive as dangerous or dirty, may well lead to pseudo-guilt. (4) If a married couple were to eschew perfectly acceptable forms of experimentation with sexual technique in order to remain within the bounds of what they perceive to be a conventional approach to sexual expression, they would most likely do so in order to avoid pharisaical or conventional guilt.

A Summary Word
on Guilt

The topic of guilt is not a popular one. It makes too many people wince inside. It is unpopular enough to make some scoff when even an attempt is made to deal with it in some kind of scientific context. But guilt is part of the human condition; it is unavoidable in human living. It is a two-edged sword. If mismanaged or not managed at all, it tends to become psychological deadweight; if faced and handled, it can become an important growth factor. Concealment of guilt from self and others, which initially appears to be the least painful, if not the only, solution, eventually exacts its price in terms of human growth. Self-revelation, on the other hand, is almost always initially painful. But once guilt is hidden from oneself and from others, it is liable to psychological translation or transformation. A sense of failure, for instance, becomes fatigue, boredom, depression, or touchiness in interpersonal relationships. It is the assumption here that a certain degree of self-revelation in a contract group can open up new perspectives with respect to the effective handling of guilt, whether the guilt be moral, existential, pharisaical, or even pseudo- or neurotic. These different types of guilt are usually not found in the pure state. They are intermingled and confused in the ordinary man's life, and only when a man dares let others see his life for what it is is there hope that the complexities of guilt may not make him less than he really is.

Shame and
Self-Disclosure

Even though Talland and Clark (1964) treated "shame and guilt" as a single topic in their study, there are reasons for separating the two here. Erikson (1963, 1968) rightly calls shame an "emotion insufficiently studied [1968, p. 110]." While it is true that the discussion of failures that have led to guilt may evoke shame, the experience of guilt and the experience of shame are simply not the same thing. Shame experiences can arise completely outside the context of guilt. Just as guilt experiences, if mishandled, can become psychological deadweight and stand in the way of growth or, if well managed, can have an opposite effect, so shame, too, can be either a destructive experience or a stimulus to growth. It, too, is intimately related to self-disclosure, but in a way different from guilt.

Erikson on Shame. Erikson (1963, 1968) deals with shame briefly in considering the various stages of man. The crisis of "autonomy versus shame" comes early in the life of the child. The child suddenly wants to have a choice. This tendency must be encouraged, and yet he must be protected from anarchy; he must be trained to "hold on" and "let go" with discretion. He must be encouraged to stand on his own two feet, and also be protected from meaningless experiences of shame and doubt. Shame, as Erikson sees it, implies that a person is completely exposed, conscious of being looked at, self-conscious, visible—yet not ready to be visible. The person who is ashamed would like to avert the eyes of those looking at him, but he cannot, and so he turns his rage in upon himself. Erikson, therefore, spells out the dangers inherent in shaming. If a person is shamed too much, the shaming leads to his trying to get away with things without being seen. If a child or an adult is constantly forced to consider self, body, and wishes as dirty and evil, he will either revolt—sometimes even to the point of defiant shamelessness—or he will succumb to a lasting sense of shame and doubt. Erikson believes that many adults, otherwise mature and free of neurotic symptoms, display this sensitivity, or perhaps oversensitivity, to a possible shameful loss of face.

Shame, then, is a powerful emotion and must be evoked with some caution. Shame in a group experience is even more powerful. I have participated in group experiences in which shame was evoked recklessly, causing a great deal of pain but very little healing. Evoking shame without providing adequate human support may be as dangerous and destructive of growth in adult life as it is in childhood. As Fromm (1956) notes, shame involves a deep awareness of human separation, and without reunion by love, shame is sterile. Erikson's cautions, then, are well taken. But this does not mean that shame experiences are merely negative; they can be a powerful force for growth.

Lynd on Shame. Lynd (1958) has written a most remarkable analysis of shame and its relationship to identity. The root meaning of the word is to uncover, to expose, to wound. But shame is not just being painfully exposed to another; it is primarily an exposure of self to oneself. In shame experiences, particularly sensitive and vulnerable aspects of the self are exposed, especially to one's own eyes. It is a sudden experience. In a flash one sees his unrecognized inadequacies without being ready for this revelation of self to self; much less is he ready for exposure to the eyes of others.

Shame, according to Lynd, in some way antedates the specific shaming event:

> ... I think that this public exposure of even a very private part of one's physical or mental character could not in itself have brought about shame unless one had already felt within oneself, not only dislike, but shame for these traits [p. 29].

The feeling of unexpectedness marks one of the central contrasts between shame and guilt. This unexpectedness is more than suddenness in time; it is also an astonishment at seeing different parts of ourselves, conscious and unconscious, acknowledged and unacknowledged, suddenly coming together, and coming together with aspects of the world we have not recognized [p. 34].

The external event, then, that precipitates a shame experience might be quite trivial. A casual remark or a joke might trigger a profound feeling of shame in another, while the person who made the remark often remains oblivious to what is happening inside the person who was the object of his remark. But shame could not arise, could not be touched off by "insignificant" incidents unless, deep down, one was already ashamed.

The Difference between Shame and Guilt. Shame and guilt differ. Alexander (1963) believes that shame generates feelings of weakness or inadequacy, while guilt gives rise to an "I am no good" or perhaps rather an "I am not good" feeling. He contends that inferiority feelings in shame are rooted in a deeper conflict in the personality than the sense of wrongdoing in guilt. Piers and Singer (1953) believe that guilt accompanies transgression, while shame follows upon failure. So guilt is generated whenever a boundary is transgressed or a standard is violated, while shame occurs when a goal is not being reached. Shame thus indicates a real shortcoming. Lynd (1958) says that shame lacks the inherent legal reference of guilt. It is not a question of failing to pay a debt or of violating a prescribed code. Rather, shame is much more intimately associated with failed potentiality and, as such, related to existential rather than moral guilt: "... The Ego-Ideal is in continuous inter-function with the unconscious and conscious awareness of the Ego's potentialities. . . . Shame . . . occurs whenever goals and images presented by the Ego-Ideal are not reached [Piers and Singer, 1953, pp. 14, 16]." Because shame represents a failure to be, it gets into one's guts in a way that differs from guilt: "It is pervasive as anxiety is pervasive; its focus is not a separate act, but revelation of the whole self. The thing that has been exposed is what I am [Lynd, 1958, p. 50]."

A shame experience might even be defined as an acute emotional awareness of a failure *to be* in some way. It differs from existential guilt in that it is an *acute emotional* experience and in that it is not just a realization of failed potentiality but a painful awareness of what one *is* not. For instance, one can be ashamed of one's own body (it lacks grace, beauty; it has grown old; it is crippled, deformed, etc.), but one's physical makeup is hardly a source of existential guilt.

As Lynd well notes, both shame and guilt might arise from the same situation: ". . . Shame and guilt may sometimes alternate with and reinforce each other . . . a particular situation may be experienced by an individual as shame or guilt or both according to the nature of the person. . . . [pp. 22–23]." The act of committing a murder may be experienced both as a violation of a standard and as a deep personal failure. It is an act that may suddenly reveal to a person his deepest personal inadequacies and his most tragic interpersonal failures. Less dramatic acts may do the same. A burst of uncontrolled anger may be experienced as some kind of contract failure, but it might also be a source of deep shame insofar as it reveals a person to himself and forces him to gaze at the nakedness of his own inadequacy. Both failures to be and overstepped boundaries are potentially destructive to personality integration. When these two strains meet in the same human experience, the danger is heightened markedly.

When an acute shame experience strikes, there is no defense. It rinses one's being. But few recognize the fact that such an experience has potentialities for growth. The icy clarity of self-knowledge that is part and parcel of the shame experience is usually too painful. One has to escape and forget. The wound is allowed to heal, and any situation that might possibly reopen the wound is quietly avoided. However, this not only constricts one's life space, but it makes one vulnerable to further shame experiences: "Not knowing what should be done with shame, one's first impulse is to conceal it, and this may produce further shame [Lynd, 1958, p. 32]." Yet, it is not easy to get at the source of shame, for this involves the demanding process of examining or re-examining one's "assumptive world" (Frank, 1961): "Part of the difficulty in admitting shame to oneself arises from reluctance to recognize that one has built on false assumptions about what the world one lives in is and about the way others will respond to oneself [Lynd, 1958, p. 43]." But, as with guilt, concealment is no answer: "Protection against isolation and the difficulty of communicating such experiences as shame may take the form of impersonalization and dehumanization. . . . I will deny the possibility of openness; I will protect myself against it [Lynd, 1958, p. 70]."

Erikson (1963, 1968) emphasizes the dangers in shame, or perhaps rather in shaming and being shamed, while Lynd (1958) emphasizes the potential value of dealing with shame through self-disclosure:

If, however, one can sufficiently risk uncovering oneself and sufficiently trust another person to seek means of communicating shame, the risking of exposure can be in itself an experience of release, expansion, self-revelation, a coming forward of belief in oneself, and entering into the mind and feeling of another person [p. 249].

If, as Fromm (1956) says, shame is a feeling of separateness without reunion by love, then self-disclosure can be the beginning of this reunion. And just as a refusal to deal with the roots of shame can lead to personality constriction, so faced or transcended shame can enhance personal identity:

Shame interrupts any unquestioning, unaware sense of oneself. But it is possible that experiences of shame if confronted full in the face may throw an unexpected light on who one is and point the way toward who one may become. Fully faced, shame may become not primarily something to be covered, but a positive experience of revelation [Lynd, 1958, p. 20].

Experiences of shame are a painful uncovering of hitherto unrecognized aspects of one's personality as well as of unrecognized aspects of one's society and of the world. If it is possible to face them, instead of seeking protection from what they reveal, they may throw light on who one is, and hence point the way toward who and what one may become [p. 183].

Shame, then, is a way of discovery.

Shame, Revelation of both Self and Society. Lynd refers to "unrecognized aspects of one's society and of the world." She says that some of the most acute shame experiences arise when one is ashamed of the "failure to be" of those closely related to oneself. Identification with significant others seems to be the mechanism that mediates such shame. If, then, a person is identified with the society that surrounds him, he can feel deep shame for this society when its "failures to be" are recognized. A young man came to me once for counseling. He had been playing basketball; a game was organized with "skins" against "shirts," and he had been asked to remove his T-shirt. When he manifested some reluctance to do so, one of the other players remarked that he was reluctant because he had a scrawny build. Even though his antagonist and the other players did not realize it, he was flooded with shame. The incident was trivial, but in an instant he realized with painful clarity that he was ashamed of his body. In the counseling session it came out that his shame went further than that. He also realized that he lived in a society that excessively extols physical grace, charm, or beauty, often to the extent that it becomes a condition for acceptance. He realized that he had more or less concurred with society in this attitude, so that he was ashamed of himself for having been so ashamed of his body and he was ashamed of his society for its hierarchy of values. Now he wanted to talk about his feelings about his own body and the way that he swallowed whole the values of society. His shame could have led to either constriction or growth. He chose to have it lead to growth.

A Summary Note on Shame. An attempt has been made to indicate the growth potentialities of facing shame. This means not only discussing the sources of shame within oneself but also facing the actual shame experiences that often arise both from the disclosure of guilt and shame and from other kinds of disclosure made in the group. This does not mean that, in some pollyannish fashion, self-disclosure and facing guilt and shame will constitute a panacea for the ills of the human condition. Sharing shame, for instance, does not mean that it will be dissipated: "It is also true that if one discovered that one was not alone in having these traits, shame would in one sense be alleviated by being shared; but if one still felt these characteristics as mean and ugly no matter how many people had them, shame would in another sense be extended [Lynd, 1958, p. 29]." This points up the fact that mutual self-disclosure is not designed just to relieve anxiety. It is designed to put people in more effective contact with what is. It is true that often a person needs a good deal of support in order to face what is, but such support is far more conducive to growth than giving support to another in order that he may endure the more or less self-inflicted agonies that arise from *not* facing what is.

Risk and Trust. Most people hesitate to disclose themselves to a group. They balance on the edge of self-disclosure as they would on the edge of a diving board. But just as the shock and pain of entering the water are short-lived and certainly outweighed by the pleasure of swimming, so the shock and pain associated with self-disclosure are mainly initial and short-lived and inevitably outweighed by the benefits of mutual sharing. Refusing to "enter the water" in the group because the shock and pain of self-revelation are seen as protracted is a defensive maneuver, a kind of psychological metonymy. Still the pain of self-disclosure and the possibility of rejection lurk around the corner, so group members bide their time.

Behind the feeling of shame stands not the fear of hatred, but the fear of contempt which . . . spells fear of abandonment . . . the deeper rooted shame anxiety is based on the fear of the parent who walks away "in disgust," and . . . this anxiety in turn draws its terror from the earlier established and probably ubiquital separation anxiety [Piers & Singer, 1953, pp. 11, 16].

Risk is an essential feature of growth groups. But before one takes this risk he asks himself searching questions: "Can one have faith that with certain other persons greater openness can increase understanding, respect, love? That with them increasing intimacy can be, not a corroding, but a deepening and enriching process? [Lynd, 1958, pp. 238–239]." Perhaps the "nothing ventured, nothing gained" truism has a special applicability to communication in growth groups:

Confronting, instead of quickly covering, an experience of shame as revelation of oneself and of society—facing "actual life"—requires an ability to risk, if necessary to endure, disappointment, frustration, and ridicule. . . . Engagement with life and with history—self-discovery and further discovery of the world—has always involved such risks [Lynd, p. 232].

Still, even initial risk demands a climate of trust. But to demand trust from others, one must first show that he himself is trustworthy.

And one of the principal ways of doing this is by risking self-revelation. Mowrer (1966d, 1968b) solves this "chicken-and-egg" dilemma by having the participants of his integrity groups contract, before even meeting the other members of the group, to engage in absolute self-disclosure. Very often this works. The initial interviewer usually models for the prospective group member and shows that at least he is trustworthy. But, since there is no such initial commitment in the contract group, the problem of mutual trust must be worked out. Perhaps the notion of "kairos"—the "right moment"—has some value in the contract group. The participants all contract to engage in self-disclosure, but each puts himself on the line at the moment that is right for him. Obviously such a concept could be used to rationalize away complete failure to fulfill the self-disclosure provision of the contract, but this need not detract from its possible utility. The problem of trust will be taken up more thoroughly in the chapter on support.

Shame and Fantasy. Daydreaming is a little-discussed activity. Full-length studies on daydreaming are few and literally far between (Green, 1923; Singer, 1966; Varendonck, 1921). Daydreaming or directed fantasy (rather than just letting the mind wander) is considered an adolescent activity that is outgrown with the responsibilities of adulthood. In adulthood, fantasy is encouraged if it is creative, if it is a source of growth rather than a substitute for it. If not encouraged, it is at least countenanced when it is used sparingly—with respect to both quantity and quality—to take the edge off a depressing day or a dreary life situation. In this sense, Singer (1966) calls daydreaming or directed fantasy "a neutral skill available for adaptive enrichment of the life of otherwise ordinary persons [p. 187]." But this is not the place to review theoretical considerations and empirical findings concerning daydreaming. Singer's work is both adequate and interesting.

The point here is that many men engage in some kind of fantasy in varying degrees. Only to the degree that this fantasy distorts what is and what should be (contract standards) of life in a noncreative way does it become a problem. The revelation of such fantasy can be the source of intense shame, but it can also get at some of the deepest roots of unfaced failure in a person's life. For instance, if a man, when he is having sexual relations with his wife, imagines that he is with someone else, either real or imaginary, then it seems that he has failed to integrate sexual experience with love. If he reveals his fantasy, he might feel deeply ashamed, but the revelation seems essential to his getting to the source of his inter-personal failure. Examination of fantasy, then, while often painful and productive of shame, can, at least for some, be an important factor in a growth experience.

Other Approaches to Self-Disclosure in the Training Group

Areas of guilt and shame, as important as they might be, are by no means the only topics for self-disclosure. Perhaps they may even be more accurately considered as dimensions that are sometimes in-volved in the process of self-disclosure. If a person talks about what is in his life, he will inevitably talk about areas of living that are touched or even suffused with guilt or shame. The preceding discussion indicates the importance of not avoiding discussion of an area of living because of the guilt or shame associated with it. But some other approaches to self-disclosure might be indicated here:

Values. In talking about themselves, people often shy away from two most important areas, the "best in me" and the "worst in me." The "worst in me" is the area of shame and guilt and has al-ready been discussed. But people also avoid talking about the good they do, the values they hold, the aspirations they have. In fact, when given a choice—that is, when asked simply to engage in some form of self-disclosure—most people immediately think of areas of shame and guilt. Perhaps one of the principal reasons that the area of values and aspirations is overlooked is that the good men do is often not unadulterated good. We have goals, but we fall short of them; we have values, but there are times when we ignore these values; we do good, but the good we do is not pure, unmixed, stain-less, without blemish. Thus, it is very difficult to talk about the "best in me" without also talking about the "worst in me."

It is also dangerous to talk about values in a group, because one soon discovers that it is impossible, even intolerable, to do so with-out arousing oneself from one's value lethargy and doing something about it. Uncommunicated values remain uncertain, ambiguous, in-operative in life; communicated values place demands on the com-municator. Just as self-disclosure concerning the guilt-shame dimen-sions of life demands "conversion," so self-disclosure in the area of values demands action. Some find the price of such self-disclosure too high. Finally, a person is sometimes loath to communicate his values because he lacks the courage of his convictions; he is afraid that his values will appear too naive or outmoded to others. He is afraid to say "I believe" to a world that has lost faith even with itself. He is afraid to admit values that seem inconsonant with a materialistic world. On the other hand, there may be childish elements in the values he holds. In that case, subjecting one's values to the scrutiny of a community will entail a process of purification and refinement. This, too, can be demanding and painful.

Contract System. Talking about contract failures (moral guilt) presupposes a contract system. A group experience can be an excellent opportunity for its participants to examine the expressed and implied contracts that provide the guidelines for interpersonal living. For instance, a college student living at home and commuting to school might examine some of the contractual relationships that exist between him and his parents. Is there, for example, a contract of mutual noninterference or mutual noninvolvement? Is the contract a utilitarian one: "I'll obey your rules since you are paying for my education, even though I see these rules as your way of keeping me an adolescent"? Contracts, of course, can be much more positive and open-ended. An example of such a positive, though in this case unilateral, contract might be: "I contract myself to show concern for my parents, to be open with them, even though they do not reciprocate."

How I Stand in the Group. The kind of self-disclosure that is absolutely essential to the life of the group is the revelation of what is happening inside each member with respect to the process of the group. If a participant is afraid to disclose himself, he should at least disclose that. If he is bored because what is happening in the group is actually flight from real group process, he should say so. Very often, when a member who has been silent for a long time is confronted about his silence, he will say: "I've been quiet because nothing has been going on. What you have been doing is very boring." Actually, he has been violating the expressed or implied contract of the group, which demands that he take the initiative and present his views about what is happening *when* it is happening. If group process is boring, then his silence is part of that boredom and not, as he might view it, a legitimate commentary on it.

The modality of self-disclosure, properly used, is one of the most effective ways of handling the hidden variables in the group. A person who is honest about himself and his feelings in the group does much to minimize the effect of the underground group culture—that complexus of tacit understandings that often leads to group stagnation—that was discussed in the chapter on leadership. High visibility is an essential part of this experiment in interpersonal growth. Self-disclosure with respect to the here and now adds a dimension of control to the experiment that is often lacking in other kinds of growth experiences.

In day-to-day living we seldom take the time to clear up communication problems that disrupt our interpersonal living. For instance, research has shown that there is a powerful tendency to assume that one's positive or negative feelings toward another are reciprocated (Newcomb, 1956, 1958, 1960; Tagiuri, 1958; Tagiuri, Blake, & Bruner, 1953; Tagiuri, Bruner, & Blake, 1958), and people tend to act on such assumptions, whether they are true or not. Since the training group is an experimental situation, the participants have cultural permission to find out where they stand in relation to one another. If the group culture supports a healthy feedback system, communication channels remain open and the participants can relate to one another realistically.

In a human relations laboratory that I attended, the trainer of one group called an extra session. He told the participants that a good deal was happening between different members of the group, both in and outside group sessions, that was not being discussed and that this failure in openness was suffocating group process. For several hours they discussed hitherto undisclosed love relationships and animosities and the way that the members had been pairing, with members of either this group or other groups, and working out binds and hang-ups outside the group. The trainer's demand for intragroup honesty seemed to work. The siphoning process stopped and the group was reborn. In the laboratory group, the members should demand this kind of intragroup honesty of themselves; this is the responsibility of the group and not just the leader-member.

"Processing" as a Way of Keeping the Group Honest. Once in a while a group should stop and "process" what it is doing. For instance, after the group has been discussing for a while, the leader-member (this is one of his legitimate functions, especially in the beginning sessions of the group) might interrupt the discussion and ask: "All right, what have we been doing here? What's going on; what's been happening?" The response is usually refreshing. The

group stands outside itself, as its own critic. A newfound freedom of speech, a freedom that belongs to the legitimate critic, often springs up in the group during these processing sessions and stands in vivid contrast to the hedging and fencing that was going on before.

The "fish-bowl" technique may also be used as a processing device. In this case, the group splits in two—either in a random fashion or perhaps into the quiet members and the talkative members —and half engage in discussion in an inner circle while the other half listen in an outer circle. After a predetermined length of time, the discussion is halted and, while the members of the inner circle remain silent, the members of the outer circle process the discussion. This processing usually focuses, not so much on the content of the discussion, but on process variables: was the group open and honest? were there any tacit understandings that subverted the discussion? did the members engage in contract behavior? who failed to engage in contract behavior and how? what N-interactions obstructed contract behavior? These and similar questions deal with process behavior.

The Mode or Quality of Self-Disclosure: "Story" versus "History"

The *way* in which a person reveals himself in the group is very important. In a sense it is even more important than the content of the revelation, for content, no matter how intimate in itself, can lose its intimacy and its meaning in the telling. I propose two styles or modes of self-disclosure: "history," the mode of noninvolvement, and "story," the mode of involvement.

History. A recent television documentary showed excerpts from a marathon group experience conducted at Daytop Village, a rehabilitation center for addicts. During the early hours of the marathon a young addict began talking about himself and his past life. His self-revelation was almost totally history. I was disturbed to think that what he was doing was considered acceptable group process; that is, I was disturbed until one of the group leaders finally spoke up and confronted the speaker. In effect he said: "You have been engaging in history rather than story, and mere history in this group experience is meaningless."

History is pseudo-self-disclosure. It is actuarial and analytic, and usually has a strong "there and then" flavor. It clicks off the facts of experience and even interpretations of this experience but leaves the person of the revealer relatively untouched; he is accounted for and analyzed, but unrevealed. The person relates many facts about himself, but the person within still remains unknown. History is often a long account. It is long and often steady because it fears interruption. Interruption might mean involvement, and a person engages in history to avoid, rather than invite, involvement. History has a way of saying "Be quiet" or "Don't interrupt," but these are dodges to keep others at bay. The steady clicking off of facts keeps the group focused on the revealer, but does not allow the members to deal with him.

In history the manner of self-revelation is usually somewhat detached. There is little ego-involvement and thus little risk. The speaker deals with himself as object rather than as subject. Intimate life details might be revealed, but their intimacy has no particular meaning. They are just more facts. On the other hand, history might be a concatenation of generalities—generalities poorly disguised by the first-person pronoun. But whether history consists of intimate details or generalities, the message is always the same: "Keep your distance." It is as if the revealer were trying to intimate to others that he is rather invulnerable: "This is not really affecting me; I don't see why it should affect you." Sometimes sheer quantity of intimate information about self is divulged because the historian implicitly realizes that if he relates enough, quickly enough, the others will not be able to react effectively to any particular part of it. History is also self-centered. The leader in the Daytop Village marathon took the young addict to task for his egocentricity. He told him that he had been talking a long time and had not even mentioned that he had a wife who had feelings.

Historical information does not unite speaker and listeners. Rather, the information sits there as an obstacle between them. It is a barrier rather than a bridge. It sometimes even has an "I dare you to do anything about this" aura. Even when the information disclosed is intimate, it is usually boring. The historian exudes an "I don't really care" attitude that is readily picked up by the other members of the group. The information *is* boring, because it is divorced from the person. It is flat, there is no human drama about it. To use Matson and Montagu's (1967) paradigm, history is "computorial," and, as such, calls for feedback rather than human response. Or in McLuhan's (1964) terms, history is a "hot" modality, high in definition and low in involvement. Its high definition refs not just to sheer quantity, but to its "there it all is and there is really nothing to be done about it" quality.

Story. Story lies at the other end of the continuum. It is authentic self-disclosure, for it is an attempt to reveal the person within, and more than that: it is an attempt to get him involved with his listeners. Story is an invitation for others to come in; it is an opening of the door. In group growth experiences, as in the rest of life, others often stand around waiting to come in. Story is a signal for others to move into one's presence.

Story is not actuarial; it is rather selective in detail, for the revealer intuits that it is not the transmission of fact that is important but the transmission of self. It does not avoid detail, but the choice of detail is secondary to the act of communication. Story usually avoids interpretation, too; it allows experience to remain unintellectualized and thus speak for itself. The storyteller, even if he leaves out detail, is graphic and specific; he does not hide behind generalities disguised by the first-person pronoun. Facts are selected for their impact value, for their ability to reveal the person as what he is now through what he has experienced.

The storyteller is taking a risk and he knows it. Therefore, story is always an implicit request for human support. The revealer has come to trust the group to a certain degree, but he still feels his vulnerability; his act of self-revelation is akin to Kierkegaard's "leap of faith," which is always a leap of trust. But he takes this leap because he wants to relate to the other members of the group and relate more fully to himself. He realizes that story is the way of involvement and the way of discovery, and he wants both. And so he comes to the point. He does not wander around in the there and then, but manages to make the past, the "there," and even the future define him as he is in the here and now. Story, then, is not analytical and discrete. It is synthetic; it attempts to present a totality, the complex totality that is the person himself, who takes shape out of the complexity of his experience.

The one who tells his story, in that story is not computorial and therefore not a request for feedback in a dehumanized sense, is looking for human response. Story, of its very nature, is dialogue and merits such response. Because story is not computorial and monologic, it is inevitably engaging, even when someone who is usually a bore adopts it. Some people are constantly talking about themselves, and most men find this terribly boring. Such people are boring because they are usually engaging in history rather than story. First of all, they are really saying nothing about themselves, and second, they care little for the objects of their monologue and would find real response, such as self-disclosure and confrontation, frightening. Bores speak in generalities poorly disguised under the pronoun "I." But story, on the other hand, is always engaging, for it means that the speaker has to blow his cover, drop his defenses, and stand somewhat naked in his own eyes and in the eyes of others. Men are seldom, if ever, bored with a sincere confession, because they intuitively realize its importance for the one revealing himself and respect him for what he is doing. The person who engages in story is one who stops complaining about how much he *hurts* and begins admitting who he *is*. This is most refreshing in human affairs. I think perhaps that it might be impossible to dislike someone who engages in story, for it is an act of humility, a manifestation of a need to move into community, and a surrender of egocentricity (or at least a beginning of surrender).

In McLuhan's terminology, story is a "cool" modality, low in definition and high in involvement. It is low in definition not just because it is selective of detail and thus allows others to fill in the gaps in information, but because the information transmitted is seen as a medium, a bridge instead of a barrier. Story has high impact value; it tends to change both speaker and listener. It draws the listener out of himself and toward the speaker; it changes the speaker in that it calls forth emotions that are authentic and therefore perhaps unfamiliar to the revealer. Story, then, is not maudlin, but it is shot through with emotion; it is not sensational, but it has drama in the same way that a life fully lived has drama.

The kind of self-disclosure wanted in the contract group is that in which a person *gives testimony* about himself, gives witness to his own mysteriousness, both the mystery of goodness and the mystery of evil that he is. When a person gives testimony, he asks others to trust him and he binds himself to telling the truth. Testimony, then, engages not only the mind but the will; it involves love. Testimony is involving: it involves the witness because he binds himself to his listeners, and it involves the listeners because it demands that they believe. Men have access to a person's innermost being only through testimony, and persons give testimony about themselves only under the influence of love (see Latourelle, 1962).

History and Story in the Training Group. It may be useful to imagine history and story as opposite ends of a continuum. The members of the interpersonal-growth group contract to engage in story; that is, story is a goal toward which the participants are working. In the same way, the elimination of the modality history is also a goal. History is thus an object of confrontation in the group.

Levels of
Self-Disclosure

Different kinds of face-to-face groups could be placed in a rough order according to the degree or level of self-disclosure that takes place in the context of the group meeting. From least self-revealing to most, the order might read something like this:

1. "Business" meetings—for example, managerial meetings, faculty and teachers' meetings, community council meetings.
2. Discussion groups—for example, formal or informal academic or seminar-type groups, discussion clubs.
3. Groups investigating the phenomenon of group dynamics—for example, academic groups that learn about group dynamics by being a group, unstructured groups that come together to see what human value there might be in coming together.
4. Sensitivity-training groups—for example, human-relations laboratories, personal-growth laboratories.
5. Psychotherapy groups.
6. Integrity-training groups (Mowrer, 1968b).

This does not mean that no self-disclosure takes place during a business meeting. For instance, if the members of a managerial-training group have gone through a sensitivity-training laboratory, they may work out their feelings toward one another before tackling an important managerial decision. Also, the above order is not rigid. For instance, a great deal of intimate self-disclosure might take place during a laboratory course in group dynamics, depending on the kind of group culture that develops. A particular sensitivity-training group, too, might engage in a degree of self-disclosure usually found in psychotherapy or integrity groups. The position of the contract group in the list will vary according to the nature of the contract. The contract explicated here would probably place the contract group between sensitivity-training and psychotherapy groups. We have been speaking of groups in general. However, *within* groups a good deal of individual differences with respect to self-disclosure will be manifested by the participants.

The contract group differs from the other groups (and is like the integrity group) in that self-disclosure is explicitly established as a group value. However, unlike the situation in the integrity group, the level of self-disclosure is not determined by contract. In the integrity group, the prospective participant must agree to disclose all his past contract failures and to do so sometime during the early part of the group experience. He also contracts to remain confessionally current throughout the rest of the experience. Therefore, the integrity group establishes a certain level of self-disclosure at least in one area, the area of contract failure.

The term "level" is difficult to define operationally. It seems to be an operational term in the integrity group, for there it means all those actions that the trainee believes to have been contract failures in his life. Since the scope of self-disclosure is wider in the contract group, "level" is not as easy to define. Still, group members have a kind of instinctive awareness of different levels of self-disclosure. To move to a deeper level of self-disclosure means to reveal that which is more painful to reveal, that which one is more reluctant to reveal. The deeper one goes, the closer one gets to his core, to the person within, to the person he really is. Deep self-disclosure gets at a person's identity. It gets at the repressed, the unrecognized, the ignored, the unseen, the unannounced in a person; it gets at the best in a person and the worst in him. The deeper the self-disclosure, the more it reveals the mystery of one's person. "Level," then, is not a certain set of statements about a certain area of living. What A discusses freely might be a most painful area for B; the same area of discussion represents different levels for them. "I am bored with this group" is often an honest statement that reveals something about the person who so speaks his mind. But, "My mother is an alcoholic and I find it difficult to be with her" would usually be a more painful kind of revelation, tapping areas of guilt and shame, and therefore getting closer to the core of the revealer. "I get deep satisfaction from being a Christian" or "I have deep religious convictions, but I have always been afraid to share them with anyone because I don't always live up to them" are statements about values that might tap even deeper levels in some persons.

This more or less metaphorical approach to the concept of level is quite obviously not entirely satisfactory, but perhaps it is sufficient for the purpose intended here. A more clinical and empirical approach to the concept of level is discussed by Truax and Carkhuff (1967) in terms of a self-exploration scale ranging from no self-exploration to a very high degree of self-exploration. In the first stage, no personally relevant material is communicated by the client, nor does he respond to attempts on the part of the therapist to reveal himself. In stage two, the therapist must coax material from the client, while in stage three, the client may actually make brief comments on material introduced by the therapist. In stage four, the client discusses personally relevant material, but in a mechanical fashion: he does not own what he is talking about. Spontaneous discussions and reactions on the part of the client begin with stage five. In stage six, the client reacts spontaneously and with feeling, while in stage seven, he makes tentative gestures toward discovering new material. Active interpersonal exploration is characteristic of stage eight, and stage nine is a highly developed phase of stage eight. The contract more or less demands that the participant begin at least with stage five, though many participants regress, at one time or another, to a lower stage. In a certain sense, the scale defines the manner of self-exploration but does not define content areas.

The members of the contract group and of training groups in general contract to engage in self-disclosure, but not any particular level of self-disclosure. The group has to work through the problem of the level of self-disclosure and, in this respect, the variability among groups can be great. The level of disclosure in the group will depend on a number of factors: the courage of individual members, the atmosphere of support and trust developed by the group, the ability of individual members to see the value of self-disclosure for themselves, and the spirit of cooperation in the group. It is assumed that the level of disclosure in the group will gradually deepen. The process will not be an even one: members will retreat during crises of trust; there will be plateaus of apparent stagnation and indifference when members are feeling their way; there will be sudden surges of honesty and intimacy, which most members will find deeply rewarding. The contract serves as a means of keeping the group under a certain degree of pressure with respect to self-revelation. If the level of self-disclosure in the group will usually not go beyond the limits set by the atmosphere of trust and support that exists in the group, then the contract should exert pressure on the group to create the kind of atmosphere in which disclosure is possible and profitable.

Self-Disclosure at the Service of Behavior Control: "Labeling"

Dollard and Miller (1950) emphasize the greater behavioral effectiveness of articulated over nonarticulated thoughts. As the child grows up, he undergoes a great variety of emotional experiences, but he does not have the ability to verbalize these experiences. Anxiety-ridden emotional experiences retain behavioral consequences that are more or less outside rational control because they have not been subjected to higher mental processes. The lack of verbal responses to drives such as fear, sex, and aggression increases the likelihood of maladaptive behavior or symptoms. Learned verbal cues can prevent the generalization of anxiety from the past to the present. When previously repressed material is verbalized, the result is not uninhibited behavior but rather behavior that is under better social control.

Dollard and Miller deal with labeling in the context of psychotherapy, in which the labeling process refers principally to past experience. But labeling or a similar process, with an orientation toward the future, can be used as a form of behavior control. For instance, the group members may discuss the seeds of irresponsibility or the seeds of failed potentiality within themselves; that is, they label unproductive forms of behavior to which they feel drawn. Usually when a person is tempted to do something that he thinks he should not or to fail to do something that he thinks he should, he tries not to think about it. He puts it out of mind, refuses to submit it to higher mental processes, allows the behavior to take place principally on the level of emotion. The man who knows vaguely (or not so vaguely) that if he goes to this tavern he will get drunk and irresponsibly involved with some of the women there will often put such considerations out of mind. If he does not want to engage in such behavior, he may try to reverse the process. That is, he forces himself to think about what he is tempted to do; he forces himself to label the entire sequence of undesirable behavior prior to initiating the sequence. The assumption here is that if he labels this behavior, submitting it to higher mental processes, he will be in better control of this behavior. And if he does initiate the undesirable behavior sequence, he will do so with increased responsibility (and culpability).

The contention here is that such a process is most effective when carried out in community, whether the community is a natural one (e.g., marriage partner, family) or some conventional group (e.g., a training group). It takes a certain degree of courage to discuss one's temptations to violate one's contracts or one's tendencies to fail to be in various ways, but if one does so, he enlists the resources of the community in his program of behavior control.

Labeling, to be effective, should be specific. "I feel that I won't live up to my expectations during the next semester" is too general and sounds more like a cry of despair than an attempt to control behavior. "If I go home with this chip on my shoulder, I'll have a fight with my wife, go out and get drunk, and end up in a mess" is a much more appropriate example of effective labeling. Since the overriding goal of the contract group is interpersonal growth, labeling of specific temptations to maladaptive interpersonal relating belongs in the group. Effective labeling is a way of transporting the there and then of the future into the here and now of group process in that it reveals seeds of action or inaction that are growing and maturing right here and right now.

Labeling need not be restricted to avoiding unwanted behavior; it can also be used to stimulate desired behavior. The individual rehearses something that he wants to do, noting what he will do when certain difficulties arise, but also noting the rewards associated with the desired behavior. The hypothesis is that the more concrete the labeling process is, dealing with specific behaviors in specific situations, the more effective will it be.

Possible Dangers Associated with Self-Disclosure

Self-disclosure is a powerful behavioral instrument and must be used with discretion. Under certain conditions, self-revelation will be either dangerous or useless.

If It Is Exhibitionism. Self-disclosure may be nothing more than verbal exhibitionism, a verbal exposure of self in an exhibitionism-voyeurism context (see Glatzer, 1967). Exhibitionism is a manifestation of lack of control and a symptom, therefore, of pathology. The exhibitionist is merely using his listeners to satisfy his own distorted needs. He is neither attempting to involve himself responsibly with others nor asking them to respond by involving themselves responsibly with him. The drama of the disclosure assumes a disproportionate significance in exhibitionism; its shock value is often its most important feature. Jourard (1964) believes that either too much or too little self-disclosure is a sign of disturbance. I would tend to think that the context in which it is done and the way in which it is done are more important than its quantity.

If the Person Receives No Support for His Openness. Even in an atmosphere of relative trust, self-disclosure entails risk. If a person puts himself on the line and then fails to receive support, self-disclosure can be quite traumatic. Self-revelation is a way of involving oneself with others. If they fail to respond, this is usually experienced as rejection, no matter what the real or objective state of affairs might be. Sometimes, after engaging in self-disclosure, a person will feel diminished—perhaps the next day or during the week between meetings. This seems to happen when the participant discloses himself in the wrong way (e.g., with a strain of exhibitionism) or when he fails to receive proper support. It is as if he had emptied himself and now there is nothing to fill the vacuum. Support is so essential a variable in growth groups that it will be treated separately (chapter 8).

If a Person Contracts to Engage in Self-Disclosure and Then Reneges. This is usually a case of failed potentiality. It is one of those existential failures that can confirm a person in a negativistic self-image.

If a Person Engages in History Rather than Story. In this case, self-disclosure is useless, for history puts something between the historian and his listeners and cuts off interpersonal involvement, the supposed purpose of the group.

If Self-Disclosure Is Incomplete in a Situation That Calls for Complete Openness. If a participant in Mowrer's integrity group tells only a part of his story of contract failure or refuses to stay confessionally current, then he is more or less living a lie, pursuing a false course of action in the very group that is designed to eliminate such behavior. It is easy to see how this would take its toll in terms of guilt and anxiety.

Self-disclosure is not as dangerous as some make it out to be. It is not a medical act; it is first of all a human act. Nor need it be a sign of immaturity, of adolescent behavior. If done responsibly, it is a continuation of valuable human behavior that often does begin, however imperfectly, during adolescence.

Epilog

The Johari Window. Luft and Ingham (1955) have presented a model of awareness in interpersonal relationships called "The Johari Window" (see Figure 3).

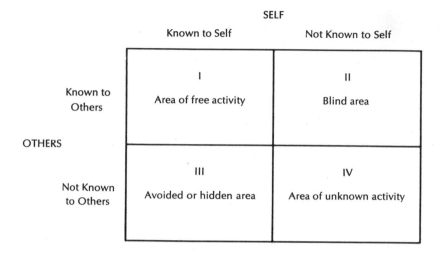

SELF

Known to Self   Not Known to Self

	Known to Self	Not Known to Self
Known to Others	I Area of free activity	II Blind area
Not Known to Others	III Avoided or hidden area	IV Area of unknown activity

OTHERS

Figure 3. The Johari Window.*

I have used this model as a basis for an exercise in a course in abnormal psychology. The figure is put on the board and the quadrants are explained. The class members are then given black three-by-five cards. They are asked to move some bit of information about themselves from Quadrant III to Quadrant I by writing it on the card. The cards are collected and a few minutes are spent eliciting the members' reactions to the exercise. Meanwhile, the person conducting the exercise shuffles the cards so that the exercise can be carried out with complete anonymity. Next he reads all the cards, without comment, one after another. Finally, he elicits the reactions of members of the class to what they have heard.

There is usually a wide variety of responses, from "I have a hole in my sock" to "I am a practicing homosexual" or "I have felt like committing suicide." The modal responses usually deal with alienation, difficulty in human relations, operating under a facade, and identity problems. The effect on class members is often quite striking. Some, for the first time, realize that there are others, many others, who have problems similar to theirs. One student once said: "Things just couldn't be the same in that class any more." The problem is that things *can* be just the same. There is a moment of open-

* Reprinted by permission from *Group Processes: An Introduction to Group Dynamics*, copyright 1963 by Joseph Luft. The Johari concept is further described in *Of Human Interaction* by the same author (Palo Alto, California: National Press Books, 1969).

ness, and its possibilities are seen, often in a dramatic way; then people return to their normal patterns of living. People really dislike being shut off from others, but few want to pay the price of change—venturing out of themselves.

The Value of Self-Disclosure: A New Kind of Communication. Mowrer deals with self-disclosure principally as a way of handling the deleterious effects of mismanaged guilt. However important this might be, it is not the focus of the contract group. Self-disclosure in the contract group is seen as leading to a new kind of communication or at least to a new freedom of communication. Dealing with one another is something like showing one another the houses we live in, houses in which one or more rooms must remain locked because of what is behind the doors. In the contract group, the participants learn the skill of opening some of these doors, and the air that sweeps through the house is refreshing. To use another metaphor, communication that is characterized by a fear of self-disclosure is like trying to talk to someone across a room filled with pillars. In the contract group, the participants learn how to remove some of these pillars, and, to their amazement, the house remains standing. The contract group is a training laboratory in which the participants learn the value of self-disclosure. If they learn well, then they return to the significant others in their lives with the potential for a new kind of communication.

Self-disclosure is not the only value in life, but it is a dimension of the interpersonally fruitful life. Only the individual can determine what part it is to play in his own interpersonal life.

Chapter Eight:
Supportive
Behavior

If a sensitivity-group contract calls for such variables as self-dis-closure in a rather demanding sense (story rather than history) and total human expression in terms of *pathos, logos,* and *poiesis,* then the contract must also provide an atmosphere which will not only sustain, but also actively encourage, such variables. In a word, the contract must provide a climate of *support.* However, the problem is that people's attempts to give solid, non-cliché support—whether these attempts are made in the context of group therapy, sensitivity training, or real life—are often clumsy and ineffective. When faced with the more dramatic dimensions of others such as their pain, their anxieties, their peak and nadir experiences, their strong emotions—positive or negative—their successes and their failures, we fumble around, babble inanities, or take refuge in silence. The contract group, then, is a laboratory in human living in which the participants learn how to react to the more dramatic dimensions of others. In the give and take of the group meetings, they learn to remedy their deficiencies in both giving and receiving support.

The need for a supportive climate in sensitivity-training laboratories is generally recognized:

The second element necessary for assuring effective feedback is what Schein and Bennis (1965) referred to as a climate of "psychological safety" and Bradford et al. (1964) called "permissiveness." That is, no matter what an individual does in a group or what he reveals about himself, the group must act in a supportive and nonevaluative way. Each individual must feel that it is safe to expose his feelings, drop his defenses, and try out new ways of interacting. Such an atmosphere has its obvious counterpart in any constructive clinical or therapeutic relationship [Campbell & Dunnette, 1968, p. 76].

Not only must a climate of psychological safety exist, but it must be communicated to the participants if it is to have any kind of thawing effect on their interpersonal behavior:

People must certainly differ greatly in their ability to accept the guarantee of psychological safety. To the extent that the feeling of safety cannot be achieved—and quickly—the prime basic ingredient for this form of learning is absent. Its importance cannot be overemphasized, nor can the difficulty of its being accomplished [Campbell & Dunnette, 1968, p. 78].

It is not difficult to find support for such suggestions in the literature dealing with interactions in small, face-to-face groups. For instance, a series of studies (Gibb, 1960; Lott, Schopler, & Gibb, 1954, 1955) indicated that feeling-oriented, positive feedback resulted in the greatest efficiency, least defensiveness, and greatest increase in participation in such groups. Supportive behavior, then, is a value in all kinds of sensitivity-training laboratories. Campbell and Dunnette (1968) suggest not only that support is essential but that it must be felt as quickly as possible. The hypothesis here is that the contract will facilitate the speedy establishment of a climate of support.

This chapter has three sections: one on listening, one on giving support, and a short section on receiving support. First of all, the participants must learn how to listen to one another; this is an absolute prerequisite for supportive behavior. But listening is much more demanding than is ordinarily supposed, since it involves much more than just hearing and registering words, sentences, and ideas.

Total Listening

For our purposes, listening means becoming aware of all the cues that the other emits, and this implies an openness to the totality of the communication of the other. In the sensitivity group, such openness requires being aware not only of individuals but also of the mood of the group as a whole. Perhaps listening to the group is even more difficult than listening to individuals because it demands an awareness of subtle interactional patterns. Ideally the leader-member is already sensitive to these patterns, and one of his functions is to point them out to the other members. Listening, then, demands work, and the work involved is difficult enough that the effort will not be readily expended unless the listener has a deep respect for the total communication process.

One does not listen with just his ears: he listens with his eyes and with his sense of touch, he listens by becoming aware of the feelings and emotions that arise within himself because of his contact with others (that is, his own emotional resonance is another "ear"), he listens with his mind, his heart, and his imagination. He listens to the words of others, but he also listens to the messages that are buried in the words or encoded in all the cues that surround the words. As Berne (1961) suggests, he listens to the voice, the demeanor, the vocabulary, and the gestures of the other, or, as Haley (1959) would have it, to the context, the verbal messages, the linguistic patterns, and the bodily movements of the other. He listens to the sounds and to the silences. He listens not only to the message but also to the context, or, in Gestalt terms, he listens to both the figure and the ground and to the way these two interact. He is aware of what Murphy (1964) calls the "world of blushing, blanching, sighing, hinting, and averting the eyes"; like Smith (1966) he is aware that "people interact not only through words but also through spatial relations . . . through temporal relations . . . and . . . through gestures and touch and many other media [p. 3]."

The contract group is a laboratory in which the participants are to learn to become more fully aware of every possible channel of communication, both verbal and nonverbal. Weick (1968) thinks that nonverbal aspects of communication are generally overlooked, much to the detriment of the communication process:

Observers who are accustomed to analyzing speech behavior in naturalistic settings may regard nonverbal actions as a redundant source of information. This point of view neglects the fact that humans spend a very small portion of their interactional time vocalizing ... [p. 381].

Although nonverbal behavior holds promise for observational research because of its visibility, naturalness, and discriminability, it can also be too subtle to record unless the observer has been trained to be sensitive to it. That persons are often unaware of the rich nonverbal language is not surprising, since much of it occurs unconsciously (Scheflen, 1965, p. 34). Jecker et al. (1964) found that teachers who were untrained in the analysis of nonverbal behavior could not predict, from filmed facial cues, whether a student had comprehended a lesson in algebra [p. 382].

We are perhaps too ideationally oriented and have a set to bypass nonideational cues. Tomkins (1962) has suggested that the face is the "primary site of affect": "the centrality of the face in affective experience may also be seen in the relationship between the hand and the face. The hand acts as if the face is the site of feeling [p. 210]." The relationship of hand to face, then, is an important source of information concerning the feeling states of the other: "It is our argument that human beings slap, hide, stimulate, support, caress, inhibit, or reassure their faces with their hands because they correctly localize the face as the primary site of their concern [p. 212]." Others have studied the face as a rich source of communication (e.g., Ekman, 1965; Haggard & Isaacs, 1966; Leventhal & Sharp, 1965; Levitt, 1964). Exline and various associates (Exline, 1963; Exline, Gray, & Schuette, 1965; Exline & Winters, 1965) have examined the phenomenon of eye contact and glances exchanged, finding them important channels for communicating such effective information as liking and various forms of interpersonal discomfort. The communication potential of both posture (Scheflen, 1964) and body movements (e.g., Katz, 1964; Mahl, Danet, & Norton, 1959; Spiegel & Machotka, 1965; Werner & Wapner, 1953) is also an area of serious study. In the laboratory setting of the training group, it is feasible to focus more attention on nonverbal aspects of communication than one would ordinarily do outside a laboratory setting, for the purpose of enhancing one's total interpersonal listening skills.

The Nonselective Character of Total Listening. Total listening is, in a sense, nonselective: it encompasses all the cues emitted by the other, even those that the other would rather conceal and those the listener would rather not hear. For instance, the weight of an obviously overweight person is a cue to be reckoned with, for through it the other is saying something to those with whom he interacts. The message may be "I am frustrated" or "I don't care about others" or merely "I have poor self-control," but it is a message that should not be overlooked. In a group therapy session in which I was an observer, the therapist asked the wife of one of the inpatients (the patient himself refused to attend the sessions) what she thought she was trying to tell others by her obvious overweight. The therapist listened to a cue, confronted the woman in a firm, kindly, responsible way, and succeeded in instituting a dialogue that proved quite useful. Therefore, good listening demands both subjectivity—that is, engagement with the other—and objectivity—that is, disengagement from the other—in order to pick up both positively and negatively valenced cues. The good listener is sensitive to what is and not just to what should be or to how I would like things to be.

Active Listening. It becomes quite apparent that the good listener is an active listener, one truly engaged in the communication process, one who goes out of himself in search of significant cues emitted by others. Listening, then, is facilitated if the listener is actively interested in others. Newcomb's (1953) "strain toward symmetry" principle leads to the prediction: the more intense one person's concern for another, the greater is the likelihood that he will be sensitive to the other's orientations toward objects in the environment. Certain studies do show that liking another person increases sensitivity toward him. Eisman and Levy (1960) showed that lipreading was more accurate the more the reader liked the communicator. Suchman (1956) discovered that people who were more favorable toward others were more accurate in estimating the feelings of these others. In a study by Fiedler (1950), it was discovered that all therapists described the good therapeutic relationship as one in which the therapist participates completely in the patient's communication, and, as Rogers (1961) has noted, this is impossible unless a mutual respect and liking arise in the therapeutic encounter.

The person who is an active listener is much less likely to stereotype others or to become guilty of univocal listening. Perhaps an analogy would make this a bit clearer. Everytime Brahms' Second Symphony is played, the untrained ear hears only the Second Symphony; it is quite a univocal experience. The individuality of different orchestras and different conductors and the nuances of different tempos and accents are all missed. However, while there is only one Second Symphony, it can be played with quite different—and distinguishable—nuances. Similarly, John Doe is only John Doe, but John Doe, too, has different nuances of orchestration at different times, and these nuances will be missed by the untrained, passive listener who finds it more comfortable to deal with him as a stereotype in univocal terms. The active, searching listener, who is open to all the nuances of John Doe, will more likely pick up many of these cues. This openness to nuance, however, does not imply that the good listener is skilled in analyzing the other, for analysis often means reducing the other to a whole series of stereotypes, and sometimes this mistake is worse than the first.

All of Rogers's works (e.g., 1942, 1951, 1961, 1967) form a magnificent treatise on total listening:

I also find the relationship is significant to the extent that I feel a continuing desire to understand—a sensitive empathy with each of the client's feelings and communications as they seem to him at that moment. Acceptance does not mean much until it involves understanding. It is only as I *understand* the feelings and thoughts which seem so horrible to you, or so weak, or so sentimental, or so bizarre—it is only as I see them as you see them, and accept them and you, that you feel really free to explore all the hidden nooks and frightening crannies of your inner and often buried experience [1961, p. 34].

Perhaps Rogers's emphasis on total listening explains in part the impact that he has had on the field of psychotherapy. He has seemed to prove that total listening is in itself therapeutic. Up to the time of Rogers's studies, total listening had been a too little-explored aspect of the therapeutic encounter.

Social Intelligence and Listening. There is no doubt that the ability to become totally aware of others demands intelligence: "... Sensitivity to the subtle aspects of the wordless communications in psychotherapy is a most important dimension of therapeutic skill. This skill is not too readily learned but rather reflects native or early acquired aptitudes that are highly correlated with general intelligence [Schofield, 1964, p. 105]." However, the intelligence required seems to be more closely related to what may be termed social intelligence—a feel for people and an ability to involve one-self creatively and responsibly with them—rather than academic intellectual interest. The socially intelligent person is capable of becoming aware of the wide range of cues emitted by others, of evaluating them, and of responding to them.

**Obstacles to
Effective Listening**

Alienation from Communication. Against the background of what it means to be a good listener, it will be helpful to review some of the obstacles that arise to prevent effective listening in the group. Goffman (1957) discusses three kinds of preoccupation that disturb the communication process. The kinds of alienation he describes actually interfere with a person's ability to listen to others in the fullest sense of that term, although what he says must be modified somewhat in order to apply it to a sensitivity-training group.

External preoccupation is the first kind of alienation: the individual neglects the prescribed focus of attention, giving his main concern to something unconnected with the other group members in their capacity as fellow participants. He is listening to something that is outside the group in some way. According to Goffman, the topic of conversation is the prescribed focus of attention; but in a sensitivity-training group, the focus of attention is wider than just the topic being discussed. For instance, in the contract group, the topic actually being discussed might well be irrelevant to contractual goals and should be challenged rather than attended to. The daydreamer is alienated in any group; but in the contract group, the person who is actively listening to the total interaction might become preoccupied with the atmosphere surrounding the discussion rather than the topic itself, perhaps because the atmosphere is speaking louder than what the participants are saying about a specific topic. The atmosphere is not external to the topic of conversation, for it is having an effect on the entire conversation. In the case described, the good listener will interrupt the conversation, bringing up the problem of the nonfacilitative atmosphere of the group.

Self-consciousness is a second cause of alienation. Self-consciousness results from one's preoccupation with himself as an interactant, and this prevents him from giving himself entirely to the topic of conversation. Whitman (1964) discusses this phenomenon in terms of perceptual defense:

The extreme type of perceptual defense is autistic perception. Here there is really no perception at all. Very often you see somebody in the group who has a dreamy look in his eyes or perhaps even listens interestedly, but a few minutes later will say, "Well, I've been thinking about what was said to me (ten minutes ago!) and I have thought of this point. . . ." This is the person who most often is responsible for contributing a thud or dud to the group discussion, because his remark is connected to his own ruminations but not to the thread of group discussion [p. 321].

In the sensitivity group, however, a certain degree of self-consciousness is expected of the participants, for they are evaluating themselves precisely as interactants. There seem to be two kinds of self-consciousness: one that draws the participant away from the interaction into himself and one that makes the participant more acutely aware of his part in the interactional process and therefore more acutely aware of all the cues generated during group meetings.

The third kind of alienation, according to Goffman, is *interaction-consciousness*. The participant is so worried about how the interaction itself is progressing that he constricts his ability to follow the topic of conversation. Again, in the training group, there is a constructive form of interaction-consciousness just as there is a destructive form. Perhaps the difference is between being interaction-conscious (Goffman also calls it being "other-conscious") and being interaction- or other-*involved*. In human relationships, "the medium is the message" to a large extent; that is, the manner in which the interactional process is conducted also communicates. Therefore, members of sensitivity-training groups are asked to become aware of interactional styles. The victim of interaction-consciousness is really so deeply involved with his personal concerns that his awareness of what others are saying and of what is happening in the group is constricted, while the interaction-involved participant is hearing more than just the conversation, for he is picking up communication cues from a variety of sources.

Listening, then, in sensitivity groups is different from listening in ordinary conversation groups, for in sensitivity groups, listening itself is a focus of study. But even in ordinary conversation groups, there is more to communication than just the topic of conversation. An awareness of all the factors involved in communicating increases one's ability to follow and evaluate a topic of conversation.

"Message Anxiety" as an Obstacle to Listening. Research indicates that the comprehensibility of a message is unfavorably in-

fluenced when the content itself is anxiety-arousing. Nunnally (1961) calls this situation "message anxiety." Gynther (1957) found that message anxiety lowered the communicative efficiency of the speaker. Kasl and Mahl (1965) discovered that it led to speaker anxiety and flustered speech, while Geer (1966) found that it produced speaker anxiety, slowed speech, and silences. Message anxiety, then, is an obstacle to effective listening in two ways: (1) it makes the speaker himself less comprehensible, so that the listener has to fill in the gaps, and (2) it is hypothesized that the speaker communicates his own anxiety plus the anxiety of the message to the listener, and the resultant listener anxiety further distorts the message. Since, in laboratory groups, there is likely to be a good deal of message anxiety, the participants should be prepared to handle the communication difficulties that arise from it. This means that both the speaker and the listener must be aware of possible communication distortions and try to minimize them. High visibility would be very helpful here; that is, if the speaker were to admit that he finds the content of the message quite disturbing, this would be a cue for the listener to listen more intently and become more aware of the anxieties that are possibly being generated within himself.

Campbell: Human Error in the Communication Process. Campbell (1958), in studying the communication process, discovered certain sources of systematic error, an understanding of which is extremely useful to anyone interested in human interaction. Both speaker and listener can profit from Campbell's findings, for these findings can be cast in terms of principles for improving the purpose of speaking (output) and the process of listening (input).

(1) *Length of the speaker's remarks.* If the only recorder present to take down a speaker's remarks is the listener himself, then both the speaker and the listener should realize that a communications leakage takes place between output and input. There is a good chance, according to Campbell, that the average listener will tend to shorten, simplify, and eliminate detail from the actual output of the speaker. The longer the speaker's remarks, the greater the leakage. Thus, if the speaker really wants to get his remarks across, he will take into account the natural leakage of the listening process and not make an unnecessarily long speech. There is an important lesson here for sensitivity groups. In such groups, there is usually little reason for anyone to speak at considerable length. Extended

speeches are out of place both because they cut down on inter-action and involvement and because they entail too much leakage. Extended history, for example, has less impact than compact story. An active, concerned listener will interrupt longer discourses pre-cisely because he does want to listen, assimilate, and interact. On the relatively rare occasions on which a participant does speak at some length in the group, he must realize that his listeners are not assimilating all the facts that he is retailing, but are rather receiving a total impact from his remarks. If he speaks at length, it must be because total impact is more important than individual facts.

(2) *The middle of the message.* "... The middle of the message will be least well retained [p. 343]." The concerned listener must make greater efforts to retain what is said as remarks lengthen, but the concerned speaker, realizing this, will try to eliminate the mid-dle, by keeping his remarks short enough so that they have only a beginning and an end.

(3) *"Rounding off" the message.* The listener tends to "round off" what he hears, "dividing the content into clear-cut 'entities,' re-ducing gradations both by exaggerating some differences and losing others [p. 344]." This seems to be a function, at least in part, of a kind of egocentricity with which every listener is afflicted: he tailors messages to fit his own needs. The good listener, then, has to take pains not to ignore subtle differences in what is said, even though these differences go contrary to opinions that he himself holds. Also, the good speaker will speak frankly, honestly, and plainly, making shadings of meaning as clear as possible. When a speaker becomes too subtle, when shadings of meaning begin to proliferate, this may mean that the speaker is unsure of himself or afraid of those to whom he is speaking. If either is the case, he should be honest enough to say so and let his message be interpreted in the light of his own misgivings.

(4) *The past haunting imperfectly transmitted messages.* "An imperfectly transmitted message will be distorted in the direction of important past messages, both *rewarding* and *punishing* past messages [p. 350]." Perhaps another way of putting this is that a listener is influenced in his listening by the way he has been reinforced by communications in the past. If a participant in a sensitivity group hears a confused, abstruse, or poorly delivered message, he has a natural tendency to interpret it in the light of past messages that have had either positive or negative (rather than merely factual) meaning for him—that is, messages that he has found important. Obviously, the good listener, being active,

will try to minimize this source of error by having the speaker clarify the message. But it is surprising how many participants, for one reason or another, allow imperfectly transmitted messages to go by without challenge. Also, a good listener will try to be aware of what the speaker is actually saying in light of previous emotional experiences he has had with the speaker. If the participant is honest enough to keep his relationship with the other members out in the open, there should be less tendency for him to distort messages for emotional reasons.

(5) *The reductive nature of listening.* The "most pervasive of the systematic biases [p. 346]" is the tendency for the listener to modify a new message so that it becomes more like previous messages. Obviously, if the speakers were never to say anything new, the listener would not be burdened with, and have to cope with, anything new. Therefore, the speaker who rarely says something new is contributing to this bias. But the good listener is one who can consistently break away from this bias. To do so, however, he must be in affective contact with the speaker, and he must allow the speaker the freedom to change. Time and again, in sensitivity groups, A, after listening to Z, will say something like: "We've really heard that story before; in fact, we have heard it over and over again," only to have B, who possibly has been listening more creatively, say: "That's not true. There is something new here. He is now saying, even though in a confused way: 'I do want to change.' Anyway, that's what I'm hearing." Unfortunately, poor listeners are a most formidable obstacle to change in group members.

(6) *Hearing what one expects to hear.* In general, according to Campbell's findings, listeners will modify messages so that they conform to the meaning expected by the listeners. The poor listener, then, either does not listen or stops listening halfway through a message, and he does so because he "knows" what the speaker is going to say. This is listening at its worst. Again, it is casting the speaker into a univocal mold, thus stripping him of his freedom. Too much listening is Kantian listening or computer listening. The listener has preset categories, and whatever is heard must fit into these molds or be handled by these banks. Whatever cannot be received into his computer banks must be shunted off and excluded. And yet, Collins and Guetzkow (1964), in reviewing the literature on group decision-making processes, find that "the most important part of conference communication may occur when another member says something that we do not expect and thus offers us a perspective or possible solution which would not have occurred to us while

working alone [p. 184]." Poor listening is poor business practice as well as poor human relations. The intelligent speaker, realizing the human tendency to stereotype, truncate, and not allow for the possibility of change, will emphasize the fact that what he is saying is different from what he has said before, that he has changed or moved away from a previously held position (if this is the case), in order to break through his listeners' natural stereotyping process. Finally, I would hypothesize that those who are uncomfortable with their own freedom or with the freedom of others tend to constrict the messages of others.

(7) *"You agree with me."* The listener tends to modify messages so that they are in better agreement with his own opinions and attitudes. Although such a tendency is nothing more than a concrete specification of the ancient scholastic principle "whatever is received is received according to the state, condition, or bias of the receiver," and, as such, is in no way new, empirical data manifest just how pervasive such a principle is in man's practical life. Thus, to a large extent, we hear what we want to hear. The sensitive listener, however, addicted as he is to what is, constantly fights this natural tendency in order to hear what is actually being said. This means that to be a good listener one must drop, or at least relax, his defenses a bit in order to be willing to explore the new.

(8) *Black-or-white listening.* "There is a tendency to distort coding assignments in the direction of an affective or evaluative coding. The most natural coding of any input by the human operator seems to be of the general nature of 'like' versus 'dislike,' 'approach' versus 'avoid,' 'good' versus 'bad,' 'beautiful' versus 'ugly,' etc. The general finding of psychologists is that whatever assignment is given tends to be distorted in the direction of this evaluative assignment. This is shown repeatedly as a 'halo' effect, or general factor in rating assignments [p. 357]." This is a reflection of the either-black-or-white tendency in man. Not only is everything a subject of evaluation, but things tend to end up in just two categories, good or bad. It seems almost natural for man to listen to messages in evaluative terms, and it is much simpler to hear a communication as bad or good in its entirety rather than to expend the effort that differential evaluation of a message would demand. This basic tendency to listen to communications in evaluative terms prevents the listener from assimilating other aspects of the message; creative aspects of the message are lost in its badness or deficiencies are swallowed up in its goodness. If the speaker realizes that his message might strike others as immediately good or bad, then

he should build a caution against this into the message itself, urging listeners to suspend, if possible, this evaluative propensity.

(9) *The pressures of the group and "filtered" listening.* "When a group of persons are exposed to a message stimulus and asked to state its meaning (size, degree of movement, amount of prejudice, etc.), they will distort their individual interpretations in the direction of their fellows [p. 361]." The average listener tends to listen, at least to some extent, through the group; that is, he filters what is said through the complex interactional and attitudinal patterns that comprise one aspect of the group culture. Although such a process can be advantageous at times—for instance, in group decision-making situations: "The social weighting given to the majority opinion (i.e., conformity) frequently causes the better alternatives to be chosen [Collins & Guetzkow, 1964, p. 55]"—this is not the case in laboratory-training groups. The good listener listens, or makes every effort to listen, directly to the other, without sifting what is said through the attitudinal filters of the group. It would seem that there is greater possibility for success in direct listening in the contract group because of the high-visibility nature of the group culture and because of the built-in cautions against tacit understandings and covert decisions in the group. But even under such contract conditions, nature will out, to a certain degree, and members will tend to modify what they hear so that it might fit more neatly into the group culture. For instance, if there is a tacit understanding in the group not to discuss sexuality, when a member does bring the subject up, others will tend to ignore what he has to say or will hear it as a digression. This tendency presents another challenge to the good listener, for he must see the individual as primary and the group as serving the needs of the individuals who constitute the group.

It is hardly necessary for sensitivity-training participants to memorize the communications obstacles described by Campbell. It is sufficient to realize that it has been demonstrated that, just in the ordinary course of events, it is difficult to be an unbiased listener. The pitfalls that he describes cannot be avoided entirely; they can only be minimized.

The Impact of the Speaker on Listening

Whenever a member speaks and really says nothing or, in the contract group, whenever he engages in various forms of flight behavior, he must realize that the quality of listening in the group will go down. As a general rule, the speaker gets the kind of attention he deserves. Some participants speak vaguely and evasively because they do not want to be read by their listeners; they thrive on the haphazard listening they receive. Such tendencies should become the object of confrontation in the group.

The "Compleat" Listener

It has been suggested that the good listener is the active listener. He is as receptive as possible to all cues generated in the group, and he is aware of, and tries to combat, the variety of obstacles, stemming from within himself and from the matrix of the group, to effective listening. The "compleat" listener, however, goes further than this, for he realizes that the proof of the pudding always lies in the eating. Therefore, once he has listened in the sense described here, he must in some way manifest to the speaker that he has listened fully, intelligently, and sympathetically (that is, he has not prejudged the speaker's remarks). In fact, this is the basic source of support in the group: the knowledge that one has been listened to actively and intelligently. Second (and this is the ultimate proof of one's listening skills), he translates what he has heard into effective interaction. That is, the good listener is hardly one who merely amasses information, however conscientiously, and communicates to the speaker that he has listened effectively. Rather, the variety of ways in which the individuals and the group itself have spoken have served as stimuli, and because he has listened well, there is a much better chance that his response will be proportioned to the stimulus. In the contract group, his response will generally take the form of one or more of the contractual modalities—direct supportive behavior, self-disclosure, expression of feeling and emotion, or some form of confrontation. All of these modalities, if carried out responsibly, are supportive.

Listening as Diagnostic

The quality of one's listening is diagnostic with respect to the quality of one's human relations. Rotter (1962) claims that it is not lack of insight into self that characterizes the person in emotional trouble, but rather a lack of insight into others. He is so poorly aware of others that his interactions with them are awkward and self-defeating. The contract group, then, is a laboratory in which the participants are to experiment with active listening. Part of the process of being an active listener—one who searches out communications cues—will include challenging participants who speak vaguely or evasively. The participant who finds out that he does not listen carefully, or that he is unable or unwilling to venture out into the group in search of clarity of communication, will profit diagnostically. On the other hand, the participant who succeeds will find himself much better prepared to provide active support in the group.

Support: Creating a Climate for Growth

The Universal Need for Interpersonal Warmth. There is almost universal recognition that a degree of warmth in interpersonal relationships is absolutely essential for psychosocial growth. This need begins at birth and, although it might undergo certain transformations throughout the maturational process, it would seem that it is a still strongly felt need during old age. Watson (1959), in reviewing the literature on the deleterious effects of maternal deprivation, found confirmatory evidence for this supposition despite the fact that there were experimental inadequacies in many of the studies (the specific kinds of design inadequacy varied from study to study). Lehrman (1960), in his clinical work, found that the need for warmth does not stop with childhood:

> The incisive work of Ackerman (1958) and others on intra-family interactions, . . . Ferenczi's (1926) demonstration that the analyst's warmth is a necessary condition for cure, and Fromm-Reichmann's (1950) brilliant sensitivity with schizophrenics all encourage the hope that precise knowledge of the effects of interpersonal warmth at the breast, in the home and role-appropriate warmth in the office can help us fulfill our task of preventing and curing mental illness [p. 1102].

The work of Rogers (1961, 1967) and others (e.g., Schofield, 1964; Truax, 1961, 1963; Truax & Carkhuff, 1964) not only supports this conclusion but also leads one to believe that warmth is necessary not just for psychotherapeutic situations but, universally, for personal and interpersonal growth.

Frank (1961) claims that "the greatest potential drawback of therapy groups is the tendency not to supply sufficient support, especially in early meetings, to enable members to cope with the stresses they generate [p. 190]." Whether this is the greatest potential drawback of sensitivity-training groups or not (some certainly think so) is still to be determined, but the fear of nonsupport is certainly one of the greatest fears of those who are considering the possibility of engaging in sensitivity training and of sensitivity-group members who are considering taking certain risks in the group (e.g., disclosing themselves, dealing openly with emotional issues, etc.). Prospective participants realize that they are to engage in some kind of self-disclosure, that they are going to be confronted or challenged by the leader or other participants, and that such interaction is, more than likely, going to arouse strong emotion. They see the possibility of some kind of shame experience, and they rightfully fear it, for, as Erikson (1959) says, "Shame supposes that one is completely exposed and conscious of being looked at. . . . One is visible and ready to be visible. . . . Shame is early expressed in an impulse to bury one's face, or to sink, right then and there, into the ground. But this, I think, is essentially rage turned against the self [pp. 142–143]." Prospective participants foresee quite easily the potential pain of the sensitivity experience, but what they do not or cannot foresee is a climate of support that will render painful interaction not only tolerable but even stimulating and deeply satisfying.

Psychological safety, then, is a legitimate concern of any kind of growth group, any kind of group in which intrapsychic and interpersonal concerns constitute the principal focus of attention, and it is a seeming lack of concern for such safety in some quarters that disturbs many professionals. However, support has always been a concern of those seriously committed to laboratory training—for example, the personnel of the National Training Laboratories (NTL):

A first purpose of the T Group is to help individuals to learn from their continuing experience in the areas of self-awareness, sensitivity to phenomena of interpersonal behavior, and understanding of the consequences of behavior—one's own and others'. Learning in these areas requires willingness to explore openly one's motivations and one's feelings; to utilize the reactions of others as feedback about the consequences of one's behavior; and to experiment with new ways of behaving. Since each of these steps requires emotional support, the T Group faces the dual task of creating a supportive climate and of developing situations in which members can learn through examining their own experience [Bradford, 1964, p. 191].

Yet, while most practitioners agree that a supportive climate in human relations laboratories is absolutely essential (and actually see to it that such a climate does develop in the group or in the community of which the group is a part), few have taken the pains to discuss either the nature of support or the ways in which a supportive climate is created in a group. Needless to say, there is little if any published research in this area.

Antecedent and Consequent Support

In the contract group, support can be discussed in terms of the kinds of interaction specified by the contract. There are basically, then, two kinds of support: antecedent and consequent. Direct or indirect encouragement to participants to engage in contractual behavior is *antecedent* support; that is, it comes before contractual behavior and is directed toward eliciting it. For example, if the leader-member models some form of contractual behavior—let us say that he engages in self-disclosure of some kind—and if he does so skillfully and sincerely, his behavior is a form of antecedent support, for it is designed to encourage members to engage in the same kind of behavior. On the other hand, reinforcement given to participants for actually engaging in contractual interaction is *consequent* support. Reinforcement, of course, can take place in many different ways, but it always says to the participant who has engaged in contractual behavior: "You have done a good thing in the group." During the early sessions, the trainer primarily (but also as many of the other participants as possible) should engage in forms of antecedent support, for it is amazing how many normal people have fears and feelings of inferiority floating immediately below the surface or lurking behind carefree facades. These feelings inhibit group process, and people need encouragement to overcome them. In the contract group, the contract itself provides one of the main sources of antecedent support in that it takes into consideration the natural fears of the participants and serves as a stimulus to participation. The contract establishes a rather large cultural island around which the participant may wander freely and with relative safety. If the participant chooses to remain on one small part of that island and remain a spectator of instead of a participant in the life of the island, this is not the fault of the island culture but rather of his exaggerated fears.

The Forms of
Antecedent Support

"I accept you because you ARE": Acceptance or Unconditional Positive Regard as Antecedent Support. The contract group recognizes that the basic attitudes its participants have toward one another as fellow human beings are crucial to the climate of interpersonal growth. Therefore, insofar as possible (though obviously one cannot change deep-seated attitudes and habitual behavioral patterns by contract or edict), the contract calls, first of all, for the basic kind of acceptance that Rogers (1961, 1967), following Standal (1954), calls "unconditional positive regard"; this attitude, considered essential for the therapeutic process, is described by Rogers and Truax (1967):

A second condition which is hypothesized as essential for therapeutic movement and change is the experiencing by the therapist of an unconditional positive regard for the client. This means that the therapist communicates to his client a deep and genuine caring for him as a person with human potentialities, a caring uncontaminated by evaluations of his thoughts, feelings, or behaviors. The therapist experiences a warm acceptance of the client's experience as being a part of the client as a person, and places no conditions on his acceptance and warmth. He prizes the client in a total rather than a conditional way. He does not accept certain feelings in the client and disapprove others. He feels an *unconditional* positive regard or warmth for this person. This is an outgoing, positive feeling without reservations and without evaluations. It means *not* making judgments. It involves as much feeling of acceptance for the client's expression of painful, hostile, defensive, or abnormal feelings as for his expression of good, positive, mature feelings. For us as therapists it may even be that it is easier to accept painful and negative feelings than the positive and self-confident feelings which sometimes come through. These latter we almost automatically regard as defensive. But unconditional positive regard involves a willingness to share equally the patient's confidence and joy, or his depression and failure. It is a non-possessive caring for the client as a separate person. The client is thus freely allowed to have his *own* feelings and his *own* experiencing. One client describes the therapist as "fostering my possession of my own experience and that I am actually having it; thinking what I think, feeling what I feel, wanting what I want, fearing what I fear; no 'ifs,' 'buts,' or 'not reallys.'" This is the type of acceptance which is expected to lead to a relationship which facilitates the engagement of the patient in the process of therapy and leads to constructive personality change. . . .

Thus, when the therapist prizes his client, and is searching for the meaning or value of his client's thoughts or behaviors within the client, he does not tend to feel a response of approval or disapproval. He feels an acceptance of what *is*.

Unconditional positive regard, when communicated by the therapist, functions to provide the non-threatening context in which it is possible for the client to explore and experience the most deeply shrouded elements of his inner self. The therapist is not paternalistic, or sentimental, or superficially social and agreeable. But his deep caring is a necessary ingredient in providing a "safe" context in which the client can come to explore himself and share deeply with another human being [pp. 102–104].

To a great extent, what Rogers and Truax describe here is the kind of acceptance ideally owed to another simply because he is a human being. It is a willingness to let the other be who he is and what he is, but it is an active, concerned letting the other to be rather than a detached "not giving a damn" what the other is like or what he does. It means allowing the other to have the psychosocial life-space that he needs in order to be himself as fully as possible. Negatively, it means a refusal to exercise various sorts of control over the other, a refusal to demand that his life style conform, generally or in specific aspects, to one's own—for example, with respect to style or modes of interpersonal interaction and to a value system. Acceptance implies an active allowing the other to be different from oneself, "active" here meaning that A's interaction with B should actually foster B's otherness, his differences, his unique way of being. In a laboratory-training group, it is as if each member of the group were to say to every other member: "You have a value that neither I nor we collectively either determine or can abrogate. We recognize you as *being* this value."

At the very minimum, acceptance demands that one allow the other to express the ways in which he is different, different from the other members of the group and perhaps different from the images of man that are currently acceptable in our society. But if such acceptance is to be active, the members must be willing to say to one another: "Your actions cannot be so different or bizarre as to open an unbridgeable gap between you and me." Insofar as acceptance is active, it approaches what Fromm (1956) calls "brotherly love," the most fundamental kind of love. This love means such things as care, respect, and the desire to further the life of the other. Such acceptance or love tends to disregard status, for it is a love between equals.

Schofield (1964) says that "this quality of 'acceptance' *in our culture at this time* is peculiarly restricted to the psychotherapeutic contract, but it is common to all such contracts. In this sense, psychotherapy provides a very special, perhaps ideal, form of friendship [p. 109]." There is no absolute reason, however, why such attitudes of acceptance cannot become more pervasive *in our culture at this time.* Perhaps one of the reasons for the proliferation of sensitivity-training laboratories *in our culture at this time* is to disseminate among the general population "growth variables" that up to now have been common only in therapeutic enterprises. Sensitivity laboratories—and certainly contract-group laboratories—are designed to stimulate the cultivation of such attitudes of acceptance among people not engaged in any strictly therapeutic situation. These laboratories encourage participants to become aware of their basic attitudes of acceptance and rejection of others and to grow in active concern for others to be who and what they are. This is essential to the kind of support in depth that creates a climate in which participants can engage freely in the modalities called for by the contract: self-disclosure, expression of feeling and emotion, and mutual confrontation. As Latourelle (1962) says, for communication and dialogue to become a reciprocal opening up—that is, a mutual revelation—the speaker and the hearer must respect each other in the mysteriousness of their personalities: there must be mutual trust and availability. One of the principal tasks of the laboratory is to find ways—direct and indirect—of communicating this basic attitude of acceptance. The laboratory is also diagnostic in this regard. If a person finds himself lacking in this basic acceptance of others, then he should explore the interactional consequences of his lack. If he decides that he should do something about it, then, for him, the laboratory will be principally remedial. If he decides that he is unwilling to change, then he must learn to live with the behavioral consequences of his decision.

Stern (1966), in discussing psychotherapy, makes a distinction that might well bridge the gap between Rogers and Truax's views on unconditional positive regard and the following section on acceptance versus approval. According to Stern, there are two approaches to experience: (1) the *instrumental,* which aims at mastery, and (2) the *sacramental,* which aims at appreciation. The therapist using the instrumental approach will see the patient's past as something to be overcome (either by emotional insight, behavioral modification, learning ways of adjusting to reality, or a combination of all of these methods). On the other hand, the therapist following the sacramental approach looks upon the patient's past with respect, even though (in the eyes of the therapist, of society in general, or of the patient himself) it may need to be transcended, and he looks upon the patient's present as an experience that can be transformed, at least in part, through concerned and appreciative confrontation. In the sacramental approach, the patient's task becomes that of learning to recognize himself as a unique and total being, while the therapist must enter into the relationship as an interacting-with-another self instead of a mirror in whose clear surface the patient can come to appreciate his own deepest feelings and how he is distorting reality. I sincerely believe that the core of what Rogers calls unconditional positive regard is compatible with the kind of respectful confrontation suggested by Stern.

Acceptance versus Approval. Acceptance—whether it is described in terms of Rogers and Truax's unconditional positive regard or in terms of giving the other respect, concern, understanding, the freedom to be, and the opportunity to make and be responsible for his own decisions—is not synonymous with approval (Rogers and Truax explicitly place it outside the pale of either approval or disapproval). But acceptance in the finest sense does not, it is contended here, exclude the kind of confrontation described in the next chapter. I do not believe that A, if he is sincerely interested in growth, wants or expects B to accept him in the sense that B must accept, overlook, discount, or even approve of modes of acting with which A himself is dissatisfied and which remain for him a source of concern, if not of contract or existential guilt. A does not (or should not) expect B to consider his own (B's) value system so cavalierly and narrowly as not to be concerned about these values among men in general and even with respect to A. Therefore, B can really accept A in a way that is consonant with such concepts as unconditional positive regard and nonpossessive warmth (and certainly this kind of acceptance does have some priority in human relationships) and still (at least eventually, if not immediately) suggest to A the hypothesis that some aspects of A's behavior might be proving deleterious to A himself, if not also to others. B can do this without in any way refusing to respect the experience of A, no matter how different from his own such experience might be. Once a person has declared effectively—perhaps by word but especially by his actions—that he is antecedently "for" another, that he is open to him and his experience—his miseries, his joys, his triumphs, his failures, his problems—then, and perhaps only then, does he have the freedom to make careful confrontational interventions in the life of the other.

Rogers and Truax (1967) and Schofield (1964), in discussing acceptance as a therapist variable, do not discuss the relationship between acceptance and confrontation, nor do they discuss approval at any length. But if, as Patterson (1966) suggests, one person manifests certain ideal qualities in his relationship to another—empathy, genuine concern, a desire to help, a belief in the ability of the other to change, an expectation or a hope that the other will change in directions indicating growth, self-congruence, and sincerity—then it would seem to follow that he simply could not tie approval to the coattails of acceptance, for this would demand a certain dishonesty on the part of one desiring to give himself to the other, and thus vitiate the concept of acceptance itself. Confrontation, at least at a certain stage of a relationship between two people, can be a manifestation of positive regard, a regard that remains unconditional in that the confronter does not make his friendship depend on a change of life in the confrontee. His positive regard is also still unconditional in that he is not trying to rob the person he is confronting of his freedom (indeed, he wants him, if possible, to be even freer than he is now).

On the other hand, wholesale approval of another either implies radical noninvolvement or nonconcern with him, or it implies unlimited, rather than unconditional, love. If A really does not care for B, then he can be lavish with his approval, because it costs him nothing. Or if A's unlimited "love" for B is really an unlimited need for B and B's affection and approval, then A might be ready to do whatever is necessary to maintain this relationship. But there is no evidence that such unlimited approval or "love" is therapeutic or otherwise growthful. On the contrary, developmental studies have demonstrated that setting limits for a child as he is growing up, if done responsibly, with the child's growth, rather than just the adult's comfort, in mind, is an obvious act of care and concern. On the other hand, there is evidence that unlimited approval is deleterious to growth. Strickland and Crowne (1963) found that patients with high need for approval terminated therapy significantly earlier than patients with low need for approval. It is true that these patients might have terminated the relationship for a number of reasons (poor therapist, spontaneous remission, failure to receive unconditional positive regard, misunderstanding of the nature of therapy, financial concerns), but it is also possible that the early terminators were, on the whole, immature people who expected to receive unlimited approval or love from the therapist. Truax and Carkhuff (1967) suggest that the need for approval (as opposed to a need for respect, concern) is an indication of disturbance rather than a remedy for it. In somewhat the same vein, Frank (1961) maintains that, in group therapy, support need not be expressed in terms of increased liking (one of the forms of approval) but may also be expressed in terms of respect and recognition for the new self that emerges from the therapeutic process. I am in no way suggesting that Rogers and Truax's concept of unconditional positive regard suffers from the inadequacies outlined here; rather, I am trying to demonstrate that there is no conflict between the concept of nonpossessive warmth and responsible confrontation, even though the latter has not been a part of the armamentarium of nondirective or client-centered approaches to therapy and other growth experiences.

Antecedent Acceptance as an Expressed Sense of Solidarity in the Human Condition. An acute awareness of the fact that man, for all his splendid accomplishments, often not only chooses unwisely but doggedly adheres to self-destructive choices—this awareness, expressed by sensitivity-group members in such a way as to make it evident that no one is exempt from human folly, is a form of antecedent acceptance. The sooner a member gives sufficient cues to indicate that he is open to both the heights and the depths of the human condition, the sooner will he find himself in community in a spirit of mutual trust. The person who can say "We are a microcommunity of men participating in both the wisdom and folly of man" expresses a kind of solidarity with others in the human condition that is both a statement of acceptance of others and a plea to be accepted by others.

Fromm-Reichmann (1950) says that the respect that the therapist has for his patient is valid only if the therapist realizes that his client's difficulties in living are not too different from his own. She also maintains that such a statement is not just a humanitarian or charitable hypothesis, but that it is a scientific conviction. Another way of putting this is that, in order to create a climate of trust, acceptance, and support, the participants in a sensitivity group must in some way denude themselves of status roles and appear in the group simply as human beings, subject to both the sublimities and follies of the human condition. Stern (1966) suggests that this should also take place in therapeutic encounters. The therapist, he says, should let his clients see some of his own problems in living, for therapy is a place where two or more people go together.

If mutual acceptance is to be accomplished, then the participants must lay aside not only formal status roles (e.g., psychiatrist, psychologist, clergyman, manager, teacher), but also any role that would interfere with free contact among group participants. For instance, if someone assumes a quasi-role based on the supposition that "problems put people in categories, problems divide," and if he translates this role into interaction in the group, saying implicitly or explicitly; "I've listened, but my hang-ups are not yours nor are yours mine; we're playing this game in different ball parks," he is assuming a role that demands that he reject others and that others reject him. This kind of psychological or interactional distance, no matter how subtle or covert, inhibits mutual acceptance and, therefore, limits or interferes with the kind of trust that is absolutely essential in the group if all the participants are to contact one another freely. This distance works in two directions. The one who says, at least by implication, "My problems are not yours; they make me less than you, they set me apart from you" sets himself apart from others, making it very difficult for them to provide him with any kind of support. Though he does this in order to make himself less vulnerable to rejection, he defeats his purpose because he creates an atmosphere in which support is not viable. If he also adds a poor-me element, he complicates matters further, for he both refuses support and, at the same time, tries to extort it. This makes the rest of the participants ambivalent toward him, if not angry. On the other hand, if a participant takes the attitude toward another: "Your problems are not mine; your problems set you apart from me," then his "support," if he gives it at all, will smell of condescension, and the one being "supported" will resent being patronized.

Support is most effectively given by one who has a feeling of involvement, of being with others, whatever the human experiences of these others might be. He has a strong feeling for what is in human living instead of what should be. He so gives himself to others that the ways in which he is like others and the ways in which he differs from them do not determine his involvement. The one who isolates himself from the experiences of others in the group is less human for doing so, no matter how he rationalizes his isolation.

Availability as Antecedent Support. Friendship—and this includes the beginnings of friendship in sensitivity or contract groups

—may be defined in terms of availability. Friends are mutually available, and the *degree* of their availability defines the strength or the depth of the relationship. Some distinction, however, must be made between physical and psychological availability. Physical availability refers to the spatiotemporal dimensions of the relationship. There is a high degree of physical availability if one person spends a good deal of time with another, if he remains geographically close, if physical presence of some sort (even contact by telephone) can be easily achieved, or if more intimate kinds of actual physical contact are a dimension of the encounter. But, as important as physical availability is for friendship, psychological availability is even more important. Physical and psychological availability are separable, and the latter is the more difficult to define. First of all, any kind of availability, whether physical or psychological, can be either active or passive. For example, A might invite B to spend some time with him or, on the other hand, he might merely allow B to be with him. These would be examples of active and passive availability. A person is actively available in a psychological way if he takes the initiative in sharing himself—his deeper thoughts, concerns, feelings, and aspirations—with another. If he merely allows the other to share such things with him—that is, if he is a more or less willing listener to the confidences of another—then he is also psychologically available, but passively so.

It is evident that there are all sorts of combinations and degrees of availability, both active and passive, physical and psychological. For instance, a prostitute might be actively available on a physical level, but not psychologically available at all. Perhaps the ideal marriage, in terms of availability, is one in which the partners are utterly psychologically available to each other and in which mutual physical availability is worked out according to the individual needs and responsibilities. Marriage partners come together with a frequency and an intimacy of contact not available to others, and their physical intimacy symbolizes, promotes, and enriches their mutual psychological availability. Both their physical and psychological intimacy reveal how deeply they are "for" each other, how deeply each wants to support the very being of the other. In like manner, failures in marriage, and in friendship in general, can be conceptualized in terms of failures in physical and psychological availability, both active and passive.

Since I had always been an at least implicit believer in the dictum that one can have very few close friends, I was taken aback once by a trainer in a sensitivity group in which I was participating when he said that he neither believed in that dictum nor lived by it. He claimed that he had many deep friends. It is true that he did not see many of them very often (physical availability was relatively low in many cases), but when he did see them, he did not need time to work his way back into the relationship. Rather, he and his friends started communicating immediately at a deep level (psychological availability was very high). It may be that our subscribing to the few-friends dictum ("don't spread yourself too thin," "don't become a psychological glutton," etc.) is a way of rationalizing our fears of getting too close to others.

In the contract group, then, members are supportive to the degree that they become available to one another. At first glance, it would seem that they are always, as long as the group is in session, physically available to one another, but even in the group itself, there are degrees of physical availability. For instance, there are certain physical cues—for example, looking at the other, modulations of voice—that indicate psychological availability or the beginnings of it, and these cues may or may not be present. One of the main purposes, in my opinion, for using nonverbal, contact exercises in the group is to allow the participants an opportunity to use physical contact both to stimulate and symbolize their psychological availability to one another. Such exercises, however antecedently anxiety-arousing or silly they may seem to be (see Kaplan, 1968), are actually serious and fear-reductive, for they usually reveal others as more psychologically available than one had realized. The sooner the participants become available to one another, and the more deft they become in finding ways in which to reveal or give evidence of this availability, the sooner will they create a climate of trust that will support more than superficial manifestations of the modalities of self-disclosure, expression of feeling, and confrontation.

Participant Congruence as Antecedent Support. Rogers (1961), Rogers and Truax (1967), and others (e.g., Truax & Carkhuff, 1967) have studied the value of therapist authenticity or congruence in the therapeutic relationships, and they have come to the conclusion that it, together with unconditional positive regard and accurate empathy, is one of the most important therapist variables:

We readily sense this quality of congruence in everyday life. Each of us could name persons who always seem to be operating from behind a front, who are playing a role, who tend to say things that they do not feel. They are exhibiting incongruence. We tend not to reveal ourselves too deeply to such people. On the other hand, each of us knows individuals whom we somehow trust because we sense that they are being what they *are* in an open and transparent way and that we are dealing with the person himself, not with a polite or professional facade. This is the quality of congruence.

In relation to therapy it means that the therapist is what he *is*, during the encounter with the client. He is without front or facade, openly being the feelings and attitudes which at the moment are flowing in him. It involves the element of self-awareness, meaning that the feelings the therapist is experiencing are available to him, available to his awareness, and also that he is able to live these feelings, to be them in the relationship, and able to communicate them if appropriate. It means that he comes into a direct personal encounter with his client, meeting him on a person-to-person basis. It means that he is *being* himself, not denying himself. . . .

It is not a simple thing to achieve such reality. Being real involves the difficult task of being acquainted with the flow of experiencing going on within oneself, a flow marked especially by complexity and continuous change. . . .

It is not an easy thing for the client, or for any human being, to trust his most deeply shrouded feelings to another person. It is even more difficult for a disturbed person to share his deepest and most troubling feelings with a therapist. The genuineness, or congruence, of the therapist is one of the elements in the relationship which makes this risk of sharing easier and less fraught with dangers.

. . . At a very low level of congruence the therapist may be clearly defensive in the interaction, as evidenced by the contradiction between the content of the message and his voice qualities or the nonverbal cue which he presents. Or the therapist may respond appropriately but in so professional a manner that he gives the impression that his responses are formulated to sound good rather than being what he really feels and means. Thus incongruence may involve a contrived or rehearsed quality or a professional front.

At the upper ranges of therapist genuineness, his openness to all types of feelings and experiences, both pleasant and hurtful, without trace of defensiveness or retreat into professionalism, is usually most evident from the quality of his voice and the manner of his expression [Rogers & Truax, 1967, pp. 100–102].

It is hypothesized here that this quality of congruence is essential not only for a therapist in a therapeutic relationship but for anyone who wants to live a fully human life. Again, this variable is perhaps too closely identified with the therapeutic relationship. It is therapeutic because it is deeply human. Therefore, participants in a training group are to examine, or rather experience, their ability or inability to be congruent in the interaction of the group and attempt modes of behavior designed to develop congruence. It is evident that a group of congruent participants will be supportive provided that they effectively handle the confrontation that arises naturally from their being congruent. This problem will be dealt with in the next chapter.

Trust Formation as Antecedent Support. One way of conceptualizing antecedent support is as trust formation. Erikson (1959, 1963, 1968) sees trust versus mistrust in existence itself as the first crisis faced by the child:

What we here call trust coincides with what Therese Benedek has called confidence. If I prefer the word "trust," it is because there is more naiveté and more mutuality in it: an infant can be said to be trusting where it would go too far to say that he has confidence. The general state of trust, furthermore, implies not only that one has learned to rely on the sameness and continuity of outer providers, but also that one may trust oneself and the capacity of one's own organs to cope with urges; and that one is able to consider oneself trustworthy enough so that the providers will not need to be on guard lest they be nipped. . . .

. . . But let it be said here that the amount of trust derived from earliest infantile experience does not seem to depend on absolute quantities of food or demonstrations of love, but rather on the quality of the maternal relationship. Mothers create a sense of trust in their children by that kind of administration which in its quality combines sensitive care of the baby's individual needs and a firm sense of personal trustworthiness within the trusted framework of their culture's life style. This forms the basis in the child for a sense of identity which will later combine a sense of being "all right," of being oneself, and of becoming what other people trust one will become [1963, pp. 247–248, 249].

This trust-mistrust crisis is, of course, resolved differentially, so that even the normal participants in a sensitivity laboratory will differ in their ability to trust themselves and others. It is important for the participants to realize this as they attempt to create a climate of trust in the group.

Gibb (1964) claims that trust is absolutely essential for growth; he links defensiveness to the trust-mistrust crises:

A person learns to grow through his increasing acceptance of himself and others. Serving as the primary block to such acceptance are the defensive feelings of fear and distrust that arise from the prevailing defensive climates in most cultures. In order to participate consciously in his own growth a person must learn to create for himself, in his dyadic and group relationships, defense-reductive climates that will continue to reduce his own fears and distrusts [p. 279].

Gibb sees the participants' unresolved feelings of fear and distrust, even though these may be buried and denied, as formidable obstacles to growth through group interaction. Acceptance must precede what he calls "data flow"—that is, the free interaction of group members: "Data flow is possible only within the limits of trust formation. A free flow of data is possible only with antecedent or concurrent reduction of distrusts and fears [p. 283]." Careful research is needed in this area, but there is some evidence to back up Gibb's clinical observations. Mellinger (1956), for instance, found that scientists in a research organization tended to conceal their attitudes about a particular issue when communicating with persons in whom they lacked trust. Read (1962) found that among executives the less trust they hold for their immediate superiors, the greater the tendency toward "inaccurate communication [p. 10]" with these superiors. As Collins and Guetzkow (1964) note: "Communication behavior is a function of ... the nature of the milieu [p. 167]." If distrust colors the environment, we can expect distortions in communication.

Some of the symptoms of distrust in the group are:

... persistent defense of one's public image, attempts to change attitudes and beliefs of others, attempts to make decisions for others, avoidance of feeling, avoidance of conflict, advice giving, flattery, cynicism about the powers of the group, derogation of the group's abilities, lack of confidence in the product of the group, and denial of membership [Gibb, 1964, p. 284].

Gibb (1968) suggests other symptoms of lack of trust in groups: strategy behavior, differences between what is said inside and outside the group, and impersonal talk:

Early in groups, people are pretty closed and they operate with a certain kind of strategy. They program their communications, they plan what to say. They plan what to say on the basis of the effect it will have. ... The more I fear someone, the more I ration out my communications, the more I restrain my behavior, the more controlled I am. ...

An operational test we use in research is: Do people say the same things about each other in the group that they do in clusters going home? To their wives after they get there . . . ? If they say the same things about each other outside as they do to each other inside, that is a good feedback system. It is very rare in my experience. . . .

People tend, when they are fearful, to be impersonal. They tend to escalate the cognitive level, to say: "Isn't it interesting that people are this way—people need people," rather than to say "I need you," "I hurt," "I love you," "Sit by me" . . . [pp. 3–4].

Therefore, since little happens in a group until the participants learn to trust one another, one of the most important tasks of early group sessions is the formation of a climate of trust. It is far better to try to forestall the mistrust behavior described by Gibb than to try to remedy it. In the contract group, the process of building a climate of trust is aided by the contract itself. If one knows that all the other participants have subscribed to the same contract, then it is easier to trust them, for one can, at least to some degree, predict their behavior and reactions. However, if the contract is imposed on the group instead of being freely chosen (imposition of contract instead of entry by contract), then it is necesary to determine to what degree the participants are actually "buying" the contract before one can use the contract as a source of trust. The leader-member should be familiar with the signs of distrust within the group and bring the entire trust issue out into the open. If he does not do this, the participants themselves will do it eventually (and sometimes repeatedly); therefore, his early confrontation of the trust issue might be more economic in the long run.

The way the preposition "behind" is used in the English language casts some light on the question of support and trust. If someone is "behind" someone else, this is usually either a heartening or a threatening situation. "We are behind you all the way," is a positive and supportive situation, but if a person is merely behind another in the sense that he is in the shadows, undeclared and unknown, then his presence is experienced as threatening. If a person does not in some way declare himself "for" me—especially if my contact with him is fairly extensive—then it is not paranoid for me to wonder whether he is against me in some way. He need not declare himself "for" me directly; it is sufficient if he indicates that he is the kind of person who is "'for" others generally. Another way of saying this is that the "he who is not for me is against me" dictum has some general applicability to human relationships. Most men would prefer to have those who are not behind them in a positive sense to stand out in the open, in front of them, in honest opposition, if necessary, rather than remain in the shadows unknown. This kind of honesty in the sensitivity group goes far in establishing a facilitative climate of trust.

Misplaced trust can, as Lynd (1958) points out, lead to deep, even incapacitating, experiences of shame:

Even more than the uncovering of weakness or ineptness, exposures of misplaced confidence can be shameful—happiness, love, anticipation of a response that is not there, something personally momentous received as inconsequential. The greater the expectation, the more acute the shame; the greater the discrepancy between one's image of oneself and the image others have of one, the more one has to put on a "brave face" [pp. 43–44].

Creating a climate of trust, then, involves having others declare themselves in the group—that is, declare their attitudes (or lack of them) toward others. Still, one cannot wait to share oneself until he is absolutely sure that he will be accepted by others. There is always the chance that one's gift of oneself will be spurned or go unnoticed, at least to a degree. However, the risk of laboratory training reflects the risk of life; too many of us fail to grow because we prefer a climate of absolute or excessive safety. The laboratory, because it is life in miniature (though it is also life under a magnifying glass), has supportive resources more readily at hand, for those who take risks and fail or are failed, than do real life situations.

Someone once called belief "prophetic of reality"; that is, if a person believes deeply enough in something, his faith will enable him to muster the forces needed to create that in which he believes. Trust, in the sense of entrusting oneself to others, can also be prophetic of reality: the person who dares to entrust himself to others goes far in creating a climate of trust in the group.

Consequent Support in Terms of Reinforcement

Collins and Guetzkow (1964), in reviewing the literature on communication and interaction, come to the conclusion that "communication behavior is a function of . . . the kinds of reward particularly valued by the individual (his motives and needs). A communicator initiates communication when he expects a reward on the basis of his own past experience with this or similar task environments and fellow group members [p. 167]." Therefore, if the various forms of antecedent support are instrumental in getting effective group interaction started and in contributing to the formation of a viable interactional climate, it is consequent support in terms of reinforcement that keeps the interaction going and brings it to term.

Recognition and Appropriate Response as Reinforcement. In the contract group, reinforcement means, in general, that once a member has participated in some form of contractual behavior (e.g., self-disclosure, expression of feeling), the other members should both (1) *recognize* (actively, behaviorally) the fact that he has acted responsibly and creatively, that he has done something good in the group, and (2) *respond* appropriately to his growthful behavior. Ideally, recognition and response merge into a single act. For instance, if a person engages in meaningful self-disclosure (story), it is not enough for the group simply to recognize verbally the fact that he has acted contractually—"You have engaged in story and this is a good thing in this group"—but they should react or respond to *what* he has said (if it is story, the assumption is that it is meaningful); that is, they should react personally to the disclosure. Appropriate response means response proportioned to the modality in which the other is speaking. For example, if A, perhaps only after screwing up his courage to take a responsible risk in the group, confronts B, then B's best response to A would be to examine himself on the issues suggested by A. Such a response would both recognize and reinforce A's contractual behavior. Again, if A reveals himself significantly to the group, then B might respond by revealing himself along similar or relevant dimensions. B's act would indicate to A not only that he has listened carefully to him but also that he has felt a certain solidarity with him. Such an act would provide A with a good deal of reinforcement. On the other hand, if B were to reply to A's self-disclosure irresponsibly—for instance, by trying to upstage A with his own disclosure—then, obviously, his response would have the opposite effect.

The trouble with simple direct recognition of contractual behavior—"We recognize the fact that you have engaged in story"—as opposed to full contractual response which *includes* recognition is that recognition that stands by itself can carry overtones of separateness from the other. If A merely recognizes the fact that B has acted contractually, he stands off from B to a certain extent by not really involving himself with B. Mere recognition of the plight of another is closer to pity than empathy, and a person who pities another separates himself or stands off from the other. Sometimes, however—and this is especially true of earlier sessions in the life of the group—the only response a person is honestly capable of is to recognize the fact that another member has acted contractually. For instance, if someone reveals himself to a degree that was unexpected in the group, he might catch the other members off guard. Perhaps all they can say at the moment (if they say anything) is something like this: "This is the deepest level of self-disclosure that we have experienced in this group. But, although we appreciate the fact that someone has moved us forward by his contractual behavior, we are still at a loss for appropriate modes of response." I have participated in groups in which premature and ill-prepared-for self-revelation has, unfortunately, merely angered the group. In one group, the participants kept referring to one such disclosure as "the bomb," and the group finally ended without their really being able to handle this disclosure. Such a situation could have been avoided if the group had first discussed its goals and worked out some sort of contract to deal realistically with possible group interactions.

Jourard (1967) discusses some research that seems to support the general position taken here—that is, that more than mere recognition of contractual behavior is necessary for adequate reinforcement:

Another student, W. J. Powell, Jr. (1964), did a doctoral dissertation which was more carefully controlled than Rivenbark's exploratory study. He conducted interviews with college students, asking them to make themselves as fully known to him, the interviewer, as they cared to. He carefully controlled all extraneous variables and compared the increase in self-disclosure (using an operant-conditioning design) that occurred when, on the one hand, he responded with authentic disclosures of his own (in contrast to "reflecting" the feeling or content of their disclosures) and when, on the other hand, he responded with expressions of approval and support. He found that "approving, supporting" responses did not increase the students' disclosures at all. Reflection and restatement of their disclosures resulted in an increase in disclosures of negative self-statements, but did not affect positive, self-enhancing expressions. Self-disclosure from the researcher was associated with significant increases in the subjects' disclosures of both positive and negative self-references [p. 114].

This research tends to confirm what has been said here about approval and the value of responding by self-involvement. The implications, not only for sensitivity training but for therapy in general, are evident, even though it means a departure from more comfortable therapeutic approaches to which we have become accustomed.

The Necessity of Immediacy of Reinforcement. Collins and Guetzkow (1964), in extending the experimental data on the timing of rewards (see Hilgard & Bower, 1966), suggest that temporal immediacy has its place in social-reward situations also:

> The experimental data on the timing of rewards suggest that they are most effective when they follow behavior within a few seconds. Although the ability of humans to verbalize and plan for the future increases the effectiveness of an environmental reward, many social systems would be impossible if events in the task environment were the sole source of reward. It may take a goodly time for the group to realize its goals, but social rewards may be applied immediately by verbal and gestural behaviors in the face-to-face group [p. 77].

For instance, what is suggested here may well refer to the situation in which a sensitivity-training participant puts himself on the line in some way or other, and, once he is finished, there follows a comparatively long silence. We should find out whether such temporal gaps are deleterious to the social-reinforcement system operative in the group, and the hypothesis here is that they well might be. I remember one group in which a young man put himself on the line and, after he had finished, called for some feedback from the others. Luckily enough, this particular segment of the group experience was recorded on videotape. He received practically no immediate response from the others. In fact, when he called for response, most of the participants tried to "leave the scene" by bowing their heads or by looking off in a different direction. When I replayed the tape, I told them to watch what they did with their heads when they were asked to give some feedback. Then I asked the one who had put himself on the line how he felt at that moment. He said that he had felt alone, very much alone.

I would hypothesize that the more immediacy there is in reinforcement behavior in the sensitivity group, the greater the effect. This refers to temporal immediacy, certainly, for temporal immediacy of reinforcement means, at least, that the listener has picked up the cue "I am finished" or the cue "I would like some response." But it also refers to qualitative immediacy—that is, the degree to which the respondent really puts himself into the response. Indeed, such qualitative immediacy seems to be more important than mere temporal immediacy. One way of conceptualizing this qualitative immediacy of response is in terms of a therapist variable currently receiving a good deal of attention—accurate empathy (Rogers, 1961, 1967; Truax, 1961, 1963; Truax & Carkhuff, 1967).

Immediacy of Supportive Reinforcement in Terms of Accurate Empathy. Rogers and Truax (1967) describe accurate empathic understanding:

The ability of the therapist accurately and sensitively to understand experiences and feelings *and their meaning to the client* during the moment-to-moment encounter of psychotherapy constitutes what perhaps can be described as the "work" of the therapist after he has first provided the contextual basis for the relationship by his self-congruence . . . and his unconditional positive regard.

Accurate empathic understanding means that the therapist is completely at home in the universe of the patient. It is a moment-to-moment sensitivity that is in the "here and now," the immediate present. . . . It is of limited use to the individual if the therapist only arrives at this insightful and empathic understanding . . . as he drives home at night. Such a delayed empathy or insight may be of value if the therapist has a later chance to respond to the same theme, but its value would lie in formulating his empathic response to the patient's *immediate* living of the relationship.

The ability and sensitivity required to communicate these inner meanings back to the client in a way that allows these experiences to be "his" is the major part of empathic understanding. . . . To communicate this perception in a language attuned to the patient that allows him more clearly to sense and formulate his confusion, his fear, his rage or anger is the essence of the communicative aspect of accurate empathy.

. . . The communication is not only by the use of words that the patient might well have used, but also by the sensitive play of voice qualities which reflect the seriousness, the intentness, and the depth of feeling.

. . . The empathic understanding when it is accurately and sensitively communicated seems crucially important in making it possible for a person to get close to himself, to experience his most inward feelings, to maintain contact with his inner self-experiences, thus allowing for the recognition and resolution of incongruencies. It is this self-exploration and consequent recognition and resolution of incongruities that we believe allows the client to change and to develop his potentialities. . . .

The common element in a low level of empathy involves the therapist's doing something other than "listening" or "understanding"; he may be evaluating the client, giving advice, offering intellectual interpretations, or reflecting upon his own feelings or experiences. Indeed, a therapist may be accurately describing psychodynamics to the patient, but in a language not that of the client, or at a time when these dynamics are far removed from the current feelings of the client, so that there is a flavor of teacher-pupil interaction [pp. 104–106].

Truax and Carkhuff (1967) note that "accurate empathy which stressed diagnostic accuracy or sensitivity to feeling or experience from a slightly analytic point of view proved much more highly related to the criterion indices than did the better known variable which grew out of the client-centered tradition [p. 365]." However this statement may be reconciled with what Rogers and Truax have said above, it is hypothesized here that the accurate empathy that is effective in sensitivity groups (and indeed in human relationships generally) includes both the ability to get within the other and the willingness and ability to convey this ability to the other in terms intelligible to him. Perhaps this kind of empathy would make a therapist more active than a Rogerian therapist is generally thought to be, but if this is a development in client-centered theory, it seems to be in the right direction.

Reinforcement of the Individual Rather than the Group. Research indicates that individuals involved in some group task, rather than the group as a whole, should receive reinforcement. Rosenberg (1960) demonstrated that an individual will not learn new modes of behavior if the group as a whole is rewarded in such a way that the task-environmental rewards and punishments are not specifically coordinated to *his* behavior. Zajonc (1962) has reported that the performance of seven-man teams was inhibited when individuals received knowledge only of group success and failure and did not receive feedback on individual performances. These findings contain an important lesson for sensitivity groups. Group members frequently tend to address the group as a whole, instead of one another, when more individualized responses would be more appropriate. While this might be safer (because it is less involving), it is also self-defeating, because the participants as individuals are not rewarded for taking risks in communication. Furthermore, communications addressed to the group as a whole tend to become general and abstractive, less immediate, less personal. Certainly some communications must be addressed to the group as a whole, and all communications are directed toward the group in some way. If A reveals himself, he usually reveals himself to the group as a whole directly (unless his self-revelation is in response to a communication from another member, in which case it is made directly to the other member and indirectly to the entire group). But if B responds to what A has said by addressing the group in general, even in rewarding terms—"Now we are getting somewhere!"—his response is less effective than if he had addressed A directly. In this case, the group is best reinforced by A's being reinforced.

Failures in Support

Group members can fail to support one another in a variety of ways. Some of them are listed here.

Cliché or Ritualistic Support. Our language is filled with socially appropriate clichés expressive of support—"I know how you feel," "Is there anything I can do?" "You must feel awful," "I just didn't know"—and they usually abound in sensitivity groups. One of the more disturbing clichés is "I know just how you feel" followed immediately by "because I . . ." It is disturbing because the implication is that the authenticity of another's feelings in some way depends upon whether it can be verified in the experience of the one listening to him. This situation at its worst is represented by the person who merely uses the cliché "I know how you feel" in order to divert attention to his own experience. The problem with such ritualistic or socialized support is that it simply is not supportive. We find noncliché support difficult because it involves emotion—the other's and our own—and we simply are not comfortable with emotion. We find noncliché support difficult because it involves going out of ourselves to the other. It demands that we lay aside our egocentricity, and many of us are not ready to do that. Frequently, when we try to express positive emotions in support of one another, we sound phony because we do not deal in these emotions from day to day and we are simply gauche with the unfamiliar. In a sensitivity group, it may be more supportive (because it is more honest) for a member to admit that he is faced by one of the lessons of the

Book of Job—that is, that it is fruitless, and even inhuman, to try to engage in logical and highly socialized dialogue with someone who is suffering. If a participant frankly admits his inability to go beyond the cliché for the moment, even this can be refreshingly supportive. In fact, this honest "clearing of the decks" might make attempts at more authentic kinds of support somewhat easier.

Cheap Empathy. Some sensitivity-training participants never miss an opportunity to give support, especially to the sufferer. They resemble professional wake-goers, their motto seeming to be: "I am always at your side (in time of disaster)." Such support is ritualistic, triggered by any sign of pain in the other, and seems to be directed toward fulfilling the needs of the one giving support rather than the one in need. Actually the one supported is seen as a stereotype— "one in pain," "one needing my support"—and to the degree that this is true, support is not authentic interaction with *this* person. On the other hand, oversupport might be a person's way of manifesting his own need for support or mothering. Support should not be "mush," even though it may be tender; it should not be sentimental, even though it involves feelings and emotions. It should arise from the strength of the one who gives support and not from his weakness. The one who gives authentic support will give support in both adversity and joy, success and failure because support does not mean "propping the other up," it means being "with" him, especially when the other reveals, or is trying to come to grips with, some of the more dramatic dimensions of his life, positive or negative. Lynd (1958) suggests that we overemphasize support in adversity: "Scheler points out that the term 'sympathy' is often wrongly confined to pity or compassion. Sympathy with suffering (*Mitleid*) and sympathy with joy (*Mitfreude*) are two different things, often confused, and the second is frequently neglected in the study of the first [p. 236]." It takes both strength and skill to support the other because he *is* the other and not because he is either victim or hero. Only those who are not afraid of universal contact with the other can provide a wide range of support.

The St. Sebastian Syndrome. St. Sebastian was a Christian martyr who was killed, it is reported, by being shot full of arrows. This frequently happens in an analogous way in sensitivity groups. A person tells his story and, although it is vaguely sensed by others that support would be an appropriate response, no one knows how to go about the task of giving support. Being unskilled in the art of support, they tend to substitute a caricature. They begin to ask questions to show their "interest": "How do you feel? When did it happen? How are things now? How long has it been going on?"— etc., etc. This keeps the victim in the center of attention, of course, and does away with the need for real involvement or response. At first (at least this is my experience) the victim does not recognize the game; he thinks that the others are actually asking serious questions and he tries to answer them. Then he begins to feel that what is happening is either out of place, missing the point, or downright ludicrous, but being polite, he still answers the questions for a while (though with less and less enthusiasm). His interlocutors keep pumping him with arrows (by this time even they are tiring of the game) until he and the interaction die. This caricature of support can also be called the "Is it bigger than a breadbox" syndrome both because of the Twenty Questions nature of the game and because such a question frequently seems as meaningful as those being asked. This does not mean that an occasional question cannot be both extremely insightful and deeply supportive, but it must be appropriate, nonritualistic, sincere, pithy, forceful, and a prelude to deeper involvement with the other. A question in this vein that is actually quite confronting can be more supportive than all the clichés and vapid questions put together.

Support versus "Red Crossing." "Red crossing" is a term that originated, I believe, at Synanon and means rushing to the aid of a group member like a Red Cross worker. Its connotations are obviously pejorative. Some people cannot stand seeing another in any kind of pain, physical or psychological, even in cases in which the pain is beneficial. For instance, if someone in the group is being confronted in a responsible way and therefore necessarily undergoing the pain associated with the process of confrontation, it is the red crosser who comes to the aid of the confrontee in an effort to get him off the hook. He does so in a number of ways: he gives approval to the confrontee's behavior (whether the confrontee approves of *his own* behavior or not), he tries to rationalize away the other's guilt or responsibility, gives speeches the burden of which is that all of us are likewise sinners, and in general tries to show that the person being confronted is an innocent victim needlessly suffering. The red crosser is not at all like the person who intervenes when he believes that the confrontational process has become irresponsible, negative, and profitless in a particular case. Such intervention is often needed in sensitivity groups (less often, I believe, in contract groups). Needless to say, in the contract group, the red crosser fulfills no useful function.

Silence as Failure in Support. "They also fail who only sit and wait"—to misuse a line from Milton. A group member once talked about the hurt that she felt from the silent members. She did not feel that they were hostile, but she found it difficult to engage in self-disclosure in front of people who willed to remain strangers. Even silence that is perceived as sympathetic is harmful if it is protracted. In the contract group, there would be no silent members; in fact, there cannot be if the contract is being fulfilled.

The Problems in Receiving Support

Even when support is given responsibly and sincerely, there is no guarantee that it is going to be received as it is given. The people who attend sensitivity laboratories come with a wide range of normal problems of living, a number of which militate against their being open to even truly human supportive behavior. Some arrive with dependency problems against which they have been struggling. They see themselves as tending to be overly dependent, and they resent any kind of behavior in others which can be interpreted as playing to their dependency needs. Evidently such counter-dependent behavior interferes with their effective involvement with others. Therefore, if it becomes clear during the interaction of the group that a participant has been fending off attempts on the part of others to support him, his behavior should become the object of confrontation. If he is struggling with dependency, then, if possible, he is to share this problem with the group, he is to bring it into community where it can be handled. On the other hand, there are those who thrive on attention and uncreative forms of support. They are constantly looking for subtle signs of approval. Ideally, support, at least in the contract group, should elicit further contractual behavior from the one who seeks support or to whom support is actually given. If it does not, if supportive behavior constantly goes sour in the case of any particular participant, the group should take this tendency as diagnostic and try to get the problem out into the open. Furthermore, if the members of a group are giving one another support and still find that little or no progress is being made in effecting a viable climate of trust (even though there is a generally pleasant atmosphere in the group), then it is time to investigate whether support putatively given is also support received. Unfortunately, groups can run a long time on social pleasantness and other counterfeits of support. Support counterfeits are seen for what they really are by their effects: (1) they tend to make the group comfortable, and the participants tend to lose that edge of anxiety that frequently stirs up meaningful interaction; (2) contractual behavior diminishes, becomes emasculated, or disappears entirely.

Conclusion

No one and no contract can program the development of a climate of trust and support in a sensitivity-training group. As Gibb (1968) notes, the group, no matter how long it remains in existence, continually discovers new levels of trust and support. The initial reaction of many participants is one of hopelessness: "I could never really entrust myself to you." However, as the group moves forward, even the most timid, encouraged by the risks the other members take, begin to move out into the group. If the contract helps the participants, including the most fearful, to move into community more quickly and with a greater degree of psychological safety, then it serves its purpose well.

Chapter Nine: Confrontation in Laboratory Training

Introduction

Confrontation is an important growth variable both in the laboratory and in life, but it is one that merits careful explanation for a number of reasons. First of all, confrontation in caricature is popularly taken as the symbol of laboratory training in general and sensitivity training in particular: "I don't have to attend a laboratory to tell people off and to give them their chance at me." It *is* true that some laboratory experiences are characterized by irresponsible confrontation, but this is certainly not generally true, nor is there any reason why it *has* to be the case in any given laboratory experience. Laboratories are designed to be growth experiences, not places where the psyche is laid open to possible destruction. And yet time and again people approach me asking me whether a particular individual should take part in a laboratory experience or whether a laboratory should be allowed to operate at all lest an individual or a group be exposed to psychic harm. Well-run laboratory experiences are no more dangerous than group therapy experiences, and I assume that the latter *are* run for the benefit of the participants. Laboratories have been designed in which *all* the participants are drawn from a psychiatric population (Morton, 1965) and with apparently excellent results (Johnson, Hanson, Rothaus, Morton, Lyle, & Moyer, 1965). Other laboratories prefer to exclude those with more severe problems in living (the NTL literature specifically states that its laboratories are not designed as therapy sessions). If confrontation is responsible—that is, proportioned to both the laboratory design and population—then it will be a powerful force for growth.

Second, confrontation as a therapy variable or as a modality of mature human interaction has received practically no theoretical attention in the literature (Douds, Berenson, Carkhuff, & Pierce, 1967), and controlled research in this area has just begun (e.g., Berenson & Mitchell, 1968; Berenson, Mitchell, & Laney, 1968; Berenson, Mitchell, & Moravec, 1968; Boyd & Sisney, 1967; Truax, Fine, Moravec, & Millis, 1968). Confrontation is another therapy variable that is therapeutic because it is a fully human and growthful kind of interaction; it receives no mystic baptism because it is associated with therapy. Douds, Berenson, Carkhuff, and Pierce (1967) suggest that life itself "without confrontation is directionless, passive, and impotent [p. 172]." One of the reasons confrontation seems necessary for full human living is what might be called the bias nature of man: man, when unchallenged, tends to drift towards extremes; he becomes either too much "for" himself (Anderson, 1964) or too much "against" himself (Reik, 1949). Or he merely drifts into the psychopathology of the average, which, given his potentialities, is also an extreme. The mature man is one who has learned to challenge himself and his own behavior; he is always looking for more productive ways to be and interact with others. But, since he is really mature, when he fails to challenge himself, he is grateful when his friends (and perhaps even his enemies) are concerned enough to confront him.

Confrontation, then, has its place, first of all, in all mature human interaction. Because it is a modality of mature living, it also belongs both in interactions that attempt to explore human potentialities and deal with the psychopathology of the average (training laboratories) and in interactions designed to come to grips with more serious problems in living (psychotherapy). It is not strange to find confrontation in therapy and other interpersonal-growth experiences; rather, it is strange that normal men make such limited and ineffectual use of such a powerful growth variable.

Confrontation, Psychoanalysis, and Client-Centered Counseling.
Douds, Berenson, Carkhuff, and Pierce (1967) note the general
failure of the psychotherapies to deal with the issue of confrontation: "Confrontation, as life, continues independently of all therapeutic models. With the possible exception of the existentialists, none
of the major systems leaves room for the concept of confrontation:
the existentialists alone approach confrontation by their concept of
'encounter' [p. 170]." Many of the therapies in existence today have
been directly or indirectly, but still deeply, influenced by both the
psychoanalytic tradition and, at least in the United States, the non-
directive approach. Nondirective approaches, by definition, eliminate direct confrontation, and the therapies that have been influenced by the psychoanalytic tradition have stressed insight rather
than action (see London, 1964). Douds and his associates (1967)
believe that the absence of confrontation in therapy has produced
a rather exsanguinated therapeutic culture; they refer to the
"middle-class" therapy "which hopes to seduce the illness away
[p. 171]." With regard to the nondirective tradition, however, perhaps we have come full circle. In Hegelian terms, the *thesis* would
be therapy as advice-giving, therapy in which the therapist took
over the direction of the other's life, therapy that was too heavy-
handed, robbing the client of his freedom to grow. In the main,
the nondirective approach came into being as the *antithesis* to such
a tradition and stressed total acceptance and empathy, the ability
to get into the world of the client. The *synthesis*, the beginnings of
which are being felt today, finds a place in therapy for responsible
confrontation, but in an atmosphere of unconditional positive regard
and empathy.

Confrontation and Other Therapies. Although few writings deal
directly and separately with confrontation as a therapy variable,
therapies in which confrontation plays a key, if not central, role do
exist. Synanon and Daytop Village (Casriel, 1963; Maslow, 1967;
Patton, 1967; Shelly & Bassin, 1965; Yablonsky, 1965) have been
using confrontational encounters as an important part of their total
institutional programs; and it is with some frequency that those
participating in the programs are called to task because they are
"talking the talk but not walking the walk"—that is, their behavior
is lagging behind Daytop or Synanon expectancies. Alcoholics
Anonymous groups have long been confronting what they call the
"stinkin' thinkin'" of members who try to rationalize and excuse

their behavior. Mainord (1968a, 1968b) and Mowrer (Mowrer, 1967; Drakeford, 1967) have for years now been using contractual approaches to therapy, approaches in which contract-oriented confrontation plays a major role. For instance, Mainord suggests the following dialogue to indicate how his patients are held to the contract:

Patient A: How did you get along sexually?
Patient B: Not very well.
Patient A: What do you mean?
Patient B: I'd rather not talk about that—it gives me this terrible feeling just to think about it.
Therapist: Your agreement was to be completely honest, and that withholding information was to be considered dishonest. You didn't agree to be honest *only* when it felt good, if you'll remember [1968b, p. 1].

Ellis (1962) uses logic, reasoning, suggestions, persuasion, and prescription of activities in his rational-emotive psychotherapy, all of which contain a large element of confrontation:

Therapist: Let's get back to changing, John. *Would* it be so terrible if you got refused, even by a girl you didn't know that there was a good chance beforehand she was going to refuse you, and you didn't know at all what was going to be? Or *would* it be so terrible if you grandiosely didn't get exactly what you wanted without any effort and without their selecting you?
Patient: No, it, it, uh, it wouldn't be bad. This I, you know, I, this I can logically believe this.
Therapist: At *times.*
Patient: Yeah, at times.
Therapist: But *most* of the time, more strongly, you still believe the other things . . . [Patterson, 1966, pp. 128–129].

Bach (1966) conducts "Marathon" groups according to rules that demand a kind of total confrontation or what he calls "constructive aggression [p. 998]." The ordinary rules of tact are suspended for the duration of the Marathon. Stoller (1968b) also outlines a kind of marathon therapy in which confrontation plays an important part. Beier (1966) has written on the use of the "asocial" response as a means used by the therapist to free himself from the games of his client and to confront the client with what he is really saying or implying. Corsini's (1968) "immediate therapy" is a form of group therapy in which both self-confrontation in community and confrontation by others play a central role. The existentialists (e.g., Frankl, 1962; May, 1958, 1961; May & Van Kaam, 1963; Van Kaam, 1962) place such emphasis on the client's "possibilities" and on his freedom and responsibility that confrontational encounters between patient and therapist are inevitable.

The list of those who use confrontation as one of their therapeutic tools could, I am sure, be lengthened considerably, but the point here is that confrontation is not new to therapy, any more than it is new to life (Plato long ago said that the unexamined life is not worth living, and the unchallenged life tends to be the unexamined life). Moreover, a good deal of informal experimentation with confrontation is taking place, both in therapy and in laboratory-training situations. As a powerful element of human interaction, confrontation can both stimulate personal and interpersonal growth and cause extensive harm. In inept hands, it becomes the tool of the user's own deficits and pathology. On the other hand, when used responsibly, it becomes another avenue of involvement with and concern for the other. What follows is an attempt to describe confrontation and its caricatures and to indicate some of its uses in a variety of growth-group experiences.

Toward a Description of Confrontation. Berne (1966) defines confrontation in terms of his transactional system:

In confrontation the therapist uses information previously elicited and specified, in order to disconcert the patient's Parent, Child, or contaminated Adult by pointing out an inconsistency. The patient is stirred up and his psyche is thrown out of balance, and this tends to cause a redistribution of cathexis. . . .

To the patient's Child, a confrontation may represent a Parental move in a game that stimulates defensive operations learned early in life. . . . To his Adult it may represent an intellectual challenge for which he is grateful ("I never noticed that before"). To his Parent it may represent an incursion on Parental authority . . . [p. 235].

Confrontation, therefore, has the purpose of ending a game type of interaction, but if it is not reacted to properly, it becomes a stimulus for further game involvement. Douds and his associates (1967) describe confrontation of a type that is adaptable to the needs of a sensitivity group:

Direct confrontation is an act, not a reaction. It is initiated by the therapist, based on his core understanding of the client. It brings the client into more direct contact with himself, his strengths and resources, as well as his self-destructive behavior. The purpose of confrontation is to reduce the ambiguity and incongruities in the client's experiencing and communication. In effect, it is a challenge to the client to become integrated; that is, at one with his own experience. It is directed at discrepancies within the client (his ideal versus real self); between what the client says and does (insight and action); and between illusion and reality (the therapist's experience of the client versus the client's expression of his experience of himself and the therapist). The therapeutic goal is non-destructive and emerging unity within the client. It implies a constructive attack upon an unhealthy confederation of miscellaneous illusions, fantasies, and life avoidance techniques in order to create a reintegration at a higher level of health [p. 171].

This is the kind of confrontation that people engage in who are concerned about one another.

The Measurement of Confrontation in Research.   Berenson and his associates (Berenson, Mitchell, & Laney, 1968; Berenson, Mitchell, & Moravec, 1968) have distinguished five major types of confrontation for the purpose of research:

Five major types of confrontation were employed: Experiential, Didactic, Strength, Weakness and Encouragement to Action. . . . Experiential confrontation was defined as the therapist's specific response to any discrepancy between patient and therapist's experiencing of the patient, or to any discrepancy between patient statement about himself and patient's inner experience of himself, or to any discrepancy between patient and therapist's experience of the therapist. A didactic confrontation was defined as the therapist's direct clarification of the patient's misinformation or lack of information. This type of confrontation may include the therapist's efforts to offer the patient information based on test data, behavior, or data about some aspect of the world as well as details about the therapist or the structure and function of the therapy process. Confrontation of Strength referred to an experiential confrontation which focused on the patient's resources. Weakness referred to an experiential confrontation which focused on the patient's liabilities or pathology. Finally, Encouragement to Action involved the therapist pressing the patient to act on his world in some constructive manner and discouraging a passive stance toward life. Frequency and type of confrontation were accepted only when the two independent judges agreed upon both presence and type of confrontation [Berenson, Mitchell, & Laney, 1968, pp. 111–112].

In a sense, then, there are only three types, for Strength and Weakness are both subdivisions of Experiential confrontation. Results seem to indicate that high-level therapists use experiential confrontation more frequently, while low-level therapists tend to confront the client's weaknesses (however, confrontation of weakness is defined in the article as a kind of experiential confrontation). Whether these are the categories of confrontation that will eventually prove most helpful in research remains to be seen, but certainly a much clearer theoretical discussion of the bases for classification is needed.

Truax and his associates (Truax, Fine, Moravec, & Millis, 1968) have studied the effects of the therapist's persuasive potency in individual psychotherapy. A therapist is high in persuasive potency if during an interview he "is the kind of person that communicates a socially influential or potent person [p. 360—again, a clearer operational definition of persuasive potency would have made this article more meaningful]." The results suggested "that therapist persuasiveness operates to effect patient improvement somewhat independently of other personal qualities of the therapist (specifically his level of accurate empathy and nonpossessive warmth for the patient) [p. 362]." I would hypothesize that there is a positive relationship between the therapist's persuasive potency and his ability to engage in growthful confrontation. Indeed, the relationship between persuasion (see Frank, 1961) and confrontation in therapy and other growth experiences is an intriguing one, but little can be said until more effective operational definitions for and measurement of both persuasion and confrontation have been devised and research has been carried out. I would now like to dissect the act of confrontation and suggest ways in which it can become an effective variable in interpersonal-growth experiences.

The Anatomy of Confrontation

Generally, confrontation takes place when one person (the confronter), either deliberately or inadvertently, does something that causes or directs another person (the confrontee) to advert to, reflect upon, examine, question, or change some particular aspect of his behavior. In other words, some act on the part of the confronter—whether he is aware of it or not—acts as a stimulus to the confrontee, and this stimulus act has a specific effect on the confrontee: it challenges him, "pulls him up short," directs him to reflect upon or change some aspect of his behavior (behavior, that is, in the wide sense: overt acts, inaction, attitudes, moods, etc.). I believe that confrontation must be described or defined as generally as this if it is to include all behavior that is referred to in the literature as confrontational. Moreover, if it is defined this generally, it becomes quite easy to see that there are many different forms (both growthful and destructive) and many different degrees of confrontation. It is extremely important for sensitivity-training participants to understand the nature of confrontation and to become acquainted with the different forms it can take, for it can be one of the most potent forms of interpersonal behavior, and its power should be respected.

At first glance, confrontation is a simple process, but it can become extremely complicated because of the variables involved: (1) the nature of the stimulus act, (2) the natural bias of the confronter, (3) the relationship between the confronter and the confrontee, (4) the motivation of the confronter, (5) the manner in which the confrontation takes place, (6) the effect which the stimulus act has on the confrontee, (7) the manner in which the confrontee responds to the confrontation. Each of these elements of the confrontational process merits separate consideration.

The Nature of the Stimulus Act: The Forms of Confrontation

A wide variety of acts, both verbal and nonverbal, may have a confrontational effect upon any particular person. If the confronter realizes or suspects that an act of his will have a confrontational effect on someone else, then he is deliberately engaging in the modality of confrontation. However, if an act has a confrontational effect that he neither foresaw nor intended, then the confrontation is not deliberate. It is evident that group members should become as aware as possible of the effects of the acts they place, for indeliberate (and thus uncontrolled) confrontation can be destructive. A review of some of the kinds of stimulus acts that can have confrontational effects is a starting point for making confrontation a more rational process.

Confrontation can take place through a variety of stimulus acts. The following are the confrontational stimuli dealt with in this chapter: giving the confrontee information he does not possess or is considered to possess in an inadequate way; interpretation of the confrontee's behavior; directly challenging the other's behavior; self-involvement of confronter with confrontee as a mode of confrontation; group situational variables that are considered confrontational—for example, group exercises, the contract itself in a contract group, being with strangers; "processing"—that is, group self-criticism; withdrawal of reinforcement; the use of videotape. Each of these stimuli will be taken up in order.

Confrontation through Information. One of the basic forms of confrontation is to transmit to another some information concerning his person. Again, such information transmission may or may not be deliberate, and it may not be foreseen that it will have a confrontational effect. One way of illustrating this process is by means of "The Johari Window" (Luft & Ingham, 1955), which we have already seen in Chapter 7. Each quadrant of the window (see

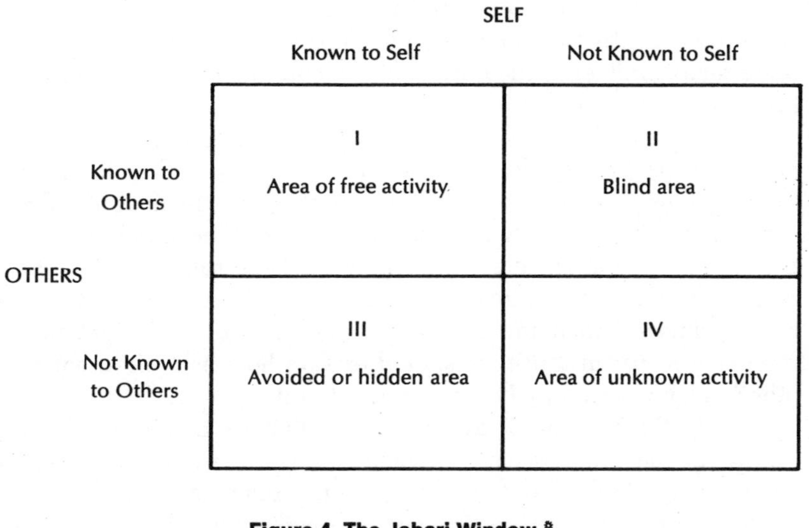

SELF

	Known to Self	Not Known to Self
Known to Others	I Area of free activity	II Blind area
Not Known to Others	III Avoided or hidden area	IV Area of unknown activity

OTHERS

Figure 4. The Johari Window. *

* Reprinted by permission from *Group Processes: An Introduction to Group Dynamics,* copyright 1963 by Joseph Luft. The Johari concept is further described in *Of Human Interaction* by the same author (Palo Alto, California: National Press Books, 1969).

Figure 4) is defined by its coordinates. Therefore, Quadrant II (blind area) involves those things that a person does not know about himself but that are known by at least some others. In confrontation through information, the confronter moves some kind of information that has some relationship to the confrontee from Quadrant II into Quadrant I. By the very fact that one man stands outside another, he has a view of the other of which the other is metaphysically incapable. In this sense, those that surround us are, at least potentially, valuable sources of information about our own persons, for they have sources of evidence that are not directly available to us.

If confrontation were merely the transmission of correct and meaningful information by a concerned observer to a willing listener in order that the latter might engage in and grow through self-examination and subsequent behavioral change, then everything would be simple indeed. In reality, however, such simplicity has to be learned: it is a goal rather than a starting point. In confrontation through information, there are a number of important variables: the nature of the information transmitted (its veridical status or hypothetical character), the person (confronter, confrontee, or other) to whom it principally refers, whether or not the confrontee already possesses the information, the seriousness of the information, and the differential meaning the information has for confronter, confrontee, and the other members of the group. Since these factors influence the quality of the confrontation, they must be taken into consideration.

Does the confrontee already possess the information? If the confronter suspects or knows that what he has to say is already known by the confrontee, then he should weigh the consequences of telling someone what he already knows. For instance, if he says to another participant: "You have not said a word here this evening," undoubtedly the other already realizes this. If the information is already known, then the confronter should manifest his intent in repeating it; for instance, he should explain how he feels about the other's silence and why he has interrupted it.

Usually the confronter assumes that what he has to say is unknown to the other person in some sense. For instance, the confronter may think that the information, though known, bears repeating, that it should be brought into community, that repeating it here and now would have a specific effect, or that it needs to be dramatized. In this case, he assumes that the confrontee does not know the information well enough to act upon it; that is, the information is unknown in the sense that it either has made little impression on the confrontee or has not had any behavioral consequences. On the other hand, if the confronter realizes that it is most likely that the confrontee simply does not possess the information that he is about to transmit, then he should first weigh the consequences of his act, its surprise or shock value, and the impact it will have on the group. In other words, the confronter should have a healthy respect for the power of knowledge and use it reasonably.

The importance of the information and its differential meaning to confronter and confrontee. "Your tie is crooked" is a relatively unimportant piece of information, while "You have bad breath" or "I notice that John never sits close to you" might be relatively more important. The seriousness or the objective importance of a piece of information will usually determine its impact on the group as a whole, including the confrontee, but the subjective meaning of any particular bit of information might differ greatly between confronter, confrontee, and other members of the group. For instance, if the confronter says, "Your tie is on crooked," this statement might be accepted by the confrontee and the group as a whole with indifference, but a crooked tie on *this particular person* might bother the confronter quite a bit. On the other hand, the confrontee might be particularly sensitive to information that is relatively meaningless to the confronter and the group as a whole. The intelligent and considerate confronter is one who can judge not only the absolute importance of any piece of information but also its relative importance to the confrontee and to the others. If there is a good deal of discrepancy between the objective importance of what the confronter has to say and its subjective meaning to him, it might be best if he were to lay the entire problem before the group: "You know, your tie is crooked and that has been bothering me. I tend to be compulsive, I know, but I really think it bothers me because it is *your* tie that is crooked. I think that I have something to work out with you." This keeps the real issue before the group. Furthermore, if the confronter suspects that there is a good deal of discrepancy between the objective importance of the information and the subjective meaning it has for the confrontee, he will have to decide what constructive use may be made of the information.

Interpretation as a Stimulus Act. Interpretation of the behavior of another as a mode of confrontation is a two-edged sword: either it can be a powerful stimulus to fruitful self-examination, or it can lead to irrelevant and meaningless speculation and be used as a means of flight by an individual and by an entire group. If interpretations are nothing more than detached intellectualized exercises on the part of the confronter, then he is playing "psychiatrist" in a game of "psychiatry," the purpose of the game being to avoid intimacy. Interpretation as a game is at best an exercise in logic; at worst it is a destructive form of manipulation of the other. On the other hand, interpretation, if carried out with skill, integrity, and empathy, can be a powerful stimulus to growth.

Theoretically, interpretation leads to insight, and insight is supposed to be a key to better psychological living. This point of view, however, is currently being strongly challenged:

As for goals of therapy, the actionists allege that Insight therapists delude themselves and at their worst, defraud society, by claiming to sell self-knowledge, for this is what practically nobody comes to them to buy. Even knowing that their clients seek relief, not information, they stock their bazaars with certificates that license dispensation of a balm they do not have. Face to face with customers, they then produce a diagram of illness and a blueprint for repair, both always the same—they say he suffers from illusions that must dissipate when once he knows himself. Chief among them, and most illusory of all—he thinks that what he thinks is his trouble really is his trouble. Almost by sleight of mind, the sufferer's surface troubles are made secondary, and the rationalization with which the therapist diverted his attention from them to begin with, launches him on his introspective voyage, and perhaps keeps him there forever—for when does a man really know himself? [London, 1964, pp. 75–76].

London goes on to maintain that the Action therapists, too, have their problems, and he suggests that a combination of the best of both action and insight might be the road that therapy must travel. Douds, Berenson, Carkhuff, and Pierce (1967) also have problems with insight as a vehicle of growth and suggest that too often it leads to psychological paralysis:

In his helplessness and confusion he [the client] seeks therapy. More often than not, he receives insight in the form of a conceptual integration of himself. He may choose insight as a way of life, a culturally higher, secondary gain. Insight may, seemingly, reduce confusion by subsuming the conceptualizations he has about himself in a neater package, allowing him the illusory belief of being "on the top of his problems"—he can now explain his anxiousness on high level terms. Victimized by a wishful need for a magic solution, he accumulates insights based on his *reactions* to different people and situations, hoping for *THE ULTI-MATE INSIGHT* which will be an answer to everything. Still paralyzed to act, he remains dependent and passive, noticeably lacking action and directionality in his existence [pp. 172–173].

Insight gives the client an out, a way to not deal with his behavior. Insight, in the sense in which it is under attack here, deals principally with cognitive systems and the relationships between cognitive systems. The problem is that, in the client, cognitive systems and behavior are in separate compartments. The critics of insight might well paraphrase Kierkegaard's criticism of Hegel and say to the client: "Your insights are beautiful castles; too bad you do not live in them."

However, this does not mean that insight and the interpretations that produce insight are useless. Interpretations as therapeutic variables are certainly prone to defects; they are too often presented as facts instead of hypotheses, and they frequently come as packaged answers to questions instead of stimuli designed to goad the confrontee into finding his own answers. Moreover, the focus of interpretation has been on the dynamics underlying behavior, the hypothetical sources of behavior, rather than behavior itself. But, in the final analysis, both interpretation and insight are valuable to the degree that they lead to constructive behavioral modification:

A comprehensive psychotherapy of the kind implied by this argument would be one that uses both insight and action to attack complex psychological problems. But insight, within this system, would no longer focus so much on motives as on those *behaviors,* present and historical, that produced disorder by violating one's relationship with the functional context that lends meaning to one's life. And its primary purpose, once achieved, would be to steer the development of a new action system, one which channels the individual's behavior in ways intended to restore his functioning within that context. And the context, the referent that makes the action system meaningful, would be neither the painful symptom, nor the wounded selfhood that may lie beneath it, but something external to the individual. For most such therapies, a social system, real or hypothesized, must provide that context [London, 1964, p. 133].

Effective interpersonal living is the ultimate goal of therapy or any other kind of growth experience, and the value of any therapy variable must be judged according to this criterion. Interpretations, then, are valuable to the degree that they are points of departure for growthful action, whether insight intervenes or not. An interpretation is valid and an insight is meaningful if the action which follows from it on the part of the confrontee is growthful—that is, if it leads him to more effective interpersonal relating.

What, then, can we say about interpretation as the stimulus in an act of confrontation? What antecedent validity must it have before it is proffered? Slater (1966) suggests that we need not worry much about the validity of an interpretation, because, in a sense, *all* interpretations are valid.

> . . . In psychotherapy, an interpretation can never be incorrect, unless it is stated comparatively or quantitatively, since human beings are so complex and ambivalent that any statement will be accurate at some level. (This follows from the psychological law that every motive has an equal and opposite contramotive.) From a theoretical viewpoint, the issue is whether it is *salient* or not; from the practical one it is whether or not it is well timed [p. 152, fn 57].

I cannot agree with his epistemological views concerning interpretation (and I will say why presently), but I am in complete accord that the *saliency* (which I consider a practical issue) of the interpretation and other variables associated with the conditions under which it is presented to the confrontee are extremely important. The goodness of an interpretation is measured by its positive or growthful *impact* value: it must cause the confrontee to examine his concrete behavior, some aspect of his life style, in such a way that he is moved to modify this behavior in ways that improve his ability to involve himself with others. It is only the empathic confronter who can come up with salient interpretations, for he alone is both outside and inside the confrontee enough to put his finger on issues that are central to the confrontee's behavior and life style. Timing, too, is important: the good confronter knows when the confrontee has opened, at least enough to receive the full impact of an interpretation. Furthermore, confrontation must be related to the ongoing process of the group and not just appear from nowhere; it should flow from the group experience and be integrated into it. Finally, it should be pithy, the starting point for interaction between the confronter and the confrontee (and the rest of the group) and not a long-winded statement with an air of finality. In general, long-winded speeches in groups, no matter what their "pith and moment," tend to "lose the name of action."

The epistemology of interpretation. Interpretations transmit "information" that is hypothetical, conjectural, inferential: "You know, Bill, I think that you have real sexual hang-ups with women and that maybe you are even latently homosexual." Such a statement is a *hypothesis* and, as such, is the conclusion of an inferential process. Since it is a conclusion, it has premises: certain behavioral cues emitted by the confrontee and a subjective element, the feelings or "clinical" judgment or insight of the confronter. For instance, the premises of the hypothesis stated above might have been: "When you talk with the males in the group, you are usually animated and interested, but your conversations with the females are guarded, short, and sometimes clipped" and other such behavioral observations *together with* the feelings and insights that led to the confronter's *interpretation* of the behavioral cues. Thus, such hypotheses are inferences based on both fact (the behavior of the confrontee) and feeling (the feelings of the confronter, which arise from the impact the confrontee has on him).

Since hypothetical statements arise from the process of clinical inference, it should be remembered that such judgments suffer from all the problems with which the inferential process is plagued. O'Neill (1968) points out the bases of clinical inference and the problems to which each kind of inference is subject: no matter whether one reasons from definitions and categories ("She is obviously schizophrenic"), uses empirical tools of varying accuracy and sophistication ("She has an elevated Pd score," "There is a poverty of M responses"), engages in interpretation of symbols ("She shows a preference for asparagus"), deals in "causal" explanations of behavior ("He probably has some minimum brain damage," "It is a question of an excessively strong superego"), or uses his own emotional reactions, whatever their integrity or sensitivity, as the basis of his inferences ("I can tell you are ripped up inside," "I feel a tremendous warmth when you talk to me")—whatever the bases of one's inferences, when confrontation is involved, it is essential to communicate to the confrontee that one *is* dealing in inferences and not in self-evident facts. Moreover, the confronter should convey to the confrontee some indication of the degree of certitude he believes underlies his hypothesis. The certitude underlying a statement like "You are anxious" will probably differ from the certitude underlying "You are dishonest." Every hypothesis, by definition, falls short of certitude in some way. The high visibility of the contract group demands that the confronter give some indication of just how hypothetical his statement is.

The point is this: in the group, facts should be presented as facts, feelings as feelings, and hypotheses as hypotheses. The problem is that too often in sensitivity groups the confronter presents his feelings and his hypotheses abruptly and apodictically as facts concerning the person of the confrontee. As a rule, this simply should not take place in the contract group. The contract calls for high visibility. In this case, this means that the confronter should share with the confrontee the bases of his feelings and the premises of his inferences and not wait until they erupt abruptly as "facts" (for then they are really accusations). If the more apodictic "You are arrogant" is preceded by the less apodictic "I feel that you are more or less patronizing me" and "Your tone then was pretty harsh" and "At times you don't seem to give the rest of us much credit," it is likely that there will be more mutual honesty and involvement and less need for destructive sledgehammer confrontation. If I bring my feelings and my premises into community as quickly as possible, then the other person can share in the inferential process and is more likely to accept a reasonable hypothesis concerning his behavior, especially if it contains a realistic suggestion for growth. If the participants are willing to be this open, then at least facts will sound like facts, feelings will sound like feelings, and hypotheses will sound like hypotheses, and failed epistemology will not muddy the waters of the group experience.

The Direct Challenge. Although there is an element of challenge in any kind of deliberate confrontation, the explicit verbal challenge can be a specific kind of stimulus act. In its simplest form, the challenge is a suggestion, request, or demand that the confrontee change his behavior in some way: "I don't deny that it might be painful, but maybe it would be more growthful if you were to try to involve yourself with us more," "Do you think that you could honestly answer a few direct questions about our relationship, yours and mine?," "Stop monopolizing the conversation." These are examples of bald challenges, whereas most challenges are situated in a much wider context of information and explanation.

The direct challenge, as such, is neutral; that is, its growth value for the confrontee (and for the group) depends on a number of confronter, confrontee, and situation variables. For instance, the confronter may act for a number of reasons: annoyance, concern for the confrontee, concern for the group or others influenced by the behavior of the confrontee, a feeling that he should say something.

He may challenge the confrontee to do something that is growthful or nongrowthful, relevant to the confrontee's needs or irrelevant, possible or impossible; the confrontee may or may not be prepared for the challenge: he may be hurt and not ready to listen, he may be very anxious, there may or may not be a climate of trust and support strong enough to sustain the kind of challenge made. If the confronter fails to take these variables into consideration, he may end up blowing in the wind, much to his own frustration.

It is usually a mistake if the confronter deals in demands, rather than suggestions and requests, when he challenges the behavior of others. Even if he does not intend to play God or omnipotent father, he may give the impression that he is doing so, and this tends to destroy any value that the confrontation might otherwise have. Since no one can predict with absolute certainty whether a change in another's behavior will benefit the other or not, there is always an element of hypothesis in every challenge. Therefore, as in confrontation through information, the degree of certitude associated with the hypothesis should dictate the manner in which the challenge is made. If the confrontee's behavior is obviously self-destructive or destructive of those around him, then the challenge to change can be put quite directly and forcefully. If, on the other hand, the confronter only suspects that a change in behavior will benefit the confrontee or others, the force or the demand element in the challenge must be proportioned to the certitude of the hypothesis underlying the challenge. For instance, whenever a confronter says to a confrontee: "You talk too much here," there are certain hypotheses and attitudes underlying such a challenge—for example, that the confrontee talks but says nothing, that he monopolizes the time of the group, that he is exhibitionistic, that he prevents other members who want to interact from interacting. Perhaps it would be more realistic to say that no matter how forcefully the confronter challenges the behavior of the confrontee, honesty demands that he deal openly with whatever is implicit in his challenge. If the confronter is willing to do this, he will soon learn whether he tends to challenge others because of his concern for them or because of his own needs.

Calling the other's game. A special and quite effective form of direct challenge consists of "calling the other's game." According to Beier (1966—a book well worth reading in its entirety), many patients in therapy attempt to engage the therapist either by their verbalizations or other communications; that is, they try to get the therapist to play their game. The patient tries to hide his game under the guise of certain conventions, his real intent lying in subtle cues rather than in the overt message:

Subtle clues are actually the means by which a sender *constricts* the response outcome. He uses these subtle cues to influence and control another person's responses to his own ends with only a minimal risk of being exposed for his attempts. . . .

In addition to constructing the respondent's possible recognition of his intentions, an individual can, as stated earlier, also hide the meaning of his manipulation from his own awareness. With his subtle hidden cues he can influence the respondent and bid for and provoke certain responses, yet maintain that he is quite innocent, that he really had no share in triggering these response activities. . . .

The mechanism described here allows the sender to "engage" the respondent and at the same time reduce the possibility of exposing his own intentions. The concept of engagement leads to new observations helpful in the analysis of the communicative process, particularly with reference to understanding certain practices in the psychotherapeutic process [pp. 280–281].

The purpose of engagement is to keep the environment as safe as possible:

Vulnerability, then, gives rise to certain preferred behaviors in interaction, which are ways of engaging and involving another person. When carefully analyzed, these messages seem to yield the ideas that made the individual vulnerable in the first place. An individual's preferred modes of interaction are not merely defenses; they are also behaviors that seek out certain responses in the environment. They trigger responses that are safe (as the sender has created an emotional climate in the respondent by which the response activity has been constricted) and apparently are also rewarding. They give the patient the experience that he is still dealing, still "alive" in the area of his vulnerability [p. 281].

The effective therapist disengages himself from the patient's game, affording the latter an opportunity to grow:

The therapist is most effective when he provides disengaged responses that do not reinforce the patient's present behavior. The therapist's responses not only interrupt the patient's expectancies (and in this manner extinguish association) but, being disengaged, are actually designed to give the patient the experience of "beneficial uncertainty." This experience provides a challenge to explore new choices in a nonthreatening situation. The patient should experience with the therapist, message by message, that he can tolerate the uncertainty and even utilize it for the discovery of territory previously prohibited to him. He will experience that in this "sanctuary" he can forgo the dangers and pleasures of being misunderstood, and so his messages will become less discordant.

Through the disengaged response, the therapist trains the patient to give more freedom to the people he encounters [p. 283].

This is one example where withdrawal of reinforcement is an effective mode of confrontation.

The general instrument of disengagement is what Beier calls the asocial response, a response that indicates a refusal on the part of the therapist to give conventional replies to the conventions the patient uses to restrict the therapist's interaction. It is a response that fails to reinforce the patient's expectations. A few samples of such responses will illustrate what is meant:

Patient: I hate you.
Therapist: Go on [p. 51].

Patient: You are sure a quack. I don't think I should come to see you again.
Therapist: To seek help from an ignorant man like myself, this is crazy [p. 53].

A patient who claims she has been raped says: I like you very much, I even dream of you.
Therapist: You want me to lie with you on the couch? [p. 61].

Member 1:   Nice weather today.
Member 2:   Oh, yes, I love a blue sky.
Therapist: And the clouds are just beautiful. And the wind is blowing so sweetly. And the sun is sparkling, bright and handsome.
Member 1:   Let's get going [p. 149].

Patient: You only see me for the money.
Therapist: Why would anyone want to see a fellow like you for anything but money? [p. 60].

The asocial response disengages the patient, thus placing him in a state of beneficial uncertainty, but it is a growthful type of uncertainty because it takes place in an atmosphere of acceptance and support.

Others suggest a variety of approaches to catch patients in their attempts to keep growth at a distance and to ward off constructive interpersonal contacts. Dreikurs (1967) suggests that patients in psychotherapy use their symptoms to cover up their real intentions, and he considers one of the goals of the therapeutic process the revelation of this game: "As Adler pointed out, one of the most effective therapeutic means is 'spitting in the patient's soup.' He can continue what he is doing, but it no longer 'tastes so good' [p. 230]." Ellis (1962) challenges the illogicalities to which the patient is addicted and which he (the patient) perpetuates by his verbalizations. Beier claims that although what he proposes may sound like Ellis's rational-emotive therapy, it is really different: "Ellis argues the patient into behaving rationally, while we propose to provide the patient with responses that give him the experience of beneficial uncertainty about his previous expectations. We propose that with the proper, disengaged response by a therapist, the patient is placed in a position where he can make more adequate choices [p. 55]." That is, Beier jolts the client into experiencing his own freedom, while Ellis is much more interested (or more exclusively interested) in the client's behavioral changes.

What Beier proposes pertains, I would suggest, not just to therapy but to sensitivity training, other growth experiences, and life itself. We would be better off if others were to respond to us asocially more often, catch us in our games, pull us up short. Beier (1966), in discussing family group therapy, offers three guidelines for effective confrontation. He suggests that the therapist should intervene (1) when a member says or implies that someone else must change to solve his (the speaker's) problem ("If John would only stop drinking..."), (2) when any member makes a statement designed to maintain the past ("Well, this is the way my father was and his before him," "My wife wants me to be more aggressive, but I am what I am, and I can't help it"), and (3) when a member constricts communication by asking loaded questions or by giving connotations of which he may not be aware ("We always talk things over, don't we, dear?" "Isn't that the way you have always treated me?"). These kinds of communications always crop up in sensitivity-training groups, and they should be challenged, but not just by the leader; in the contract group, all the members agree to challenge such response-restricting communications.

Involvement of Self as a Stimulus Act. Not every kind of confrontation is explicit and direct. If a person tries to live up to the implicit contract of any sensitivity-training group or the explicit one of the contract group, he will take an active role in contacting others in various ways, especially through the modalities of the contract—for example, self-disclosure, expression of feeling, and support. In short, he will reach out to others in attempts to establish varying degrees of intimacy. Such contact is confronting because intimacy itself is confronting. The person being contacted, the confrontee, feels himself being reached out to, he feels himself as the object of unconditional positive regard and empathy, he feels the impact of the other's congruence, he experiences the other as a locus of deep feelings and emotions. But in many ways he is probably not used to such behavior, especially such focused behavior, and it pulls him up short, it makes him take stock of himself, it makes him reach for responses that are not usually at hand. Intimacy, in our culture, is almost bound to have a confrontational effect, especially when it is set in sharp focus through the experiences of the laboratory. Since these indirect forms of confrontation can be as strong as or even stronger than more direct forms such as challenges of the other's behavior, the participants should be as aware as possible of the impact their behavior is having on the other. Some of the conflicts that arise in the laboratory stem from the fact that a participant's whole mode of behavior has been confrontational without his realizing it. For instance, the way a participant interacts with another may place the other under extreme emotional pressure. If this is the case, and it is not sensed by the confronter, then the confrontee or someone else should advert to what is happening: "John, you are making tremendous emotional demands of me right now, and I do not think that I can reply to them at this time or under these conditions." Indirect forms of confrontation have the same effects, generally speaking, as more direct forms and should be pursued in the same way.

Group Situation Variables as Confrontational. Certain aspects of the laboratory experience itself are designed to have a confrontational effect on the participants. In the contract group, the contract itself is an instrument of confrontation: it outlines a rather demanding set of interpersonal behaviors and usually sends the prospective participant searching into himself to see if he has the resources necessary to engage in such behaviors. That a certain degree of intimacy is demanded in any sensitivity-training group is confronting enough, but the confrontational quality is compounded by the fact that the participant finds himself in a stranger group: he does not choose his bedfellows. As he looks around the group, it is as if each of the other participants were saying: "Here I am; you have to deal with me." It is not that any of the participants verbalizes or even conceptualizes such a challenge; rather, each *is* the challenge by his very being.

The verbal and nonverbal exercises used to stimulate communication in the group constitute another source of confrontation. The participant finds himself touching others or looking at others without using words, and such focusing in on relatively molecular aspects of the interactional process is foreign to him and therefore places its own set of demands on him. One commonly used exercise, called prescription, is directly confrontational. If this exercise is used, then somewhere toward the middle of the life of the group, each member takes his turn leaving the group while the others work out a prescription for him—that is, a set of suggestions for improving the quality of his interpersonal living. When he returns to the group, the prescription is presented to him and he can use it, if he wants, as a basis for further experimentation with his behavior in the group. These are just a few of the group variables that can have a confrontational effect; whether they do or not depends on how they are perceived by the individual participant.

Processing as a Group Mode of Self-Confrontation. Processing is a very useful form of group interaction. After the participants have been interacting for a while, the interaction is stopped and the members process what has been taking place—that is, they try to examine the nature of the interaction and answer such questions as: "What have we been doing here? How have we been interacting with one another? Who has been interacting with whom? What have been our communication blocks? Who has been active? Who has been silent? Which participants have assumed leadership roles? Who has been bored?" Processing gives the group an opportunity to be its own critic. The members receive a kind of cultural permission to stand outside themselves and act as critics of their own behavior. Remarks made during this period are not taken as critical in a negative sense, because responsible criticism is the very meaning of this processing interlude. Very often, because of the cultural permission, participants will find themselves saying things that they simply had not been able to say during the group interaction itself: "We have really been beating the air," "John, I think you wanted to get us going, but you really monopolized the situation," "Bill, I am not so sure now that I was really honest with you," "I think we showed how really afraid of self-disclosure we are," "I was just too anxious to say anything." In the early stages of the group life, processing is something that stands outside the regular interaction of the group and thus gives the members an opportunity to realize that self-criticism can be quite constructive. Gradually, however, the members learn to incorporate processing into the regular group interaction itself. Until such incorporation is possible, processing periods provide excellent opportunities for groups to confront themselves, to admit and frankly examine the modes of flight that individuals and the group as a whole have been using, and to do so without arousing intolerable anxiety.

Withdrawal of Reinforcement as Confrontational. Beier's asocial response is one that fails to reinforce certain behaviors that are seen as nongrowthful. Other such withdrawals of reinforcement in sensitivity groups can also serve as stimuli with confrontational effects. For instance, the person who uses humor to flee intimacy or to interrupt interactions that are uncomfortable for him is reinforced in such behavior when others laugh. Tension dissipates, and uncomfortable issues are sidetracked. A refusal to reinforce such behavior —that is, a refusal to laugh or to abandon an uncomfortable issue— is confrontational. Another example is the noninvolving monologue: if group participants tend to deliver monologues that prevent mutual interaction, then passive attentiveness will be an effective reinforcer. Confrontation in this case means interrupting and engaging the speaker. Part of the processing of group interaction should consist of pointing out the ways in which unproductive forms of behavior in the group are reinforced and in determining effective ways of withdrawing such reinforcement. If the participants fail to support a- or anti-contractual behavior, the group will become less diffuse and more productive.

Videotape as a Vehicle of Confrontation. Since about 1960, an increasing amount of research has taken place in which attempts have been made to alter the behavior of psychiatric patients by confronting them with photographs, movies, or videotape recordings of their appearance and behavior (e.g., Boyd & Sisney, 1967; Cornelison & Arsenian, 1960; Kagan, Krathwohl, & Miller, 1963; Miller, 1962; Moore & West, 1965; Pascal, Cottrell, & Baugh, 1967; Rogers, 1968; Stoller, 1968; Ward & Bendak, 1964). This technique has also been used with cardiac patients (Verwoerdt, Nowlin, & Agnello, 1965) and in the training of counselors and psychotherapists (Schiff & Reivich, 1964; Walz & Johnston, 1963). Boyd and Sisney (1967), using videotape playbacks, found that "interpersonal concepts of the self, the ideal self, and the public self became less pathological and less discrepant with one another following the self-image confrontation [p. 291]." One of the primary advantages of feedback by videotape is its objectivity, its "cleanness." The confrontee is confronted by himself, and, since he cannot charge bias, rationalizations are relatively useless. Furthermore, the confrontee sees his behavior in context, he gets a view of the molar realities of his interaction that ordinarily escape him. He can more readily see those aspects of his behavior that elicit what Stoller (1968) calls discrepant feedback—that is, response to his behavior other than what he believed he would receive. I find that immediate playback of the tape tends to have the greatest impact value, for, as Rogers (1968) notes, "the closeness in time to the behavior that has just happened makes it difficult to disown what has occurred [p. 38]." In time, videotape feedback should become one of the most potent sources of confrontation in both individual and group therapy and in laboratory-training experiences.

The Natural Bias of the Confronter

A second factor to be noted in the confrontation process is the possible bias of the confronter. If the confronter, merely by the fact that he is not the other, by the fact that he stands outside the other, is in a metaphysical position to know the other in ways that are not available to the latter, it is also true that his separateness is a source of bias. The information that he feeds to the other is processed through the subjective filtering systems (e.g., the philosophical, value, and natural psychological systems) of the confronter and takes on the latter's color. Though this bias can be minimized (depending in large part on how close the confronter is to his own experiencing), it cannot be avoided altogether. Therefore, both confronter and confrontee should be aware of this phenomenon, for it is another source of possible error in the confrontational process. Even when the stimulus act does not consist of information, interpretations, or direct challenges on the part of the confronter but, rather, of the emotional impact he has on the confrontee, the confrontation may still be quite biased. The confronter's emotions are real, but they are not necessarily realistic. He may confront by expressing anger toward someone who really did nothing to provoke it (that is, he may be projecting the anger he feels toward himself). In such cases his emotions are biased (in some sense of the word), and thus the confrontee cannot be expected to respond as if he had actively provoked these emotions. In general, confronter bias should be controlled by group members other than the confrontee, for this latter should be as open as possible to constructive confrontation. But this very openness makes him less sensitive to sources of confrontational error. The others, therefore, are in a better position to pick up elements of bias and deal with them openly.

The Relationship between the Confronter and the Confrontee

Both the long-range and the *ad hoc* aspects of this relationship affect the quality of the confrontational process. Confronter and confrontee might love, hate, or be indifferent or neutral toward each other, or the relationship might be a confused or muddled one, marked by an admixture of feelings, conscious and semiconscious, strong and weak, positive and negative. Moreover, such feelings may be mutual or one-sided. But even if the confronter loves the confrontee, at the moment of confrontation he might be acting from some lesser motive such as pique, jealousy, or momentary irritation. On the other hand, a confronter who generally dislikes another might rise above his feelings and engage in an act of concerned, growthful confrontation. In the contract group, the participants are asked to be as aware as possible of their relationship to those they confront, including the quality of the relationship at the moment of confrontation. If the confronter has really done nothing to establish a relationship between himself and the confrontee, or if he has even rejected overtures of friendship on the part of the confrontee, this is obviously going to affect the dynamics of confrontation. Some research evidence corroborates what seems to be a common-sense observation: the behavior of liked persons is seen in a more favorable light than the behavior of disliked persons, even when the favorable perception is not accurate (Berkowitz, 1956, 1957; Horo-witz, Lyons, & Perlmutter, 1951; Sherif, White, & Harvey, 1955). The responsible participant will first of all be aware of the quality of his relationships and then try to rectify whatever bias might exist in his perceptions. An ideal atmosphere for confrontation is one in which the quality of the relationships is highly visible. This means a group culture in which members know where they stand in relation to one another because their relationships have been dealt with in community. It is evident, then, that confrontations that take place early in the group will often center around clarifying relationships ("We have really never spoken to each other, so I'm not sure where I stand"). The more real the relationships within the group are—that is, the more frank, open, and motivated by concern they are—the greater the chance of eliminating some of the natural bias factors mentioned.

The Motivation of
the Confronter

An analysis of the motivation underlying confrontation has two distinct dimensions: (a) the purpose or function of an act of confrontation in itself and (b) the motivation of the confronter. Ideally, a high degree of correlation will exist between these two dimensions; that is, the confronter will choose to confront because of the growth functions he sees inherent in an act of responsible confrontation. These two dimensions, however, are separable, and the confronter can choose to confront out of motives that are less than ideal.

The Purpose of an Act of Confrontation. In general, confrontation is just one more modality of interpersonal contact and as such stems, ideally, from a desire on the part of the confronter to involve himself more deeply with the confrontee. The term "confrontation," when used in the context of international politics, connotes a standoff, a refusal to yield, an impasse, an irreducible separateness on the part of the nations involved. However, "confrontation," as used in the context of growth experiences, has the opposite connotation: an act of constructive confrontation is an attempt on the part of one person to involve himself with another, a way of expressing his concern, a way of showing the confrontee that he is "for" him. Confrontation is a way of being with, rather than being against, the other, even though the confronter might disagree strongly with the confrontee. In training groups, then, the rule is simple: do not confront if you do not intend to involve yourself with the other. The person who confronts in such a way that he either does not want or fails to exhibit concern or a willingness to become involved with the confrontee is actually an intruder. Since the intruder merely wants to get inside the other, for some reason or another, without fostering any kind of mutuality, it is hypothesized here that such intrusive presence is inimical to interpersonal growth and is to be avoided in sensitivity groups.

The direct purpose of an act of confrontation is not to change the behavior of the other but to create a situation in which it becomes possible for *him* to change his behavior. Confrontation is an invitation to the other to engage in self-examination. The confronter invites the confrontee into community to reflect on his behavior—whether the community be a dyad or a larger group. The purpose of confrontation is not to restrict the other but to free him. The confrontee is given an opportunity—in an atmosphere of trust and security—to step back from his behavior in order to see it in a different light and from a different viewpoint—that is, as it strikes others. It is possible, then, that he will be challenged to consider more fruitful, or at least less destructive, modes of behavior or to take a longer look at the human possibilities that are in and around him, but he will grow only if *he* chooses from these possibilities. In other words, one of the purposes of confrontation is to bring the confrontee into more direct contact with his own experiencing. Gendlin (1962) suggests that a person need not be forced to live with the introjected values of alienated man. Rather, through therapy or some other growth experience, he can become psychologically open; that is, he can learn to trust his own experience and use it as a direct referent and source of wisdom. Rogers (1964) develops the same theme:

Most importantly [in therapy], he can begin, with much difficulty at first, to sense and to feel what is going on within him, what he is feeling, what he is experiencing, how he is reacting. He uses his experiencing as a direct referent to which he can turn in forming accurate conceptualizations and as a guide to his behavior. . . . As his experiencing becomes more and more open to him, as he is able to live more freely in the process of his feelings, then significant changes begin to occur in his approach to values [p. 20].

Confrontation, then, becomes a way of inviting the other to become himself more fully.

Another way of looking at confrontation is to see it as an instrument that might help the other reduce the amount of "cognitive dissonance" (Festinger, 1957) in his life. One way of reducing such dissonance is to tailor reality to one's own inner needs, and there is an extensive (though hardly unchallenged) literature suggesting that such tailoring is quite common. Confrontation offers the possibility of realistic resolution to dissonant cognitions. For instance, as Newcomb (1963) points out, there is a very strong tendency to assume that the associates one ranks highest on a scale of preference return the compliment, however unwarranted such an assumption might be. Furthermore, the ability to judge the attraction of others toward oneself does not become more accurate with increasing acquaintance. Now, if I think that another has more interest in me than he really has, I may try to ignore whatever cues he emits that would indicate disinterest. On the other hand, I could try to be sure where I really stand with him, realizing that positive regard is not always reciprocated. Concerned mutual confrontation, then, though it is sometimes painful, is a powerful tool for the reduction of dissonance. In the contract group, the participants are asked to be open with one another, establishing a group culture that is as dissonance-free as possible. Responsible confrontation goes far in making reality the measure of one's thinking instead of one's thinking the measure of reality.

The Motives of the Confronter. Ideally, the confronter engages in confrontation for the reasons listed above: he involves himself with the confrontee so that they might grow together. However, he may engage in confrontation for more idiosyncratic and less growthful reasons: to relieve his boredom, to ward off confrontation of himself ("the best defense is a good offense"), to punish the confrontee or the entire group, to take flight by engaging the group in game behavior, to relieve his own frustration and anxiety, to fulfill a need to dominate. Moreover, his motivation might be mixed; that is, he might confront for a variety of reasons, both good and bad. Although it would be futile for the confronter himself or the group as a whole to try to unravel the confronter's entire motivational skein, still it is useful for the participants to realize that confrontational behavior, like most human behavior, is multi-determined, multi-motivated. If, as far as the confronter is able to determine, his personal motives are in general agreement with the purpose of confrontation in the group, then he need not worry about ancillary motives. However, if he or the group suspects that ancillary motives are quite important or even predominant, then high visibility demands that he qualify his confrontation ("I may well be biased in my remarks because John and I have never gotten along") or, if he fails to do so, that his remarks be challenged by the other participants.

Confrontation implies some kind of separateness, some kind of gap between confronter and confrontee that the former desires or feels impelled to close. His reasons for doing so, as we have seen, can either enhance or vitiate the act of confrontation. However, good motivation is not enough, for even the well-motivated confronter may confront in such a way as to thwart the desirable effects of confrontation.

Punishment as a Dimension of Confrontation. This question is a thorny one, one that does not yield to ready answers. But it must be dealt with, because every act of confrontation, however responsible, seems to have a punitive dimension. Some people confront in order to punish and succeed in doing so, but, on the other hand, an act of confrontation not intended to be punitive may have quite punitive effects. This punitive tendency is a problem because research has not yet given us clear-cut answers about the growth value of punishment in human interactional situations. Research so far has shown that punishment, depending on the conditions under which it is administered, can have both positive and negative effects (see Bandura, 1962; Church, 1963; Hilgard & Bower, 1966; Solomon, 1964). Studies indicate that punishment may be ineffective if it is delayed too long (thus losing its association with the punishable act), that it can serve as a cue for selecting an appropriate response (provided that the subject is aware of alternative responses), that mild punishment may merely suppress a response temporarily rather than eliminating it (though during the time of suppression the subject has an opportunity to learn alternative responses), that punishment that produces only emotional excitement tends to fixate the punished response, and that it is important that punishment be given in the presence of the discriminative cues for the response. Because the evidence on punishment is not all in, and because what we have leads to different conclusions, it is quite difficult to map out an intelligent plan for the use of punishment in psychotherapy and other growth experiences. To my knowledge, there has been no systematic attempt to do so.

Most of the research on punishment so far has been carried out on animals or on molecular aspects of human behavior, so that the problem of application to more molar aspects of human behavior is necessarily an unresolved one: "This series of experiments by Estes, with their interpretations, show how, within the experimental and theoretical framework of Skinner's system, it is possible to experiment upon problems genuinely relevant to the practical control of learning situations. The challenging difficulty is finding appropriate ways to test the implications *in a social context* [Hilgard & Bower, 1966, p. 139, emphasis added]." Perhaps sensitivity-training groups and other forms of laboratory experience will provide a realistic social context for such research, but this has not yet happened.

French and Raven (1960) touch on the question of punishment in social behavior:

> At times, there is some difficulty in distinguishing between reward power and coercive power. Is the withholding of a reward really equivalent to a punishment? Is the withdrawal of punishment equivalent to a reward? The answer must be a psychological one—it depends upon the situation as it exists for P [a person]. But ordinarily we would answer these questions in the affirmative; for P, receiving a reward is a positive valence as is the relief of suffering. There is some evidence (Dittes & Kelley, 1956) that conformity to group norms in order to gain acceptance (reward power) should be distinguished from conformity as a means of forestalling rejection (coercive power).
>
> The distinction between these two types of power is important because the dynamics are different. The concept of sanctions sometimes lumps the two together despite their opposite effects. While reward power may eventually result in independent systems, the effects of coercive power will continue to be dependent. Reward power will tend to increase the attractions of P to O [some social agent]; coercive power will decrease this attraction (Raven & French, 1958). The valence of the region of behavior will become negative, acquiring some negative valence from the threatened punishment. The negative valence of punishment would also spread to other regions of the life space. Lewin (1935) has pointed out this distinction between the effects of rewards and punishments. In the case of threatened punishment, there will be a resultant force on P to leave the field entirely. Thus, to achieve conformity, O must not only place a strong negative valence in certain regions through threat of punishment, but O must also introduce restraining forces, or other strong valences, so as to prevent P from withdrawing completely from O's range of coercive power. Otherwise, the probability of receiving the punishment, if P does not conform, will be too low to be effective [pp. 614–615].

While much of what is said here is thought-provoking and in some way applicable not only to sensitivity groups in general but specifically to the act of confrontation in the context of such groups, still it is quite theoretical and in need of confirmation by research.

In view of the shaky research foundation upon which the social value of punishment rests, one might imagine that it would be excluded from such interactions as confrontations in growth groups. Not only has this not been the case, but there is a rather interesting body of evidence which indicates that punitive—and sometimes extremely punitive—confrontation has quite a salubrious effect on the confrontee. Grinker and his associates (1957) attempted to evoke anxiety in hospitalized patients by means of a stressful interview, but, to their chagrin, the patients tended to look upon the interview as helpful no matter how threatening the interpretations made to them (Hawthorne effects?). Heller, Davis, and Myers (1966) studied the activity-passivity and the friendliness-hostility dimensions of interviews conducted with patients. The most noteworthy point of the experiment was that the only clear advantage of interviewer friendliness was that it was overwhelmingly preferred by the subjects. Despite this preference, however, there was no indication that verbal behavior during the interview changed in any way as a result of friendliness. In fact, there was some evidence that the subjects may have felt more pressure to discuss some possibly threatening topics (e.g., sex) with hostile interviewers. Kushner and Sanalu (1966) found that punishment therapy may be used to best advantage when there are other factors, such as social pressure, working on the patient to reduce undesirable behavior. They suggest that in aversion therapy the level of punishment should be clearly noxious, but not so intense as to immobilize the organism. These considerations, it would seem, could well apply to confrontation.

More striking than these considerations, however, is the apparent success of groups in which rather punitive confrontation forms the central core of the therapeutic or growth process. Bach (1966) works in the context of the group Marathon in which group pressure "is a major vehicle which can move people effectively and quickly from impression making and manipulative behavior toward honest, responsible, spontaneous *levelling* with one another [p. 995]." The Marathon situation may be called totally confrontational: "It takes devotion mixed with CONSTRUCTIVE AGGRESSION to get people to take off image-masks and put on honest faces. It takes patience and energy to break down resistances against change which all well-entrenched behavioral patterns ... will put up as part of a person's phoney 'self-esteem.' ... Tired people tend to be truthful! They do not have energy to play games [p. 998]." Bach admits that, at times, the confrontation can be quite brutal: "In the 'feedback' reactions to the expression, no holds are barred! Candid *'levelling'* is expected from everyone, which means participants explicitly share and do *not* hide or mask their here-and-now, on the spot reactions to one another! Tact is 'out' and brutal frankness is 'in' [p. 1001]." An even more brutal approach is taken at Daytop Village; Drakeford (1967) describes an encounter at Daytop:

Three nights a week the whole population of Daytop musters for a ninety-minute session of encounter. This unique event, described as "the principal formal medium for effecting value and behavioral changes," commences with a gathering in the assembly room. The leader stands to read the names of the participants in each group and designates their meeting places. It is the prerogative of any member of the community to fill out a slip indicating his desire to be in a group with a certain other individual. There may have been some difficulty of relationship and he wants to tell this other person what is "on his chest.". . .

I tried to look nonchalant and unconcerned as I sat in the dining room with my assigned group. A man led off with a blast of abuse at . . . his superior who had offended him by his attitude in a work relationship. To say that the statements of the offended one were candid would be a gross understatement. In a couple of minutes the protestor was pouring out a torrent of abuse . . . [p. 72].

Maslow (1967) was pulled up short by what he witnessed at Daytop Village. He found himself re-evaluating his position on the value of confrontation and asking himself questions he had not asked before:

I have a lot of impressions and thoughts rushing in on me. . . . Let me say it this way: Do you think that this straight honesty, this bluntness that even sounds cruel at times, provides a basis for safety, affection, and respect? It hurts, it must hurt. . . . It seems possible that this brutal honesty, rather than being an insult, implies a kind of respect. You can take it as you find it, as it really is. And this can be a basis for respect and friendship [p. 30].

A similar type of therapeutic process called the Synanon game is played at Synanon three times a week. Patton (1967) describes the game:

The Synanon game has been described as "intense group interaction" —which it is. It has also been called "attack therapy," which tells nothing at all about the actual game experience. One sociologist described the game as "verbal street fighting," a threatening analogy, though not an entirely inaccurate one, in spite of the limited backgrounds of most Synanon residents in street fighting, verbal or other. For Synanon people the game is a group situation where one can spill out his fears and hostility, where he can expect to hear the kinds of truths he cannot see in himself, where he can tell others what he really thinks of them without retribution, where he can solve the confusions and conflicts of his working day and his interpersonal relationships, where he can be as spontaneous, creative, rigid, angry, loud or passive as he chooses with no authority or rules save one, the proscription against physical violence or the threat of it. ... Its weapons are the language of truth and accuracy, which always hit a moving target; both have a place in the Synanon game— itself ever changing and becoming [p. 5].

No attempt is made here to imply that the populations of such centers as Daytop Village and Synanon are comparable to those that engage in sensitivity-training laboratories, nor is it suggested that "brutality therapy" become a way of life in such laboratories. Rather, the point is this: severely punishing, even brutal, confrontation in each of the contexts described above apparently works, and somehow this fact must be integrated into a theory of confrontation. The use of punishment in the control of behavior is a very complex question. One simply cannot say: "I am going to punish John by this act of confrontation, but it is for his own good," unless one has some basic understanding of both the effects of punishment in general and of how particular punishment is inflicted. As Solomon (1964) notes:

The effects of punishment are partly determined by those events that directly precede it and those that directly follow it. A punishment is not just a punishment. It is an event in a temporal and spatial flow of stimulation and behavior, and its effects will be produced by its temporal and spatial point of insertion in that flow [p. 242].

Thus, to predict in even the grossest way the action of punishment on a response, one has to know *how* that particular response was originally inserted in the subject's response repertoire [p. 243].

Campbell and Dunnette (1968) apply some of Solomon's theorizing to laboratory training:

Based on his and others' research, Solomon theorized that learning as a consequence of punishment occurs in a two-stage process: First, a conditioned emotional reaction must be established to temporarily suppress the unwanted behavior. Second, and most important, responses incompatible with the punished response must then be reinforced and established; only in this way can one guard against the rapid extinction of the conditioned emotional reaction and the corresponding reappearance of the unwanted behavior. In the context of the T group, this means that "punishment" in the form of anxiety arousal must be accompanied by the reinforcement and shaping of responses incompatible with those responsible for originally inducing the anxiety. In a sense this is what the T group tries to do; however, it seems reasonable to ask whether or not the usual T group is sufficiently structured to assure the sophisticated control of stimuli and reinforcement configurations necessary in the two-stage process suggested by Solomon. Given the variability of contingencies that this lack of structure probably produces, some possible alternative outcomes might be either that simply no learning occurs or that some of the negative side effects are incurred [p. 78].

It is hypothesized here that a contract, especially one that deals specifically with confrontation as a possibly punitive stimulus, might help to control some of the contingencies of which Campbell and Dunnette speak. Finally, all of this is said, not to discourage the use of confrontation, even though it almost inevitably has punitive side effects, but to make the confronter realize that he can expect, at times, quite negative responses to what he might consider most benevolent acts of necessarily punitive confrontation.

Confrontation and Domination. While confrontation can be used to punish, it can also be used to control and dominate. If A confronts B because A thinks that he is right and B is wrong, he should be careful of his motivation. As Gibb (1968) notes, when people are fearful, they tend to try to control. If there is an atmosphere of trust in the group, tendencies to confront in order to control should diminish. However, if such confrontation continues to be a part of any participant's interactional style, this pattern should become a matter for group reflection.

Confrontation in the Context of Acceptance and Empathy. Research is beginning to show that therapists who supply ample amounts of empathy, positive regard, and genuineness are more likely to occasion deeper levels of self-exploration in their clients than therapists lacking in these qualities (Berenson, Mitchell, & Moravec, 1968; Holder, Carkhuff, & Berenson, 1967; Piaget, Berenson, & Carkhuff, 1967; Rogers, 1967; Truax, 1966; Truax & Carkhuff, 1965). Therefore, if one of the most important functions of confrontation is to invite the other to responsible self-examination in community, then it seems that confrontation would be most effective if carried out under the conditions mentioned—that is, under conditions of empathy and positive regard. Good therapists confront more often than poor therapists (Berenson, Mitchell, & Laney, 1968), but they also provide the conditions that sustain confrontation by various group members. The results of research on confrontation are in keeping with the theory underlying Stern's (1966) "sacramental" approach to psychotherapy: he sees a person's present as an experience that is to be transformed and, if necessary, transcended through concerned and appreciative confrontation. A study by Torrance (1966) suggests that confrontation will be more effective if it is positive and constructive rather than negative or merely evaluative. Somehow, these facts, too, must contribute to a total theory of confrontation.

The Manner of Confrontation: Reconciling Diverse Elements. My own experience with confrontation in different kinds of growth groups has been mixed. I have seen confrontations that fulfilled the caricature of sensitivity training ("a place where people tell one another off") and that did a good deal of harm (e.g., apparently pushed someone into a short-lived psychotic episode—though some claimed that even this was a beneficial episode), and yet I have also seen bitter confrontations produce not only realistic self-exploration and growthful behavioral changes but even increased intimacy between confronter and confrontee. On the other hand, I have witnessed nonpunitive, high-regard confrontations both succeed and fail. Confrontation is a growth-experience variable with great potential although it is not entirely clear under what conditions this potential is released.

Proportion as a Key to Growthful Encounter. The question here is: how can one strip confrontation of its tendencies to attack and destroy without stripping it of its impact? An attempt will be made here to formulate certain hypotheses about the manner in which confrontation must take place if it is to be a growthful rather than a neutral or even destructive experience. These remarks take on the nature of hypotheses because they are based on evidence that is principally observational and has not been confirmed by experimentation. The evidence so far suggests that the *proportional* nature of confrontation is most important; that is, confrontation, if it is to be effective, must be proportioned to a number of confronter, confrontee, and situational variables. In other words, the interaction of confrontation variables is as important as the variables themselves. It is assumed here that it is the socially intelligent person who can perceive the importance of these interactions and act upon them. In fact, this *is* one definition of social intelligence.

The strength of any confrontation arises principally from two variables: the sensitivity, or closeness to core, of the subject matter of the confrontation (e.g., under ordinary circumstances the area of sex would be a more sensitive one, closer to the core of the confrontee, than, say, personal neatness) and the vehemence with which the confrontation is delivered (e.g., the Daytop Village approach would score very high on a scale of vehemence). These variables are additive, so that vehement confrontation in a highly sensitive area would represent the strongest kind of confrontation. If confrontation is to be responsible, its strength must be proportioned to a number of variables, among which are (1) the quality of the relationship between confronter and confrontee, (2) the current psychological state of the confrontee, (3) the possible disorganization that the confrontee will undergo as a result of the confrontation, (4) the limits of the confrontee's capabilities, (5) certain group conditions, and (6) the contract, either implicit or expressed, that governs the group experience.

(1) *The quality of the relationship between confronter and confrontee.* The confronter must ask himself: "What can the relationship between the other and me bear?" To use metaphorical language, the more solid, the healthier, the more substantial the relationship is, the more powerful the confrontation may be (other conditions being equal). If the confronter has done little to build a solid relationship between himself and the confrontee, then he cannot expect to engage in strong confrontational encounter, for it has nothing on which to stand. However, if a participant has tried to build a relationship and has received no response, then he would be justified in engaging in comparatively strong confrontation, especially with respect to the lack of communication on the part of the confrontee, for mutual involvement is one of the expressed goals of the group. In general, then, the confronter must realistically assess the quality of the relationship between himself and the other—his degree of acceptance and concern for the other, the degree of sup-

port of which he is capable *and* which he is willing to provide the other, etc.—and then proportion his confrontation to these variables.

(2) *The current psychological state of the confrontee.* The strength of the confrontation must be proportioned to the current ability of the confrontee to support and act upon the confrontation. This means a number of things. If, for instance, the confrontee is already laboring under a good deal of anxiety, his immediate need might be for encouragement and support, and the confronter should ask himself whether it would be fruitful to confront him at this time (timing is always an important concern) or in this area of sensitivity or with this degree of vehemence. No participant is expected to be free of anxiety, but the level of anxiety should stimulate rather than paralyze. Confrontation should also be proportioned to the other's ability to change, and, to some extent, his desire to change. One of the purposes of confrontation is to try to show the other that he does have the personal or community resources necessary to change an unproductive or destructive style of life. But if the confrontee is relatively eager to change, then he can ordinarily tolerate much stronger confrontation than a person who is not convinced that he can or should change. If the confronter is interested in the other, he will not mount a strong frontal attack when he knows that it has little or no chance of being effective. The confronter who, knowing that the confrontee has little or no interest in change, still hits him with an extremely strong confrontation is dealing in a form of shock therapy ("kick the TV and see what happens"). I have seen such tactics work, but they seem to be a last resort and effective only in the hands of an extremely socially intelligent person.

Some people, without being masochistic, are looking for strong medicine in terms of confrontation and are quite ready to respond favorably to it. I would hypothesize that this is especially true for those who voluntarily attend sensitivity-training laboratories (especially if they have an accurate basic idea of what such a laboratory entails). It should be true to an even greater extent of those who join a contract group. Others, again without being masochistic, welcome even the punitive aspect of confrontational process, for, if I may use an analogy from religious experience, they see in it an element of cleansing or expiation. They pay the price of reintegrating themselves more fully into community. On the other hand, it is possible that a person might seek confrontation precisely to prove to himself his own lack of self worth. But such a situation in sensitivity groups is relatively rare and usually easy to discover; for that person, confrontation becomes an end in itself and is divorced from subsequent behavioral change.

(3) *The risk of disorganization.* Effective confrontation will usually induce some degree of disorganization in the other:

> The therapeutic risk will . . . depend upon the amount of disorganiza-tion both the therapist and the client can handle. . . . The closer the deci-sion affects the inner core of a person, the greater the fear of the life and death choice. A constructive therapeutic confrontation frequently does result in death of a sort: the death of illusion, hence, an illusory death. . . . After an initial experience of death to the illusory self, the void which is temporarily created has a chance to fill up with the person's real be-ing. . . . The therapist, by active confrontation, precipitates an awareness of crisis; he did not precipitate the crisis [Douds, Berenson, Carkhuff, & Pierce, 1967, pp. 171, 173, 175].

Confrontation is usually in some way directed toward the defense mechanisms of the confrontee. This questioning of defenses, al-though ultimately growthful, does entail disorganization.

> Almost every individual has an established self-image protected by a number of defense mechanisms. Such mechanisms have become resistant to change because of their repeated association with the reinforcing prop-erties of anxiety reduction; that is, they protect the self-image from threat. Thus, in the T group, when an individual's usual mode of inter-acting is thwarted and his defense mechanisms are made a direct topic of conversation, considerable anxiety results. Such anxiety then constitutes a force for new learning because, if the group experience is a successful one, new methods of anxiety reduction will be learned. If the T group is successful, these methods will be more in line with the goals of the training and will have more utility for the individual in coping with his environment than his old methods which may indeed have been dys-functional. Thus, anxiety serves the purpose of shaking up or jarring loose the participant from his preconceived notions and habitual forms of interacting so that feedback may have its maximum effect. Without such "unfreezing," feedback may be ineffectual . . . [Campbell & Dun-nette, 1968, p. 76].

The strength of the confrontation must be proportioned to the de-gree of disorganization foreseen and the ability of the confrontee, in the context of the group, to handle this disorganization. Confrontation means in some way challenging the unrealities of the world of the other, which, though unreal, feels "solid" to him. Maslow (1967), however, after his experience at Daytop Village, suggested or hypothesized that, in therapy in general, we have looked upon the client as too delicate, too fragile, too incapable of handling strong confrontation and its disorganizing effects, and so we have been afraid to use this tool. Douds and his associates (1967) suggest that we fail to confront because *we* are afraid of the consequences for ourselves, for he who confronts opens himself to confrontation: "Much of the time it is the fear of exposure that is at the base of the therapist's avoidance [p. 176]." The "disorganization" that Douds and his associates speak of sounds a good deal like Beier's (1966) "beneficial uncertainty," which is a step toward growth rather than toward dissolution.

(4) *The limits of the confrontee's capabilities.* The contract group should be diagnostic in the best sense of the word; that is, the participants should get a feel for one another's areas of potential and of deficit. While the participants should allow one another a wide latitude for growth, they should also come to a realistic understanding of one another's limits. Confrontation should be proportioned to these limits. Certainly the object of confrontation is to help the confrontee to move beyond his present limits, but even concerned confrontation cannot create potential where it does not exist. It may well be that the confrontee is not capable of the interpersonal styles that are preferred by the confronter, and it is a mistake to use confrontation in an attempt to get the confrontee to assume a style of relating that is not consonant with his capabilities. I have seen individuals and even groups spend unreasonable amounts of time trying to get the confrontee to assume an interpersonal style more similar to their own. This is a waste of time and also a way of avoiding one's own problems.

(5) *Group conditions.* Confrontation must be proportioned to certain group variables; that is, the group must create a climate in which confrontation is viable. For instance, if the participants have achieved a certain degree of mutual trust and support, then relatively strong confrontation can be handled, even if the confronter himself fails to provide proportional support, for the other members will supply his deficiency. Confrontation is also much more possible in a group that has developed an open culture—that is, a group that has refused to tolerate the tacit understandings that tend to constrict or eliminate effective communication. In a group in which the participants show that they are willing both to confront and to be

confronted, confrontation soon becomes a constructive dimension of the group culture. In a word, confrontation must be proportioned to the culture of the group.

(6) *Contract, implicit or expressed.* It was suggested earlier that every group operates on some contract, whether expressed or implied. The trouble with implicit contracts in sensitivity-training situations is that they may or may not effectively provide for confrontation, and, even if they do, the conditions that regulate its use always remain vague. It seems only reasonable to assume that making confrontation one of the specific provisions of an overt group contract goes far in preparing the group for this variable. Through the contract, confrontation and other variables receive a high degree of legitimacy. French and Raven (1960), in discussing coercive power (and there is an element of coercion in confrontation), suggest that "the more legitimate the coercion the less it will produce resistance and decreased attraction [p. 622]." The hypothesis is that contractual legitimation of confrontation will increase its frequency, responsibility, acceptability, and effectiveness. Such legitimation will also allow stronger degrees of confrontation to be used. The group, then, becomes a laboratory in which the participants, through their successes and failures, learn how to make responsible confrontation part of their interpersonal styles of life.

The success of such therapeutic communities as Daytop Village and Synanon and of Bach's Marathon groups rests, in part, on the fact that the participants contract, more or less explicitly, to confrontation. They know what they are getting into, but their desire for change outweighs the pain they foresee. At one time I was tempted to call such experiences "supportless" groups, but this, I believe, is inaccurate. They ban from the beginning more effete or unsubstantial kinds of support and even, to a large extent, the approaches to support outlined in the previous chapter. Support arises, rather, from the fact that severe confrontation takes place in a total institutional setting (even Bach's groups are in residence for the entire time of the Marathon), that there are no observers, but just participants (leaders and clients together), that everyone realizes that there is work to be done and gets down to doing it in community, that everyone present is striving for interpersonal growth. Motivation, too, is quite high in such groups. Bach, for instance, chooses only those who can demonstrate a sincere willingness to change. It cannot be assumed that the rank and file of those who participate in sensitivity-training laboratories, or even contract-group programs, possess the same degree of motivation as Synanists or Marathon participants.

The Effect Confrontation
Has on the Confrontee

There is no absolute way to predict the precise effect that any particular act of confrontation will have on the confrontee. His immediate emotional response might be one of elation, depression, or indifference, regardless of whether the confrontation is responsible or irresponsible. The high visibility of the contract group would suggest that the confrontee reveal to the confronter and the group in general what impact, positive or negative, the confrontation has had upon him ("I guess for the moment I really do not know what to say, because frankly you really took me by surprise," "My immediate reaction is elation over the fact that you are concerned enough about me to confront me," "You've made me so angry that I have to get my wits about me before I could possibly make a rational response"). If someone says to John, "John, your contributions here have been both marginal and minimal and I really feel your absence in our interaction," John may be relieved, appreciative, anxious, shocked, or angry, but if he reveals his emotional response, he will go far in preventing unproductive ambiguity, confusion, uncertainty, or "stickiness" from arising in the group. Once the confrontee has gotten his emotional reaction into community so that it can be dealt with productively there, then he will be much freer to channel his energies into the open and constructive reaction to confrontation called for by the contract. Precisely how a person should react, or rather respond, to confrontation is the subject that concerns us next.

Growthful Response
to Confrontation

Up to now we have been dealing with what the confronter should do in order to make confrontation a responsible interactional process. We now turn to the confrontee and what he should do in response to objectively growthful confrontation. Most of us naturally tend to *react* to confrontation, autonomically and emotionally, but few of us develop the art of *responding* to confrontation. The contract group is a laboratory in which this art is to be learned. The most common reactions to confrontation are various forms of defensiveness ("My family has always been this way," "But I'm like this only in *this* group") and counterattack ("You haven't put out much in the group yourself"). Pilisuk (1962) showed that subjects tended to retain favorable estimates of their own performance in the face of adverse criticism, and it made little difference whether the criticism came from a friend or a stranger. However, if the subject thought that the criticism came from a friend, he used different forms of rationalization to explain away the friend's behavior. Harvey, Kelley, and Shapiro (1957) found that criticisms were distorted by confrontees when they were thought to come from friends; confrontees also tended to devalue friends who engaged in such criticism. It is not easy to respond nondefensively to confrontation. However, it is assumed here that awareness of this difficulty is a step toward taking a more positive attitude toward confrontation. Kirtner (1955) found that the client who sees his problems as involving his relationships with others and who feels that he has contributed to these problems and wants to change is likely to be successful in a therapeutic encounter, while the client who externalizes his problems, feeling little responsibility, is much more likely to be a failure. Motivation, then, is crucial to the confrontational process. If the participant wants to change, he will want to be confronted and be willing to endure the unpleasant dimensions of confrontation. The ideal is that the confrontee enter actively into the confrontational process, that he become an agent in a dialogic process rather than just a patient suffering through something that is for his own good. Now we will try to clarify such confrontee agency.

Accepting the Invitation of Self-Examination. If growth-provoking confrontation is, in one sense, an invitation to self-examination as a prelude to possible behavioral change, then actual self-examination on the issues in question is the proper response to confrontation. Research in psychotherapy is beginning to show that successful outcome is related to the client's ability or willingness to explore his behavior. Wagstaff, Rice, and Butler (1960) found that successful patients tended to explore themselves more, while those who failed engaged in little self-exploration and in general manifested little emotional involvement. Braaten (1961) found that therapeutic success was related to exploration of the private self. Truax (1961) found, from a schizophrenic population, significantly more depth of experiencing in therapeutic successes than in therapeutic failures. Similar results have been reported by Truax and Carkhuff (1963), Holder, Carkhuff, and Berenson (1967), Piaget, Berenson, and Carkhuff (1967), and Tomlinson and Hart (1962), among others. Pratt & Tooley (1966) calls the striving on the part of individuals or groups to understand themselves and their conditions and to take part in changing themselves and their contractual surroundings their "reflexivity quotient." As Pratt implies, the kind of self-exploration desired is one geared to the examination of behavior and focused on behavioral change. Too many people equate self-examination with a kind of amateur psychoanalytic self-exploration. The person who sees himself only through a maze (or haze) of interpretations can too easily become convinced that responsibility for him lies either outside himself or in hidden layers of his personality that are almost impossible to fathom.

Getting a Feel for How One Is Experienced by Others. The participant cannot respond to confrontation unless he is willing to venture outside himself. One of the most effective ways for him to learn is to drop his defensiveness, at least partially and temporarily, and try to understand the way in which he is experienced by the others in the group. Ideally, the confrontee—admittedly under some-what adverse conditions—tries to become as accurately empathetic as he can during the confrontational encounter; that is, he tries to get inside the world of the confronter and actually feel how he is being experienced by the other.

Self-Confrontation. The contract calls for self-exploration in community as the response to confrontation, but such self-explora-tion may be either self-initiated or undertaken in response to a challenge by another. If the question is looked at a bit abstractedly, a certain gradation appears: it is good for a participant to respond appropriately to unsolicited confrontation, but it may even be better if he actively seeks it—that is, if he manifests to the other members that he is open to meaningful hypotheses about himself and his behavior. It might even be best if the participant were to confront himself ("It strikes me that I have been coming across rather punitively in our interactions here; I'm dissatisfied with my behavior and would like to deal with it"), for such self-confrontation in community indicates a very high degree of responsibility or agency on his part. The self-confronter takes the initiative, but he realizes that he needs the community, both for support and for a corrective outside view of himself. The person who does nothing more than respond appropriately to confrontation seems to imply that motivation for change must come principally from others; it is they who make him want what is essential to his own growth. Learning how to confront oneself, then, is one of the goals of the group. There are, however, counterfeits of self-confrontation: some participants "get" themselves first so that the other members will not "get" them in areas more sensitive and more in need of attention. They want to avoid certain issues, so they take the initiative in less sensitive areas. Since many groups fall for this ploy, it would seem that a healthy confrontation culture would call for a combination of self-initiated and other-initiated confrontations.

Differential Response to Different Modes of Confrontation. There is absolutely no reason why group participants should respond univocally to different kinds of confrontation. It may well be that any given participant will respond quite differentially to the various forms of confrontation that arise in the group. For instance, a person's ability to respond to highly intellectualized or rational verbal confrontation might differ drastically from his ability to respond to the confrontation implicit in the others' emotional approaches to him. Such a person might be quite frightened by manifestations of affection. The contract asks such a person to try to respond to such a confrontation as he would to more intellectualized or strictly verbal forms of confrontation: "I feel your concern and your warmth, and frankly they frighten me, they make me want to turn you off and run away, but that's precisely why I think I should take a good look at what's going on inside me and between you and me." Since it is usually much more difficult to deal with a feeling than with a rational confrontation, the confrontee has to take greater pains to be honest with himself and others, and the group participants have to provide the support necessary to sustain such confrontation. Very often only the confrontee knows what kind of stimulus acts pull him up short, and the responsibility is his to reveal this to the group so that he may reap the benefits of confrontation.

An Openness to Temporary Disorganization. The confrontee should be ready to accept (in some sense of the term) the disorganization induced by effective confrontation. Confrontation almost always demands some kind of reorganization of perceptions, attitudes, and feelings, and such reorganization is impossible without some kind of uprooting. However, if the participant is prepared for this disorganization, then his chances of responding, rather than merely reacting, to confrontation are greatly increased. If, in addition, the group culture itself and the participants individually provide support proportioned to the degree of disorganization, the possibility of successful confrontational interaction is further enhanced. Confrontation without support is disastrous; support without confrontation is anemic.

Over-Response. A person is not supposed to soak up confrontation like a sponge. This might be as bad as, or even worse than, being closed to confrontation, for it implies a lack of agency and of contact with one's own experiencing, both of which are essential to change: "Other people can give us feedback, and we can sense when their reporting is accurate, if their view resonates with an organismic sensing within us of what we have been doing, and consequently we can change our course of action [A. H. Rogers, 1968, p. 37]." While those who are relatively socially adjusted do not count on continual social reinforcement in order to operate effectively on an interpersonal level, passive absorption of any and every confrontation cannot be termed responsible openness to confrontation. If this takes place in a group, getting at the roots of such masochism (psychoanalytically defined or not) would not be out of place. Over-response to confrontation should be challenged and, if possible, unmasked.

Confrontation and Conflict. Even though the correct response to confrontation is self-examination in view of possible behavioral change, conflict and differences of opinion are not eliminated. Once the confrontee has assimilated the point of view of the confronter and has examined himself on the issues proposed, then together they might examine both areas of agreement and areas of conflict. Conflict differs from defensiveness, attack, hostility, and aggression. It may be intense, but it is constructive rather than argumentative. It is a challenge for those who participate in it to accept one another's otherness. Hoffman, Harburg, and Maier (1962) offer some evidence suggesting that conflict can increase the number of alternatives that group members generate. It is quite likely that the same can be said of interpersonal contacts. When conflict is merely a front for a defensive refusal to examine oneself or a disguise for counterattack, it is usually unproductive. The group participants themselves—especially during confrontational interactions—should monitor the conflicts that arise in order to keep them honest.

Responding to Irresponsible Confrontation. There are those who take advantage of the relatively nondefensive climate of the group in order to ride roughshod over the other participants. If confrontation is irresponsible—if it is nothing more than attack, if its primary aim is punishment rather than involvement—then the leader and the group as a whole should intervene and confront the confronter. Little is gained if the confrontee merely becomes angry and fights it out with his aggressor. However, if the confrontee can ignore the irresponsibilities of the other, he can often sift out elements of truth that otherwise might never have come up: "I really thought that John's primary purpose was to attack and punish me and that he exaggerated quite a bit, but as I look at myself I am beginning to realize that his basic point is true: I am fundamentally a very selfish person and I do try to disguise this at times by 'do-good' tactics." Honesty, whenever and wherever it can be found, is a valuable commodity.

Areas of Confrontation

Behavior Rather than Motivation. The direct object of confrontation should be a person's overt behavior rather than the conjectural foundations of that behavior—that is, what is should be the primary object of confrontation rather than what may be. The closer confrontation comes to motivation, the more hypothetical it becomes and thus the more abstract. For instance, one way of conceptualizing neurosis is in terms of a set of central strategies:

A conceptualization of the problem of neurosis in terms of information storage and retrieval is based on the fundamental idea that what is learned in a neurosis is a set of central strategies (or a program) which guide the individual's adaptation to his environment. Neuroses are not symptoms (responses) but are strategies of a particular kind which lead to certain observable (tics, compulsive acts, etc.) and certain less observable, phenomena (fears, feelings of depression, etc.). The whole problem of symptom substitution is thus seen as an instance of response substitution or response equipotentiality, concepts which are supported by abundant laboratory evidence [Breger & McGaugh, 1965, p. 355].

A person might emit behavioral cues that reveal his program, but the fact remains that his behavior is quite real, while the program is a construct. If the construct is the object of confrontation, it should be confronted as construct and confronted primarily through the behavioral cues through which it is revealed.

Strength as Well as Weakness. Since the purpose of the contract group is not unmasking but rather interpersonal growth, it would be meaningless if the participants were to confront one another only in areas of interpersonal deficit without touching on one another's constructive resources. To do so would be to fall into the error of the low-functioning therapists studied by Berenson, Mitchell, and Laney (1968) and by Berenson, Mitchell, and Moravec (1968): low-functioning therapists tend to confront weaknesses rather than resources. "You say little in the group" differs quite a bit from "You don't say much, but when you do speak you always contact someone and without clichés." The remark is still confrontation, but now it is directed toward unused or little-used potential. If a participant always deals with the deficits, rather than the resources, of others, his tendency is diagnostic in itself and should become a subject of discussion in the group.

Self-Underestimation. Self-underestimation is possibly a form of flight and as such should be confronted. Some informal research that Dr. Barbara Powell and I did with sensitivity groups while we were at Galesburg State Research Hospital indicated that there is a rather high correlation between self-estimate measures on group-process variables (administered before regular group sessions began) and actual performance in the group. In other words, participants seem to place a limit on their own desire or ability to participate, and their performance becomes a self-fulfilling prophecy. Therefore, if participants are to move beyond their own self-estimated limits, they must be confronted with their tendency to underestimate their ability to participate in the give and take of group interaction. This is a specific example of confrontation of strength.

Behavior in the Group: Confrontation and Contract. It is relatively easy to delineate what kind of behavior should be confronted in the contract group: (1) any behavior that violates any of the provisions of the contract and (2) the different forms of flight over contract fulfillment (these will be considered separately in the next chapter). In groups in which there is only an implicit contract, areas of confrontation cannot be as clearly delineated. Also, the high visibility demanded in the contract group suggests certain areas of confrontation—that is, the hidden aspects of the group culture, such as tacit understandings, hidden agenda, and hidden goals.

Differential Intragroup Relationships. The contract does not demand that the participants involve themselves with one another in any univocal way. Each participant becomes involved in different ways and to different degrees with his fellows. However, much can be learned by confronting the participants with these differences in involvement. For instance, if A involves himself deeply with B but only superficially with C, the situation says something about A, B, and C.

Behavior Outside the Group. Behavior outside the group is relevant only to the degree that it can be made a here-and-now concern for the participants in general. As a rule, story is relevant, while history is not. Once a person reveals extra-group behavior, it, too, can become an object of confrontation. However, the group should not deal exclusively with the out-there behavior of the participants. This leads to loss of immediacy, loss of interest, and eventually to the stagnation or the death of the group. The way a person behaves out there affects his in-here relationships, but the out there and the in here should be dealt with concomitantly.

**Summary: Suggested
Rules for Confrontation**

In summary, the following rules may help to make confrontation in the group a constructive process:

(1) Confront in order to manifest your concern for the other.

(2) Make confrontation a way of becoming involved with the other.

(3) Before confronting, become aware of your bias either for or against the confrontee. Do not refrain from confrontation because you are for him or use confrontation as a means of punishment, revenge, or domination because you are against him.

(4) Before confronting the other, try to understand the relationship that exists between you and him, and try to proportion your confrontation to what the relationship will bear.

(5) Before confronting, try to take into consideration the possible punitive side effects of your confrontation.

(6) Try to be sure that the strength or vehemence of your confrontation and the areas of sensitivity you deal with are proportioned to the needs, sensitivities, and capabilities of the confrontee.

(7) Confront behavior primarily; be slow to confront motivation.

(8) Confront clearly: indicate what is fact, what is feeling, and

what is hypothesis. Do not state interpretations as facts. Do not engage in constant or long-winded interpretations of the behavior of others.

(9) Remember that much of your behavior in the group can have confrontational effects (e.g., not talking to others, your emotional attitudes, etc.).

(10) Be willing to confront yourself honestly in the group.

No set of rules will provide assurance that confrontation will always be a growthful process in the sensitivity-training group. But groups can learn much from both the use and abuse of confrontation.

Chapter Ten:
A Stance
against
Flight

Introduction

It is not easy to engage in the kinds of interaction outlined in the previous chapters. Thus, human nature being what it is, there is a natural tendency for group participants to find ways either to resist or to flee the work at hand. Even though participants engage in sensitivity-training experiences because they want to, it can still be expected that they will resist the process, because it is anxiety-arousing and demanding. Not only are the common defense mechanisms such as projection, rationalization, reaction formation, and insulation used, but they are used in ways peculiar to the group situation. The group situation threatens the participants with both self-knowledge and intimacy, and the defenses of the participants rise to the challenge.

Flight tendencies seem to appear whenever the human organism is threatened by the often painful processes associated with intra-psychic and interpersonal growth. It is not surprising, then, to find flight a constant problem in both psychotherapy and other kinds of growth situations. Gibb (1964), for instance, notes that "a person may . . . engage in frenetic off-target work in an effort to find himself or to keep from finding himself [p. 282]." Whitman (1964) suggests that group participants defend themselves against involvement by overintellectualization, overaffective behavior, and selected inattention. In Grinker's transactional therapy, the patient is not permitted to become anonymous, to intellectualize, or to talk persistently about others. Mowrer (1950), Dollard and Miller (1950), and Rotter (1954) all see the maladjusted person as one who fails to learn adjustive or growthful behavior automatically, because he persistently engages in avoidance behavior, which keeps him from situations in which he could learn more adaptive and growthful behavior. Although such avoidance behavior is not really satisfying in the long run (flight never is) and is eventually punished, it is immediately satisfying and, therefore, persists. Whitaker and Lieberman (1964) define failure in therapy in terms of various forms of flight: "Failure to benefit from therapy occurs (1) when a patient succeeds consistently in maintaining a habitual maladaptive solution in the group, thus remaining uncomfortable but affectively untouched by the situation; (2) when a patient resorts to physical or psychological flight, thus insulating himself from the affective forces of the group; or (3) when a patient reacts to threat with the breakdown of previously established solutions and the substitution of disorganized, inadequate behavior [p. 180]." Whatever the immediate rewards of flight behavior, it is ultimately self-destructive.

Flight can be conceptualized in various ways—for instance, along overt-covert and mild-severe dimensions (see Figure 5).

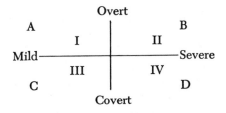

Figure 5. Flight Behavior.

At point A (mild-overt) in quadrant I we might find a remark such as "We don't have to overdo it here," or "It's better to let this thing develop gradually," at point B (severe-overt) in quadrant II actual physical flight, at point C (mild-covert) in quadrant III a passing joke that breaks the tension of the interaction, and at point D (severe-covert) in quadrant IV disruptive, aggressive, and punitive behavior on the part of some group member.

Flight from growth is easily conceptualized in the contract group: it refers to failures to engage in the contractual behaviors outlined and to substituting a- or anti-contractual behavior. Therefore, we have already dealt with a number of different kinds of flight—for instance, engaging in history rather than story in the modality of self-disclosure. It is our purpose here, not to repeat what has been said above, but briefly to classify and clarify the major modes of flight used in groups in the hope that such exposure of flight modalities will reduce flight behavior in actual group interaction. Nor are all possible flight modalities detailed here, for, given the ingeniousness of the human spirit in both devising modes of flight and disguising them, this would be an endless task.

This chapter, then, is an attempt to "spit in the soup" of the group member in flight. The members of the contract group are asked to become aware of the principal kinds of flight behavior and to take a stance against flight by confronting themselves and one another when such behavior arises. Refusal to withdraw from the enterprise is extremely important, for flight in the group mirrors the flight behavior in the participant's day-to-day life.

Since not only individuals, but also entire groups, may engage in flight, the following discussion is divided into two sections: the individual in flight and the group in flight.

The Individual in Flight

Cynicism, Initial and Otherwise. The participant who comes to the group experience with a closed mind and whose principal defense is a cynical attitude toward what is happening in the group will find it extremely difficult, if not impossible, to engage in the group interaction. Watson and his associates (1961) found that those who came to a laboratory experience ready to give themselves to it showed positive results afterwards, while those who expected the laboratory to be irrelevant found it irrelevant. Perhaps the most incapacitating failure of the cynic is that he refuses to initiate anything in the group. To initiate is to show interest, and he cannot be caught showing interest in an enterprise that is in some way below him. He waits until someone else initiates something, and then he sits in judgment on what is happening. In fact, his usual posture is one of silent judgment on the proceedings of the group. Thus he is all but invulnerable, for he can maintain the same posture even when he becomes the object of confrontation. At times he may be swept along by the action of the group, and when the group situation calls for sincerity, he is sincere. But he returns almost immediately to his former posture and hangs albatross-like around the neck of the group.

Silence. Some have tried to rationalize silence by claiming that there is no evidence that the silent person is not benefiting from the group experience; others say that the silent member is a point of rest in the group or that he is dynamic in the sense that the group must deal with him. There are a number of errors here. The silent person may well be *learning* something in the group, but he certainly is not *growing* interpersonally, for it is ludicrous to assume that interpersonal growth takes place without interpersonal exchange. Growth means, in part, that the person becomes an agent instead of a patient in his interpersonal contacts. Even if the silent member is considered dynamic in that he contributes to the dynamics of the group—his silence is a felt force, or he mobilizes the energies of the group, for they must deal with him—his silence is implicitly or explicitly manipulative and deleterious to interpersonal growth. The silent member frequently arouses the concern of the group ("Why is he silent?" "What is happening inside?"), creates feelings of guilt ("We have been neglecting him"), or provokes anger ("Why does he choose to remain an outsider?" "Why does he sit there in judgment of the rest of us?"). Thus, silence *does* manipulate, whether manipulation is the intention of the silent member or not. Furthermore, in the contract group, silence and contract fulfillment are simply antithetical. By definition, the silent member is not growing in the contract group insofar as contract fulfillment can be considered a sign of growth. It has already been mentioned that one sensitivity-group member felt hurt by the silent members: she did not know where they stood in the group, and this constricted her ability to interact with them. Smith (1957) found that group productivity was negatively affected by the presence of two silent members in five-person groups, for the silent members were perceived as *unpredictable.*

Slavson (1966) sees silence in group psychotherapy as a form of communication, even though it is also a form of resistance. The reasons for silence, he says, are either characterological (e.g., the person never says much, he has developed habits of silence) or neurotic (e.g., the result of anxiety or guilt). An individual may also be selectively silent—that is, he might be silent because he feels that the topic of discussion has no relevance to his current needs or preoccupations or that it might constitute an area of threat for him. In the contract group, however, such selective silences violate certain provisions of the contract, for the participants are asked to deal openly with their boredom and, at least in a general way, with their areas of threat. Slavson calls an attempt on the part of a member to impose silence on the group because the interaction threatens him "endogenic" silence; if, on the other hand, the members of a group turn off an overassertive member, this is "imposed" silence. In the contract group, however, anxiety arising from threat should be handled as openly as possible, and the overassertive member should be confronted and not merely silenced. Imposing silence on others usually constitutes a form of flight. Finally, Slavson talks about "iatrogenic" silence—that is, silence that ensues in the group when the leader is abrupt or becomes angry. In the contract group, the leader is a leader-member and his behavior, too, is open to confrontation. The group that responds to leader behavior by falling silent is in flight.

Sometimes the entire group becomes silent, but naturally so. The meaning of such silence varies, but by no means is it always a sign of flight. If such silences occur with any frequency, or if they occur at dramatic moments in the life of the group, their practical meaning for the group should be investigated.

Silence as flight, although it has varying degrees, tends to limit growth. What Whitaker and Lieberman (1964) say of the silent patient also refers to the participant in any kind of interpersonal growth experience:

Therapeutic benefit is limited for the consistently silent patient. He can experience affect associated with crucial personal conflicts in the group, can observe the consequences of others' yielding maladaptive solutions similar to his own, and can achieve insight through being exposed to relevant group information. Direct interpretations and feedback are less available to him and less likely to be accurate and usable. He cannot directly experience the actual testing of the reality of his fears or the necessity for maintaining habitual maladaptive solutions [p. 180].

Although quality of participation is, absolutely speaking, more important than quantity, there is a point at which lack of quantity is deleterious to the overall quality of an individual's participation.

The marriage of quantity and quality of participation is something that must be learned in the actual give and take of group interaction.

Interpretation and the Pursuit of Insight. Interpretation and insight go together, for supposedly the former leads to the latter. The values of both interpretation and insight in therapeutic practice are currently being challenged from a number of quarters. Whatever the outcome of the struggle between insight and action therapists (London, 1964), the point is that in all growth experiences, including sensitivity-training situations, the use of interpretation and the pursuit of insight too often constitute flight behavior. Our culture tends to make us think that the only kind of real knowing is scientific knowing. In growth groups, then, the participants think that they are doing the scientific thing when they attempt to tease out the conjectural foundations of their own and others' behavior. The person in the group who makes interpretation one of the principal components of his style of interaction is either misled or in flight. Not only does the understanding of behavior become an end in itself, but there even comes a point at which interpretation and insight no longer refer to actual behavior, and they become merely internally consistent logical systems with their own axioms and postulates.

Rogers and Truax (1967) maintain that accurate empathy is a far cry from the interpretation-insight dyad under attack here:

An accurate empathic grasp of the patient's conflicts and problems is perhaps most sharply contrasted with the more usual diagnostic formulation of the patient's experiences. This diagnostic understanding which is so different but so common involves the "I understand what is wrong with you" or "I understand the dynamics which make you act that way" approach. These evaluative understandings are external and even impersonal. While they may at times be very useful in developing external understanding, they are in sharp contrast to an accurate and sensitive grasp of events and experiences and their *personal meaning to the client.* The external and evaluative understanding tends to focus the client's being on externals or upon intellectualizations which remove him from an ongoing contact with the deeper elements of his self [p. 105].

Insight cultures are often flight cultures because they keep the group from coming to grips with the affective behavioral dimensions of interpersonal living. Frank (1961) reflects on the problems inherent in an overintellectualized approach to therapy. At least in American psychotherapy the scientific ideal reinforces the democratic one by valuing lack of dogmatism. It also values objectivity and intellectual comprehension and these features may not be entirely advantageous for psychotherapy. They tend to result in an overevaluation of its cognitive aspects. From the patient's standpoint, "insight" in the sense of the ability to verbalize self-understanding may be mistaken for genuine attitude change. From the therapist's standpoint, the scientific attitude may lead to undue stress on the niceties of interpretation and avoidance of frankly emotion-arousing techniques such as group rituals and dramatic activities, even though there is universal agreement that in order to succeed psychotherapy must involve the patient's emotions [pp. 219–220].

Insight is not considered meaningless. Rather, insight through action might be more interesting, and ultimately more productive, than a more intellectualized and abstractive form of insight. As Goroff (1967) notes, "the development of 'insight' comes not from interpretations, but from experiencing . . . changes in . . . behavior [p. 432]." The participants in the contract group are asked to do just that: change their behavior, attempt to be with one another in new, noncliché ways. The sharing of resulting emotional reactions and insights is a far cry from the sterile insight searching that goes on too frequently, both in and out of therapy. Douds and his associates (1967), too, severely criticize the insight game:

At best, insight inundates affect with ideas and drowns it in a whirlpool of words. At worst, the person is left with the feeling of being splintered into a thousand pieces, in contact with the fact that he has no identity of his own, only fitting in relation to specific people and situations. Feeling alone, without action, leads to no change. Thus, the alienated person who seeks *only* insight slowly decays while having the illusion of making progress [p. 177].

Our fear of feelings and emotions moves us to try to substitute logic for them. It is a poor substitute. There are two ways in which the interpretation-insight game may be played. First, a participant may play the role of interpreter: he feels free to discuss the dynamics underlying his own behavior and that of others. Another way of playing the game, however, is to demand that the other come up with proper interpretations of and insights into his own behavior. The favorite ploy of the person who plays the game is the question "why?" His immediate response to disclosure is not support but "why?" If the respondent plays his game, he usually has to venture into intellectualized conjecture, which is usually quite boring and does not lead to either fruitful insight or behavioral change. However, the game does prevent group members from interacting affectively with one another, and this might well be its whole purpose.

Although the pursuit of interpretation and insight might be the problem of only one or two members, it can become a group problem; that is, a culture of interpretation and insight can develop within the group. If intellectualized interpretation and insight can go unchallenged early in the life of the group, the participants tend to enter into a tacit understanding to encourage, or at least to tolerate, such activities. Once the decision has been made, it is difficult to unmake. The leader-member should challenge such tacit understandings from the beginning.

This is not to say that every interpretation or all pursuit of insight constitutes flight behavior. Interpretation is valuable to the degree that it has some impact on the person whose behavior is being analyzed. Interpretation must produce some kind of focus that leads to behavioral change. Wiener (1967) suggests that "it is not the quantity of information that is important for action, but the quantity of information which can penetrate into a communication and storage apparatus sufficiently to serve as a trigger for action [p. 127]." The pithy, conjectural, impact interpretation usually produces intensive interaction in the group, while the extended interpretation almost inevitably ends in monologue and lecture. As May (1958) notes, the more detailed we become in our analysis of forces and drives, the more abstract and the more removed from living human beings we become. An interpretation culture contributes vastly to the entropy of group process. Such a culture is overly intellectual and analytic; living together in dialogue, on the other hand, is emotional and synthetic.

Humor. Humor is a two-edged sword. For instance, it can be used to ease the punitive side effects of confrontation and thus facilitate interaction, but it can also be used as a weapon to destroy attempts at deepening the level of the interaction or broaching sensitive topics. When humor is used to dissipate tension, it does just that, but it does so without getting at the issues underlying the tension. Whenever either an individual or a group adopts humor as a consistent component of interactional style (e.g., the group spends five or ten minutes in banter at the beginning of a session, or a member becomes humorous whenever a particularly sensitive issue is brought up), such behavior should be challenged.

The Questioner. It is amazing how many participants handle emotional interactions by means of questions. For instance, A reveals himself at a fairly deep level and expresses a good deal of emotion in doing so. B, unable to handle either the revelation or the emotion, begins to ask A questions instead of supporting him or engaging in counter self-sharing. Questions can be effective if they get at the guts of the interaction and also reveal something about the questioner in the process (e.g., that he is concerned or anxious). Berne (1966) uses interrogation primarily to help document points that promise to be clinically decisive ("Did you really steal the money?"). Questions put to the patient's Adult, Berne says, are thought-provoking, and, in this respect, resemble confrontations. But, on the negative side, questions can be an attempt to intellectualize emotions expressed in the group or even an expression of hostility, a way of picking at the other. Some people ask questions because they think that they should say something or interact in some way, and questions constitute the safest way of doing this. Whenever questions, especially "why" questions, become the instruments of an ineffective interpretation-insight culture, they indicate flight, and the question culture should be challenged.

Rationalizations. Rationalization plays a part in almost every defense mechanism. In sensitivity groups, an almost infinite variety of rationalizations are available to the participant who finds that he is not giving himself to the group experience. As the proverb goes, he who cannot dance says that the yard is stony. It is possible to mention here only a few of the more commonly used rationalizations. One is the distant-fields syndrome: the participant says to himself, if not to others, that he would be doing well if he were only in that other group. It is the peculiar combination of personalities in *this* group that prevents him from getting on with the work. Once he has convinced himself that the obstacle is his environment (including the trainer) rather than himself, he proportions his participation to his discovery. Sometimes it takes the form: "Even *I* cannot cope with *this* group."

Others project their own inadequacies on the laboratory experience itself: "This is a contrived situation, quite unreal; it does not facilitate real interpersonal contact." The fact is that no one claimed that the group situation was not contrived; the laboratory is both real and unreal, but the person who becomes preoccupied with its unrealities is in flight. It is too easy to blame these unrealities for one's own failures, just as it is easy, for the person who is afraid of failure or who feels he has failed, to become cynical about the powers of the group.

A rather silent member of a group once suggested an interesting rationalization for his nonparticipation: he said that he was participating *outside* the group, but found it impossible to participate inside the group. Inside the group he was *learning;* outside the group he was *doing.* Other statements that summarize rationalization processes are: "No one else is keeping the contract," "I really don't know what is holding me back," "I really don't know what's happening here," "I'll let you know whatever you want, just ask me," —and the list could be extended.

Sometimes participants who do not really give themselves to the contract (whether the contract is expressed or merely implied) not only blame the contract for their failures, but then try to rework the contract. The assumption is that if an ideal contract is worked out (if the environment is ideal), they will have no trouble fulfilling it. It is true that the contract exists for the participants and not the participants for the contract, but reworking the contract should not be allowed if such reworking is just an expression of flight on the part of individual members or the group itself. Many participants have difficulty with the here-and-now provision of the contract. They are much more comfortable when they are revealing what they were like, what they did, or what happened to them there and then, instead of merely using the there and then to let others know what they are like here and now. They tend to say that the contract is restricting and want to rewrite it to include history instead of realizing that they are afraid of the immediacy of story.

Boredom. Endured boredom is a favorite form of flight from group interaction. Goffman (1967) says that the ways of not quite concealing lack of involvement constitute the symptoms of boredom. The person in the process of becoming bored separates himself from the interaction:

When a conversation fails to capture the spontaneous involvement of an individual who is obliged to participate in it, he is likely to contrive an appearance of being really involved. This he must do to save the feelings of the other participants and their good opinion of him, regardless of his motives for wanting to effect this saving. In doing so he has a damping effect upon the repercussive consequences of misinvolvement, ensuring that while he may be disaffected his disaffection will not contaminate others. At the same time, however, he drives a wedge between himself and the world that could become real for him. And the gap that is created in this way he fills with that special kind of uneasiness that is characteristically found during conversation; the kind of uneasiness that occurs when involvement obligations can neither be laid aside nor spontaneously realized; the kind that occurs when the individual is separated from the interaction, yet at a time when interaction is all around him [Goffman, 1967, p. 126].

A number of explanations have been offered for boredom (e.g., Fenichel [1953] and Greenson [1953] offer psychoanalytic interpretations), with Goffman himself suggesting that "there is a psychological doctrine that . . . argues that when the individual is himself convinced that he is bored, he may be trying to conceal from himself that he is actually embarrassed [p. 128]." But perhaps it would be better to focus on what the bored person actually does in the process of becoming bored, instead of trying to discover the hypothetical foundations of his boredom. He witnesses an interaction that has little meaning, at least for him, but at that time he chooses to keep his disaffection to himself. Then, after perhaps an hour of enduring the interaction, the bored person, in a burst of "honesty," tells the group how bored he has been. At this point, what may appear to be honesty is, in reality, an act of censure and punishment and at the same time a confession of noninvolvement. If a participant has allowed himself to be bored for any length of time, he should not punish but apologize, for he has violated his contractual obligations in a number of ways. In the contract group, the participant who does nothing about his boredom deserves it.

Overinvolvement. Some people flee centrifugally, away from the interaction, while others (probably fewer) flee centripetally, into the action. The latter overinvolve themselves with the group and cannot tolerate what seems to be underinvolvement on the part of others. Being in the group becomes their identity (perhaps because they have little sense of identity outside the group), and what they experience inside the group is more real for them than what they experience outside the group. But the group is a means of enhancing one's interpersonal living, not a substitute for it. Perhaps the overinvolvement of some can be explained by the construct of reaction-formation: those who feel most uncomfortable and alienated from the group (or from others in general) must seem to be its most ardent supporters. Those who make a cult of growth-group experiences, both inside and outside the group, do much to alienate both fellow participants and the general population. Overinvolvement, however, is not the usual participant problem, and those who tend to flee centrifugally should be slow to accuse their fellow participants of too much involvement.

Dealing in Generalities. One of the most common failings of participants is a generality approach to the interaction. When speaking, they use "you" and "one" and "people" instead of "I," they state and restate general principles without applying them to themselves or to others, and they address themselves to the group at large instead of contacting individual participants. But being specific *does* make a difference in the sense of immediacy in the group. There is a world of difference between the statement "You get scared to bring up what is really bothering you" and "I am really afraid to talk about the things that bother me here." It does make a difference when participants talk about specific incidents and people inside the group instead of speaking generally about the group culture. It does make a difference when a participant directs a high percentage of his remarks to individuals in the group instead of speaking generally to the whole group. When a participant addresses the whole group through the immediacy of his contact with another individual, the entire interaction becomes less abstractive and more engaging. In experimenting with groups, I have arbitrarily banned the use of "people" and of "you" and "one," refused to let others make general statements, and demanded that the participants address themselves to particular individuals instead of the entire group. The resulting culture, while somewhat artificial, at least initially, dramatizes the lack of immediacy that preceded it. Rid the group of the generalities that plague it and you rid it of one of the most common sources of boredom.

Low Tolerance for Conflict and Emotion. Inevitably there are some participants who have a low tolerance for conflict or strong emotion. When conflict and emotion run high, these participants react in one of two ways (or in both ways at different times): they either withdraw from the interaction or they try to stop what is taking place. In conflict or confrontational situations, they may become mediators, saviors, or "red crossers." They defend the confrontee, chide the confronter, and in general pour oil on the waters of conflict. Nor is it just negative emotion that they find intolerable. Often strong positive emotions are just as threatening, and these, too, must be tempered by humor, changing the subject, and other ploys. This does not mean that no one should ever intervene in conflict situations; some conflict situations are unprofitable and forms of flight in themselves, and they deserve to be challenged. It does mean, however, that one should try to be aware of, and perhaps declare, his motivation when he does intervene in conflictual or other emotional situations ("intervene" is used here as distinct from "participate"). The participant who can declare his discomfort during even responsible conflict without trying to sabotage the interaction has taken the first step toward handling his low tolerance for emotion.

No Space to Move. One of the functions of growth experiences is to reveal to the participant the possibilities for growthful change. He can resist this revelation in a variety of ways. He may deny that any change, or at least the changes proposed, would be beneficial or even possible. That is, he may present himself as having no room in which to move. He sees himself as hemmed in by his heredity, environment, and history. Too often his response to confrontation is: "I can't do anything about it; that's the way I am." The problem here is not that the participant refuses to move in the directions suggested by others but that he refuses even to entertain the possibility of moving. He might refuse to do so in the name of personal freedom and integrity or from a sense of being the victim of forces outside his control, but responsible confrontation is not an attack upon a person's integrity nor a call to do the impossible. The person comes to the group not to be remade but to entertain possibilities for change. If he resists this goal, he is resisting the very *raison d'être* of the group. If a participant finds that his interactional style is heavily loaded with statements of defense or attack, he might well entertain the hypothesis that he is unwilling to examine even the possibility of change.

The Group in Flight

Obviously, some of the resistances and flight modalities outlined above could apply not only to individuals but to the group as a whole. This is especially true if the group establishes a culture in which a particular flight modality—for example, intellectualized interpretation—is tolerated or even encouraged. Certain other behaviors, however, indicate the resistance or the flight of the group as such, though here again, any particular behavior might characterize an individual rather than the group. Some of these behaviors are outlined below.

Extended Contract Talk.   In contract-group experiences, it is essential that participants have a solid understanding of the principal provisions of the contract. In other kinds of growth-group experiences, especially experiences characterized by goallessness or planned ambiguity, it is necessary for the participants to work out some kind of contract among themselves. In both groups, then, early meetings are characterized by contract talk, which includes a discussion of goals and the group structures necessary to achieve these goals. However, when the group persists in contract talk, when it keeps formulating and reformulating its goals, when it keeps restructuring the contract, then it is quite likely that the group is allowing talk about the contract to take the place of fulfilling the contract. It is much easier to discuss a contract (expressed or implied) than to engage in fulfilling it. This does not mean that a group should not discuss the contract or reformulate its goals from time to time. Reformulation, however, should be quite concrete—that is, goals should be discussed not in themselves but in terms of the individuals, interactions, and incidents of the group. If this is done, occasional contract talk will become just another modality through which the participants contact one another.

Analysis of Past Interactions.   Detailed analysis of past interactions in the group is both a caricature of processing and a seemingly popular form of flight. For instance, the group, in an afternoon meeting, discusses in detail the dynamics of the morning meeting. This discussion takes place under the guise of "working things out" and "getting things straight," but the hidden purpose is frequently to gain a respite from intimate interaction. The group analyzes not to put things in perspective but to put the interaction at a distance. Sometimes these historical analyses take place during the same meeting; that is, the participants interact for a while, and then its interchange degenerates into a "This happened and then that happened" or a "No, B got angry and *then* A got angry" situation in which the here and now is abandoned for a safer there and then. In worthwhile processing, the participants become critics of the group culture and of their own interactions, with a view to improving both. Historical analyses, on the other hand, usually become ends in themselves; the group treads water, as it were, in order to avoid involvement. It is

interesting to see what happens after the group concludes an historical analysis of its interaction; frequently it merely drops silent
for a while, which is some indication of the relevance of the analysis.

Serious A-contractual Conversations. Sometimes groups flee the
expressed or implied contract by engaging in worthwhile discussions
that really have no relation to the goals of the groups. I sat in on a
sensitivity group once and listened for a while to a rather high-level
discussion of some of the most important social issues of the day.
Had a total stranger come into the group without knowing its general
purpose, I am sure that he would have thought that it was a social-
action group that was taking itself seriously. Such conversation
would have been most appropriate at another time in another place,
but in the training group, it was merely an expression of discomfort
and anxiety and a flight from the real purpose of the group. Usually,
such serious discussions take place early in the life of the group,
for most people assume that when they are talking intellectually
about serious issues, they are in close contact with their fellow dis-
cussants. Such conversations are difficult to challenge, too, for it
seems ignoble to interrupt something that is so worthwhile in itself.
I tend to interrupt the conversation and have the group process
what it is doing. Soon the participants realize that they are avoiding
the real issues at hand. The point is that such conversations should
be interrupted immediately so that serious intellectual discussions
do not become part of the group culture.

Turn-Taking and Dependence on Exercises. Some of the exercises
which are commonly introduced into human relations laboratories
involve "turn-taking" or "going around." For instance, early in the life
of the group, each member might be asked to give his first impressions of every other member. Turn-taking provides a structure that
both forces each member to participate and provides a certain
amount of institutionalized safety. As the group moves forward,
however, there should be less and less reliance on such artificial
methods of stimulating meaningful interaction and of getting everyone to interact. If the group goes dead, or if any particular participant is failing to interact, these issues should be dealt with directly
without resorting to artificial communication stimulators. Sometimes
a group has to live with its own inertness in order to discover that
it has within itself the resources to deal with its own problems.
Exercises can be used effectively to introduce different kinds of ex-

periences into the group, to stimulate interaction, and to break through communication blocks, but if they are used excessively, they rob the group of its initiative. If the leader feels that he must make frequent use of exercises in order to keep the interaction going, his feeling is probably more a sign of his own flight from anxiety than of his interest in group communication. As the participants grow, they will resist artificiality and attempts to manipulate them into doing what they know they should do themselves.

Dealing with One. A common occurrence in groups is the phenomenon of one person's becoming the focal point of the group interaction for a relatively extended period of time. In its extreme form, this means that eventually each member has his turn as the focal point of the group (and this results in a kind of amplified version of "going around"). There is no particular reason that the group may not give extended attention to the problems of an individual member, but, in practice, the way in which such attention is given frequently involves elements of flight. Once a single individual becomes the focal point of the interaction, usually a number of members fall silent, becoming interested listeners because they have nothing to say to the participant in question, perhaps because they do not have the same problems. These silent members are in flight. No structure that significantly reduces the involvement of a number of members (or serves as an excuse for their noninvolvement) should be tolerated; if dealing with one has this effect, then it is not being handled properly. It is possible, however, to deal with one in a way that does not cut down on the involvement of the participants. First of all, no participant should be allowed to excuse himself from the interaction simply because another participant is the focal point of the discussion. Second, dealing with one does not exclude interactions between participants other than the focal participant. Too often it is assumed that if the group is dealing with one, the only permissible interactions are those between the focal participant and someone else. The situation thus produced is artificial and stultifying. Third, the focal participant, himself realizing that there is a tendency on the part of some to withdraw from the interaction in a "dealing with one" situation, should take the initiative in bringing silent members back into the discussion. The problem is that most focal participants become somewhat passive and merely allow themselves to be dealt with. Another danger inherent in a "dealing with one" situation is the tendency to focus on there-and-then incidents and concerns rather than the here and now. This tendency serves the cause of alienation. The responsibility for maintaining a here-and-now culture in a "dealing with one" situation falls, to a great degree, on the shoulders of the focal participant. He cannot escape talking about there-and-then concerns, but it is his responsibility to make these concerns relevant to the here and now. For instance, it may be that the there and then limits his ability to involve himself with the other participants—that is, his past history affects his here-and-now participation and involvement: or, on the other hand, it may be that he has found it both easy and rewarding to involve himself with group members, a fact that stands in stark contrast to his there-and-then situations. Whatever the case might be, he must make there-and-then concerns relevant to this group. If he fails to do so, his fellow participants should challenge him.

Sometimes, when a person other than the focal participant brings up concerns of his own that are similar or relevant to those of the focal participant, he will be silenced and chided for not giving the other enough time. This defeats the very purpose of the group, which is not to deal with one another serially as problem but rather to engage in mutual self-sharing. Giving the focal participant enough time ("I don't think that we are finished with Ted") frequently means keeping him artificially in the limelight, making him a case, constituting him as a problem, which the group must in some way solve. Those who mother the focal participant, protecting his time and interests, should examine their motivation for doing so.

Personally, I prefer group cultures that do not make a habit of dealing with a single individual in an extended way. Even the most dramatic aspects of the lives of the participants can be dealt with in the give and take of a culture that calls for the more or less continued participation of all members. If a member reveals a dramatic dimension of his life, he needs support rather than time. To assume that this support can take place only by his becoming the central actor (or patient) on the stage for an extended period of time is unwarranted. One of the most effective forms of support is mutual self-sharing, for it is a way of saying "Thank you for trusting me, I trust you, too" or "Thank you for sharing yourself with me, it gives me the courage to share myself with you." It is also unwarranted to assume that the group can work completely through any participant's self-revelation at any one time. Such grandiosity covers a multitude of uncertainties and anxieties in groups. The group should feel free to return again and again to anything that has been said in the group and to look at new facets of self-disclosure in the light of subsequent group interaction.

Interruptions and Moods. If the group culture is too polite, it will not allow one participant to interrupt another, nor will it allow anyone to interrupt a group procedure such as dealing with one. Perhaps a distinction should be made between relevant and irrelevant interruptions or interventions. To interrupt in order to change the topic is one thing; to intervene because one has something important and relevant to say is another. On the one hand, the group culture should not encourage boorishness, but, on the other, it should promote a freer atmosphere than that found in polite conversations. With good purpose, one should be able to break into a conversation without being made to feel that he is an intruder or a bull in a china shop. Although it had been thought that the number of interruptions that would occur when members of families of schizophrenics interacted would be significantly higher than the number of interruptions during the conversations carried on by the families of normals, Mishler and Waxler (1966) found that the opposite was true. The data suggest that the families of acute schizophrenic patients have the fewest interruptions, and families of normal children have the most. Such data may indicate that interruptions are even an essential part of good conversational interaction.

If the interaction is so fragile that any interruption can destroy it, then perhaps the participants should work at making it more robust rather than pouring energies into protecting it. Sometimes participants claim that through interruptions the magic of the moment is lost: "We never got back to it." This statement, however, may mean "We did not want to get back to it"—relief being disguised as altruistic annoyance. The group does have its moods, and mood can be a facilitating factor, but the group should not be too dependent on mood in order to get its work done. There are right times for dealing with certain issues, but it is up to the group to create these right times rather than wait for them to happen.

Problem-Solution Cultures. No matter how applicable a problem-solution model might be to such sciences as mathematics and physics, it leaves much to be desired when applied to intrapsychic and interpersonal living. As soon as a group participant mentions that he has certain problems, the other participants react predictably: they want to solve his problems, have him solve them himself, or help him solve them. In fact, the group usually welcomes talk of problems, because it is much easier to deal with problems than to involve oneself with persons. If certain of his behaviors can be separated from him and labeled as problem-causing, then one's approach to him can be relatively simple and clean.

This seems to be more than just a question of semantics. Problems and implied solutions simply are not persons but ways of setting persons at a distance. In fact, people are beginning to substitute other terms for the word "problem." For instance, they talk about their "hang-ups." It may be that the term "hang-up" is just a current substitution for the cliché "problem," but the former term implies that the person who is "hung up" is in some way responsible for his behavior and that behavioral change is within his power. At least "hang-ups" do not seem to have "solutions."

Life is not the compartmentalized or atomistic entity that proponents of the problem-solution paradigm envision. Life is principally interpersonal living, but to cast interpersonal living in terms of problems and solutions tends to make objects out of people. Even though most interpersonal-growth groups, at least in the beginning, identify depth of involvement in the group process with the revelation of problems, depth of involvement entails their sharing themselves rather than their problems. If the participants insist upon sharing problems, this might be because they cannot share themselves. When two people find it difficult to involve themselves with each other, they seldom sit down and solve this problem they have with each other. Rather, through dialogue, they begin to transcend attitudes and behaviors that keep them apart. Once they become more available to each other, a new synthesis (rather than a solution) takes place in their relationship. They grow in relationship to each other, and growth does not fit in well with a problem-solution paradigm.

If a person always talks about himself in terms of his problems, he tends to maintain the false hope that if he solves his problems, then things will be all right: Utopia is the land of solved problems. Perhaps the use of such terms as "problem" and "solution" appears unhealthy or inappropriate because such language is symptomatic of overly mechanistic attitudes toward oneself and one's relationships with others.

Tacit Decisions. The tendency of the group to make tacit decisions or come to tacit understandings has been mentioned, but it bears repeating here in that it is one of the principal ways in which groups as such take flight. As Whitaker and Lieberman (1964) note, unchallenged modes of behavior tend to pass into the group culture as laws, and once these laws are made, they become very difficult to change or abrogate. Tacit understandings can affect almost any aspect of group life: the content of discussions ("We do not talk about sex here"), procedure ("When one person is talking, no one should interrupt him and he should be given all the time he wants"), depth of interaction ("We really don't want to wash our dirty linen here" or "There are some things that we should just keep to ourselves"), rules ("Coming late or absenting oneself from this group is not an offense"), style ("Humor is allowed almost anytime during interaction"), goals ("Our purpose is to decrease the discomfort that we feel in being together with one another" or "Cooperation with one another is not a group value in this situation"). Since flight by tacit decision can take place very early in the life of the group, it is up to the leader-member to explain both the process involved and the consequences of such understandings and to challenge them as soon as he sees them being formulated in the group.

Tacit decisions can begin with clearly expressed statements that go unchallenged in the group. For instance, in a group that was slated to meet once a week for twelve weeks in three-and-a-half-hour sessions, one of the participants said during the first meeting: "This set-up really doesn't allow us much time to get involved with one another; the time is short and we don't see one another between sessions." One hypothesis might be that he was afraid of getting involved with the others and that he really feared that there was *too* much time. His statement, however, went unchallenged in the group and kept coming up like a refrain in subsequent meetings. The participants tacitly accepted his analysis of the limitation of the possibilities of the group and spent the following weeks trying to live with the frustration that such limitation entailed. There are always tendencies to blame the group structure (time, length of meeting, lack of specific things to say and do, etc.) for group inaction, but to allow these tendencies to be made concrete in the group culture can mean the suffocation of the group.

Ritual Behavior. Alexander (1963) warns against what he calls "standardizing the treatment" in psychotherapy—that is, allowing it to degenerate into an interaction ritual between therapist and client. The interpersonal-growth group, too, can easily take on a ritualistic atmosphere, devoid of eruptions of any kind, in which sameness soothes. Although the participants become quite comfortable in such a ritual, there is still the illusion that something serious and worthwhile is really taking place. In a ritualistic group culture, not only do the same issues come up over and over again, but they are handled in the same way. For instance, X's silence and general lack of involvement is dealt with from time to time, but little is done between ritualistic confrontations to bring X into the interaction. It is almost as if the participants were to say to themselves from time to time: "Since nothing in particular is taking place right now, we might as well make a group assault on X again." One way to dramatize the ritualization of the group is to replay a videotape of, let us say, session three, together with a tape of session eight. If the same issues are being dealt with in the same way—that is, if it would be impossible for a stranger to determine which was the earlier and which the later session—then it may well be that the group has ritualized itself as a form of resistance or flight. A ritualized group culture is a sterile thing, of which boredom and resistance to attending (reluctance to come, coming late, actual absences) are the inevitable signs.

Exceeding Contractual Limits and the Question of Loyalty. The following situation comes up again and again in groups. The meeting is scheduled to last from seven until ten o'clock. Little happens until about nine-thirty, so that by ten o'clock the group is "in the middle of things." Most members take it as a sign of involvement in and loyalty to the group to extend the group session until ten-thirty or eleven o'clock. Not only that, but they implicitly or explicitly accuse anyone who wants to leave at the contracted time of disloyalty. Frequently this mode of proceeding is established early in the life of the group by means of a tacit understanding and becomes an important factor in the group culture. The group attempts to take flight by substituting sheer quantity of participation (time spent together) for quality. In my opinion, meetings should, in general, start and stop on time. Loyalty should be demonstrated not by a willingness to give oneself to endless discussions (quite often such discussions entail dealing with one in a way that precludes the involvement of the majority of the members) but by a willingness to get down to work from the start. The person who opens up five minutes before the scheduled end of the meeting should continue in the following meeting. If, in the following meeting, he finds that the golden moment has passed, it is more than likely that he was only teasing the group in the first place. Or if mood is so important for him, then the interactions that take place when the mood is upon him might well have little learning value. His moods are perhaps analogous to drugged states in which real learning either does not take place or does not transfer to non-drugged conditions.

Flight as Nongrowthful Avoidance Learning. Avoidance learning has been used, in varying degrees, in treating such problems as alcoholism and sexually deviant behavior (Kalish, 1965). The client must learn to stay away from a certain situation, avoid a certain stimulus, or place a certain act in order to prevent some unwanted consequence. For instance, an alcoholic treated with Antabuse might learn that nausea and violent retching are too high a price to pay for drinking, so he avoids the stimulus that results in such a noxious response. In groups, the participants soon learn that, at least initially, a certain degree of pain and discomfort is associated with involving themselves effectively with one another. They also learn that there are certain behaviors (the flight behaviors previously outlined) that put off, circumvent, or in other ways avoid painful self-actualizing interactions. Each time a participant engages in some sort of flight and not only avoids painful interaction but even receives some kind of positive response from his fellow participants, the flight behavior in question is reinforced, and the group is on its way toward a flight culture.

Participation versus Involvement. Some members participate quite a bit in the group interaction but involve themselves minimally. In reviewing the videotape of a group session recently, I began scoring the interactions, using (X) to indicate a contractual interaction, (O) a noncontractual interaction, and (N) a kind of neutral interaction, designed to keep things moving though not constituting a real contribution in itself. Participation styles began to emerge. For instance, one participant ended up with a long string of (N's). He had participated quite a bit in the interaction but had contributed little of himself. He had really assumed the role of facilitator without even realizing what he was doing (for he was quite surprised later when his fellow participants told him that he was playing the role of leader). The participants who have long strings of (O's) and (N's) are certainly participating, but they are not involving themselves. It would be better if these members were to cut down on their participation and increase their involvement.

Flight versus Maintaining Adequate Defenses. Sensitivity-training experiences, if carried out responsibly, give the participants a relatively safe opportunity to lower some of their defenses in the name of growth. No growth experience, however, should demand that the participant divest himself of his defenses entirely. But maintaining adequate defenses (even in the process of lowering them) and resistance flight are two different processes. The more common danger is that the participant will not drop his defenses enough to allow the experience to have its impact on him. The person with crumbling defenses either refuses to participate in such experiences because he senses the danger, or he reveals his tenuous defense system behaviorally early in the life of the group. Selection procedures should screen out those with crumbling defenses so that the group culture can bring to bear fairly strong pressures on those with more than adequate defenses.

Flight as Entropic. Group interaction tends to entropy unless it is fed information from outside the system—that is, outside the systems of defense and convention that enclose the participants. Clichés are entropic, a cause and a sign of the decline of the system. Long-winded, intellectualized interpretation-insight systems are entropic. Story, on the other hand, has high message or information value, for it keeps the system open, reverses the entropic process, and leads to an enclave of anti-entropic organization (see Wiener, 1967 and Rosenblith, 1967). Flight is always identifiable by its entropic effect. No matter how engaging or entertaining it might be at the moment, it has no sustaining effect, and the system that is constituted by the interrelationships between members runs down. If nothing is done, it dies. Again, no contract, implicit or explicit, can ban the various forms of flight that take place during sensitivity-training laboratories, but if the participants are willing to examine the modes of flight in which they do engage, they can learn much about themselves.

Chapter Eleven:
Epilog

The Problem of Agency

An assumption throughout this book has been that the relatively active participant will benefit most from the training experience. The group has no miraculous powers: it cannot serve the personal and interpersonal growth of the participant who actively resists the experience or who remains a passive spectator of the group interaction. However, as Bion (1961) notes, it is impossible to do nothing in a group, even by doing nothing. A refusal to accept the challenge of agency in a group is a refusal to face one's potential. The assumption here is that such refusals are deleterious to personal and interpersonal growth. Erikson (1964) speaks generally about the agency-passivity dimension of psychic life:

Patiens, then, would denote a state of being exposed from within or from without to superior forces which cannot be overcome without prolonged patience or energetic redeeming help; while *agens* connotes an inner state of being unbroken in initiative and in acting in the service of a cause which sanctions this initiative. You will see immediately that the state of *agens* is what all clients, or patients, in groups or alone, are groping for and need our help to achieve [p. 87].

Indeed, one of the common marks of emotional disturbance is the surrender of agency, especially the refusal to be an agent in interpersonal situations. Perhaps one of the most important goals of laboratory training in interpersonal relations is experimenting with one's power of agency in interpersonal living. In order to do this, the individual participant must take responsibility for what is happening in the group: "The group (including the trainers) is responsible for itself; each of us must exercise his personal and joint responsibility if any degree of 'self-actualization' is to be achieved [Bugental & Tannenbaum, 1965, p. 110]." The group will be as good as *I* make it—this seems to be the cold, hard logic of sensitivity-training groups.

Agency, like independence, cannot be conferred; it must be seized:

In the last analysis independence cannot be conferred; it can only be seized. . . . We can only say that it has become manifest in an individual or group when it no longer occurs to that group or individual to seek the solution of its problems by an agent outside itself. To "demand one's independence" . . . is of course a contradiction in terms [Slater, 1966, p. 150].

"Initiative," therefore, is an important concept in training groups. In the contract group this is made abundantly clear: the member, for all practical purposes, contracts to be an initiator, to move out of himself and contact the group and its individual participants. It is unlikely that the group will transform a passive person into a high initiator, but an increased sense of agency is an important goal for every participant. If a person participates only by responding when he is contacted in some way, then his participation, rated in terms of seconds spent talking, might well be high; but if his participation is rated in terms of number of acts initiated (see Mann, 1959, p. 244), then his participation will be low. The contract calls for participation by initiation—at least this is an ideal to be pursued.

It is not suggested here that universal active participation is characteristic of face-to-face groups. The evidence indicates that ordinarily "interaction is unevenly distributed among group members [Collins & Guetzkow, 1964, p. 170]." There is a characteristic tendency for a few people to dominate group interaction, and this tendency increases with the size of the group. In training groups, however, tendencies toward domination and passivity are to be resisted. This is essential if the participants are to work toward cohesiveness. The group-dynamics literature indicates that cohesiveness, defined in terms of intermember attraction or liking, increases with increased positive interaction (for a summary see the work of Lott & Lott, 1965). Collins and Guetzkow (1964) also cite evidence indicating that the "more interactions initiated by a group member, the more interactions will be directed to him by other group members [p. 170]." In other words, group cohesiveness depends on intermember activity, and intermember activity depends, at least in part, on the willingness of the individual participant to assume a certain degree of agency in the interpersonal life of the group. Mann (1959) indicates that initiators in groups are usually more intelligent, better adjusted, and more extroverted than noninitiators. Since group members usually possess different amounts of intelligence, adjustment, and extroversion, this means that the group as a whole will have to strive to keep the interaction distributed in such a way as to benefit all members. This is not to say that all members must participate equally (nor is mere quantity rather than quality of participation being urged), but it does mean that care should be taken to give all members an opportunity to become initiators and that the relatively passive should be encouraged to initiate interaction. It is hypothesized here that a certain quantity of participation (and initiation) is essential to overall quality of participation. Every group session starts with an emptiness that can be filled only by the initiative of the participants. Filling this emptiness must be a cooperative effort.

Bunker (1965), in studying the effects of laboratory training in the participants' day-to-day lives subsequent to the training sessions, found no differences between participants and controls in effective initation of action, assertiveness, and self-confidence—all factors in the agency dimension of living. However, we do not know how much initiative, assertiveness, and self-confidence was displayed by the experimental group in the laboratory itself. Nor do we know whether increasing initiative, assertiveness, and self-confidence were explicit goals of the laboratory experience or not. A laboratory will not magically increase these qualities unless it is designed to do so and unless the participants experiment with and exercise their power of agency within the group. In the contract group, the exercise of agency is an explicit goal. I would like to see Bunker's experiment replicated with an experimental group that has been explicitly encouraged, by the laboratory experience itself, to strive for responsible agency.

**Research: Issues
and Applications**

A number of reviews have covered the research literature on laboratory learning from a variety of points of view (Buchanan, 1965; Campbell & Dunnette, 1968; House, 1967; Stock, 1964). While most of the research has had a direct or indirect managerial or organizational orientation, still it raises issues and suggests applications to laboratory experiences the goals of which are self-actualization and interpersonal growth. Unfortunately, despite the phenomenal growth and spread of these latter experiences, there is little research dealing directly with them. In fact, the research that seems most relevant to such groups is that pertaining to psychotherapy and to a number of areas of social psychology. However, no one has yet synthesized the pertinent aspects of this literature and used it as a starting point for research into interpersonal-growth-oriented sensitivity-training groups. Yet it is only fitting to comment on some of the research findings in the general area of laboratory training and discuss their relevance to the kind of experience outlined in the past ten chapters. Since these comments will not be exhaustive, the reader interested in a more comprehensive review of research problems and findings is referred to the reviews listed.

The Lack of a Unitary Phenomenon. The consensus of those who have reviewed the literature is that the evidence concerning the value of laboratory-training experiences is contradictory, confusing, and inconclusive. Since most of the research deals with the use of laboratory training for the purpose of increasing managerial skills and organizational effectiveness, the evidence may be best summarized as follows: "Examination of the research literature leads to the conclusion that while T-group training seems to produce observable changes in behavior, the utility of these changes for the performance of individuals in their organizational roles remains to be demonstrated [Campbell & Dunnette, 1968, p. 73]." This conclusion does not deal with the use of laboratory techniques as means of increasing self-actualization processes and interpersonal growth. One of the principal causes of the confusing and contradictory evidence obtained so far is undoubtedly the fact that "sensitivity training," the "T-group," and "laboratory-training" are very broad terms and do not indicate any kind of unitary phenomenon. Laboratories use a variety of techniques—for example, lectures, exercises, both verbal and nonverbal, and face-to-face conversation of various kinds; trainers use a variety of styles, some being quite passive while others are quite active; laboratories take place in a variety of settings with different kinds of populations—volunteers who attend a residential laboratory, students in courses, nonvolunteers who represent a cross-section of a particular organization, volunteers in weekly local groups conducted by nonprofessionals. Perhaps it is the phenomenon itself, and not the evidence, that is confusing. As Campbell and Dunnette (1968) put it:

Research concerning the relative contributions of specific technological features of the T group is also sparse. For example, there are no systematic studies examining the influence of differences in trainer personality and/or style on the outcomes achieved by participants. Case reports and anecdotal evidence are all that exist [p. 97].

It is practically impossible at times to replicate studies, for descriptions of what took place in the training situations are either nonexistent or too sparse to be meaningful. The variables of the laboratory situation must be described carefully if replication is to become possible.

Because the contract-group approach delineates goals, leadership style, and the kinds of interaction expected of the members, it offers a kind of unitary phenomenon for study. If, in addition, a log is kept indicating the sequence of such events as exercises, greater control is possible in replication studies. This does not mean that research with laboratories characterized by goallessness and planned ambiguity is impossible (though it is probably more difficult). However, the essential characteristics of such experiences should be carefully described so that research efforts center around the same phenomena. A contract approach to self-actualization through the small group experience may standardize the experience in a way that does not appeal to some, but if such standardization is impossible, then so is research, and all that an interested party can do is listen to the witness, both positive and negative, given by those who engage in laboratory training.

Methodological Problems and the Question of Outcome. It is a truism to say that enormous methodological problems face the researcher interested in the macro-aspects of human behavior. Furthermore, once one has read the extant research literature dealing with laboratory training, it is easy to criticize the efforts that have been made to measure this phenomenon. For instance, one glaring defect in these studies (among many in the design of research) has been the failure to use control groups (Gassner, Gold & Snadowsky, 1964). One of the serious problems facing the researcher is how to measure outcome. In this respect, a kind of dilemma exists: on the one hand, traditional psychological tests are not sensitive to the changes that take place in training groups, and yet, on the other, *ad hoc* scales and tests are unvalidated. For instance, Dunnette (1962) reports a study in which the California Psychological Inventory was used to assess change in 70 business students who had engaged in 48 hours of laboratory training. Although the results were termed negative, perhaps it would have been more exact to say that they were irrelevant, for there is no reason the CPI should measure the outcome of laboratory training. Haiman (1963) found significant shifts in attitude as measured by a composite open-mindedness scale, and indeed, as Campbell and Dunnette (1968) suggest, the whole area of attitude change as one of the principal outcomes of laboratory experiences is one that has been little studied even though it is an area of great promise. Some of the tests that have been used to measure outcome have been of limited use because of ceiling effects: laboratory participants score high on the pretest, and thus have little room to move. Better tests of self-actualization of the relatively normal person are needed. After a laboratory experience, a participant might feel better and be more satisfied with the quality of his interpersonal interaction, but many are wary of such subjective measures.

In summary it seems relatively well established that the way in which an individual sees himself may indeed change during the course of a T group. However, there is no firm evidence indicating that such changes are produced by the T-group training as compared with other types of training, merely by the passage of time, or even by the simple expedient of retaking a self-descriptive inventory after a period of thinking about one's previous responses to the same inventory [Campbell & Dunnette, 1968, p. 91].

Furthermore, while it is possible to ask the associates of a person who has participated in a laboratory whether he has changed for the better or not (Bunker, 1965), measurement by this method is awkward and of unknown accuracy. Moreover, even the positive changes might be unrelated to both the kinds of interactions and the goals of laboratory experience. It might even be that the participant merely used the laboratory experience as an occasion to engage in some kind of conversion experience that is relatively unrelated to the goals, operations, interactions, and exercises of the laboratory. But if this is the case, are we to say that the laboratory has been successful or not?

Most outcome studies deal with group scores. The problem with group scores, however, is that individual differences are lost, and ceiling effects are frequently operative. During the same laboratory experience, some participants improve their interpersonal skills while others seem to regress.

So far research focused on the "average" effects of T-group or laboratory training has been considered. That is, the crucial question has been whether or not training makes a difference for the group as a whole. Such a generalized interpretation might cover up important interactions between individual differences and training methods. Given a particular kind of outcome, certain kinds of people might benefit from T-group training while others may actually be harmed. The same reasoning may be applied to the interaction of differences in situational and organizational variables with the training experience. However, very few studies have investigated interactive effects [Campbell & Dunnette, 1968, p. 96].

What is it that causes some to succeed and some to fail? What does the successful person do that the unsuccessful person does not?

Finally, the question of baseline measurements seems to be important in outcome studies. In a study by Zand, Steele, and Zalkind (1967) it was found that individuals rated as most involved in the laboratory experience also tended to be rated as the most involved in follow-up activities. At first glance, this evidence would seem to bear on the question of agency previously discussed. But since no baseline with respect to involvement has been determined, it is not clear whether it was evidence of increased agency or merely of consistency of behavior. There was no baseline against which to measure improvement in involvement or agency.

Perhaps it is time to review the criteria we use to judge the success or failure of sensitivity-training experiences. If measurement is to have any meaning at all, it is necessary to delineate clearly the specific goals of any given laboratory experience, to determine what means are associated with achieving these goals, and to devise measures to determine whether these goals have been reached or not. Perhaps the criteria we have used to measure success or failure have been too gross or have not reflected the real goals of the experience. For instance, managerial-training laboratories aside, can success be indicated by the very fact that the participant believes that he has benefited by the training experience and somehow feels enriched for having involved himself rather intimately with this set of people at this time? Does the criterion of success always or exclusively have to be what constructive changes take place in the home situation subsequent to the laboratory experience? Perhaps, at this stage of laboratory-training development, we should be more modest in looking for results. But we can be neither modest nor exact unless we get a clearer picture of what takes place within the laboratory and of the component parts of the goals set for training experiences.

Research and the Goals of Laboratory Learning. To say that "interpersonal sensitivity" is the goal of laboratory learning is to say almost nothing. Campbell and Dunnette (1968) discuss the vagueness of such a goal:

The major purpose here is simply to emphasize that interpersonal sensitivity is not only an elusive, but also a highly complex phenomenon. Persons involved in a T-group training program may indeed become more "sensitive," but the nature and underlying strategies of the sensitivities developed may differ widely from person to person and from program to program. Unless the various components and strategies involved in interpersonal sensitivity are taken into account during the design of measuring instruments and during the design and implementation of research investigations, little new knowledge concerning T-group training effects or the likelihood of transferring skills back to the work setting will accrue. So far . . . most investigators have not attempted to cope with the serious measurement and design problems in this area [p. 80].

Later in the same article, the authors run up against the very complexity they speak of. They suppose that one of the goals of laboratory learning should be accurate empathy, and they tend to define such empathy in terms of the ability of an individual to predict the values and attitudes of others. Then they conclude on this negative note: "In sum, the studies incorporating a measure of how well an individual can predict the attitudes and values of others before and after T-group training have yielded largely negative results [p. 91]." Yet it is doubtful that such predictive ability *is* the goal of interpersonal-growth-oriented laboratory training. Accurate empathy refers to the ability to get some kind of feeling for what is going on inside another here and now and is not necessarily related to conceptual accuracy or predictive ability. Sensitivity training should produce more openness to the attributes, attitudes, opinions, feelings, and reactions of others. Accuracy, however, is something that depends upon both the one who emits the communication and the one who receives it. A person perceives another more accurately both if he gets rid of his own barriers to perceiving and if the other emits communications more directly and accurately. The central point is this: it is difficult to measure attainment of goals unless there is agreement on the part of the participant, trainer, and researcher that the particular laboratory experience is designed to achieve a certain goal and that the participants see it as a goal worth achieving.

It would be better to set more modest goals for laboratory experiences. Perhaps the laboratory is a success for any participant who experiments with his behavior sufficiently to get some kind of feel for his interpersonal potentialities and deficiencies. The laboratory, then, would be an instrument of exploration rather than a vehicle of immediate change. It would be much easier to determine whether a participant experiments with certain kinds of behavior than to determine whether his life style has changed. It might well be that it is the participant who explores his possibilities who ultimately changes. If this is the case, then it is not surprising that Harrison (1966) and Schutz and Allen (1966) have found that some of the principal effects of laboratory training, in terms of behavorial change, did not take place until months after the training experience. Perhaps there is a period of fermentation or incubation characterized by subtle behavioral changes (e.g., changes in interpersonal attitudes).

The Psychotherapy Research Paradigm. Research in laboratory learning could well take some cues from some of the more effective research taking place in psychotherapy. First of all, the goals of any particular kind of laboratory training should be quite clear and operationalized in terms of specific behaviors. In the contract group, engaging in self-disclosure, expression of feeling, support, confrontation, and self-exploration as a response to confrontation are the specific interactional behaviors that define the group goal of interpersonal growth. The immediate goal of the contract group is experimentation with these behaviors on the part of the participants. The laboratory is a success, in one sense, if the participants actually do (increasingly) engage in such behaviors, for it is hypothesized that through these behaviors they come in more effective contact with themselves and with others. The laboratory becomes diagnostic in a good sense of that term: the participants come face to face with their interpersonal deficits and potentialities. It is hypothesized that if the participants do experiment constructively with such behavior in the context of the group, then possibilities for growthful behavioral change arise in real-life situations.

The laboratory must provide a climate in which the kind of experimentation described above becomes possible. Certain participant, trainer, relationship, and situation variables facilitate such a climate. It is the function of research to determine precisely what these variables are.

(1) *Participant behaviors*. Friedman (1963) found that a patient who enters a therapeutic relationship expecting to be helped in that relationship usually does find help in the form of symptom reduction; that is, patient expectancy is related to symptom reduction. Similarly, it seems that the person who enters a laboratory experience expecting to benefit from it will tend to profit from the experience. The person who enters a laboratory with a closed mind and a cynical attitude is likely to leave the experience the same way (and then perhaps blame the experience itself for being ineffective). Truax and Carkhuff (1964) have suggested that concreteness or specificity of expression is a highly desirable patient variable; that is, they find some evidence that it is related to successful outcome. Concreteness also seems to be a participant variable that adds to the effectiveness of training sessions. The question is: what participant variables are related to positive and negative outcomes?

(2) *Trainer variables*. Rogers and his associates (1967) discuss the differences between high-functioning and low-functioning therapists, outlining the qualities that make for high functioning— for example, acceptance and warmth, genuineness, and accurate empathy. Others (e.g., Berenson & Mitchell, 1968; Berenson, Mitchell, & Laney, 1968; Berenson, Mitchell, & Moravec, 1968; Douds, Berenson, Carkhuff, & Pierce, 1967) have added confrontation to the repertoire of high-functioning therapists. Patients in therapy with high-functioning therapists tend to make progress, while those in therapy with low-functioning therapists tend to stay

the same or deteriorate. Now, given the wide variety of trainer styles in laboratory experiences, there are probably certain kinds of behavior that help create a climate of growth for participants and other kinds of behavior which inhibit such growth. It is the function of research to determine precisely what trainers should and should not do in order to facilitate growth in the laboratory. In the contract group, the function of the trainer is spelled out with a good deal of clarity: he manifests the growth-facilitating behaviors suggested by Rogers (1967), he clarifies the contract, he suggests problems that might arise because of his role as leader or leader-member, and he models the kind of interactional behavior called for by the contract. It is hypothesized that if he does these things well, he will help provide a climate in which interpersonal growth (defined by the participants' fulfilling the contract by experimenting with the kinds of behavior it calls for) is facilitated.

Situation and relationship variables, too, should be studied in laboratory settings, especially with respect to the impact they have on outcome.

Outcomes: Success, Indifference, Disappointment, and Damage. Though Bunker (1965), Boyd and Elliss (1962), and Valiquet (1964), in more or less objective studies, have showed that laboratory experiences caused increased sensitivity, more open communication, and increased flexibility in role behavior, still most of the evidence that exists concerning the outcome of laboratory training is in the form of personal testimonials. Most volunteers believe that they have been helped in some way (although at times they have difficulty in specifying just what ways), though it is also true that while the participant might believe that he has changed greatly, his associates do not perceive the changes. This may mean that the laboratory participant is inept in externalizing the change, that his associates are inept in recognizing change, or that change simply has not taken place. On the other hand, a certain percentage of participants leave the laboratory experience feeling indifferent, disappointed, or even disturbed. Klaw (1965), for instance, found one in ten liking themselves less after a training period and not knowing what to do about it. It is not uncommon that people change after laboratory experiences, but the changes are not always in the expected or "right" direction. A study of the Foundation for Research on Human Behavior (1960) showed that participants believed that they had changed in seven or eight areas, but it also showed that they thought that half of these changes were negative. Boyd and Elliss (1962) studied three groups: one laboratory trained, the second conventionally trained, and the third not trained at all. Of 22 reported changes judged to be unfavorable (e.g., increase in irritability or loss of tolerance) 20 were attributed to members of laboratory-trained groups. Underwood (1965) showed that laboratory training produced more observable changes in participants than in controls with respect to job behavior, but it also produced a higher percentage of unfavorable changes. Even if the participant changes for the good during the laboratory experience, the change does not mean that his life will proceed more smoothly than before, for his friends and the organizations to which he belongs might not be ready for these changes. For example, Schein and Bennis (1965) report three incidents of participants who suffered more tension after they returned to the job. It may well be that these participants changed for the better but the laboratory did not help them handle the problem of reentry into a society that had not changed. In fact, some of the unfavorable changes reported above might merely reflect resistance to growth on the part of the back-home associates who rated the trainees' behavior subsequent to the training experience. In sum, the whole problem of the transfer of training effects to real-life situations is an unsolved one.

As to the question of whether laboratory experiences are psychologically harmful or not, House (1967), in a review of the literature, states: "Instances of reported collapse as a result of participation in T-Group training are rare and completely undocumented ... [p. 29]." Seashore (1968) corroborates this: "The incidence of serious stress and mental disturbance during training is difficult to measure, but it is estimated to be less than one per cent of participants and in almost all cases occurs in persons with a history of prior disturbances [p. 2]." Such assurances are important because it seems that, in the mythology of sensitivity training, almost everyone knows a person who has suffered tragic emotional upset because of some laboratory experience. These assurances do not mean that laboratory experiences do not have risks, but then it is also somewhat dangerous to fly, to drive, to get married, or to set one's goals high; that is, there is a certain danger associated with living, especially with living a full human life, but men usually do not become preoccupied with these dangers. Safeguards should certainly be built into laboratory experiences, but people should not become obsessed by potential dangers.

The Power of the Laboratory Experience. The evidence we have indicates that the laboratory is a powerful force for behavorial change, but it also indicates that we have an imperfect understanding of the sources of its power and of ways to channel it into constructive change. An enlightened and integrated process-outcome research program is essential if laboratory programs are to become growthful vehicles of personal and cultural change.

The Ending of the Group

While most sensitivity-training laboratories are relatively short (a two-week residential laboratory, a semester course, a weekend marathon, etc.), this is not always the case. Some people are beginning to integrate a group experience into the pattern of their lives. Even in the short-lived laboratory, many of the participants get to know one another quite intimately and, in a sense, do not want to see the group experience come to an end. There is often a certain nostalgia associated with the last meeting, but usually there is no choice: because of real-life needs, the group must end. Perhaps Mills (1964) describes the feeling tone of the last meeting most poignantly: "Yearning for a benediction from some source, the group dies [p. 79]." Those who belong to groups that do not die probably do so for a number of reasons, such as security, companionship, stimulation, intimacy, and interpersonal growth. Little can be said about these variables, however, since little or no published research refers to such ongoing groups. Some, I imagine, would feel uneasy about such groups, seeing them as fostering dependency needs, substituting for real interpersonal living, or serving as a means of fleeing the larger social issues of life and the action these issues demand. Certainly encounter groups could be misused in these and other ways, but there is nothing in the structure of these groups that would necessitate such misuse. If I were to risk a prediction, I would say that the ongoing-group phenomenon will increase and that at its best it will both contribute significantly to interpersonal growth and stimulate its members to become more effective agents of constructive social change within the communities and organizations to which they belong.

References

Abrahams, R. D. Public drama and common values in two Caribbean islands. *Trans-action*, 1968, **5** (8), 62–71.

Ackerman, N. W. *Psychodynamics of family life.* New York: Basic Books, 1958.

Adler, A. *Social interest.* J: Linton & R. Vaughn (Trans.). New York: Capricorn Books, 1964.

Alexander, F. *Fundamentals of psychoanalysis.* New York: Norton, 1963.

Allport, F. H. A structuronomic conception of behavior: individual and collective. *Journal of Abnormal & Social Psychology*, 1962, **64**, 3–30.

Allport, G. *Becoming.* New Haven: Yale University Press, 1955.

Allport, G. Values and our youth. *Teachers College Record*, 1961, **63**, 211–219.

Allport, G. Psychological models for guidance. *Harvard Education Review*, 1962, **32**, 373–381.

Anderson, C. M. Guilt is not the problem. *The Pastoral Counselor*, 1964.

Anderson, S. Level of therapist functioning and confrontation. Unpublished manuscript, University of Massachusetts, 1966.

Anderson, S., Douds, J., & Carkhuff, R. R. The effects of confrontation by high and low functioning therapists. Unpublished research, University of Massachusetts, 1967.

Anonymous. Housewives and the psychotherapy gap. *Harper's Magazine*, 1967, **235** (November), 71.

Anonymous. The group experience: A personal account. *Chicago Daily News*, Panorama section, March 2, 1968, 4.

Ansbacher, J. L. Life style: A historical and systematic review. *Journal of Individual Psychology*, 1967, **23**, 191–212.

Arnold, M. B. *Emotion and Personality*. Vol. 1: Psychological aspects. New York: Columbia University Press, 1960.

Aronson, E., & Carlsmith, J. M. Experimentation in social psychology. In G. Lindzey & E. Aronson (Eds.), *The handbook of social psychology*. (2nd ed.) Vol. II. Reading, Mass.: Addison-Wesley, 1968. Pp. 9–79.

Ausubel, D. P. *The psychology of meaningful verbal learning*. New York: Grune & Stratton, 1963.

Ayllon, T., & Ayllon, M. The psychiatric nurse as a behavior engineer. *Journal of the Experimental Analysis of Behavior*, 1959, **2**, 323–334.

Ayllon, T., & Azrin, N. H. Reinforcement and instructions in mental patients. *Journal of the Experimental Analysis of Behavior*, 1964, **7**, 327–331.

Ayllon, T., & Haughton, E. Control of schizophrenic patients by food. *Journal of the Experimental Analysis of Behavior*, 1962, **5**, 343–352.

Bach, G. R. The Marathon group: Intensive practice of intimate interaction. *Psychological Reports*, 1966, **18**, 995–1002.

Bales, R. F. *Interaction process analysis*. Cambridge, Mass.: Addison-Wesley, 1950.

Bales, R. F. Interaction process analysis. In D. L. Sills (Ed.), *International encyclopedia of the social sciences*. New York: Crowell Collier & Macmillan, in press.

Bandura, A. Punishment revisited. *Journal of Consulting Psychology*, 1962, **26**, 298–301.

Bandura, A., Lipsher, D. H., & Miller, P. E. Psychotherapists' approach-avoidance reactions to patients' expressions of hostility. *Journal of Consulting Psychology*, 1960, **24**, 1–8.

Becker, R. J. Sin, illness and guilt. *The Christian Century*, 1966, **83**, 1007–1009.

Beier, E. G. *The silent language of psychotherapy*. Chicago: Aldine, 1966.

Benne, K. D. From polarization to paradox. In L. P. Bradford, J. R. Gibb, & K. D. Benne (Eds.), *T-Group theory and laboratory method*. New York: Wiley, 1964a. Pp. 216–247.

Benne, K. D. History of the T Group in the laboratory setting. In L. P. Bradford, J. R. Gibb, & K. D. Benne (Eds.), *T-Group theory and laboratory method*. New York: Wiley, 1964b. Pp. 80–135.

Benne, K. D., Bradford, L. P., & Lippitt, R. The laboratory method. In L. P. Bradford, J. R. Gibb, & K. D. Benne (Eds.), *T-Group theory and laboratory method*. New York: Wiley, 1964. Pp. 15–44.

Bennett, C. C. What price privacy? *American Psychologist*, 1967, **22**, 371–376.

Bennis, W. G. The relationship between some personality dimensions and group development. Unpublished material, Boston University Human Relations Center, 1956.

Bennis, W. G. Patterns and vicissitudes in T-Group development. In L. P. Bradford, J. R. Gibb, & K. D. Benne (Eds.), *T-Group theory and laboratory method*. New York: Wiley, 1964. Pp. 80–135.

Bennis, W., Burke, R., Culter, H., Harrington, H., & Hoffman, J. A note on some problems of measurement and prediction in a training group. *Group Psychotherapy*, 1957, **10**, 328–341.

Berenson, B. G., & Mitchell, K. M. Therapeutic conditions after therapist-initiated confrontation. *Journal of Clinical Psychology*, 1968, **24**, 363–364.

Berenson, B. G., Mitchell, K. M., & Laney, R. C. Level of therapist functioning, types of confrontation and type of patient. *Journal of Clinical Psychology*, 1968, **24**, 111–113.

Berenson, B. G., Mitchell, K. M., & Moravec, J. A. Level of therapist functioning, patient depth of exploration, and type of confrontation. *Journal of Counseling Psychology*, 1968, **15**, 136–139.

Berkowitz, L. Group norms among bomber crews: Patterns of perceived crew attitudes, "actual" crew attitudes, and crew liking related to aircrew effectiveness in Far East combat. *Sociometry*, 1956, **19**, 141–153.

Berkowitz, L. Liking for the group and the perceived merit of the group's behavior. *Journal of Abnormal and Social Psychology*, 1957, **54**, 353–357.

Berne, E. Ego states in psychotherapy. *American Journal of Psychotherapy*, 1957, **11**, 293–309.

Berne, E. *Transactional analysis in psychotherapy*. New York: Grove Press, 1961.

Berne, E. *Games people play*. New York: Grove Press, 1964.

Berne, E. *Principles of group treatment*. New York: Oxford University Press, 1966.

Bernstein, A. The psychoanalytic technique. In B. B. Wolman (Ed.), *Handbook of clinical psychology*. New York: McGraw-Hill, 1965. Pp. 1168–1199.

Berzon, B., & Solomon, L. N. Research frontiers. The self-directed therapeutic group: Three studies. *Journal of Counseling Psychology*, 1966, **13**, 491–497.

Bettelheim, B. *The empty fortress.* New York: Collier-Macmillan, 1967.

Bion, W. R. *Experience in Groups.* London: Tavistock, 1959.

Bion, W. R. *Experiences in groups, and other papers.* London & New York: Tavistock & Basic Books, 1961.

Birdwhistell, R. L. *Introduction to kinesics.* Louisville: University of Kentucky Press, 1952.

Birdwhistell, R. L. Paralanguage: 25 years after Sapir. In H. W. Brosin (Ed.), *Lectures in experimental psychiatry.* Pittsburgh: University of Pittsburgh Press, 1961.

Birdwhistell, R. L. Body signals: Normal and pathological. Paper read at Annual Meeting, American Psychological Association, Philadelphia, August–September, 1963a.

Birdwhistell, R. L. The kinesic level in the investigation of emotions. In P. H. Knapp (Ed.), *Expression of the emotions in man.* New York: International Universities Press, 1963b. Pp. 123–139.

Bixler, R. H. Limits are therapy. *Journal of Consulting Psychology,* 1949, **13,** 1–11.

Blake, R. R. Studying group action. In L. P. Bradford, J. R. Gibb, & K. D. Benne (Eds.), *T-Group theory and laboratory method.* New York: Wiley, 1964. Pp. 336–364.

Blake, R. R., & Mouton, J. S. *Group dynamics: Key to decision making.* Houston, Texas: Gulf Publishing, 1961.

Blake, R. R., & Mouton, J. S. The instrumented training laboratory. In I. R. Weschler & E. H. Schein (Eds.), *Issues in training.* Washington, D.C.: National Training Laboratories, 1962. Pp. 61–76.

Blake, R. R., & Mouton, J. S. *The managerial grid.* Houston, Texas: Gulf Publishing, 1964.

Blake, R. R., & Mouton, J. S. A 9,9 approach for increasing organizational productivity. In E. H. Schein & W. G. Bennis (Eds.), *Personal and organizational change through group methods.* New York: Wiley, 1965. Pp. 169–183.

Bloch, H. S. An open-ended crisis-oriented group for the poor who are sick. *Archives of General Psychiatry,* 1968, **18,** 178–185.

Borgatta, E. F., & Crowther, B. *A workbook for the study of social interaction processes.* Chicago: Rand McNally, 1965.

Boss, M. *Psychoanalyse und Daseinsanalytik.* Bern and Stuttgart: Verlag Hans Huber, 1957.

Boy, A. V., & Pine, G. J. *Client-centered counseling in the secondary school.* Boston: Houghton Mifflin, 1963.

Boyd, H. S., & Sisney, V. V. Immediate self-image confrontation and change in self-concept. *Journal of Consulting Psychology,* 1968, 31 (3), 291–294.

Boyd, J. B., & Elliss, J. D. *Findings of research into senior management seminars.* Toronto: Hydro-Electric Power Commission on Ontario, 1962.

Braaten, L. J. The movement from nonself to self in client-centered psychotherapy. *Journal of Counseling Psychology,* 1961, 8, 20–24.

Bradford, L. P. Membership and the learning process. In L. P. Bradford, J. R. Gibb, & K. D. Benne (Eds.), *T-Group theory and laboratory method.* New York: Wiley, 1964. Pp. 190–215.

Bradford, L. P., Gibb, J. R., & Benne, K. D. (Eds.) *T-Group theory and laboratory method.* New York: Wiley, 1964.

Breger, L., & McGaugh, J. L. Critique and reformulation of "learning-theory" approaches to psychotherapy and neurosis. *Psychological Bulletin,* 1965, 63, 338–358.

Bronson, G. W. Identity diffusion in late adolescents. *Journal of Abnormal and Social Psychology,* 1959, 59, 414–417.

Buber, M. *I and Thou.* Edinburgh: T. & T. Clark, 1937.

Buber, M. *The knowledge of man.* New York: Harper Torchbooks, 1965.

Buchanan, P. C. Evaluating the effectiveness of laboratory training in industry. In *Exploitations in human relations training and research.* No. 1. Washington, D.C.: National Training Laboratories, 1965.

Bugental, J. F. T. *The search for authenticity.* New York: Holt, Rinehart and Winston, 1965.

Bugental, J. F. T., & Tannenbaum, R. Sensitivity training and being motivation. In E. H. Schein & W. G. Bennis (Eds.), *Personal and organizational change through group methods: the laboratory approach.* New York: Wiley, 1965. Pp. 107–113.

Buhler, K. *Sprach theorie.* Jena: Gustav Fisher, 1934.

Bunker, D. R. Individual applications of laboratory training. *Journal of Applied Behavioral Science,* 1965, 1, 131–148.

Bunker, D. R., & Knowles, E. S. Comparison of behavioral changes resulting from human relations training laboratories of different lengths. *Journal of Applied Behavioral Science,* 1967, 2, 505–524.

Burgess, A. The future of Anglo-American. *Harper's,* 1968, **236,** 53–56.

Burton, A. The psychotherapy of a non-diseased person. In A. Burton (Ed.), *Modern psychotherapeutic practice.* Palo Alto, Calif.: Science & Behavior Books, 1965, Pp. 381–399.

Burton, R. V., & Whiting, J. W. M. The absent father and cross-sex identity. *Merrill-Palmer Quarterly,* 1961, 7, 80–85.

Cameron, N. *Personality development & psychopathology.* Boston: Houghton Mifflin, 1963.

Campbell, D. T. Systematic error on the part of human links in communication systems. *Information and Control,* 1958, 1, 334–369.

Campbell, J. P., & Dunnette, M. D. Effectiveness of T-group experiences in managerial training and development. *Psychological Bulletin,* 1968, **70,** 73–104.

Carkhuff, R. R., & Berenson, B. G. *Beyond counseling and psychotherapy.* New York: Holt, Rinehart and Winston, 1967.

Carroll, J. B. *Language, thought, and reality: Selected writings of Benjamin Lee Whorf.* New York: Wiley, 1956.

Cartwright, D., & Zander, A. Individual motives and group goals: Introduction. In D. Cartwright & A. Zander (Eds.), *Group dynamics: Research and theory.* (2nd ed.) New York: Harper & Row, 1960. Pp. 345–369.

Cartwright, D., & Zander, A. (Eds.) *Group dynamics: Research and theory.* (3rd ed.) New York: Harper & Row, 1968.

Casriel, D. *So fair a house: The story of Synanon.* Englewood Cliffs, N.J.: Prentice-Hall, 1963.

Cassirer, E. *The philosophy of symbolic forms. I: Language.* New Haven: Yale University Press, 1953.

Cattell, R. B. New concepts for measuring leadership, in terms of group syntality. *Human Relations,* 1951, **4,** 161–184.

Cattell, R. B. New concepts for measuring leadership, in terms of group syntality. In D. Cartwright & A. Zander (Eds.), *Group dynamics: Research and theory.* New York: Harper & Row, 1953. Pp. 14–29.

Church, R. M. The varied effects of punishment on behavior. *Psychological Review,* 1963, **70,** 369–402.

Cioran, E. M. *The temptation to exist.* R. Howard (Trans.). Chicago: Quadrangle, 1968.

Clark, J. V. Toward a theory and practice of religious experience. In J. F. T. Bugental (Ed.), *Challenges of humanistic psychology.* New York: McGraw-Hill, 1967. Pp. 253–258.

Cofer, C. N., & Musgrave, B. S. (Eds.). *Verbal behavior and learning problems and processes.* New York: McGraw-Hill, 1963.

Coles, R. Doppelganger for Freud. *Psychiatry and Social Science Review,* 1967, **1** (12), 14–17.

Collins, B. E., & Guetzkow, H. *A social psychology of group processes for decision-making.* New York: Wiley, 1964.

Cornelison, F. S., & Arsenian, J. A study of the response of psychotic patients to photographic self-image experience. *Psychiatric Quarterly,* 1960, **34,** 1–8.

Corsini, R. J. Immediate therapy in groups. In G. M. Gazda (Ed.), *Innovations to group psychotherapy.* Springfield, Ill.: Charles C Thomas, 1968. Pp. 15–41.

Craig, R. L., & Bittel, L. R. *Training and development handbook.* New York: McGraw-Hill, 1967.

Curran, C. A. Structuring the counseling relationship: A case report. *Journal of Abnormal and Social Psychology,* 1944, **39,** 189–216.

Darley, J. M. Fear and social comparison as determinants of conformity behavior. *Journal of Personality and Social Psychology,* 1966, 4, 73–78.

Davitz, J. R. *The communication of emotional meaning.* New York: McGraw-Hill, 1964.

Deutsch, M. The effects of cooperation and competition upon group process. *Human Relations,* 1949, 2, 129–152, 199–231.

Deutsch, M. Field theory in social psychology. In G. Lindzey (Ed.), *The handbook of social psychology.* Vol. I. Cambridge, Mass.: Addison-Wesley, 1954. Pp. 181–222.

Deutsch, M. Trust and suspicion. *Journal of Conflict Resolution,* 1958, 4, 265–279.

Dittes, J., & Kelley, H. Effects of different conditions of acceptance upon conformity to group norms. *Journal of Abnormal and Social Psychology,* 1956, **53,** 629–636.

Dittmann, A. T. Kinesic research and therapeutic process: Further discussion. In P. H. Knapp (Ed.), *Expression of the emotions in man.* New York: International Universities Press, 1963.

Dixon, T. R., & Horton, D. L. (Eds.). *Verbal behavior and general behavior theory.* Englewood Cliffs, N.J.: Prentice-Hall, 1968.

Dollard, J., & Miller, N. E. *Personality and psychotherapy.* New York: McGraw-Hill, 1950.

Douds, J., Berenson, B. G., Carkhuff, R. R., & Pierce, R. In search of an honest experience: Confrontation in counseling and life. In R. R. Carkhuff & B. G. Berenson, *Beyond counseling and therapy.* New York: Holt, Rinehart and Winston, 1967. Pp. 170–179.

Drakeford, J. W. *Integrity therapy.* Nashville, Tenn.: Broadman Press, 1967.

Dreikurs, R. *Fundamentals of Adlerian psychology.* Chicago: Alfred Adler Institute, 1950.

Dreikurs, R. Goals of psychotherapy. In A. Mahrer (Ed.), *The goals of psychotherapy.* New York: Appleton-Century-Crofts, 1967. Pp. 221–237.

References

Dunnette, M. D. Personnel management. *Annual Review of Psychology*, 1962, **13**, 285–314.

Eisman, B., & Levy, J. The influence of certain communicator characteristics on lip reading efficiency. *Journal of Social Psychology*, 1960, **51**, 419–425.

Ekman, P. Communication through nonverbal behavior: A source of information about an interpersonal relationship. In S. S. Tomkins & C. E. Izard (Eds.), *Affect, cognition, and personality*. New York: Springer, 1965. Pp. 390–442.

Ekman, P. Differential communication of affect by head and body cues. *Journal of Personality and Social Psychology*, 1965, **2**, 726–735.

Ekman, P., & Friesen, W. V. Head and body cues in the judgment of emotion: A reformulation. *Journal of Perceptual and Motor Skills*, 1967, **24**, 711–724.

Ellenberger, H. R. The pathogenic secret and its therapeutics. *Journal of the History of the Behavioral Sciences*, 1966, **2**, 29–42.

Ellis, A. *Reason and emotion in psychotherapy*. New York: Lyle Stuart, 1962.

Ellis, A. Should some people be labeled mentally ill? *Journal of Consulting Psychology*, 1967, **31**, 435–446.

Erikson, E. H. On the sense of inner identity. In R. P. Knight & C. R. Friedman (Eds.), *Psychoanalytical psychiatry and psychology: Clinical and theoretical papers*. Vol. I. New York: International Universities Press, 1954.

Erikson, E. H. The problem of ego identity. *Journal of the American Psychoanalytic Association*, 1956, **4**, 56–121.

Erikson, E. H. *Identity and the life cycle*. New York: International Universities Press, 1959.

Erikson, E. H. *Childhood and society* (2nd ed.) New York: Norton, 1963.

Erikson, E. H. *Insight and responsibility*. New York: Norton, 1964.

Erikson, E. H. *Identity: Youth and crisis*. New York: Norton, 1968.

Exline, R. V. Explorations in the process of person perception: Visual interaction in relation to competition, sex, and need for affiliation. *Journal of Personality*, 1963, 31, 1–20.

Exline, R. V., Gray, D., & Schuette, D. The incidence of mutual glances in dyads as a form of communication: Avoidance as a function of interview content and sex of interviewee. *Journal of Personality and Social Psychology*, 1965, 1, 201–209.

Exline, R. V., & Winters, L. C. Affective relations and mutual glances in dyads. In S. S. Tomkins & C. E. Izard (Eds.), *Affect, cognition, and personality*. New York: Springer, 1965. Pp. 319–350.

Eysenck, H. J. Learning theory and behavior therapy. *Journal of Mental Science*, 1959, 105, 61–75.

Feifel, H. & Eells, J. Patients and therapists assess the same psychotherapy. *Journal of Consulting Psychology*, 1963, 27, 310–318.

Fenichel, O. The psychology of boredom. No. 26 in the *Collected papers of Otto Fenichel*. First Series. New York: Norton, 1953.

Ferenczi, S. *Further contributions to the theory and technique of psychoanalysis*. London: Hogarth Press, 1926.

Festinger, L. *A theory of cognitive dissonance*. New York: Harper & Row, 1957.

Fiedler, F. E. A comparison of therapeutic relationships in psychoanalytic, non-directive, and Adlerian therapy. *Journal of Consulting Psychology*, 1950, 14, 436–445.

Fiedler, F. E. The concept of an ideal therapeutic relationship. *Journal of Consulting Psychology*, 1950, 14, 239–245.

Fiedler, F. E. The leader's psychological distance and group effectiveness. In D. Cartwright & A. Zander (Eds.), *Group dynamics*. 2nd ed. New York: Harper & Row, 1960. Pp. 586–606.

Fleishman, E. A., & Harris, E. F. Patterns of leadership behavior related to employee grievances and turnover. *Personnel Psychology*, 1962, 15, 43–56.

Forrest, D. V. Poiesis and the language of schizophrenia. *Psychiatry*, 1965, 28, 1–18.

Foundation for Research on Human Behavior. *An action program for organization improvement.* Ann Arbor, Mich., 1960.

Fouriezos, N. T., Hutt, M. L., & Guetzkow, H. Measurement of self-oriented needs in discussion groups. *Journal of Abnormal and Social Psychology,* 1950, **45**, 682–690.

Fox, R. S., & Lippitt, R. The innovation of classroom mental health practices. In M. B. Miles (Ed.), *Innovation in education.* New York: Columbia University, Teachers College, 1964. Pp. 271–297.

Frank, J. D. *Persuasion and healing.* Baltimore: The Johns Hopkins University Press, 1961.

Frank, J. D. Training and therapy. In L. P. Bradford, J. R. Gibb, & K. D. Benne (Eds.), *T-Group theory and laboratory method.* New York: Wiley, 1964. Pp. 442–451.

Frank, L. K. Tactile communication. *Genetic Psychology Monographs,* 1957, **56**, 209–255.

Frankl, V. E. *Man's search for meaning.* Boston: Beacon Press, 1962.

French, J. R. P., Jr. The disruption and cohesion of groups. *Journal of Abnormal and Social Psychology,* 1941, **36**, 361–377.

French, J. R. P., & Raven, B. The bases of social power. In D. Cartwright & A. Zander (Eds.), *Group dynamics.* New York: Harper & Row, 1960. (Reprinted from D. Cartwright [Ed.], *Studies in social power.* Ann Arbor, Mich.: Institute for Social Research, 1959.)

Friedenberg, E. Z. *Coming of age in America.* New York: Random House, 1963.

Friedman, H. J. Patient-expectancy and symptom reduction. *Archives of General Psychiatry,* 1963, **8**, 61–67.

Fromm, E. *Escape from freedom.* New York: Farrar & Rinehart, 1941.

Fromm, E. *Man for himself.* New York: Holt, Rinehart, & Winston, 1947.

Fromm, E. *The sane society.* New York: Rinehart, 1955.

Fromm, E. *The art of loving.* New York: Harper & Row, 1956.

Fromm-Reichmann, R. *Principles of intensive psychotherapy.* Chicago: University of Chicago Press, 1950.

Garfield, S. L., & Wolpin, M. Expectations regarding psychotherapy. *Journal of Nervous and Mental Disorders,* 1963, **137**, 353–362.

Gassner, S., Gold, J., & Snadowsky, A. M. Changes in the phenomenal field as a result of human relations training. *Journal of Psychology,* 1964, **58**, 33–41.

Geer, J. H. Effect of fear arousal upon task performance and verbal behavior. *Journal of Abnormal and Social Psychology.* 1966, **71**, 119–123.

Gendlin, E. T. *Experiencing and the creation of meaning.* New York: Free Press, 1962.

Getzels, J. W. A stable identity in a world of shifting values. *Education Leadership,* 1957, **14**, 237–240.

Gibb, C. A. The sociometry of leadership in temporary groups. *Sociometry,* 1950, **13**, 226–243.

Gibb, J. R. Defense level and influence potential in small groups. *Research Reprint Series,* No. 3, National Training Laboratories, Washington, D.C., 1960.

Gibb, J. R. Climate for trust formation. In L. P. Bradford, J. R. Gibb & K. D. Benne (Eds.), *T-Group theory and laboratory method.* New York: Wiley, 1964a. Pp. 279–309.

Gibb, J. R. The present status of T-group theory. In L. P. Bradford, J. R. Gibb, & K. D. Benne (Eds.), *T-Group theory and laboratory method.* New York: Wiley, 1964b. Pp. 168–189.

Gibb, J. R. Fear and facade: Defensive management. In R. Farson (Ed.), *Science and human affairs.* Palo Alto, Calif.: Science & Behavior Books, 1965.

Gibb, J. R. Dimensions of fear and trust. Unpublished paper, Human Relations Laboratory, Cedar City, Utah, August 1968.

Glatzer, H. Neurotic factors of voyeurism and exhibitionism in group psychotherapy. *International Journal of Group Psychotherapy,* 1967, **17**, 3–9.

Glauber, I. P. Speech characteristics of psychoneurotic patients. *Journal of Speech Disorders*, 1944, **9**, 18–30.

Goffman, E. Alienation from interaction. *Human Relations*, 1957, **10**, 47–60.

Goffman, E. *Interaction ritual: Essays on face-to-face behavior.* Garden City, N.Y.: Anchor Books (Doubleday), 1967.

Goldstein, A. P., Heller, K., & Sechrest, L. B. *Psychotherapy and the psychology of behavior change.* New York: Wiley, 1966.

Golembiewski, R. T. *The small group: An analysis of research concepts and operations.* Chicago: University of Chicago Press, 1962.

Goroff, N. N. Confrontation with reality: A social group work approach. *Mental Hygiene*, 1967, **51**, 426–432.

Gottschalk, L. A. (Ed.) *Comparative psycholinguistic analysis of two psychotherapeutic interviews.* New York: International Universities Press, 1961.

Green, G. H. *The daydream: A study in development.* London: University of London Press, 1923.

Greenson, R. On boredom. *Journal of the American Psychoanalytic Association*, 1953, **1**, 7–21.

Grinker, R. R., MacGregor, H., Selan, K., Klein, A., & Kohrman, J. *Psychiatric social work: A transactional casebook.* New York: Basic Books, 1961.

Grinker, R. R., Sabshin, M., Hamburg, D. A., Board, F. A., Bosowitz, H., Korchin, S. J., Porsky, H., & Chevalier, J. A. The use of an anxiety-producing interview and its meaning to the subject. *Archives of Neurology and Psychiatry*, 1957, **77**, 406–419.

Grossack, M. M. Some effects of cooperation and competition upon small group behavior. *Journal of Abnormal and Social Psychology*, 1954, **49**, 341–348.

Guilford, J. P. Factors that aid and hinder creativity. *Teachers College Record*, 1962, **63**, 380–392.

Gunther, B. *Sense relaxation: Below your mind.* New York: Collier, 1968.

Gynther, R. A. The effects of anxiety and of situational stress on communicative efficiency. *Journal of Abnormal and Social Psychology,* 1957, **54,** 274–276.

Haggard, E. A., & Isaacs, K. S. Micromomentary facial expressions as indicators of ego mechanisms in psychotherapy. In L. A. Gottschalk & A. H. Auerbach (Eds.), *Methods of research in psychotherapy.* New York: Appleton-Century-Crofts, 1966. Pp. 154–165.

Haiman, F. S. Effects of training in group processes on open-mindedness. *Journal of Communication,* 1963, **13,** 236–245.

Haley, J. An interactional description of schizophrenia. *Psychiatry,* 1959, **22,** 321–332.

Hall, E. T. *The silent language.* New York: Fawcett, 1959.

Hall, E. T. Proxemics: The study of man's spatial relations. In I. Galdston (Ed.), *Man's image in medicine and anthropology.* New York: International Universities Press, 1963a. Pp. 422–445.

Hall, E. T. A system for the notation of proxemic behavior. *American Anthropologist,* 1963b, **65,** 1003–1026.

Hall, E. T. Silent assumptions in social communication. *Disorders of Communication,* 1964, **42,** 41–55.

Hall, E. T. *The hidden dimension.* Garden City, N.Y.: Doubleday, 1966.

Hall, M. H. A conversation with Carl Rogers. *Psychology Today,* 1967, **1** (7), 19–21, 62–66.

Halpin, A. W. The leader behavior and effectiveness of aircraft commanders. In R. M. Stogdill & A. E. Coons (Eds.), *Leader behavior: Its description and measurement.* Monograph 88, Bureau of Business Research, The Ohio State University, 1957. Pp. 39–51.

Hampden-Turner, C. M. An existential learning theory and the integration of T-group research. *Journal of Applied Behavioral Science,* 1966, **2,** 367–386.

Hare, P. A., Borgatta, E. F., & Bales, R. F. *Small groups: Studies in social interaction.* New York: Knopf, 1962.

Harper, R. A. *Psychoanalysis & psychotherapy.* Englewood Cliffs, N.J.: Prentice-Hall, 1959.

Harrison, R. Cognitive change and participation in a sensitivity training laboratory. *Journal of Consulting Psychology,* 1966, **30,** 517–520.

Harrow, M., Astrachan, B. M., Becker, R. E., Miller, J. C., & Schwartz, A. Influence of the psychotherapist on the emotional climate in group therapy. *Human Relations,* 1967, **20,** 49–64.

Harvey, O. J., Kelley, H. H., & Shapiro, M. M. Reactions to unfavorable evaluations of the self made by other persons. *Journal of Personality,* 1957, **25,** 393–411.

Hathaway, S. R., & Meehl, P. E. *An atlas for the clinical use of the MMPI.* Minneapolis: University of Minnesota Press, 1951.

Hathaway, S. R., & McKinley, J. C. *Minnesota Multiplastic Personality Inventory.* Minneapolis: University of Minnesota Press, 1942.

Heller, K., Davis, J. D., & Myers, R. A. The effects of interviewer style in a standardized interview. *Journal of Consulting Psychology,* 1966, **30,** 501–508.

Hendin, H., Gaylin, W., & Carr, A. *Psychoanalysis and social research: The psychoanalytic study of the non-patient.* Garden City, N.J.: Doubleday, 1965 (Anchor Books Edition published 1966).

Henry, J. *Culture against man.* New York: Random House, 1963.

Hess, R. D. High school antecedents of young adult achievement. In R. E. Grinder (Ed.), *Studies in adolescence.* New York: Macmillan, 1963. Pp. 401–414.

Hilgard, E. R., & Bower, G. H. *Theories of learning.* New York: Appleton-Century-Crofts, 1966.

Hobbs, N. Sources of gain in psychotherapy. *American Psychologist,* 1962, **17,** 18–34.

Hodges, H. A. *The philosophy of Wilhem Dilthey.* London: Routledge & Kegan Paul, 1952.

Hoehn-Saric, R., Frank, J. D., Imber, S. D., Nash, E. H., Stone, A. R., & Battle, C. C. Systematic preparation of patients for psychotherapy: 1. Effects on therapy behavior and outcome. *Journal of Psychiatric Research*, 1965, 2, 267–281.

Hoffman, L. R., Harburg, E., & Maier, N. R. F. Differences and disagreement as factors in creative group problem solving. *Journal of Abnormal and Social Psychology*, 1962, **64**, 206–214.

Holder, T., Carkhuff, R. R., & Berenson, B. G. Differential effects of the manipulation of therapeutic conditions upon high- and low-functioning clients. *Journal of Counseling Psychology*, 1967, **14**, 63–66.

Holland, G. A. *Fundamentals of psychotherapy.* New York: Holt, 1965.

Holland, J. L. Creative and academic performance among talented adolescents. *Journal of Educational Psychology*, 1961, **52**, 136–147.

Holsti, O. R. Content analysis. In G. Lindzey & E. Aronson (Eds.), *The handbook of social psychology.* (2nd ed.) Vol. II. Reading, Mass.: Addison-Wesley, 1968. Pp. 596–692.

Homan, G. C. *The human group.* New York: Harcourt, 1950.

Honigfeld, G., Platz, A., & Gillis, R. D. Verbal style and personality authoritarianism. *Journal of Communication*, 1964, **14**, 215–218.

Horney, K. *Our inner conflicts: A constructive theory of neurosis.* New York: Norton, 1945.

Horowitz, M. W., Lyons, J., & Perlmutter, H. V. Induction of forces in discussion groups. *Human Relations*, 1951, **4**, 57–76.

Horwitz, M. Training in conflict resolution. In L. P. Bradford, J. R. Gibb, & K. D. Benne (Eds.), *T-Group theory and laboratory method.* New York: Wiley, 1964. Pp. 365–378.

House, R. J. T-group education and leadership effectiveness: A review of the empiric literature and a critical evaluation. *Personnel Psychology*, 1967, **20**, 1–32.

Hunt, J. McV. Concerning the impact of group psychotherapy on psychology. *International Journal of Group Psychotherapy*, 1964, **14**, 3–31.

Ingham, H. V., & Love, L. R. *The process of psychotherapy.* New York: McGraw-Hill, 1954.

Israel, J. *Self-evaluation and rejection in groups.* Stockholm: Almquist & Wiksell, 1956.

Jacob, P. E. *Changing values in college.* New York: Harper, 1957.

Jecker, J., Macoby, N., Breitrose, H. S., & Rose, E. O. Teacher accuracy in assessing cognitive visual feedback from students. *Journal of Applied Psychology,* 1964, **48**, 393–397.

Johnson, D. L., Hanson, P. G., Rothaus, P., Morton, R. B., Lyle, F. A., & Moyer, R. Follow-up evaluation of human relations training for psychiatric patients. In E. H. Schein & W. G. Bennis (Eds.), *Personal and organizational change through group methods.* New York: Wiley, 1965. Pp. 152–168.

Jourard, S. M. *Personal adjustment.* (2nd ed.) New York: Macmillan, 1963.

Jourard, S. M. *The transparent self.* Princeton, N.J.: Van Nostrand, 1964.

Jourard, S. M. Experimenter-subject dialogue: A paradigm for a humanistic science of psychology. In J. F. T. Bugental (Ed.), *Challenges of humanistic psychology.* New York: McGraw-Hill, 1967. Pp. 109–116.

Jourard, S. M. *Disclosing man to himself.* Princeton, N.J.: Van Nostrand, 1968.

Kagan, N., Krathwohl, D. R., & Miller, R. Stimulated recall in therapy using video tape: A case study. *Journal of Counseling Psychology,* 1963, **10**, 237–243.

Kalish, H. I. Behavior therapy. In B. B. Wolman (Ed.), *Handbook of clinical psychology.* New York: McGraw-Hill, 1965. Pp. 1230–1253.

Kanfer, F. H., & Saslow, G. Behavior analysis: An alternative to diagnostic classification. *Archives of General Psychiatry,* 1965, **12**, 529–538.

Kansler, D. H. (Ed.). *Readings in verbal learning: Contemporary theory and research.* New York: Wiley, 1966.

Kaplan, D. M. Expanding human expansiveness. *Psychiatric and Social Science Review,* 1968, **2** (9), 7–9.

Kasl, S. V., & Mahl, G. F. The relationship of disturbances and hesitations in spontaneous speech to anxiety. *Journal of Personality and Social Psychology,* 1965, **1,** 425–433.

Katz, E. W. A content-analytic method for studying interpersonal behavior. Unpublished technical report No. 19, University of Illinois, 1964.

Katz, R. Body language: A study in unintentional communication. Unpublished doctoral dissertation, Harvard University, 1964.

Kelly, G. A. *The psychology of personal constructs.* Vol. 1. *A theory of personality.* New York: Norton, 1955a.

Kelly, G. A. *The psychology of personal constructs.* Vol. 2. *Clinical diagnosis and psychotherapy.* New York: Norton, 1955b.

Kelman, H. C. Human use of human subjects: the problem of deception in social psychological experiments. *Psychological Bulletin,* 1967, **67,** 1–11.

Keniston, K. *The uncommitted: Alienated youth in American society.* New York: Harcourt, Brace & World, 1965.

Kirtner, W. L. Success and failure in client-centered therapy as a function of personality variables. Unpublished master's thesis, University of Chicago, 1955.

Klaw, S. Inside a T-group. *Think,* 1965, **31** (November–December), 26–30.

Klein, D. C. Sensitivity training and community development. In E. H. Schein & W. G. Bennis (Eds.), *Personal and organizational change through group methods.* New York: Wiley, 1965. Pp. 184–200.

Kohn, M. L. Social class and parental values. *American Journal of Sociology,* 1959, **64,** 337–351.

Krasner, L. Reinforcement, verbal behavior, and psychotherapy. *American Journal of Orthopsychiatry,* 1963, **33,** 601–613.

Kris, E. *Psychoanalytic explorations in art.* New York: International Universities Press, 1952.

Kushner, M., & Sanalu, J. Aversion theory and the concept of punishment. *Behavior Research and Therapy*, 1966, 4, 179–186.

La Barre, W. Paralinguistics, kinesics, and cultural anthropology. In T. A. Sebeok, A. S. Hayes, & M. C. Bateson (Eds.), *Approaches to semiotics*. The Hague: Mouton, 1964. Pp. 191–220.

Laing, R. D. *The divided self*. London: Tavistock, 1960.

Laing, R. D. *The politics of experience*. New York: Pantheon Books (Random House), 1967.

Latourelle, R. La revelation comme parole, temoignage et recontre. *Gregorianum*, 1962, 43, 39–54.

Lehrman, N. S. Precision in psychoanalysis. *American Journal of Psychiatry*, 1960, 116, 1097–1103.

Leventhal, H., & Sharp, E. Facial expressions as indicators of distress. In S. S. Tomkins & C. E. Izard (Eds.), *Affect, cognition, and personality*. New York: Springer, 1965. Pp. 296–318.

Levitt, E. A. The relationship between abilities to express emotional meanings vocally and facially. In J. Davitz (Ed.), *The communication of emotional meaning*. New York: McGraw-Hill, 1964. Pp. 87–100.

Levitt, E. E. Psychotherapy research and the expectation-reality discrepancy. *Psychotherapy: Theory, Research and Practice*, 1966, 3, 163–166.

Levitt, E. E. *The psychology of anxiety*. Indianapolis: Bobbs-Merrill, 1967.

Lewin, K. *Dynamic theory of personality*. New York: McGraw-Hill, 1935.

Lieberman, M. A. The relationship of group climate to individual change. Unpublished doctoral dissertation, University of Chicago, 1958.

Lieberman, M. A., Lakin, M., & Whitaker, D. S. The group as a unique context for therapy. *Psychotherapy: Theory, Research, and Practice*, 1968, 5, 29–36.

Limbacher, W. J. An approach to elementary training in mental health. *Journal of School Psychology*, 1967a, 5, 225–234.

Limbacher, W. J. *Mental health: A dynamic approach to instructing children in matters of emotional adjustment and personal happiness in life.* Dayton, Ohio: George A. Pflaum, 1967b.

Lindzey, G., & Byrne, D. Measurement of social choice and interpersonal attractiveness. In G. Lindzey & E. Aronson (Eds.), *The handbook of social psychology.* (2nd ed.) Vol. 2. Reading, Mass.: Addison-Wesley, 1968. Pp. 452–525.

Lippitt, R., Polansky, N., Redl, F., & Rosen, S. The dynamics of power. *Human Relations,* 1952, **5**, 37–64.

Locke, N. M. *Group psychoanalysis.* New York: New York University Press, 1961.

London, P. *The modes and morals of psychotherapy.* New York: Holt, Rinehart and Winston, 1964.

London, P., & Rosenhan, D. (Eds.) *Foundations of abnormal psychology.* New York: Holt, Rinehart and Winston, 1968.

Lorenz, M. Expressive behavior and language patterns. *Psychiatry,* 1955, **18**, 353–366.

Lorge, I., Fox, D., Davitz, J., & Brenner, M. A survey of studies contrasting the quality of group performance and individual performance, 1920–1957. *Psychological Bulletin,* 1958, **55**, 337–372.

Lorr, M. Research problems in group psychotherapy. Paper read at the meeting of the American Group Psychotherapy Association, Washington, D.C., January, 1963.

Lott, A. J., & Lott, B. E. Group cohesiveness as interpersonal attraction: A review of relationships with antecedent and consequent variables. *Psychological Bulletin,* 1965, **64**, 259–309.

Lott, A. J., Schopler, J. H., & Gibb, J. R. The effects of feedback on group processes. Paper read at the Rocky Mountain Psychological Association Meeting, 1954.

Lott, A. J., Schopler, J. H., & Gibb, J. R. Effects of feeling-oriented and task-oriented feedback upon defensive behavior in small problem-solving groups. Paper read at the American Psychological Association Meeting, 1955.

Lowe, M. C. The equivalence of guilt and anxiety as psychological constructs. *Journal of Consulting Psychology*, 1964, **28**, 553–554.

Lowrey, L. G. Group therapy for mothers. *American Journal of Orthopsychiatry*, 1944, **14**, 589–592.

Luft, J., & Ingham, H. The Johari window, a graphic model for interpersonal relations. Western Training Laboratory in Group Development, University of California at Los Angeles, Extension Office, August 1955.

Lynch, W. F. Counterrevolution in the movies. *Commonweal*, 1967, **87**, 77–86.

Lynd, H. M. *On shame and the search for identity*. New York: Science Editions, 1958.

Mahl, G. F., Danet, B., & Norton, N. Reflections of major personality characteristics in gestures and body movement. Paper presented at the meeting of the American Psychological Association, 1959.

Mahl, G. F., & Schulze, G. Psychological research in the extra-linguistic area. In T. A. Sebeok, A. S. Hayes, & M. C. Bateson (Eds.), *Approaches to semiotics*. The Hague: Mouton, 1964. Pp. 51–125.

Mailer, N. The steps of the pentagon. *Harper's*, 1968, **236** (March), 47–142.

Mainord, W. A. Operant group psychotherapy in a total institution setting. *The Dis-Coverer*, 1968a, **5** (Nos. 1 & 2, entire issues).

Mainord, W. A. Therapy #52: The truth. Mimeographed paper, University of Louisville, 1968b.

Malamud, D. I., & Machover, S. *Toward self-understanding: Group techniques in self-confrontation*. Springfield, Ill.: Charles C Thomas, 1965.

Mandelbaum, D. G. (Ed.). *Selected writings of Edward Sapir in language, culture, and personality*. Berkeley: University of California Press, 1949.

Mann, J. H., & Mann, C. H. The importance of a group task in producing group member personality and behavior changes. *Human Relations*, 1959, **12**, 75–80.

Mann, R. D. A review of the relationships between personality and performance in small groups. *Psychological Bulletin*, 1959, **56**, 241–270.

Mann, R. D. *Interpersonal styles and group development.* New York: Wiley, 1967.

March, J. G., & Simon, H. A. *Organizations.* New York: Wiley, 1958.

Maritain, J. *Man and the state.* Chicago: University of Chicago Press, 1951.

Maslow, A. H. (Ed.) *New knowledge in human values.* New York: Harper, 1959.

Maslow, A. H. Isomorphic interrelationships between knower and known. In F. W. Matson & A. Montagu (Eds.), *The human dialogue.* New York: Free Press, 1967a. (Previously printed in G. Kepes [Ed.], *Sign, image, symbol.* New York: George Braziller, 1966.)

Maslow, A. H. Synanon and Eupsychia. *Journal of Humanistic Psychology,* 1967b, **7,** 28–35.

Maslow, A. H. *Toward a psychology of being* (2nd ed.). Princeton, N.J.: Van Nostrand, 1968.

Matarazzo, J. D., Ulett, G. A., & Saslow, G. Human maze performance as a function of increasing levels of anxiety. *Journal of General Psychology,* 1955, **53,** 79–95.

Matson, F. W., & Montagu, A. (Eds.). *The human dialogue.* New York: Free Press, 1967.

May, R. Contributions of existential psychotherapy. In R. May, E. Angel, & H. F. Ellenberger (Eds.), *Existence: A new dimension in psychiatry and psychology.* New York: Basic Books, 1958. Pp. 37–91.

May, R. *Existential psychology.* New York: Random House, 1961.

May, R., Angel, E., & Ellenberger, H. (Eds.) *Existence.* New York: Basic Books, 1958.

May, R., & van Kaam, A. Existential theory and therapy. In J. H. Masserman (Ed.), *Current psychiatric therapies.* Vol. 3. New York: Grune & Stratton, 1963. Pp. 74–81.

McLuhan, M. *Understanding media: The extensions of man.* New York: McGraw-Hill, 1964.

McReynolds, P., Acker, M., & Pietila, C. Relation of object curiosity to psychological adjustment in children. *Child Development,* 1961, **32,** 393–400.

Meerloo, J. *Conversation and communication: A psychological inquiry into language and human relations.* New York: International Universities Press, 1952.

Meerloo, J. *The rape of the mind.* Cleveland: World, 1956.

Mehrabian, A. Immediacy: An indicator of attitudes in linguistic communication. *Journal of Personality,* 1966, **34,** 26–34.

Mellinger, G. D. Interpersonal trust as a factor in communication. *Journal of Abnormal and Social Psychology,* 1956, **52,** 304–309.

Miles, M. B. *Learning to work in groups.* New York: Columbia University, Teachers College, 1959.

Miles, M. B. Educational innovation: The nature of the problem. In M. B. Miles (Ed.), *Innovation in education.* New York: Columbia University, Teachers College, 1964. Pp. 1–46.

Milgram, S. Behavioral study of obedience. *Journal of Abnormal and Social Psychology,* 1963, **67,** 371–378.

Miller, M. F. Response of psychiatric patients to their photographed images. *Diseases of the Nervous System,* 1962, **23,** 296–298.

Mills, T. M. Authority and group emotion. In W. G. Bennis, E. H. Schein, D. E. Berlew, & F. I. Steele (Eds.), *Interpersonal dynamics.* Homewood, Ill.: Dorsey, 1964a.

Mills, T. M. *Group transformation: An analysis of a learning group.* Englewood Cliffs, N.J.: Prentice-Hall, 1964b.

Mishler, E. G., & Waxler, N. Power structure and power strategies in schizophrenic and normal families. Unpublished manuscript, 1966.

Moore, F. J., Chernell, E., & West, M. J. Television as therapeutic tool. *Archives of General Psychiatry,* 1965, **12,** 217–220.

Morton, R. B. The patient training laboratory: An adaptation of the instrumented training laboratory. In E. H. Schein & W. G. Bennis (Eds.),

Personal and organizational change through group methods. New York: Wiley, 1965. Pp. 114–151.

Moscovici, S. Communication processes and the properties of language. In L. Berkowitz (Ed.), *Advances in experimental social psychology.* Vol. 3. New York: Academic Press, 1967. Pp. 225–270.

Moustakas, C. (Ed.) *The self.* New York: Harper, 1956.

Mowrer, O. H. *Learning theory and personality dynamics.* New York: Ronald Press, 1950a.

Mowrer, O. H. Pain, punishment, guilt, and anxiety. In P. H. Hoch & J. Zubin (Eds.), *Anxiety.* New York: Grune & Stratton, 1950b.

Mowrer, O. H. Learning theory and the neurotic fallacy. *American Journal of Orthopsychiatry,* 1952a, **22,** 679–689.

Mowrer, O. H. Neurosis and its treatment as learning phenomena. In L. Abt (Ed.), *Progress in clinical psychology.* New York: Grune & Stratton, 1952b.

Mowrer, O. H. Neurosis: A disorder of conditioning or problem solving? *Annals of the New York Academy of Science,* 1953a, **56,** 273–288.

Mowrer, O. H. (Ed.) *Psychotherapy: Theory and research.* New York: Ronald Press, 1953b.

Mowrer, O. H. *The crisis in psychiatry and religion.* Princeton, N.J.: Van Nostrand, 1961.

Mowrer, O. H. *The new group therapy.* Princeton, N.J.: Van Nostrand, 1964.

Mowrer, O. H. Learning theory and behavior therapy. In B. Wolman (Ed.), *Handbook of clinical psychology.* New York: McGraw-Hill, 1965.

Mowrer, O. H. Abnormal reactions or actions?—An autobiographical answer. In J. Vernon (Ed.), *Introduction to general psychology.* Dubuque, Iowa: Brown, 1966a. Pp. 1–42.

Mowrer, O. H. The basis of psychopathology: Malconditioning or misbehavior? In C. Spielberger (Ed.), *Anxiety and behavior.* New York: Academic Press, 1966b. Pp. 143–156.

Mowrer, O. H. The behavior therapies, with special references to "modeling" and imitation. *Journal of the Association for the Advancement of Psychotherapy*, 1966c, **20**, 439–461.

Mowrer, O. H. Integrity therapy: A self-help approach. *Psychotherapy: Theory, Research, and Practice*, 1966d, **3**, 114–119.

Mowrer, O. H. Loss and recovery of community: A guide to the theory and practice of integrity therapy. In G. M. Gazda (Ed.), *Theories and methods of group psychotherapy and counseling*. Springfield, Ill.: Charles C Thomas, 1967a.

Mowrer, O. H. Some notes and notions on integrity training. *The Dis-Coverer*, 1967b, **4**, 8.

Mowrer, O. H. Conflict, contract, conscience, and confession. Unpublished paper, University of Illinois, 1968a.

Mowrer, O. H. Loss and recovery of community: A guide to the theory and practice of integrity therapy. In G. M. Gazda (Ed.), *Innovations to group psychotherapy*. Springfield, Ill.: Charles C Thomas, 1968b. Pp. 130–189.

Mowrer, O. H. New evidence concerning the nature of psychopathology. In M. J. Feldman (Ed.), *Studies in psychotherapy and behavioral change*, Buffalo, N.Y.: University of New York at Buffalo, 1968c. Pp. 113–193.

Mullin, C. S., Jr. Some psychological aspects of isolated antarctic living. *American Journal of Psychiatry*, 1960, **117**, 323–325.

Munroe, R. *Schools of psychoanalytic thought*. New York: Holt, Rinehart and Winston, 1955.

Murphy, G. *Human potentialities*. New York: Basic Books, 1958.

Murphy, G. Communications and mental health. *Psychiatry*, 1964, **27**, 100–106.

Nardini, J. E. Navy psychiatric assessment program in the antarctic. *American Journal of Psychiatry*, 1962, **119**, 91–105.

Neill, A. S. "Can I come to Summerhill? I hate my school." *Psychology Today*, 1968, **1** (12), 34–40.

Newcomb, T. M. An approach to the study of communicative acts. *Psychological Review*, 1953, **60**, 393–404.

Newcomb, T. M. The prediction of interpersonal attraction. *American Psychologist*, 1956, **11**, 575–586.

Newcomb, T. M. The cognition of persons as cognizers. In R. Tagiuri & L. Petrullo (Eds.), *Person perception and interpersonal behavior.* Stanford, Calif.: Stanford University Press, 1958. Pp. 179–190.

Newcomb, T. M. Varieties of interpersonal attraction. In D. Cartwright & A. Zander (Eds.), *Group dynamics: Research & theory.* (2nd ed.) New York: Harper & Row, 1960. Pp. 104–119.

Newcomb, T. M. Stabilities underlying changes in interpersonal attraction. *Journal of Abnormal and Social Psychiatry*, 1963, **66**, 376–386.

Newman, S., & Mather, V. G. Analysis of spoken language of patients with affective disorders. *American Journal of Psychiatry*, 1938, **94**, 913–942.

Nunnally, J. C. *Popular conceptions of mental health.* New York: Holt, Rinehart and Winston, 1961.

Oaklander, H., & Fleishman, E. A. Patterns of leadership in hospital settings. *Administrative Science Quarterly*, 1964, **8**, 521–532.

Ogilvie, D. M. An exploration of identification following aggressive acts. Unpublished honors thesis, Harvard University, 1961.

O'Neill, A. M. The bases of clinical inference. *Journal of Clinical Psychology*, 1968, **24**, 366–372.

Oskamp, E., & Perlman, D. Factors affecting cooperation in a Prisoner's Dilemma game. *Journal of Conflict Resolution*, 1965, **9**, 359–374.

Otto, H. A. (Ed.) *Explorations in human potentialities.* Springfield, Ill.: Charles C Thomas, 1966.

Panel on Privacy and Behavioral Research. Privacy and behavioral research: Preliminary summary. *Science*, 1967, **155**, 535–538.

Pascal, G. R., Cottrell, T. B., & Baugh, J. R. A methodological note on the use of video tape in group psychotherapy with juvenile delinquents. *International Journal of Group Psychotherapy*, 1967, **17**, 248–251.

Patterson, C. H. *Theories of counseling and psychotherapy*. New York: Harper & Row, 1966.

Patton, T. Synanists play self-growth game. *The Dis-Coverer*, 1967, **4** (3), 4–7.

Penney, R. K. Reactive curiosity and manifest anxiety in children. *Child Development*, 1965, **36**, 697–702.

Penney, R. K. The children's reactive curiosity scale. *Psychological Reports*, 1964, **15**, 323–334.

Phillips, E. L. *Psychotherapy: A modern theory and practice*. Englewood Cliffs, N.J.: Prentice-Hall, 1956.

Piaget, G. W., Berenson, B. G., & Carkhuff, R. R. Differential effects of the manipulation of therapeutic conditions by high- and moderate-functioning therapists upon high- and low-functioning clients. *Journal of Consulting Psychology*, 1967, **31**, 481–486.

Piaget, J. *The language and thought of the child*. London: Routledge & Kegan Paul, 1952.

Piers, G., & Singer, M. B. *Shame and guilt*. Springfield, Ill.: Charles C Thomas, 1953.

Pilisuk, M. Cognitive balance and self-relevant attitudes. *Journal of Abnormal and Social Psychology*, 1962, **65**, 95–103.

Pittenger, R. E., Hockett, C. F., & Danehy, J. J. *The first five minutes: A sample of microscopic interview analysis*. Ithaca, N.Y.: Paul Martineau, 1960.

Poser, E. G. The effect of therapists' training on group therapeutic outcome. *Journal of Consulting Psychology*, 1966, **30**, 283–289.

Pratt, S., & Tooley, J. Contract psychology and the actualizing transactional field. *International Journal of Social Psychiatry*, Congress issue, 1964, 51–69.

Pratt, S., & Tooley, J. Human actualization teams: The perspective of contract psychology. *American Journal of Orthopsychiatry*, 1966, **36**, 881–895.

Rapoport, A. *Strategy and conscience*. New York: Harper & Row, 1964.

Raven, B., & French, J. R. P. Legitimate power, coercive power, and observability in social influence. *Sociometry*, 1958, **21**, 83–97.

Raven, B. H., & Rietsema, J. The effects of varied clarity of goal and group path upon the individual and his relation to his group. *Human Relations*, 1957, **10**, 29–44.

Read, W. H. Upward communication in industrial hierarchies. *Human Relations*, 1962, **15**, 3–15.

Redl, F. Group emotion and leadership. *Psychiatry*, 1942, **5**, 573–596.

Reik, T. *Masochism in modern man*. M. H. Beigel & G. M. Kurth (Trans.). New York: Farrar, Straus, 1949 (also New York: Grove Press, 1959).

Riecken, H. Some problems of consensus development. *Rural Sociology*, 1952, **17**, 245–252.

Riesman, D. *The lonely crowd: A study of the changing American character*. New Haven: Yale University Press, 1950.

Rioch, D. Theories of psychotherapy. In W. Dennis (Ed.), *Current trends in psychological theory*. Pittsburgh: University of Pittsburgh Press, 1951.

Rioch, M. J., Elkes, C., Flint, A. A., Usdansky, B. S., Newman, R. G., & Silber, E. National Institute of Mental Health pilot study in training mental health counselors. *American Journal of Orthopsychiatry*, 1963, **33**, 678–689.

Rogers, A. H. Videotape feedback in group psychotherapy. *Psychotherapy: Theory, Research, and Practice*, 1968, **5**, 37–39.

Rogers, C. R. *Counseling and psychotherapy*. Boston: Houghton Mifflin, 1942.

Rogers, C. R. *Client-centered therapy*. Boston: Houghton Mifflin, 1951.

Rogers, C. R. *On becoming a person*. Boston: Houghton Mifflin, 1961a.

Rogers, C. R. The process equation of psychotherapy. *American Journal of Psychotherapy*, 1961b, **15**, 27–45.

Rogers, C. R. The actualizing tendency in relation to "motives" and consciousness. In *Nebraska symposium on motivation*. Lincoln: University of Nebraska Press, 1963.

Rogers, C. R. Toward a modern approach to values: The valuing process in the mature person. In C. R. Rogers & B. Stevens, *Person to Person*. Lafayette, Calif.: Real People Press, 1967. Pp. 13–28 (reprinted from *Journal of Abnormal and Social Psychology*, 1964, **68**, 160–167).

Rogers, C. R. Some learnings from a study of psychotherapy with schizophrenics. In A. P. Goldstein & S. J. Dean (Eds.), *The investigation of psychotherapy*. New York: Wiley, 1966. Pp. 5–13. (Reprinted from *Pennsylvania Psychiatric Quarterly*, 1962, 3–15.)

Rogers, C. R. The process of the basic encounter group. In J. F. T. Bugental (Ed.), *Challenges of humanistic psychology*. New York: McGraw-Hill, 1967. Pp. 261–276.

Rogers, C. R. (Ed.) *The therapeutic relationship and its impact: A study of psychotherapy with schizophrenics*. Madison: The University of Wisconsin Press, 1967.

Rogers, C. R., & Skinner, B. F. Some issues concerning the control of human behavior: A symposium. *Science*, 1956, **124**, 1057–1066.

Rogers, C. R., & Truax, C. B. The therapeutic conditions antecedent to change: A theroetical view. In C. R. Rogers (Ed.), *The therapeutic relationship and its impact*. Madison: The University of Wisconsin Press, 1967. Pp. 97–108.

Rohrer, J. H. Interpersonal relations in isolated small groups. In B. E. Flaherty (Ed.), *Psychophysiological aspects of space flight*. New York: Columbia University Press, 1961. Pp. 263–271.

Rome, S., & Rome, B. Humanistic research on large social organizations. In J. F. T. Bugental (Ed.), *Challenges of humanistic psychology*. New York: McGraw-Hill, 1967. Pp. 109–116.

Rosenberg, S. Cooperative behavior in dyads as a function of reinforcement parameters. *Journal of Abnormal and Social Psychology*, 1960, **60**, 318–333.

Rosenblith, W. A. Afterword. In N. Wiener, *The human use of human beings*. New York: Avon Books, 1967. Pp. 265–281.

Rotter, J. *Social learning and clinical psychology*. Englewood Cliffs, N.J.: Prentice-Hall, 1954.

Rotter, J. Some implications of a social learning theory for the practice of psychotherapy. Mimeographed paper, 1962.

Ruesch, J. *Disturbed communication*. New York: Norton, 1957.

Ruesch, J. The role of communication in therapeutic transactions. *The Journal of Communications*, 1963, **13**, 132–139.

Ruesch, J., & Bateson, G. *Communication, the social matrix of psychiatry*. New York: Norton, 1951.

Rush, C. H., Jr. Leader behavior and group characteristics. In R. M. Stogdill & A. E. Coons (Eds.), *Leader behavior: Its description and measurement*. Monograph 88, Bureau of Business Research, The Ohio State University, 1957. Pp. 69–73.

Salter, A. *Conditioned reflex therapy*. New York: Creative Age Press, 1949 (Capricorn, 1961).

Salzberg, H. C. Verbal behavior in group psychotherapy with and without a therapist. *Journal of Counseling Psychology*, 1967, **14**, 24–27.

Salzinger, K. (Ed.) *Research in verbal behavior and some neurophysiological implications*. New York: Academic Press, 1967.

Salzinger, K., Portnoy, S., & Feldman, R. S. Verbal behavior of schizophrenic and normal subjects. *Annals of the New York Academy of Science*, 1964, **105**, 845–860.

Sanford, F. H. Speech and personality: A comparative case study. *Character and Personality*, 1942, **10**, 169–198.

Sarbin, T. R. On the futility of the proposition that some people be labeled "mentally ill." *Journal of Consulting Psychology*, 1967, **31**, 447–453.

Schachtel, E. G. On memory and childhood amnesia. *Psychiatry*, 1947, **10**, 1–26.

Schachter, S. Deviation, rejection, and communication. *Journal of Abnormal and Social Psychology*, 1951, **46**, 190–207.

Schachter, S. *The psychology of affiliation.* Stanford, Calif.: Stanford University Press, 1959.

Scheff, T. J. *Being mentally ill: A sociological theory.* Chicago: Aldine, 1966.

Scheflen, A. E. The significance of posture in communication systems. *Psychiatry,* 1964, **27,** 316–331.

Scheflen, A. E. Communication systems such as psychotherapy. In J. H. Masserman (Ed.), *Current psychiatric therapies.* Vol. 5. New York: Grune & Stratton, 1965. Pp. 33–41.

Schein, E. H., & Bennis, W. G. Overview of laboratory training. In E. H. Schein & W. G. Bennis (Eds.), *Personal and organizational change through group methods.* New York: Wiley, 1965a. Pp. 28–54.

Schein, E. H., & Bennis, W. G. (Eds.) *Personal and organizational change through group methods: The laboratory approach.* New York: Wiley, 1965b.

Schein, E. H., & Bennis, W. G. What is laboratory training: Description of a typical residential laboratory. In E. H. Schein & W. G. Bennis (Eds.), *Personal and organizational change through group methods.* New York: Wiley, 1965c. Pp. 10–27.

Schiff, S. B., & Reivich, R. Use of television as an aid to psychotherapy supervision. *Archives of General Psychiatry,* 1964, **10,** 84–88.

Schneider, L. A proposed conceptual integration of group dynamics and therapy. *Journal of Social Psychology,* 1955, **42,** 173–191.

Schofield, W. *Psychotherapy: The purchase of friendship.* Englewood Cliffs, N.J.: Prentice-Hall, 1964.

Schutz, W. C. *Joy.* New York: Grove Press, 1967.

Schutz, W. C., & Allen, V. L. The effects of a T-group laboratory on interpersonal behavior. *Journal of Applied Behavioral Science,* 1966, **2,** 265–286.

Seashore, C. What is sensitivity training? *NTL Institute News and Reports,* 1968, **2** (2), 1–2.

Shaffer, L. F., & Shoben, E. J., Jr. *The psychology of adjustment.* Boston: Houghton Mifflin, 1956.

Shelly, J. A., & Bassin, A. Daytop Lodge: A new treatment approach for drug addicts. *Corrective Psychiatry,* 1965, 11, 186–195.

Sherif, M., White, B. J., & Harvey, O. J. Status in experimentally produced groups. *American Journal of Sociology,* 1955, 60, 370–379.

Sherman, D. An analysis of the dynamic relationships between counselor techniques and outcomes in larger units of the interview situation. Unpublished doctoral dissertation, Ohio State University, 1945.

Sherrill, L. J. *Guilt and redemption.* Richmond, Va.: John Knox Press, 1945.

Sidowski, J. R. (Ed.) *Experimental methods and instrumentation in psychology.* New York: McGraw-Hill, 1966.

Singer, J. L. *Daydreaming: An introduction to the experimental study of inner experience.* New York: Random House, 1966.

Slater, P. E. *Microcosm: Structural, psychological, and religious evolution in groups.* New York: Wiley, 1966.

Slavson, S. R. The phenomenology of silence in psychotherapy groups. *International Journal of Group Psychotherapy,* 1966, 16, 395–404.

Smith, A. G. Introduction: Communication and culture. In A. G. Smith (Ed.), *Communication and culture.* New York: Holt, Rinehart and Winston, 1966.

Smith, E. E. The effects of clear and unclear role expectations on group productivity and defensiveness. *Journal of Abnormal and Social Psychology,* 1957, 55, 213–217.

Snoek, J. D. Some effects of rejection upon attraction to a group. *Journal of Abnormal and Social Psychology,* 1962, 64, 175–182.

Solomon, R. L. Punishment. *American Psychologist,* 1964, 19, 239–253.

Spiegel, J. P. The resolution of role conflict within the family. *Psychiatry,* 1957, 20, 1–16.

Spiegel, J. P., & Machotka, P. A program for somatotactical testing. Unpublished manuscript, Harvard University, 1965.

Spiegel, R. Specific problems of communication in psychiatric conditions. In S. Arieti (Ed.), *American handbook of psychiatry.* New York: Basic Books, 1959. Pp. 909–949.

Standal, S. The need for positive regard: A contribution to client-centered theory. Unpublished doctoral dissertation, University of Chicago, 1954.

Steinzor, B. *The healing partnership: The patient as colleague in psychotherapy.* New York: Harper & Row, 1967.

Steinzor, B. Psychotherapy as a way of life. *Psychiatry and Social Science Review,* 1968, **2** (4), 5–9.

Stennett, R. G. The relationship of performance level to level of arousal. *Journal of Experimental Psychology,* 1957, **54,** 54–61.

Stern, E. M. Psychotherapy: Reverence for experience. *Journal of Existentialism,* 1966, **6,** 279–287.

Stern, K. *The third revolution.* New York: Harcourt, Brace & World, 1954.

Stock, D. A. A survey of research on T-groups. In L. P. Bradford, J. R. Gibb, & K. D. Benne (Eds.), *T-group theory and laboratory method.* New York: Wiley, 1964. Pp. 395–441.

Stock, D., & Thelen, H. A. *Emotional dynamics and group culture.* New York: New York University Press, 1958.

Stoller, F. H. Focused feedback with videotape: Extending the group's functions. In G. M. Gazda (Ed.), *Innovations to group psychotherapy.* Springfield, Ill.: Charles C Thomas, 1968a.

Stoller, F. H. Marathon group therapy. In G. M. Gazda (Ed.), *Innovations to group psychotherapy.* Springfield, Ill.: Charles C Thomas, 1968b. Pp. 42–95.

Stoller, F. H. A synergic model for human growth. An outline prepared for the American Psychological Association Symposium on "Marathon Groups," San Francisco, 1968c.

Stout, G. F. *Analytic psychology*. Vol. 2. New York: Macmillan, 1902.

Strickland, B. R., & Crowne, D. P. Need for approval and the premature termination of psychotherapy. *Journal of Consulting Psychology*, 1963, **27**, 95–101.

Suchman, J. R. Social sensitivity in the small task-oriented group. *Journal of Abnormal and Social Psychology*, 1956, **52**, 75–83.

Sullivan, H. S. Conceptions of modern psychiatry. *Psychiatry*, 1940, **3**, 1–117.

Szasz, T. S. The myth of mental illness. *American Psychologist*, 1960, **15**, 113–118.

Szasz, T. S. *The myth of mental illness*. New York: Harper, 1961.

Tagiuri, R. Social preference and its perception. In R. Tagiuri & L. Petrullo (Eds.), *Person perception and interpersonal behavior*. Stanford, Calif.: Stanford University Press, 1958. Pp. 316–336.

Tagiuri, R., Blake, R. R., & Bruner, J. S. Some determinants of the perception of positive and negative feelings in others. *Journal of Abnormal and Social Psychology*, 1953, **48**, 585–592.

Tagiuri, R., Bruner, J. S., & Blake, R. R. On the relation between feelings and perception of feelings among members of small groups. In E. Maccoby, T. Newcomb, & E. Hartley (Eds.), *Readings in social psychology*. (3rd ed.) New York: Holt, Rinehart and Winston, 1958. Pp. 110–116.

Talland, G. A., & Clark, D. H. Evaluation of topics in therapy group discussion. *Journal of Clinical Psychology*, 1954, **10**, 131–137.

Tannenbaum, R., Weschler, I. R., & Massarik, F. *Leadership and organization: A behavioral science approach*. New York: McGraw-Hill, 1961.

Thomas, H. F. Self-actualization through the group experience. *Journal of Humanistic Psychology*, 1964, **4**, 39–44.

Thomas, H. F. An existential attitude in working with individuals and groups. In J. F. T. Bugental (Ed.), *Challenges of humanistic psychology*. New York: McGraw-Hill, 1967. Pp. 227–232.

Thorne, F. C. *Principles of personality counseling.* Brandon, Vt.: *Journal of Clinical Psychology,* 1950.

Tomkins, S. S. *Affect, imagery, and consciousness: The positive affects.* Vol. 1. New York: Springer, 1962.

Tomlinson, T. M., & Hart, J. T., Jr. A validation study of the process scale. *Journal of Consulting Psychology,* 1962, **26,** 74–78.

Torrance, E. P., & Witt, G. Experimental grouping on the basis of creative abilities and motivations. *Gifted Child Quarterly,* 1966, **10,** 9–14.

Tournier, P. *Guilt and grace.* London: Hodder & Stoughton, 1962.

Truax, C. B. The process of group psychotherapy. *Psychological Monographs,* 1961a, **75** (14, Whole No. 511).

Truax, C. B. Therapeutic conditions. *Discussion papers, Wisconsin Psychiatric Institute,* University of Wisconsin, 1961b, **13.**

Truax, C. B. Effective ingredients in psychotherapy: An approach to unraveling the patient-therapist interaction. *Journal of Counseling Psychology,* 1963, **10,** 256–263.

Truax, C. B. Some implications of behavior therapy for psychotherapy. *Journal of Counseling Psychology,* 1966, **13,** 160–170.

Truax, C. B., & Carkhuff, R. R. For better or for worse: The process of psychotherapeutic personality change. Invited address: Recent advances in the study of behavior change. Academic Assembly on Clinical Psychology, McGill University, Montreal, Canada, June 4, 1963.

Truax, C. B., & Carkhuff, R. R. Concreteness: A neglected variable in research in psychotherapy. *Journal of Clinical Psychology,* 1964a, **20,** 264–267.

Truax, C. B., & Carkhuff, R. R. The old and the new: The changing scene in theory and research in counseling and psychotherapy. *Personnel Guidance Journal,* 1964b, **42,** 860–866.

Truax, C. B., & Carkhuff, R. R. Significant developments in psychotherapy research. In L. E. Abt & B. F. Reiss (Eds.), *Progress in clinical psychology.* New York: Grune & Stratton, 1964c. Pp. 124–155.

Truax, C. B., & Carkhuff, R. R. Experimental manipulation of therapeutic conditions. *Journal of Consulting Psychology*, 1965, **29**, 119–124.

Truax, C. B., & Carkhuff, R. R. *Toward effective counseling and psychotherapy*. Chicago: Aldine, 1967.

Truax, C. B., Fine, H., Moravec, J., & Millis, W. Effects of therapist persuasive potency in individual psychotherapy. *Journal of Clinical Psychology*, 1968, **24**, 359–362.

Tuckman, B. W. Developmental sequence in small groups. *Psychological Bulletin*, 1965, **63**, 384–399.

Underwood, W. J. Evaluation of laboratory method training. *Training Directors Journal*, 1965, **19**, 34–40.

Valiquet, I. M. Contribution to the evaluation of a managerial development program. Unpublished master's thesis, Massachusetts Institute of Technology, 1964.

Van Kaam, A. *The third force in European psychology: Its expression in a theory of psychotherapy*. Psychosynthesis Research Foundation, Greenville, Del., 1960.

Van Kaam, A. Counseling from the viewpoint of existential psychology. *Harvard Educational Review*, 1962, **32**, 403–415.

Varendonck, J. *The psychology of daydreams*. London: Allen & Unwin, 1921.

Verwoerdt, A., Nowlin, J. B., & Agnello, S. A. A technique for studying effects of self-confrontation in cardiac patients. *Health Services TV Bulletin*, 1965, **2**, 1–6.

Von Hartmann, E. *Philosophy of the unconscious*. New York: Macmillan, 1884.

Wagstaff, A. K., Rice, L. N., & Butler, J. M. Factors of client verbal participation in therapy. *Counseling Center Discussion Papers*, University of Chicago, 1960, **6** (9), 1–14.

Walz, G. R., & Johnston, J. A. Counselors look at themselves on video tape. *Journal of Counseling Psychology*, 1963, **10**, 232–236.

Ward, W. D., & Bendak, S. The response of psychiatric patients to photographic self-image experience. *Newsletter for Research in Psychology*, Veterans Administration, 1964, **6**, 29–30.

Watson, J. R., Lippitt, R., Kallen, D., & Zipf, S. Evaluation of a human relations laboratory program. Typewritten manuscript, Research Center for Group Dynamics, University of Michigan, 1961.

Watson, R. I. *Psychology of the child*. New York: Wiley, 1959.

Weick, K. E. Systematic observational methods. In G. Lindzey & E. Aronson (Eds.), *The handbook of social psychology*. (2nd ed.) Vol. 2. Reading, Mass.: Addison-Wesley, 1968. Pp. 357–451.

Wender, P. H. Communication unclarity: Some comments on the rhetoric of confusion. *Psychiatry*, 1967, **30**, 332–349.

Werner, H., & Wapner, S. Changes in psychological distance under conditions of danger. *Journal of Personality*, 1953, **24**, 153–167.

Werry, J. S. The psychiatrist and society. *The Dis-Coverer*, 1968, **5** (3), 1–12 (The 1967 Velde Lecture, Bradley University, Peoria, Illinois, April 26–27).

Weschler, I. R., Massarik, F., & Tannenbaum, R. The self in process: A sensitivity training emphasis. In I. R. Weschler & E. Schein (Eds.), *Issues in human relations training*. Washington, D.C.: National Training Laboratories, 1962. Pp. 33–46.

Wheelis, A. *The quest for identity*. New York: Norton, 1958.

Wheelis, A. *The seeker*. New York: Random House, 1960.

Whitaker, D. S., & Lieberman, M. A. *Psychotherapy through the group process*. New York: Atherton, 1964.

White, R. W. *The abnormal personality*. (3rd ed.) New York: Ronald Press, 1964.

Whitman, R. M. Psychodynamic principles underlying T-Group processes. In L. P. Bradford, J. R. Gibb, & K. D. Benne (Eds.), *T-Group theory and laboratory method*. New York: Wiley, 1964. Pp. 310–335.

Whyte, W. H., Jr. *The organization man*. New York: Simon & Schuster, 1956.

Wiener, N. *The human use of human beings.* New York: Discus Books (Avon), 1967 (original Houghton Mifflin, 1950).

Wiener, M., & Mehrabian, A. *Language within language: Immediacy, a channel in verbal communication.* New York: Appleton-Century-Crofts, 1968.

Williams, M. The group phenomenon, *Chicago Daily News,* Panorama Section, March 2, 1968, 3–4.

Wittgenstein, L. *Tractatus logico-philosophicus.* London: Routledge & Kegan Paul, 1955 (originally published in 1922).

Wolberg, L. R. *The technique of psychotherapy.* New York: Grune & Stratton, 1954.

Wolf, A., & Schwartz, E. K. *Psychoanalysis in groups.* New York: Grune & Stratton, 1962.

Yablonsky, L. Synanon: The anticriminal society. *Federal Probation,* 1962, **26,** 50–57.

Yablonsky, L. *The tunnel back: Synanon.* New York: Macmillan, 1965.

Yerkes, F. M., & Dodson, J. D. The relation of strength of stimulus to rapidity of habit-formation. *Journal of Comparative Neurology and Psychology,* 1908, **18,** 459–482.

Zajonc, R. B. The effects of feedback and probability of group success on individual and group performance. *Human Relations,* 1962, **15,** 149–161.

Zand, D. E., Steele, F. I., & Zalkind, S. S. The impact of an organizational development program on perceptions of interpersonal, group, and organizational functioning. In S. S. Zalkind (Chm.), Research on the impact of using different laboratory methods for interpersonal and organizational change. Symposium presented at the meeting of the American Psychological Association, Washington, D.C., September 1967.

Zuckerman, M., Kolin, E. A., Price, L., & Zoob, I. Development of a sensation-seeking scale. *Journal of Consulting Psychology,* 1964, **28,** 477–482.

Author Index

Abrahams, R. D., 162
Acker, M., 102, 152
Ackerman, N. W., 260
Adler, A., 194, 306
Agnello, S. A., 309
Albee, E., 188
Alexander, F., 219, 225, 355
Allen, V. L., 367
Allport, F. H., 221
Allport, G., 11, 19, 81
Anderson, C. M., 210, 211, 288
Ansbacher, J. L., 194
Arnold, M., 148
Aronson, E., 41, 120
Arsenian, J., 309
Ausubel, D. P., 37
Ayllon, M., 210
Ayllon, T., 210
Azrin, N. H., 210
Bach, G. R., 20–22, 62, 136, 290, 317, 326
Bales, R. F., 28, 30, 65

Bandura, A., 187, 315
Bassin, A., 2, 289
Bateson, G., 170
Baugh, J. R., 309
Becker, R. J., 215, 217
Beier, E. J., 42, 290, 303, 305–306, 325
Bendak, S., 309
Benedek, T., 273
Benedikt, M., 199
Benne, K. D., 1, 3–4, 8, 30, 71–72, 109, 137, 191, 202
Bennett, C. C., 202–204
Bennis, W. G., 3, 4, 8, 11, 71–72, 129–131, 247, 370
Berenson, B. G., 164, 201, 288–289, 292–293, 298, 320–321, 324, 328, 333, 368
Berkowitz, L., 311
Berne, E., 81, 82, 98, 158, 164, 170, 209, 220, 248, 291, 344

Bernstein, A., 131
Berzon, B., 137
Bettelheim, B., 160
Bion, W. R., 30, 33, 129, 131, 359
Birdwhistell, R. L., 176
Bittel, L. R., 3
Bixler, R. H., 39
Blake, R. R., 1–3, 105, 107, 136–137, 233
Bloch, H. S., 184
Borgatta, E. F., 28, 30
Boss, M., 215
Bower, G. H., 279, 315, 316
Boy, A. V., 60
Boyd, H. S., 288, 309–310
Boyd, J. B., 64, 369–370
Braaten, L. J., 212, 328
Bradford, L. P., 3, 4, 8, 30, 109, 247, 261
Breger, L., 332
Bronson, G. W., 172
Bruner, J. S., 233
Buber, M., 11, 81, 216
Buchanan, P. C., 4, 362
Bugental, J. F. T., 3, 16, 17, 46, 216, 360
Buhler, K., 159, 167
Bunker, D. R., 63, 114, 361, 365, 369
Burgess, A., 162
Burton, A., 14, 28
Burton, R. V., 187
Butler, J. M., 212, 328
Byrne, D., 123
Cameron, N., 213
Campbell, D. T., 254, 256, 258
Campbell, J. P., 1, 3, 64, 68, 100, 102, 111, 135, 139, 247, 319, 320, 324, 362, 363, 364, 365, 366
Carkhuff, R. R., 23, 36, 40, 45, 65, 95, 137, 164, 201, 212, 239, 260, 268, 271, 280, 281, 288, 289, 298, 320, 321, 324, 328, 368
Carlsmith, J. M., 41, 120
Carr, A., 15, 28
Carroll, J. B., 169
Cartwright, D., 26, 28, 30, 32, 83, 89
Casriel, D., 2, 289

Cassirer, E., 159
Cattell, R. B., 67, 86, 135
Church, R. M., 315
Cioran, E. M., 162
Clark, D. H., 212, 223
Clark, J. V., 216
Cofer, C. N., 159
Coles, R., 82
Collins, B. E., 7, 29, 108, 135, 221, 222, 256, 258, 274, 276, 279, 360, 361
Cornelison, F. S., 309
Corsini, R. J., 291
Cottrell, T. B., 309
Craig, R. L., 3
Crowne, D. P., 267
Crowther, B., 30
Curran, C. A., 35
Danet, B., 249
Darley, J. M., 92
Davis, J. D., 317
Davitz, J. R., 176
Deutsch, M., 89, 95
Dittes, J., 316
Dittmann, A. T., 176
Dixon, T. R., 159
Dodson, J. D., 48
Dollard, J., 191, 219, 240, 241, 337
Douds, J., 288, 289, 291, 298, 324, 325, 342, 368
Drakeford, J. W., 290, 318
Dreikurs, R., 88, 194, 306
Dunnette, M. D., 1, 3, 64, 68, 100, 102, 111, 135, 139, 247, 319, 320, 324, 362, 363, 364, 365, 366
Eells, J., 36
Eisman, B., 250
Ekman, P., 176, 249
Elkes, C., 22, 122
Ellenberger, H. R., 199
Ellis, A., 15, 166, 290, 306
Elliss, J. D., 64, 369–370
Erikson, E. H., 79, 80, 97, 101, 160, 172, 173, 205, 213, 219, 223, 224, 227, 261, 273, 359
Estes, W. K., 315
Exline, R. V., 249
Eysenck, H. J., 131

Feifel, H., 36
Fenichel, O., 346
Ferenczi, S., 260
Festinger, L., 149, 150, 313
Fiedler, F. E., 88, 150, 250
Fine, H., 288, 293
Fleishman, E. A., 139
Flint, A. A., 22, 122
Forrest, D. V., 159, 182
Fouriezos, N. T., 87
Fox, R. S., 1
Frank, J. D., 37, 38, 100, 202, 227, 260, 268, 293, 341
Frank, L. K., 157
Frankl, V. E., 291
French, J. R. P., 72, 316, 326
Freud, S., 42, 201
Friedenberg, E. Z., 12, 98
Friedman, H. J., 368
Friel, B., 162
Friesen, W. V., 176
Fromm, E., 92, 144, 207, 224, 227, 264
Fromm-Reichmann, R., 39, 79, 260, 268
Garfield, S. L., 36
Gassner, S., 364
Gaylin, W., 15, 28
Geer, J. H., 254
Gendlin, E. T., 183, 313
Getzels, J. W., 92
Gibb, C. A., 123
Gibb, J. R., 3, 4, 8, 30, 72, 136, 138, 247, 273, 274, 275, 286, 320, 336
Gillis, R. D., 159
Glatzer, H., 242
Glauber, I. P., 159
Goffman, E., 89, 140, 166, 174, 252, 253, 345, 346
Gold, J., 364
Goldstein, A. P., 20, 37, 38, 39
Golembiewski, R. T., 34, 65
Goroff, N. N., 342
Gottschalk, L. A., 159
Gray, D., 249
Green, G. H., 230
Greenson, R., 346
Grinker, R. R., 96, 317, 337
Grossack, M. M., 89

Guetzkow, H., 7, 29, 87, 108, 135, 221, 222, 256, 258, 274, 276, 279, 360, 361
Guilford, J. P., 12, 98
Gunther, B., 2, 153, 178, 181
Gynther, R. A., 254
Haggard, E. A., 249
Hanson, P. G., 9, 288
Harburg, E., 331
Haiman, F. S., 364
Haley, J., 248
Hall, E. T., 176
Hall, M. H., 3
Halpin, A. W., 139
Hampden-Turner, C. M., 108
Hare, P. A., 28, 30
Harper, R. A., 196
Harris, E. F., 139
Harrison, R., 367
Harrow, M., 137
Hart, J. T., Jr., 212, 328
Harvey, O. J., 311, 328
Hathaway, S. R., 206
Haughton, E., 210
Hegel, G. W. F., 299
Heller, K., 20, 37, 38, 39, 317
Hendin, H., 15, 28
Henry, J., 97, 206
Hess, R. D., 172
Hilgard, E. R., 279, 315, 316
Hobbs, N., 152
Hodges, H. A., 159
Hoehn-Saric, R., 36, 38, 39
Hoffmann, L. R., 331
Holder, T., 320, 328
Holland, G. A., 39
Holland, J. L., 12
Holsti, O. R., 66
Homan, G. C., 30
Honigfeld, G., 159
Horney, K., 88
Horowitz, M. W., 311
Horton, D. L., 159
Horwitz, M., 73, 77
House, R. J., 1, 2, 3, 10, 35, 47, 362, 370
Hunt, J. McV., 21
Hutt, M. L., 87
Ingham, H. V., 35, 39, 243, 295
Isaacs, K. S., 249
Israel, J., 87

Jacob, P. E., 12, 81
James, W., 11
Jecker, J., 249
Johnson, D. L., 9, 138, 288
Johnston, J. A., 310
Jourard, S. M., 11, 41, 116, 117, 198, 199, 203, 204, 207, 242, 278
Kagan, N., 309
Kalish, H. I., 357
Kanfer, F. H., 15
Kansler, D. H., 159
Kaplan, D. M., 271
Kasl, S. V., 254
Katz, E. W., 66
Katz, R., 249
Kelley, H. H., 316, 328
Kelly, G. A., 109
Kelman, H. C., 41
Keniston, K., 98, 144, 221
Kierkegaard, S., 236, 299
Kirtner, W. L., 328
Klaw, S., 369
Klein, A., 96
Klein, D. C., 1, 104, 105
Knowles, E. S., 114
Kohn, M. L., 204
Kohrman, J., 96
Kolin, E. A., 152
Krasner, L., 188
Krathwohl, D. R., 309
Kris, E., 48
Kushner, M., 317
LaBarre, W., 176
Laing, R. D., 11, 146, 151, 167
Lakin, M., 156
Laney, R. C., 288, 292, 293, 321, 333, 368
Latourelle, R., 237, 265
Lehrman, N. S., 260
Leventhal, H., 249
Levitt, E. A., 249
Levitt, E. E., 36, 49, 213
Levy, J., 250
Lewin, K., 316
Lieberman, M. A., 2, 30, 127, 130, 131, 156, 157, 337, 340, 354
Limbacher, W. J., 12
Lindzey, G., 123
Lippitt, R., 1, 109, 138
Lipsher, D. H., 187

Locke, N. M., 20
London, P., 164, 201, 213, 289, 298, 299, 341
Lorenz, M., 159
Lorge, I., 73
Lorr, M., 21
Lott, A. J., 20, 89, 128, 247, 361
Lott, B. E., 20, 89, 128, 361
Love, L. R., 35, 39
Lowe, M. C., 213
Lowrey, L. G., 20
Luft, J., 243, 244, 295
Lyle, F. A., 9, 288
Lynch, W. F., 182
Lynd, H. M., 80, 144, 163, 169, 170, 188, 189, 193, 200, 213, 224, 225, 226, 227, 228, 229, 276, 283
Lyons, J., 311
MacGregor, H., 96
Machotka, P., 249
Machover, S., 181
Mahl, G. F., 142, 175, 249, 254
Maier, N. R. F., 331
Mailer, N., 206
Mainord, W. A., 9, 21, 197, 198, 204, 210, 290
Malamud, D. I., 181
Mandelbaum, D. G., 169
Mann, C. H., 37
Mann, J. H., 37
Mann, R. D., 30, 124, 125, 129, 186, 360, 361
March, J. G., 32, 75, 192
Maritain, J., 45
Maslow, A. H., 2, 11, 12, 13, 15, 92, 102, 188, 289, 318, 325
Massarik, F., 3, 202
Matarazzo, J. D., 48
Mather, V. G., 159
Matson, F. W., 164, 235
May, R., 11, 131, 213, 215, 291, 343
McGaugh, J. L., 332
McKinley, J. C., 206
McLuhan, M., 43, 165, 235, 237
McReynolds, P., 102, 152, 153
Meehl, P. E., 23, 206
Meerloo, J., 209
Mehrabian, A., 142, 159, 169, 175
Mellinger, G. D., 274

Miles, M. B., 3, 12
Milgram, S., 117
Miller, M. F., 309
Miller, N. E., 191, 219, 240, 241, 337
Miller, P. E., 187
Miller, R., 309
Millis, W., 288, 293
Mills, T. M., 30, 187, 371
Mishler, E. G., 353
Mitchell, K. M., 288, 292, 293, 320, 321, 333, 368
Montagu, A., 164, 235
Moore, F. J., 309
Moravec, J. A., 288, 292, 293, 320, 333, 368
Morton, R. B., 9, 288
Moscovici, S., 159
Moustakas, C., 11
Mouton, J. S., 1, 2, 3, 105, 107, 137
Mowrer, O. H., 2, 9, 11, 21, 86, 136, 193, 194, 195, 196, 197, 198, 199, 200, 204, 205, 210, 213, 214, 215, 218, 230, 238, 243, 245, 290, 337
Moyer, R., 9, 288
Mullin, C. S., Jr., 142
Munroe, R., 97, 205
Murphy, G., 11, 155, 248
Musgrave, B. S., 159
Myers, R. A., 217
Nardine, J. E., 142
Neill, A. S., 143
Newcomb, T. M., 233, 250, 314
Newman, S., 22, 122, 159
Norton, N., 249
Nowlin, J. B., 309
Nunnally, J. C., 254
Oaklander, H., 139
Ogilvie, D. M., 187
O'Neill, A. M., 301
Oskamp, E., 89
Otto, H. A., 2, 11
Pascal, G. R., 309
Patterson, C. H., 42, 183, 267, 290
Patton, T., 289, 318
Penney, R. K., 102, 152
Perlman, D., 89
Perlmutter, H. V., 311

Phillips, E. L., 14
Piaget, G. W., 320, 328
Piaget, J., 159
Pierce, R., 288, 289, 298, 324, 368
Piers, G., 225, 226, 229
Pietila, C., 102, 152
Pilisuk, M., 327
Pine, G. J., 60
Plato, 101, 205, 291
Platz, A., 159
Polansky, N., 138
Poser, E. G., 23
Powell, B., 333
Powell, W. J., 278
Pratt, S., 194, 214, 328, 329
Price, L., 152
Rapoport, A., 164
Raven, B. H., 33, 75, 316, 326
Read, W. H., 274
Redl, F., 126, 138
Reik, T., 288
Reivich, R., 310
Rice, L. N., 212, 328
Riecken, H., 185
Riesman, D., 92, 207
Rietsema, J., 33, 75
Rioch, D., 21
Rioch, M. J., 22, 23, 122
Rogers, A. H., 309, 310
Rogers, C. R., 3, 11, 12, 15, 37, 38, 42, 43, 95, 125, 133, 152, 154, 155, 250, 251, 260, 263, 264, 265, 266, 267, 268, 271, 272, 280, 281, 313, 321, 331, 341, 368, 369
Rohner, J. H., 142
Rome, B., 117
Rome, S., 117
Rosen, S., 138
Rosenberg, S., 281
Rosenblith, W. A., 139, 358
Rosenhan, D., 213
Rothaus, P., 9, 288
Rotter, J., 39, 171, 259, 337
Ruesch, J., 101, 161, 170
Rush, C. H., 139
Ryle, G., 173
Salter, A., 184
Salzberg, H. C., 137
Salzinger, K., 159

Sanalu, J., 317
Sanford, F. H., 159
Sapir, E., 169
Sarbin, T. R., 15, 201
Saslow, G., 15, 48
Schachtel, E. G., 169, 170
Schachter, S., 48, 93
Scheff, T. J., 15
Scheflen, A. E., 249
Schein, E. H., 3, 4, 8, 11, 247, 370
Scheler, M., 283
Schiff, S. B., 310
Schneider, L., 21
Schofield, W., 12, 14, 15, 22, 23,
    48, 88, 121, 200, 251, 260,
    265, 267
Schopler, J. H., 247
Schuette, D., 249
Schulze, G., 142, 175
Schutz, W. C., 144, 150, 181, 367
Schwartz, E. K., 20
Seashore, C., 7, 370
Sechrest, L. B., 21, 37, 38, 39
Selan, K., 96
Shaffer, L. F., 212
Shapiro, M. M., 328
Sharp, E., 249
Shaw, G. B., 172
Shelly, J. A., 2, 289
Sherif, M., 311
Sherman, D., 36
Sherrill, L. J., 207
Shoben, E. J., 212
Sidowski, J. R., 203
Silber, E., 22, 122
Simon, H. A., 32, 75, 192
Singer, J. L., 230
Singer, M. B., 225, 226, 229
Sisney, V. V., 288, 309, 310
Skinner, B. F., 37
Slater, P. E., 17, 30, 35, 44, 73,
    107, 129, 131, 140, 187,
    188, 300, 360
Slavson, S. R., 339, 340
Smith, A. G., 155, 248
Smith, E. E., 339
Snadowsky, A. M., 364
Snoek, J. D., 66
Solomon, L. N., 137, 315, 319, 320
Spiegel, J. P., 91, 249
Spiegel, R., 159

Standal, S., 263
Steele, F. I., 365
Steinzor, B., 12, 42, 43, 88
Stennett, R. G., 48
Stern, E. M., 88, 265, 266, 268,
    321
Stern, K., 218
Stock, D. A., 30, 133, 362
Stoller, F. H., 108, 290, 309, 310
Stout, G. F., 159, 162
Strickland, B. R., 267
Suchman, J. R., 250
Sullivan, H. S., 79
Szasz, T. S., 15, 201
Tagiuri, R., 233
Talland, G. A., 212, 223
Tannenbaum, R., 3, 46, 202, 360
Thelen, H. A., 30
Thomas, H. F., 3
Thorne, F. C., 205
Tomkins, S. S., 249
Tomlinson, T. M., 212, 328
Tooley, J., 194, 214, 328
Torrance, E. P., 321
Tournier, P., 215, 217
Truax, C. B., 23, 36, 40, 45, 65,
    95, 137, 212, 239, 260,
    263, 264, 265, 266, 267,
    268, 271, 272, 280, 281,
    288, 293, 321, 328, 341,
    368
Tuckman, B. W., 69, 70, 74, 88,
    92, 129
Ulett, G. A., 48
Underwood, W. J., 370
Usdansky, B. S., 22, 122
Valiquet, I. M., 369
Van Kaam, A., 11, 291
Varendonck, J., 230
Verivoerdt, A., 309
Von Hartmann, E., 159
Wagstaff, A. K., 212, 328
Walz, G. R., 310
Wapner, S., 249
Ward, W. D., 309
Watson, J. R., 338
Watson, R. I., 260
Waxler, N., 353
Weick, K. E., 66, 248
Wender, P. H., 159
Werner, H., 249

Werry, J. S., 15, 23, 201
Weschler, I. R., 3, 202
West, M. J., 309
Wheelis, A., 11
Whitaker, D. S., 30, 127, 130, 131, 156, 337, 340, 354
White, B. J., 311
White, R. W., 200
Whiting, J. W. M., 187
Whitman, R. M., 98, 124, 126, 129, 130, 131, 132, 252, 337
Whorf, B. L., 169
Whyte, W. H., Jr., 222
Wiener, M., 142, 159, 169, 175
Wiener, N., 140, 164, 204, 343, 358

Williams, M., 1
Winters, L. C., 249
Wittgenstein, L., 159, 162
Wolberg, L. R., 39
Wolf, A., 20
Wolpin, M., 36
Woolf, V., 162
Yablonsky, L., 2, 289
Yerkes, F. M., 48
Zajonc, R. B., 281
Zalkind, S. S., 365
Zand, D. E., 365
Zander, A., 26, 28, 30, 32, 83, 89
Zoob, I., 152
Zuckerman, M., 152

Subject Index

Acceptance (*see* Support)
Acting out, 185f
Action therapists, 298
Advertising, 206
Agency, 329, 359–362
Agenda, hidden, 132
Aggression, 187f, 317
Alcoholics Anonymous, 289f
Alienation, 146, 252
Ambiguity in groups, 8, 18,
    35–41, 71–75
Anti-logos, 166f
Anxiety, 6, 18, 47–50, 179,
    213, 253f
Approval, 266f
Artificiality-reality in groups, 117ff
Asocial response, 290, 305
Assumptive world, 227
Attitude change, 102
Attraction, 314
Authority problems, 129ff
Availability, 269ff

Avoidance behavior (*see* Flight)
Awareness, 148f, 243

Baseline measurements, 365
Behavioral change, 103
Beneficial uncertainty, 325
Bias, 310–311
B-needs, 13–14, 16–17
Boredom, 345–346

Central strategies, 332
Challenge, 302f
Clarity in group experiences,
    35–41, 71–75
Cliché support, 282f
Cliché talk, 165f
Client-centered counseling, 289
Clinical judgment, 301
Coercive power, 316

Cohesion, 70
Commercial speech, 165
Common good, 35
Communication, 7, 141–189
Concealment, 193ff, 198f
Concreteness, 96
Conflict, 70, 331, 347
Conformity, 91f, 97ff, 221f
Confrontation, 58–59, 267,
    287–335
  Berenson's types, 292
  rules for, 334–335
Confusion in groups, 71ff
Congruence, 271ff
Contract, 25–67
  artificiality, 118
  cautions, 62–64
  confrontation, 333
  conversation group, 26
  defining life, 194f, 232
  focused, 61
  implicit, 326
  imposed, 61
  leader, 27
  limits, 356
  Mainord's, 197
  member, 27–28
  Mowrer's, 196
  objections to, 43–50
  operationality, 31ff
  reality, 119f
  sample, 51–60
Contract groups, 17–22, 25ff
Contract talk, 349
Controls, experimental, 65–66, 115
Cooperation, 53–54, 87–92
Countertransference, 130f
Cultural permission, 5, 110–111,
    200ff
Cultural taboo, 199ff
Culture, 122
Cynicism, 338–339

Data flow, 274
Daytop Village, 2, 289, 318, 326
Dealing with one, 351–352
Deception, 193ff
Defenses, 151, 357–358
Deprivation, social, 142–143

Developmental sequence of
    groups, 69–71
Deviant members, 92–93, 132f
Diagnosis, 100–102, 259f
Disorganization, 324f, 330f
Dispositional verbs, 173
Dissonance, 313f
Distance, psychological, 269
D-needs, 13–14, 16–17, 46
Domination, 320

Education, 12–13, 143
Emotion, 7, 55, 57, 143ff, 185ff,
    307, 347
Empathy, 320f
  accurate, 280f, 341
  cheap, 283
Encounter groups, 1
Ending the group, 371
Endogenic silence, 340
Exercises, 9, 118, 120, 157–158,
    180–181, 308, 350
Exhibitionism, 242
Existential guilt, 215ff
Experiencing, 183, 313
Experimental realism, 120f
Experimentation, 2, 5, 53
Expression, total human, 141–189

Family, 144f
Fantasy, 230f
Feedback, 6, 53, 111f
Fish-bowl, 234
Flight, 59–60, 336–358
Freedom, 45, 60

Game communication, 164f, 188,
    303f
Generalities, 347
Goallessness, 72, 74
Goals, 8, 10–11, 31ff, 51, 68–103,
    191f
  altruistic, 83f
  content, 77, 96–97
  contract, 76, 78–82
  interaction, 76, 82

Goals (continued)
  need, 77–78
  process, 77, 82–96
  research, 366f
  self-oriented, 83f
Group dynamics, 19–21, 30
Groups
  contractual, 25ff
  natural, 25
Growth, interpersonal, 79ff, 99f
Guilt, 213–223

Harm, 370
Here and now, 5, 53, 93f
History, 234–238, 243
Hostility, 186ff
Human potential, 11–12
Humanistic psychology, 11–12
Humor, 343

Iatrogenic silence, 340
Identification, 187f
Identity, self-, 172f, 346
Identity problems, 79–80
Immediacy, 53–54, 95–96, 347
Impact, emotional, 150ff
Incompetence, interpersonal, 113f
Initiative, 329, 359–362
Insight, 70, 259, 298ff, 341–343
Interrupting, 353
Instrumented laboratories, 137–
  138
Integrity training, 2, 21, 196f
Interaction consciousness, 140,
  253
Interactions
  contractual (C-), 28–31
  natural (N-), 28–31, 128–129
Interpretation, 297–302, 341–343
Intimacy, 81, 208f, 336

Johari window, 243f, 295
Judgment, suspension of, 115f

Labeling, 240ff
Laboratory learning (see
  Laboratory training)

Laboratory training, 4–11, 52–54,
  104–122
  artificiality, 117–118
  nature, 4
  reality, 118ff
  sensitivity training, 10
  uses, 1, 2, 9, 104ff
  variability of, 4, 9–10, 137f
  what it is not, 116f
Language, 55, 159–189
  extra-linguistic dimensions of,
    175
  organizing reality, 169f
  self-identity, 172–173
Leaderless groups, 136f
Leader-member, 125–126 (see
  also Trainer)
Leadership, 6–7, 27–28, 30, 51–
  52, 123–140
  diffusion of, 135f
  guarding the contract, 133f
Legitimacy of power, 326
Listening, 57, 248–260
Logos, 141ff, 159–182
Lowest-common-denominatorism,
  132f

Manipulation, 41–42, 188, 339
Marathon, 21–22, 290, 317, 326
Medical model, 15, 200ff
Members as mutual "therapists,"
  42–43
Membership, psychological versus
  formal, 34–35
Message anxiety, 253f
Messages, 170ff
Metacommunication, 170ff
Methodological problems, 364
Micro-lab, 180
M-needs, 13–14, 16–17, 46
Modal verbs, 173
Modeling, 134f, 230
Mood, 353
Moral guilt, 213ff
Motivation, 133, 312ff
Mundane realism, 120f

Needs (see B-needs, D-needs,
  M-needs)

Neurosis, 332
Neurosis, philosophical, 121
Neurotic guilt, 217ff
Non-diseased person, 14
Non-patient, 15, 28
Nonverbal communication, 154,
155, 175ff
Novels, 161

Openness (*see* Self-disclosure)
Operationality, 32
Operationalizing the group, 31–34
Outcome, 364ff, 369–370
Outer-directed, 207
Overinvolvement, 346–347

Parallel learning, 13
Pathogenic secret, 199
Pathos, 141ff, 143–159
Persuasive potency, 293
Pharisaical guilt, 220f
Poetry, 55
Poiesis, 141ff, 182–189
Populations, 9, 14, 288
Privacy, 202ff
Problem-solution cultures,
353–354
Processing, 233f
Provocation, experimental, 66
Pseudo-guilt, 217ff
Psychoanalysis, 204f, 289
Psychopathology, 196
Psychopathology of the average,
11–12, 20, 198, 288
Psychotherapy, 7, 11–17, 19–21,
28, 35–41, 81, 146, 289f,
367ff
Punishment, 315–320

Questions, 283f, 344

Rational-emotive therapy, 290
Rationalization, 344–345
Reaction-formation, 346
Red crossing, 284f, 347
Reinforcement, 276–282, 309
Research, 64–67, 362–370

Response to confrontation, 327ff
Responsibility, fear of, 209f
Reverse halo effect, 211
Reward power, 316
Risk, 229f
Ritual, 222, 355–356
Role induction interview (RII),
39

Safety, psychological, 113, 247,
261
St. Sebastian Syndrome, 283f
Scoring systems, 66–67
Selectivity, 45
Self-confrontation, 329
Self-consciousness, 252f
Self-disclosure, 55–57, 190–245
dangers of, 242f
levels of, 238ff
Self-examination, 328ff
Self-exploration, 212, 239f, 320f,
328ff
Self-knowledge, flight from, 207f
Semi-led groups, 138f
Sensitivity training, 1, 3, 4, 10–11
(*see also* Laboratory
training)
Sensory awareness, 153–154
Shame, 223–231, 276
Silence, 285, 339–341, 345
Siphoning, 54, 233
Size of groups, 6
Social intelligence, 251f
Sociometric status, 123
Solidarity, 268f
Story, 234–238, 243
Structure in group experiences,
18–19, 25–67, 69–71, 126
Success (*see* Outcome)
Support, 8, 57–59, 242f, 246–286
antecedent, 262ff
consequent, 262ff
Suppression, 185
Symptoms, 195f
Synanon, 2, 289, 318f, 326
Synergy, 67

Tacit decisions or understandings,
131f, 354–355
Testimony, 237

Third-force psychology, 193f
Trainer, 2, 10–11, 22–23, 123–
  140, 368f (*see also*
  Leadership)
Transactional therapy, 291, 337
Transfer of learning, 114f
Transference, 130f
Trust, 229f, 273–276
Turn-taking, 350

Unconditional positive regard,
  263f

Unfreezing, 324

Value guilt, 215
Values, 231f
Vicarious therapy pre-training
  (VTP), 40
Videotaping, 40, 309–310
Visibility in groups, 18–19, 130

Wasteful design in clinical
  settings, 33–34